QuickBooks®
Online

7th Edition

by David H. Ringstrom, CPA

A Wiley Brand

QuickBooks® Online For Dummies®, 7th Edition

Published by: **John Wiley & Sons, Inc.,** 111 River Street, Hoboken, NJ 07030-5774, www.wiley.com

Copyright © 2022 by John Wiley & Sons, Inc., Hoboken, New Jersey

Published simultaneously in Canada

For general information on our other products and services, please contact our Customer Care Department within the U.S. at 877-762-2974, outside the U.S. at 317-572-3993, or fax 317-572-4002. For technical support, please visit https://hub.wiley.com/community/support/dummies.

Wiley publishes in a variety of print and electronic formats and by print-on-demand. Some material included with standard print versions of this book may not be included in e-books or in print-on-demand. If this book refers to media such as a CD or DVD that is not included in the version you purchased, you may download this material at http://booksupport.wiley.com. For more information about Wiley products, visit www.wiley.com.

Library of Congress Control Number: 2022930197

ISBN: 978-1-119-81727-7 (pbk); 978-1-119-81728-4 (ebk); 978-1-119-81729-1 (ebk)

SKY10032532_011422

Contents at a Glance

Table of Contents

Introduction

I get it: Small-business owners have many other things they'd rather be doing with their time than accounting. We're legally mandated to maintain a set of accounting records for our businesses, so avoidance isn't an option — but working smarter is. This book will help you get there. What's more, certain tasks, such as reporting earnings and paying employees, are markedly more difficult if you don't use accounting software.

Accounting programs such as QuickBooks Online help take the pain out of accounting, and in some cases, they even make it easy. In this book, I explore QuickBooks Online, which is aimed at business users, and QuickBooks Online Accountant (QB Accountant), which is aimed at — you guessed it — accountants and bookkeepers. Both programs are web-based products that offer mobile versions, so your accounting records are at your fingertips no matter which device you have at hand. The benefit of an online accounting system such as QuickBooks is that it enables you to access your books from anywhere and share access with your accountant as well. QB Accountant helps accountants streamline various aspects of supporting multiple clients who use QuickBooks Online.

Intuit, the maker of QuickBooks Online and QB Accountant, also offers QuickBooks Desktop, which is a version of the software that you must purchase a license for and then install on individual computers. In the appendix, I discuss migrating QuickBooks Desktop to QuickBooks Online. But if you're looking for a QuickBooks Desktop reference, please get a copy of Stephen L. Nelson's *QuickBooks All-in-One For Dummies* 2022 (John Wiley & Sons, Inc.).

About This Book

Everything that can be done in QuickBooks Online can be accomplished in QB Accountant as well. QB Accountant offers additional tools that are useful to accountants who manage multiple clients and/or multiple companies. As you'll see, QuickBooks Online requires a subscription fee for every set of books you want to maintain, whereas accountants get free access to QB Accountant for overseeing their clients' books.

QuickBooks Online and QuickBooks Online Accountant aren't for everyone. Before you commit to Intuit's web-based solution, you need to explore the available editions and examine the requirements for the products. In that regard, I've divided the book into five parts:

>> Part 1, "Getting Started with QuickBooks and QuickBooks Online Accountant," helps you get oriented within the respective environments.

>> Part 2, "Managing Your Books," covers the nuts and bolts of getting started with QuickBooks, establishing your books, and carrying out common accounting transactions.

>> Part 3, "Reporting and Analysis," shows you how to run reports within QuickBooks Online, and then how to crunch your numbers in Excel.

>> Part 4, "Working in QuickBooks Online Accountant." helps accountants set up shop in QB Accountant and explore the software's accountant-specific features.

>> Part 5, "The Part of Tens," covers ten features of the Chrome browser that help you optimize your use of QuickBooks.

Appendix A offers guidance on migrating to QuickBooks Online from QuickBooks Desktop.

REMEMBER

As I discuss in Chapter 2, QuickBooks Online offers different subscription levels. I used QuickBooks Online Advanced to write this book because it is the most feature-laden offering.

Before diving in, I have to get a few technical conventions out of the way:

>> Text that you're meant to type as it appears in the book is **bold**. The exception is when you're working through a list of steps: Because each step is bold, the text to type is not bold.

>> Web addresses and programming code appear in monofont. If you're reading a digital version of this book on a device connected to the internet, note that you can tap or click a web address to visit that website, like this: www.dummies.com.

>> You can use QuickBooks Online and QB Accountant in a web browser or a mobile app. Example web browsers include Microsoft Edge, Google Chrome, Mozilla Firefox, and Apple's Safari. QuickBooks and QB Accountant mobile apps are available for Android and iOS. QuickBooks Advanced subscribers and QB Accountant users also have a desktop app available.

>> When I discuss a command to choose, I separate the elements of the sequence with a command arrow that looks like this: ⇨. When you see Chrome Menu ⇨ Settings, for example, that command means that you should click the Chrome Menu button (on the right side of the screen; see Chapter 18 for a description of Chrome's screen elements) and then click Settings in the drop-down menu that appears.

>> You may be surprised to learn that QuickBooks Online has more than one version of its navigation bar that appears along the left-hand side. Your navigation is mostly likely set to the Business View, which consolidates commands into fewer top-level choices. In this book, I used the Accountant View, which provides more top-level choices. To change your view, click the Settings button at the top right-hand corner of the screen, and then toggle the view setting at the bottom right-hand corner of the menu that displays.

   However, you don't have to change to Accountant View to follow along in this book. When necessary, I list the Accountant View commands first, and then parenthetically list the Business View commands. For instance, a reference to the Invoices screen looks like this: Sales ⇨ Invoices (Sales & Expenses ⇨ Invoices).

   As this book was going to press, Intuit started rolling out yet another tweak to the Business View for users who identify as owners or partners. If you have any problems finding a command that I reference, you can briefly switch to Accountant View to carry out your task and then toggle back to Business View if that's more your speed.

Foolish Assumptions

I had to assume some things about you to write this book, so here are the educated guesses I made:

>> You know that you need to manage a set of accounting records for one or more businesses, and you might even have some sort of setup in place already. I *did not* assume that you know how to do all those things on a computer.

>> You may want to analyze some of your accounting data outside QuickBooks, which is why I include a couple of chapters on using Microsoft Excel, some of which translate to Google Sheets as well.

>> You have a personal computer running Windows 10 or Windows 11 (I wrote this book in Windows 10) or a Mac running macOS 10.11 or later.

>> You have a copy of Microsoft Excel or another spreadsheet program on your computer.

Icons Used in This Book

Throughout the book, I use icons to draw your attention to various concepts that I want to make sure you don't skip over in the main part of the text. Sometimes, I share information to help you save time; in other cases, the goal is to keep your accounting records safe.

This icon points out time-saving tricks or quirks that you may encounter in QuickBooks.

This icon points out tricky aspects of QuickBooks that you'll want to keep in mind.

This product can burn eyes. Oh, sorry, wrong type of warning. Don't worry, you're safe! Pay careful attention to warnings that you encounter so that you can avoid problems that could wreak havoc in your accounting records or cause you frustration.

At some points, I may include some geeky stuff about QuickBooks, your web browser, or your computer. You can safely skip over the technical stuff if that's not your cup of tea.

Beyond the Book

In addition to the book content, this product comes with a free, access-anywhere Cheat Sheet that lists keyboard shortcuts for QBO and QBOA and handy toolbar buttons in QBO. To get this Cheat Sheet, go to www.dummies.com and search for "QuickBooks Online For Dummies Cheat Sheet."

You can keep the learning going with the most up-to-date information and tutorials from School of Bookkeeping (https://schoolofbookkeeping.com/). The folks there (one of which is the technical editor of this book) have broken down every version of QuickBooks Online, QuickBooks services (Payments and Payroll), and other tasks into bite-sized lessons you can watch and get back to business. Use promo code QBO4DUMMIES to save 20% on any membership.

Where to Go from Here

Simply turn the page. Seriously. You can dive in anywhere you want and come back as often as you like. You don't have to read through this book cover to cover, as you would a Lee Child thriller, because each chapter stands alone and provides step-by-step instructions for common tasks. You should consider this book to be a reference that you can use when you need it.

That said, if you're getting started with QBO or QBOA, you may want read the chapters in Part 1 in order. Then feel free to explore any chapter you want, using the table of contents or the index to find topics that interest you.

1

Getting Started with QBO and QBOA

Chapter **1**

Presenting QuickBooks Online

QuickBooks Online is a web-based platform you can use to manage accounting records for a business. Business owners and employees will use QuickBooks Online, whereas accounting professionals will use QuickBooks Online Accountant. In this book, I often refer to QuickBooks Online as simply QuickBooks, and QuickBooks Online Accountant as QB Accountant. In this chapter, I introduce these products and discuss whether you should move your accounting tasks to the cloud.

REMEMBER

When I mention *the cloud,* I mean that you'll access your accounting records remotely from an internet server instead of from your local hard drive. I also explain the system requirements for cloud-based products.

Comparing QuickBooks and QB Accountant

If you own or work for a business that is looking to maintain accounting records more effectively, QuickBooks Online may be just the ticket; you can use it to manage customers, vendors, employees, and contractors, as well as the panoply of related accounting transactions. Any experience you have in QuickBooks Desktop will help you understand accounting software as a whole, but keep in mind that QuickBooks Online is a separate, distinct product written specifically for the internet. This version of QuickBooks was written from scratch, so you're not going to see any screens that mirror QuickBooks Desktop. Also, QuickBooks Desktop certainly does some things better than its online counterpart, such as inventory tracking. But QuickBooks Desktop allows you to access your books only from certain computers, whereas you can access QuickBooks Online from any device that's connected to the internet.

QuickBooks Online Accountant (QB Accountant) is a free cloud-based portal that accounting professionals use to access clients' QuickBooks Online companies and communicate with clients. QB Accountant includes a QuickBooks Online company that accountants can use to account for their own businesses, but the standard subscription fees apply for any additional QuickBooks Online companies that accountants establish for themselves or their clients.

Comparing interfaces

QuickBooks Online was initially written and optimized to be used only in web browsers such as Google Chrome, Mozilla Firefox, Apple's Safari, and Microsoft Edge. Now you can use QuickBooks apps on iOS and Android mobile devices as well. A short-lived QuickBooks Online app for Mac and Windows computers has been discontinued. If you previously installed the desktop app, you can continue to use it, but it's no longer available to install due to low use and the product will no longer be updated.

QuickBooks ONLINE ADVANCED APP

QB Accountant users can download the QuickBooks Online Advanced App for Windows by using the following steps:

1. Log into QuickBooks Online Accountant.

2. Click the Settings button.

3. Click Get the Desktop App.

4. Click Download for Windows.

5. Follow the onscreen instructions once you launch the installation file.

In a browser, an open QuickBooks company looks similar to the one shown in Figure 1-1. I cover the interface in more detail in Chapter 3, but for the time being, the most important thing to notice is the navigation bar that runs down the left side of the screen. QuickBooks Desktop offers a similar navigation aid, so this bar may feel familiar. Click any link to navigate to that portion of the program.

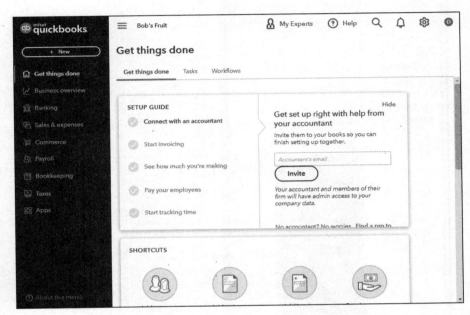

 Clicking the collapse/expand (three stripes) button next to the QuickBooks logo at the top of the screen enables you to collapse the navigation bar to view just the icons. Click the button again to expand the navigation bar. Collapsing the navigation bar gives you more screen space to view the main area of the QuickBooks interface. Additional commands at the top of the screen allow you to create transactions, search for existing transactions, and view settings for the QuickBooks company.

Figure 1-2 shows what an accountant sees immediately upon logging into QB Accountant.

As you can see in Figure 1-3, when an accountant opens a client's company, the QB Accountant interface resembles what a client sees in QuickBooks Online, apart from some minor differences that are mostly additional tools for accountants. In short, the functionality is the same; QB Accountant users simply have more options than QuickBooks users do. In Chapter 12, I tell you more about how the navigation bar changes to support an accountant's needs.

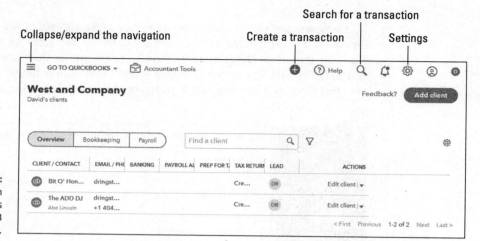

Collapse/expand the navigation   Create a transaction   Search for a transaction   Settings

FIGURE 1-2:
The first view an accountant has when opening QB Accountant.

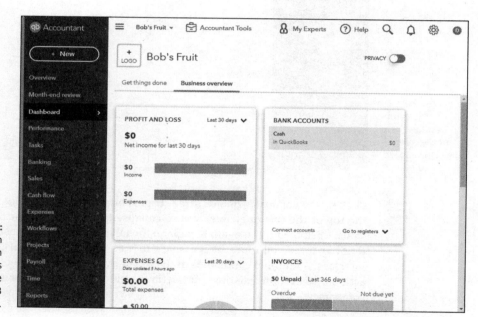

FIGURE 1-3:
An open company in QuickBooks Online Accountant (QB Accountant).

REMEMBER

Because QB Accountant contains functionality that QuickBooks doesn't have, I've organized this book so that QuickBooks users can focus on Part 2 when using the product, whereas QB Accountant users can use the information in both Parts 3 and 4.

Taking a look at QuickBooks Online Mobile

Your QuickBooks subscription includes mobile apps that are also available for iOS/ iPadOS and Android devices. These apps are optimized for touch interaction and on-the-go workflows such as customer management, invoicing, estimates, and signatures. You can also use the mobile apps to track the status of invoices, take payments, reconcile bank accounts, capture expenses, and check reports. Pinch and zoom functionality works in both the apps and browsers on mobile devices.

You can get the mobile apps from the app store for your device or request a link at `https://quickbooks.intuit.com/accounting/mobile`. Alternatively, you can use your mobile device to log into your books at `https://qbo.intuit.com` without installing anything. Keep in mind that the mobile apps offer a subset of the functionality, so you may still need to use a web browser to carry out certain tasks, such as customizing templates.

Understanding the Cloud

Just to make sure we're on the same page here, I'm defining *the cloud* as software and data housed securely in remote data centers (not on your office premises) and accessed securely over the internet. Working in the cloud can increase your efficiency by offering you the opportunity to work anywhere, communicate easily with others, and collaborate in real time. Further, your data is backed up automatically, which can help you avoid disasters such as fire or flood, which can take out not only your workspace, but also your accounting records.

REMEMBER

Regardless of whether you use QuickBooks in a browser or in an app, both the software and the data are housed on servers controlled by Intuit and accessible via the internet.

Historically, we bought software and installed it on our computers, or we bought the software and installed it on a vendor's server. However, QuickBooks Online and QB Accountant fall into the category of Software as a Service (SaaS). You don't buy SaaS software; instead, you rent it by purchasing a subscription.

You typically access SaaS software such as QuickBooks over the internet by using a browser. A *browser* is software installed on your local computer or the mobile device that you use to . . . well, browse the internet, looking up cool stuff like what the stock market is doing today, what kind of weather you can expect on Friday (when your vacation starts), how to get to your boss's house for the party they're having, and — yes — how to work with web-based software such as QuickBooks Online.

SHOULD YOU MOVE TO THE CLOUD?

Before you decide to move your accounting records to the cloud, you should consider the needs of your business in the following areas:

- Invoicing, point of sale, electronic payment, and customer relationship management
- Financial and tax reporting
- Budgeting
- Time tracking and payroll
- Inventory, job costing, and job scheduling
- Management of company expenses and vendor bills

Beyond the advantages described in this section, the needs of your business may dictate whether you can use QuickBooks Online. The platform won't work for you if your business has industry-specific needs or is midsize, for example. In addition, QuickBooks Online won't work for you if you need to do any of the following things:

- Track your balance sheet by class.
- Track labor costs.
- Manage a robust inventory that supports making and selling finished goods.

In any of these cases, you'd probably be better off with Intuit's desktop-based QuickBooks Enterprise or perhaps QuickBooks Premier.

Using web-based software can be attractive for several reasons. For one thing, when you use web-based software, you have access to that software's information anywhere, at any time, from any device — stationary or mobile.

REMEMBER

Some folks see the "anywhere, anytime" feature as a potential disadvantage because it makes information too readily available — and therefore a target for hackers. Rest assured that Intuit stores your data on servers that use bank-level security and encryption, and it backs up your data for you automatically.

In addition, web-based software like QuickBooks promotes collaboration and can help you save time. Accountants, bookkeepers, and clients can communicate about issues that arise, as described in Chapter 16.

Web-based software also eliminates the issue of keeping software up to date. The desktop version of QuickBooks typically receives a major update once each year, along with periodic software patches that must be installed manually. Conversely, QuickBooks is updated automatically every two to four weeks, so there's never a new version to install or a patch to deal with. Most modern computers should exceed the minimum requirements, but you can get the nitty-gritty computer specification details here: https://intuit.me/3yEaSJL.

REMEMBER

Because updates occur so frequently in QuickBooks, by the time this book is published, some features (and screens) may have changed. Make that *will* have changed.

TIP

My technical editor extraordinaire Dan DeLong has created a free QuickBooks Chooser chatbot that will help you choose the right version of QuickBooks Online based upon your specific business needs. Check it out at https://sob.drift. click/QBChooser.

Chapter **2**

Embracing QuickBooks Online

QuickBooks Online and QuickBooks Online Accountant are cloud-based accounting software programs. Actually, it's more apt to call them *accounting ecospheres,* because as you'll see throughout the book, you can layer on functionality with add-ons from Intuit and third-party developers. In this chapter, I help you determine which version of QuickBooks fits your needs best from both functionality and cost standpoints.

I'll Subscribe to That

QuickBooks Online isn't your father's accounting software. Back in the day, you'd pay once for a software license and use it as far into the future as you chose. Such perpetual licenses have mostly fallen by the wayside in favor of subscriptions, often referred to as Software as a Service (SaaS). The good news for accounting professionals is that QuickBooks Online Accountant is free and includes one free QuickBooks Online Advanced subscription for you to use for your own use. Everyone else must choose and pay for a QuickBooks Online subscription. Unlike old accounting software, you don't have to install QuickBooks Online on your desktop computer, which means there are no software patches to keep up with. Any changes or improvements appear automatically the next time that you log in. If you end your subscription, however, you also end your access to the software, apart from a one-year period during which you can view transactions and run reports.

QuickBooks Online is available at five price and functionality levels:

>> Self-Employed

>> Simple Start

>> Essentials

>> Plus

>> Advanced

All versions of QuickBooks Online have three features in common:

>> You can use a tablet, Android or iOS smartphone, or desktop computer to access your data.

>> Your data is backed up online automatically.

>> All versions use 128-bit Secure Sockets Layer (SSL), the same security and encryption that banks use to secure data sent over the internet.

After you assess your needs, as described in Chapter 1, use the following information to identify the lowest subscription level that will meet your requirements. You can upgrade to a higher level at any time, but you can't downgrade.

TIP

Whether you're a business user or an accountant, you can easily add payroll to a QBO subscription at any time. For details, see "Payroll Options" later in this chapter.

QuickBooks Online Self-Employed

This version is aimed at freelancers and self-employed people who file Schedule C of IRS Form 1040. Unlike the higher level offerings, QuickBooks Self-Employed allows you to mix business with pleasure, meaning that you can separate personal and business expenses and mileage. It's best suited to someone with a side hustle who wants to keep track of their business and simplify income tax filing.

QuickBooks Simple Start

A QuickBooks Simple Start subscription is great for a new business with basic bookkeeping needs. With Simple Start, you can

>> Track your income and expenses

>> Download transactions from your bank and credit card accounts

>> Create an unlimited number of customers

>> Send unlimited estimates and invoices

>> Print checks and record transactions to track expenses

>> Track and pay sales taxes

>> Track, create, and send 1099 forms

>> Import data from Microsoft Excel or QuickBooks Desktop

>> Invite up to two accountants to access your data

>> Integrate with available apps in QuickBooks Online App Center

Although the Simple Start version supports accounts-receivable functions, you can't set up invoices to bill customers on a recurring basis or track unpaid bills. It does include a trial balance and a general ledger, however.

Although the Simple Start version allows two accountants to work in the client's company, Simple Start is still designed for a single user, so an accountant who uses QuickBooks Online Accountant can't establish a Simple Start company for a client.

This version offers more than 50 reports that you can customize and save. Go to this address to establish a QuickBooks Simple Start subscription: `https://quickbooks.intuit.com/pricing`. If you're on the fence between Self-Employed and Simple Start, you'll have more options in the future with Simple Start.

QuickBooks Online Essentials

A QuickBooks Essentials subscription builds on the Simple Start functionality by allowing you to

>> Set up invoices to bill automatically on a recurring schedule

>> Use accounts-payable functions, including scheduling payment of vendor bills

>> Create and post recurring transactions

>> Track time

>> Control the areas of QuickBooks that your users can access

An Essentials subscription permits up to three simultaneous users and two accountant users, as well as an unlimited number of users who log in only to use time-tracking tools. In addition, Essentials subscribers can access 85 reports.

QuickBooks Online Plus

A Plus subscription goes beyond the Essentials level by adding the ability to

>> Create, send, and track purchase orders.

>> Track inventory using the first in, first out (FIFO) inventory valuation method. QuickBooks Online supports light inventory needs: If you sell finished goods you should be able to manage your needs. But if you need to assemble finished goods to sell, QuickBooks Online won't meet your needs on its own. You can look for an add-on app to supplement your inventory needs; I talk about add-on apps at the end of this chapter.

>> Categorize income and expenses by using class tracking.

>> Track sales and profitability by business location. You can assign only one location to a transaction, but you can assign multiple classes to a transaction.

>> Give employees and subcontractors limited access to the QuickBooks company to enter time worked.

>> Track billable hours by customer. QuickBooks Online supports light job-costing needs, but it doesn't allow you to cost labor automatically.

>> Track projects.

>> Create budgets to estimate future income and expenses. You can create multiple budgets per year, location, class, or customer.

A Plus subscription allows five simultaneous billed users and two accountant users, as well as an unlimited number of users who log in only to use reports or time-tracking tools. Plus subscribers have 124 reports. You can get the lay of the land in QuickBooks Online Plus by way of the free test drive at https// qbo.intuit.com/redir/testdrive.

QuickBooks Online Advanced

QuickBooks Online Advanced is the flagship subscription for users who have out-grown QuickBooks Online Plus, which allows you to

>> Have unlimited accounts, transactions, and classes.

>> Connect with a dedicated customer success manager to handle support questions; support calls go to the front of the line instead of waiting in queue. Customer success managers also provide information on online training and QuickBooks products; Advanced subscribers are entitled to five free online training courses annually.

>> Establish custom permissions for your users.

>> Efficiently import hundreds of invoice transactions into QuickBooks by way of a comma-separated-values (CSV) file. You can create such a file in Microsoft Excel or Google Sheets.

>> Edit or delete multiple invoices.

>> Batch-reclassify and batch-create transactions, including invoices, bills, checks, and expenses.

>> Enable workflows to trigger reminders for customers and team members.

>> Use up to 48 custom fields.

>> Visualize your data in the Performance Center with customizable chart widgets.

>> Employ premium app integration with services such as Bill.com, HubSpot, Salesforce, LeanLaw, and DocuSign. (Third-party subscription fees apply.)

>> Restore QuickBooks data to a particular date and time. You can also schedule automatic backups and reverse changes made to customers, vendors, and company settings.

>> Take advantage of a license for enhanced reporting capabilities called Smart Reporting, powered by Fathom.

TECHNICAL STUFF

Fathom requires that your chart of accounts have no more than 3,000 active or inactive accounts and no more than 60 classes. Smart Reporting is included at no cost in Advanced subscriptions, or you can add it to a lower level QuickBooks subscription for $44 per month as of this writing.

QuickBooks Online Advanced subscribers have only two real limitations: They can have up to 25 billed users and 3 unbilled accountant users. For more information on the Advanced subscription level, see `https://quickbooks.intuit.com/accounting/advanced`.

REMEMBER

I used a QuickBooks Online Advanced subscription as I wrote this book because it offers the whole enchilada with regard to QuickBooks functionality. Accordingly, there's a good chance that you'll see references to features you don't have. If you're curious, kick the tires for free in the Advanced sample company at `https://qbo.intuit.com/redir/testdrive_us_advanced`.

Usage limits for QuickBooks Simple Start, Essentials, and Plus

Intuit applied updated use limits to Simple Start, Essentials, and Plus subscriptions (see Table 2-1) when it introduced the Advanced level. Customers with these subscriptions who already exceed their use limits can continue with their current subscription and their existing data, but they won't be able to manually add to any element that exceeds the use limit without upgrading to a higher-level plan.

TABLE 2-1   **Use Limits for Simple Start, Essentials, and Plus Subscriptions**

QBO Element	Use Limit
Chart of accounts	250
Classes and locations	40 combined
Billed users	1 for Simple Start, 3 for Essentials, 5 for Plus
Unbilled users	2 Accountant users for all plans; for Plus, unlimited users who have access for reports only; for Essentials and Plus, unlimited users who have access for time tracking only

Suppose that your QuickBooks company requires more than 250 accounts or more than a combination of 40 classes and locations. If your company already exceeds these limits, you won't be able to add accounts or any combination of classes and locations until you delete or deactivate these elements to bring your total down to the limits listed in the table. If you can't reduce your accounts or combination of classes and locations, you'll need to upgrade to an Advanced subscription.

The Dollars and Cents of QuickBooks Subscriptions

One thing to keep in mind is that QuickBooks subscription fees continue month after month, year after year. This fact can result in some sticker shock if you're accustomed to paying one time for a perpetual software license for, say, QuickBooks Desktop. You can run, but you can't hide though, as QuickBooks Desktop requires a subscription for the 2022 version and beyond. Table 2-2 shows the current monthly and annual costs so that you can budget accordingly.

TABLE 2-2 **QuickBooks Online Subscription Pricing**

Version	Sale Price (Per Month)	Regular Price (Per Month)	Annual Cost
Self-Employed	$7.50	$15	$180
Simple Start	$12.50	$25	$30
Essentials	$25	$50	$600
Plus	$40	$80	$960
Advanced	$90	$180	$2,160

REMEMBER

The sale and regular prices shown in Table 2-2 are monthly subscription prices. The sale price is typically good for three months.

TIP

At the time I wrote this chapter, Intuit allowed Simple Start, Essentials, Plus, and Advanced users to add full-service payroll for the sale prices of $22.50 per month plus $4 per employee per month, Payroll Premium for $37.50 per month plus $8 per employee per month, or Payroll Elite for $62.50 per month plus $10 per employee per month. *Full-service* means that Intuit handles your payroll tax deposits and payroll tax returns for you.

Payroll charges are billed monthly as part of your QuickBooks subscription. You can test-drive payroll processing at no charge for up to 30 days. After that period, your overall subscription fee increases to include payroll. Conversely, QuickBooks Payments feature, which allows you to accept online payments from your customers, doesn't have a monthly fee; you'll pay per transaction instead. As of this writing, the rates are 2.4 percent for swiped credit card transactions, 2.9 percent for e-invoiced transactions, and 3.4 percent for key-entered transactions, plus a 25-cent fee per transaction. Automated Clearing House (ACH) transactions incur a 1 percent fee up to a maximum of $10.

As I write this chapter, QuickBooks is rolling out an additional subscription-based feature called QuickBooks Commerce, which is designed to make it easy to place and sell your inventory products on a variety of major online shopping platforms. You can bet that additional premium offerings will become available in Quick-Books as time goes on.

You have to choose between a 30-day free trial and the 3-month sale price, although Intuit sometimes offers the sale price to trial users. If you're offered this deal, be prepare to act on it immediately because the offer won't be repeated. Or you can start your full-price subscription immediately by choosing Buy Now. You can cancel your subscription at any time, but the service is billed in monthly periods with no refunds or prorations.

Accounting professionals can use QuickBooks Online Accounting for free and also sign up for the Wholesale Pricing program, which offers you discounted pricing on QBO subscriptions for companies that you create or manage. Your credit card is charged each month for all the subscription fees, and you can pass along the discounted price to your clients or charge the market rate. As discussed in Chapter 12, Intuit will send you a single consolidated bill for all the QBO subscriptions you manage.

The 30-day free trial isn't available if an accounting professional creates a company through QBOA because a payment method must be provided when the company is created.

If your client initially sets up their own QBO subscription, you can move it to your consolidated bill at the discounted wholesale rate. If your arrangement with your client doesn't work out, you can remove the client from your consolidated bill, which means that the client will resume paying for their own subscription.

Payroll Options

When you establish your QBO subscription, you can choose add-on payroll from the start or elect to incorporate payroll later from the Employees screen (see Figure 2-1). Alternatively, your accountant can enable payroll on your behalf by way of QBOA. In the past, QuickBooks offered self-service versus full-service plans, but now all plans are full-service, meaning that QBO will handle your payroll tax deposits and payroll tax returns. If you opt in to QBO Payroll, you can't complete those tasks your own even if you want to. But who would want to?

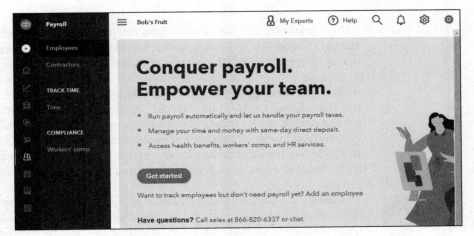

FIGURE 2-1:
If you sign up for QBO on your own, you can turn on Payroll from the Employees screen.

All QBO Payroll services include the following features:

>> Paying employees with printed checks or by direct deposit

>> Calculating tax payments automatically and paying them electronically

>> Processing federal and state quarterly and annual reports, and preparing W-2 forms

>> Processing payroll for employees who work in your company's state or another state

>> Keeping payroll tax tables up to date without having to install updates (as you do with the QuickBooks Desktop product)

>> Using the QBO Payroll mobile app to pay employees, view past paychecks, file tax forms electronically, and pay taxes electronically

WARNING

When you establish QBO Payroll, you must connect your bank account and provide your tax identification numbers. Make sure that you're ready to start processing payroll immediately before you embark on a QBO Payroll subscription. If you'd like to try before you buy, use the online test drives I mention earlier for QBO Plus and QBO Advanced.

Migration from QuickBooks Desktop

Yes, you can migrate your accounting records from QuickBooks Desktop to QBO, as I discuss in Chapter 13. This process won't affect your original desktop company; it's still available via the desktop product. After you import your data into

QBO, you should run the Profit & Loss report and the Balance Sheet, using the accrual method for all dates from both QBO and QuickBooks Desktop, to ensure that both versions show the same information.

If you want to keep one foot on the ground while you reach for the cloud, you can run QuickBooks Desktop and QBO in parallel for a brief period. Doing so does require double work because you'll have to enter your transactions in both platforms. Then you'll be able to run reports from both platforms to confirm that you're seeing the same results in both places. Plan carefully if you opt to run parallel; things can quickly turn confusing if you're not disciplined about the process.

WARNING

You should discontinue using QuickBooks Desktop when you make the switch to QBO, except for running reports and viewing historical data. No synchronization occurs between QuickBooks Desktop and QBO; the transfer that you perform from QuickBooks Desktop to QBO is one-time and one-way.

An App for That

It's very likely that you'll have accounting needs that aren't met by a base subscription for QBO. As I discussed earlier, for example, payroll is an add-on that entails additional monthly costs. The Intuit Payments app, which supports electronic customer payment processing and integrates with QBO, doesn't have a monthly cost, but it does have per-transaction fees.

Many add-on apps are available for QBO. Intuit rose to the top of the small-business accounting world by empowering third-party developers to create apps that enhance the functionality of QBO, and over time, you can expect more apps to be developed.

REMEMBER

In Chapter 1, I use the term *apps* to describe the versions of QBO available from mobile device stores (such as Google Play and Apple's App Store). In this section, when I refer to *apps,* I mean add-ons developed to enhance the functionality of QBO. You can browse the available offerings at this slightly unwieldy address: https://quickbooks.intuit.com/app/apps. Or you can choose Apps from the navigation bar, as shown in Figure 2-2.

As shown in Figure 2-3, you can click any app to view a description, price information, and sometimes a video tutorial.

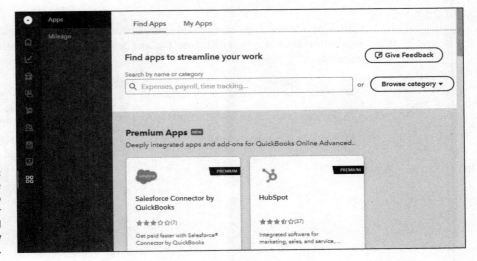

FIGURE 2-2:
Take a trip to the App Center to search for additional functionality for QBO.

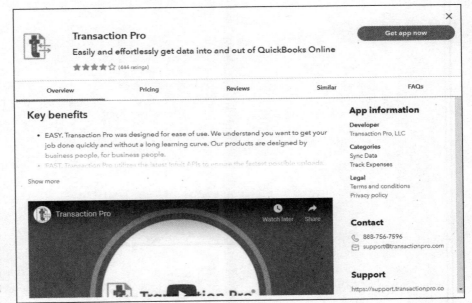

FIGURE 2-3:
Choose any app in the App Center to view the underlying details.

Although add-on apps can provide additional functionality in QBO, you may still encounter limitations. QBO won't allow you to do the following things, for example:

>> Track your balance sheet by class.

>> Process more than 350,000 transactions annually without QBO Advanced.

>> Manage a robust inventory.

2
Managing Your Books

Chapter **3**

Creating a QuickBooks Online Company

After you subscribe to QuickBooks Online, the next step is creating your company. If you're migrating from QuickBooks Desktop, you can import most of your data, or you can allow the QuickBooks Setup Wizard to walk you through the process, as shown in this chapter. You even have the option to have a live bookkeeper assist you.

See Chapter 13 or ask your accountant for help if you're migrating from Quick-Books Desktop. You can choose a full migration, which includes most transactions, or you can import only the lists, which I cover in Chapter 4.

TIP

If you're in the market for an accountant or bookkeeper, visit the ProAdvisor marketplace at https://quickbooks.intuit.com/find-an-accountant/ to seek expert advice from certified QuickBooks advisors. Or try the QuickBooks Live Bookkeeping service at quickbooks.intuit.com/live.

Signing Up for QuickBooks Online

After you complete the sign-up process for a QuickBooks Online account, the setup process begins. The process is much shorter than the one you go through to set up a QuickBooks Desktop product company, and you need the following information:

>> Your company's name and address.

>> The industry in which your company operates.

>> Whether you want to import company information from a QuickBooks Desktop product.

>> The way you want to handle payroll. (You can always opt into one of the QuickBooks Payroll (QB Payroll) offerings later.)

To purchase or start a 30-day trial of QuickBooks Online, follow these steps:

1. **Visit** `quickbooks.intuit.com/pricing`.

This page has the current pricing as well as any sale prices.

2. **Look for four boxes describing the Simple Start, Essentials, Plus, and Advanced subscriptions.**

If you're looking for QuickBooks Self-Employed, scroll down past the boxes to the Freelancer section.

REMEMBER

Typically, you can choose between a free 30-day trial and three months of reduced prices for Simple Start, Essentials, and Plus. The Advanced subscription doesn't offer a free trial, but you can access the test drive at `qbo.intuit.com/redir/testdrive_us_advanced`. For more information, see Chapter 2 and `quickbooks.intuit.com/accounting/advanced`.

3. **To sign up for a free trial, click the slider button above the QuickBooks versions to activate Free Trial for 30 Days (see Figure 3-1).**

REMEMBER

Be aware that the price you ultimately pay for QuickBooks depends on whether you choose the Buy Now option or the Free Trial for 30 Days option. If you opt to buy now, you'll pay less for your subscription because discounts don't apply to the free trials. Be aware that promotional pricing usually ends after three months. However, ask your accountant if they're able to extend a ProAdvisor Preferred Pricing discount to you, which I discuss in Chapter 12.

FIGURE 3-1:
Use the slider
button to toggle
between a
short-term
discount and a
free trial.

Choose the plan that's right for your business

Buy now for 50% off for 3 months* ⬤ Free trial for 30 days

4. **Click the Try It Free button for the version you want to try.**

   If you see a Select button instead of Try It Free, click the Free Trial for 30 Days button. The optional Add Payroll page appears; this page allows you to add a free payroll service test drive to your QuickBooks trial if you want.

5. **Click Add to Trial or Continue without Payroll to move to the Checkout screen.**

   You can always add payroll later, so don't feel that you need to make a heat-of-the-moment decision here. But your payroll trial will be free for 30 days as well.

6. **Review your choices and then click Checkout to establish your QuickBooks Online account.**

   The amounts shown are what you'll be charged each month for your subscription.

7. **Fill in your email address, mobile number, and a password (see Figure 3-2).**

   Your password must be between 8 and 32 characters and consist of a mix of uppercase and lowercase letters, numbers, and one or more special characters (such as an exclamation point or pound sign). The email address and password will serve as your credentials for accessing QuickBooks. Your mobile number will be used to recover your account if you mislay your credentials. If you already have an Intuit account, look for the tiny — and I mean tiny — Sign In link.

8. **Click the Sign Up with Email button.**

   Intuit will text you a confirmation number to enter. When I wrote this chapter, a window appeared, offering an option to skip the free trial and buy the product at a discounted rate. You can buy, but I opted to click the Continue with Trial button.

SIGNING IN TO AND OUT OF QUICKBOOKS ONLINE

If you followed the process to sign up for QuickBooks, you're currently signed in. But obviously, you don't sign up for QuickBooks every time you want to use it. Also, there's the question of how you sign out of QuickBooks each time you finish using it.

To sign out of QuickBooks, click the profile button and then click Sign Out. The profile button will most likely display your first initial; on my screen, it displays *D* for *David*. Also QuickBooks will log you out automatically after one hour of inactivity.

To sign in to QuickBooks in the future, visit qbo.intuit.com, and supply your username and password. I suggest that you bookmark this page to make signing in easy.

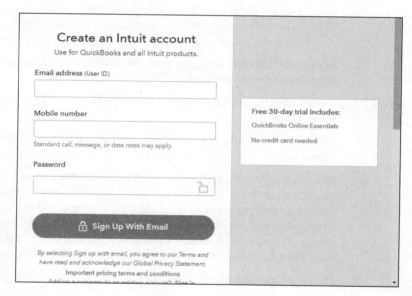

FIGURE 3-2:
Fill in the information needed to start the free trial.

Setting Up a New Company

When you've established your paid or trial subscription, the first screen of the Setup Wizard appears, as shown in Figure 3-3. Click Next after you complete each screen of the wizard, which asks you to enter your company name, industry, and type of business; your role in your company; any team members; and your goals for QuickBooks. Click Skip for Now to skip any questions that feel too personal, such as the one that asks you to link your bank and credit card accounts, and the one that asks you to list the apps that you use. You can indicate which activities you want to use QuickBooks for or skip that item as well. At long last, you'll reach the screen shown in Figure 3-4, which is the end of the Setup Wizard.

FIGURE 3-3:
A loquacious wizard walks you through the setup process.

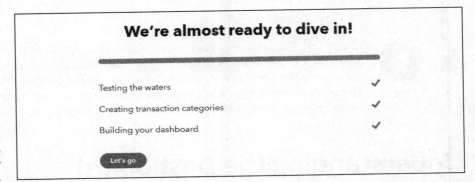

FIGURE 3-4:
This screen shows that you've prevailed over the Setup Wizard.

TIP

QuickBooks Online will ask whether you want to import your QuickBooks Desktop data, but you can defer that decision until later, as I discuss in Chapter 13. Make sure, however, that you perform the import before you enable the QB Payroll service, if you decide to go that route. You lose the ability to import your QuickBooks Desktop data after QB Payroll is enabled.

A short tour appears followed by a Get Things Done page that includes areas of QuickBooks you may want to set up (see Figure 3-5). I walk you through this page in "Understanding the Dashboard" later in this chapter.

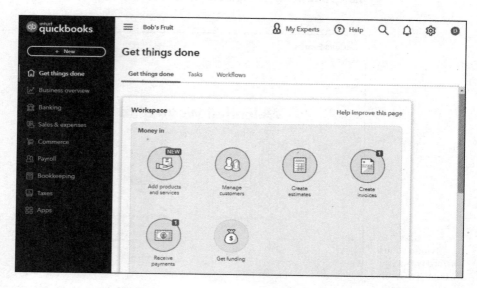

FIGURE 3-5: Your Get Things Done page after you create your company.

Essentially, you've completed much of the initial setup work. I get to the other program settings later in the chapter.

TIP

If you feel the need for QuickBooks technical support, first choose Settings ⇨ SmartLook to get a number that you can share with the support agent. This will grant temporary permission to view your QuickBooks company (but nothing else on your computer). I can attest from decades of work as a software consultant that being able to see someone's screen turbocharges the support process.

Understanding the Dashboard

Your Get Things Done page (refer to Figure 3-5) contains links to options you can use to set up features in QBO that are important to you. You can use those links and set up those options now, or you can wait until later.

The navigation bar runs down the left side of the screen. You use this bar the same way you'd use a menu; click an item to navigate to that part of QBO. You can click Sales on the navigation bar, for example, to see existing sales transactions in QBO and to create a new Sales transaction.

REMEMBER

Descriptions on the navigation bar sometimes vary, based on your version of QBO and the preferences that you've set. In place of Sales, for example, you may see Sales & Expenses or Invoicing. Regardless, the highlighted entry in the navigation bar helps you identify the section of QBO that you're using.

On the navigation bar, the option below Get Things Done is Business Overview, which serves as a dashboard for your business (see Figure 3-6).

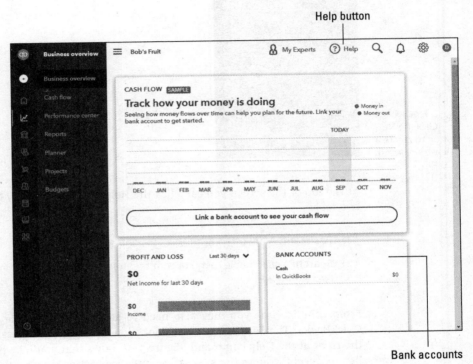

FIGURE 3-6:
The Business
Overview
dashboard.

On the right side of the dashboard page is a list of the bank accounts you've set up. If you scroll to the bottom of the list, you find options to connect your accounts to their banks, open an account's register, and review transactions that have been imported into QuickBooks. The dashboard also displays a summary of expenses and sales for periods extending as far back as the last fiscal year.

Over to the left hand side of the screen, you'll see the New button on the navigation bar, shown in Figure 3-7, which is the starting point for creating most but not all transactions in QuickBooks. If the list of options feels overwhelming, click Show Less in the bottom right-hand corner to collapse the list down to the basics: Invoice, Estimate, Expense, and Check. You can then click Show More to get the full list of transactions back again. The commands are grouped into four columns: Customers, Vendors, Employees, and Other. When you click any choice on the menu the corresponding transaction window will open in QuickBooks.

At the top of the screen you can click the Help button to display a task pane with two tabs:

>> **Assistant:** A bot offering answers to common questions

>> **Search:** A searchable menu of common topics that might be of interest to you (see Figure 3-8)

From time to time you may also need to search through prior transactions in QuickBooks. The Search command looks like a magnifying glass and appears to the right of the Help command. Figure 3-9 shows that you'll be presented with a list of recent transactions — click any transaction in the list to open that transaction — as well as a Search field. You can also click Advanced Search if you want to search based on multiple filters.

The second button from the top right, known as the Settings button, is shown in the margin. Clicking it displays the menu shown in Figure 3-10. From here, you can review and change QuickBooks settings; view lists; work with tools such as import and export, reconciliation, and budgeting tools; and view information about your QuickBooks account. Note that the Settings menu is divided into four columns that organize related commands.

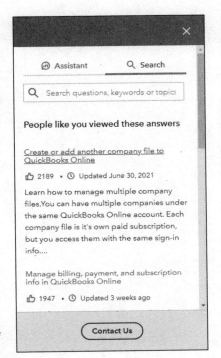

FIGURE 3-8:
The Search tab of the Help pane.

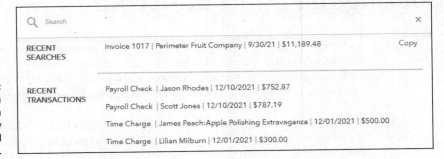

FIGURE 3-9:
Click the Search button to search for previously entered transactions.

REMEMBER

Although I couldn't fit it into Figure 3-10, the bottom right-hand corner of the Settings menu contains a link that will either display Accountant View or Business View that controls how the navigation bar in QuickBooks is displayed. Business View groups things into fewer categories, whereas Accountant View is more detailed. You can toggle between these modes to find what feels most comfortable for you. For the record, I used Accountant View for most of the images in this book, because as an accountant myself, that view resonates with me more than the Business View.

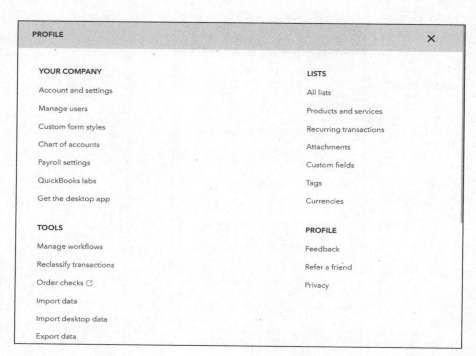

PROFILE	✕
YOUR COMPANY	**LISTS**
Account and settings	All lists
Manage users	Products and services
Custom form styles	Recurring transactions
Chart of accounts	Attachments
Payroll settings	Custom fields
QuickBooks labs	Tags
Get the desktop app	Currencies
TOOLS	**PROFILE**
Manage workflows	Feedback
Reclassify transactions	Refer a friend
Order checks ⮺	Privacy
Import data	
Import desktop data	
Export data	

FIGURE 3-10:
Use the Settings menu to work with settings, lists, tools, and your QBO account.

Updating the Chart of Accounts

As I mention earlier in this chapter, QuickBooks automatically sets up the chart of accounts it thinks you'll need when you create a new company. If you're not happy with this list, you can replace it with one you set up in Excel, in a CSV file, or in a Google Sheet. See Chapter 13 for details on importing a chart of accounts.

You'll probably want to modify the chart of accounts that QuickBooks establishes for your company. To do so, choose Settings ⮕ Chart of Accounts or Accounting ⮕ Chart of Accounts. On the page that appears, click the See Your Chart of Accounts button to display a page similar to the one shown in Figure 3-11. This page lets you perform a variety of functions. You can print a list of your accounts, for example, if you click the Run Report button at the top of the page.

If you've enabled the Multicurrency feature, you'll see a Currency column. (Read more about multicurrencies later in this chapter in the "Working with Multiple Currencies" section.)

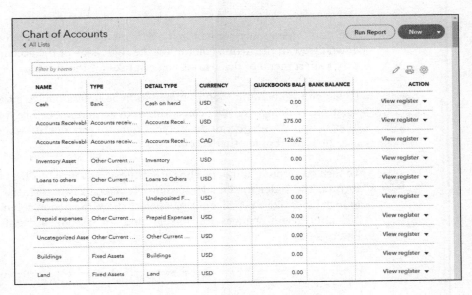

FIGURE 3-11:
The Chart of
Accounts page.

For individual accounts, you can perform a few actions. Balance Sheet accounts have registers; you can view the transactions in the account by clicking View Register in the Action column. You can identify balance sheet accounts by looking in the Type column. Balance Sheet accounts display one of the following account types:

» Bank

» Accounts Receivable

» Other Current Assets

» Fixed Assets

» Other Assets

» Credit Card

» Other Current Liabilities

» Long Term Liabilities

» Accounts Payable

» Equity

For other accounts — the ones without registers — you can run reports for the account by choosing Run Report in the Action column.

You also can edit any account and delete an account you haven't used. Click the down arrow in the Action column (at the right edge of the account's row) to display a short menu of the actions you can take for the account.

WARNING

If you edit an account, don't change its type unless you're sure that you know what you're doing. Consider consulting your accountant before you make a change in an account's category or detail type. You also can identify whether the account is a subaccount of another account.

To turn on account numbers, choose Settings ⇨ Advanced ⇨ Chart of Accounts, and turn on the slider for Enable Account Numbers. Then click the Batch Edit icon (which looks like a pencil and appears just above the Action column). The Chart of Accounts page changes to enable you to assign account numbers (see Figure 3-12).

Chart of Accounts
‹ All Lists

Cancel   Save

NUMBER	NAME	TYPE ▲	DETAIL TYPE	CURRENCY	QUICKBOOKS BALAN	BANK BALANCE
	Cash	Bank	Cash on hand	USD	0.00	
	Accounts Receiv	Accounts receiva...	Accounts Receiva...	USD	375.00	
	Accounts Receiv	Accounts receiva...	Accounts Receiva...	CAD	126.62	
	Inventory Asset	Other Current As...	Inventory	USD	0.00	
	Loans to others	Other Current As...	Loans to Others	USD	0.00	

FIGURE 3-12: The Chart of Accounts page in Batch Edit mode.

If you've enabled the Multicurrency feature, the Chart of Accounts page in Batch Edit mode contains a Currency column.

Type a number for each account, and when you finish entering all the numbers, click the Save button at the top of the page. QBO displays the account number as part of the account name on the Chart of Accounts page.

Follow these steps to add a new account to your chart of accounts (jump to Chapter 8 if you're adding a bank account):

1. Click the New button on the Chart of Accounts page to open the New Category dialog box (see Figure 3-13).

2. Confusingly, at this point QuickBooks refers to new accounts as categories, so enter your account name in the Category Name field.

3. **Click Select Category, choose an option, and then click Next.**

   Your options are Income, Expenses, Expensive Items (Assets), Loans & Money Owed (Liabilities), Owner Investment or Expenses (Equity), Bank & Credit Cards, and Other Accounts.

4. **Click the entry in the Detail Type list that most closely matches the type of account you want to add; then click Select.**

5. **(Optional) Assign a description.**

6. **If you're using account numbers, supply a number for the new account.**

   If you've enabled the Multicurrency feature, the dialog box you use to create a bank account — or any type of asset or liability account except an A/R or A/P account — also contains a list box in which you select the currency for the account. QBO automatically creates currency-related A/R and A/P accounts when you create transactions for foreign customers and vendors.

7. **Click Save.**

   QBO redisplays the Chart of Accounts page, and your new account appears in the list.

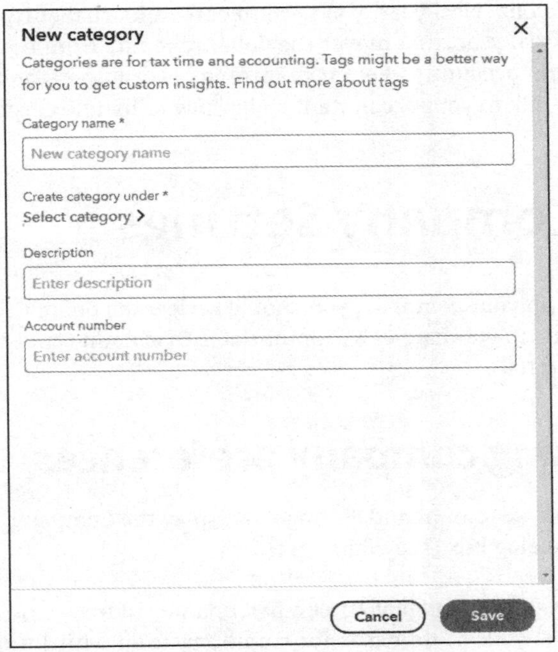

FIGURE 3-13:
The dialog box you use to create an account.

At the end of your fiscal year, you need to enter a journal entry, dated on the last day of your fiscal year, that moves the dollar amounts from the appropriate Draw or Contribution account to Retained Earnings — another equity account. If I've just lost you, talk to your accountant about how to handle closing the year.

Establishing Company Settings

After you set up your company, you should review the default settings that Intuit established and make changes as appropriate. To examine and change payroll settings, see Chapter 9.

Examining company preferences

 Choose Settings ⇨ Account and Settings to display the Company tab of the Account and Settings dialog box (see Figure 3-14).

On this tab, you can change your company name, address, and contact information, as well as your preferences for communication with Intuit. To change any setting, click anywhere in the group where the setting appears. Editable fields or controls will appear for any settings that you can change. When you finish making changes, click the Save button that appears in the group of settings and then move on to another group of settings if you want. When you finish, click Done in the bottom-right corner.

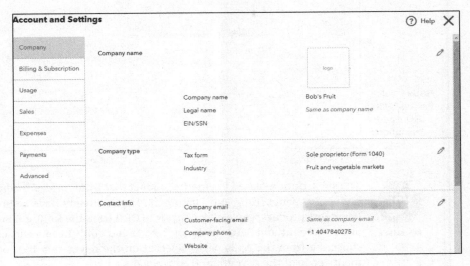

FIGURE 3-14:
Review company settings.

Examining billing and subscription settings and use limits

To review the settings related to your QBO billing and subscription, click Settings and choose the appropriate option. QBO users will choose Settings ⇨ Account and Settings to display the Account and Settings dialog box and then click Billing & Subscription in the pane on the left side. QBO Accountant users will choose Settings ⇨ Your Account.

REMEMBER

You won't see the Billing & Subscription pane if your QBO company is being managed by an accountant who participates in the ProAdvisor Preferred Pricing program, which I discuss in Chapter 12.

The page shown in Figure 3-15 shows you the status of your QuickBooks, QB Payroll, and QuickBooks Payments subscriptions. From this page, you can convert your trial version of QuickBooks and of the QB Payroll product to a regular subscription. Be aware that converting cancels any trial period that you opted into. Although I couldn't show it in Figure 3-15, if you scroll down on your screen, you'll see that you can also use this page to order checks and supplies. As of this writing, you can also reduce your QBO subscription fees by roughly 10 percent by opting into annual billing instead of monthly billing.

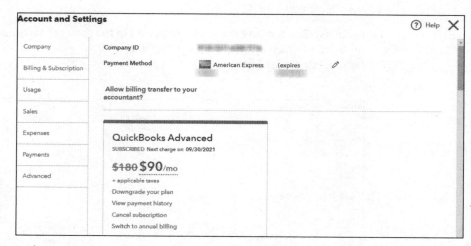

FIGURE 3-15:
Review QBO
billing and
subscription
settings.

REMEMBER

The subscription-based Payments product that Intuit offers enables you to receive online payments from your customers. If you already have a subscription to the Payments product, you can connect it to QBO from the Billing & Subscription page of the Account and Settings dialog box. If you don't have a subscription, you can subscribe from the Apps page (select it on the navigation bar) or from the Payments page of the Account and Settings dialog box.

When you click the Usage tab on the left side of the Account and Settings dialog box, QBO displays the use limits applied to your QBO company based on the version of QBO you selected when you created your company (Simple Start, Essential, Plus, or Advanced).

Setting sales preferences

To review sales preferences for your QBO company, choose Settings ⇨ Account and Settings to display the Account and Settings dialog box; then click Sales in the pane on the left side.

Taking a look at expense preferences

On the Expenses tab of the Account and Settings dialog box, you can control expenses related to purchase orders, bills, and payments you make to vendors (see Figure 3-16). To view this tab, choose Settings ⇨ Account and Settings ⇨ Expenses.

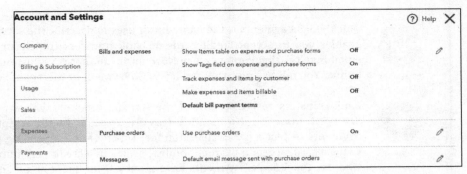

FIGURE 3-16:
Expense
preferences you
can control.

In the Bills and Expenses group of settings, you can opt to display a table on expense and purchase forms so that you can itemize and categorize the products and services you buy. If you purchase goods and services for your customers, you can

>> Add a column to the table so that you can identify the customer for whom you made the purchase.

>> Add a column where you identify expenses and items for which you want to bill customers.

You also can set default bill payment terms.

In the Purchase Orders group, you can opt to use purchase orders and manage up to three custom fields for purchase orders, as well as custom transaction numbers.

In the Messages group, you can establish the settings for the default email message sent with purchase orders, including the salutation, subject, and message. You also can opt to send yourself a copy of the message that goes out with each purchase order.

Examining options to receive customer payments

The Payments tab of the Account and Settings dialog box offers you a way to connect with Intuit Merchant Services via a QuickBooks Payments account. If you don't have a QuickBooks Payments account with Intuit and want one, click the Learn More button. If you already have a QuickBooks Payments account, you can click the Connect button to connect your QBO account with your QuickBooks Payments account.

QuickBooks Payments is the name Intuit uses to describe the service it offers that enables you to accept credit cards or bank transfers from your customers and email invoices that contain a Pay Now button so that your customers can pay you online. You might know this service as GoPayment or Merchant Services.

Bank transfers cost 1 percent of the transfer amount, with a maximum fee of $10 per transaction. No monthly fees are associated with accepting credit card payments — just a per-transaction fee, which varies depending on whether you swipe a card, accept a payment online, or key in a credit card number. QBO users who use QuickBooks Payments have money from qualifying credit or debit card transactions deposited in the bank the next business day, with no extra fees and no extra waiting.

An additional benefit of using QB Payments is that your payments and deposit transactions are entered automatically for you, based on when they're funded, so you don't have to spend time entering those transactions later.

Reviewing advanced preferences

The Advanced tab of the Account and Settings dialog box enables you to change a variety of QBO settings (see Figure 3-17). Choose Settings ⇨ Account and Settings ⇨ Advanced to view and update these settings:

>> In the Accounting group, you can control fiscal-year settings and the accounting method your company uses (cash or accrual).

>> Use the Company Type group to select the tax form your company uses, based on its legal organization.

>> When you create a new company, QBO automatically sets up the chart of accounts that it thinks you'll need. Because QBO doesn't use account numbers in the chart of accounts, you can turn them on in the Chart of Accounts group — something that most accountants prefer you do.

You can replace the chart of accounts that QBO sets up with a chart of accounts that you create outside QBO (in Excel or Google Sheets) and then import. The file you import needs to follow a particular format. You can download a sample layout file when you choose Settings ⇨ Import Data.

>> Depending on the version of QBO you use, you can use the Categories section to opt to track information by using classes, locations, or both. You can also have QBO warn you if you don't assign a class to a transaction, and you can assign a class to each line of a transaction or assign one class to the entire transaction. For locations, you can choose among seven labels; one of these choices might better describe your intended use of the Location category.

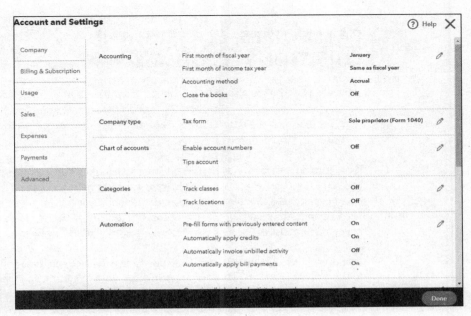

FIGURE 3-17:
The Advanced tab
of the Account
and Settings
dialog box.

>> In the Automation group, you can control some of QBO's automated behavior. If you don't want QBO to prefill new forms with information from forms you entered previously, for example, feel free to turn that setting off.

>> In the Projects section, you can enable QBO's project-tracking features; if you do, QBO organizes all job-related activity in one place. You can read more about projects in Chapter 6.

>> In the Time Tracking section, you can control the appearance of time sheets. You can add a service field to time sheets, for example, so that you can select services performed for each time entry. By default, QBO includes a customer field on time sheets so that you can optionally charge work performed for a customer.

TIP

If time tracking is an integral part of your business, you might consider purchasing the QuickBooks Time add-on app (formerly known as TSheets Time Tracking). It integrates with QBO and gives you extensive time-tracking capabilities, including scheduling employees and letting employees track billable and nonbillable time in the mobile version of the app. Visit the QBO App Center by clicking Apps on the navigation bar of QBO.

>> Use the Currency section to turn on multicurrency tracking and to set your company's home currency. If you change the home-currency symbol, QBO changes the symbol for future transactions; existing transactions will still be calculated at the original currency value. For more information, see "Working with Multiple Currencies" later in this chapter.

WARNING

Turning on multicurrency prevents you from changing your home currency, and you can't turn multicurrency off after you turn it on. Think twice, or maybe even three times, before you enable this feature.

» In the Other Preferences group, you can change a variety of settings, such as date and number formats; whether QBO warns you if you reuse a check number, bill number, or journal entry number you used previously; and how long QBO should wait before signing you out because you haven't done any work. Also, if you prefer to call your customers something other than Customer (such as Client, Patron, or Shopper), you can change the label you use to refer to them.

Customizing Sales Forms

As you'll see in a moment, the Sales section of the Account and Settings page (see Figure 3-18) allows you to change the look and feel of certain sales forms, including the following things:

» The Sales Form Content section allows you to define the fields that appear on invoices, sales receipts, and other sales forms.

>> The Products and Services section enables you to modify the product- and service-related fields that appear on sales forms. QBO Plus and Advanced users can turn on inventory tracking and try out price rules. You can read more about inventory and price rules in Chapter 4.

>> The Messages section is where you set the default email message sent to customers with sales forms, as well the default message that appears in the body of your sales forms.

>> Use the Reminders section to set the default email message that will accompany reminder notifications.

>> Unfortunately, the Online Delivery section doesn't allow you order a pizza, but you can use it to control email delivery options for sales forms. Those options include attaching the sales form as a PDF document, displaying a summary or details of the sales form in the email, and specifying formatting for invoices.

>> Finally, the Statements section lets you choose decide whether to show an aging table at the bottom of the statement.

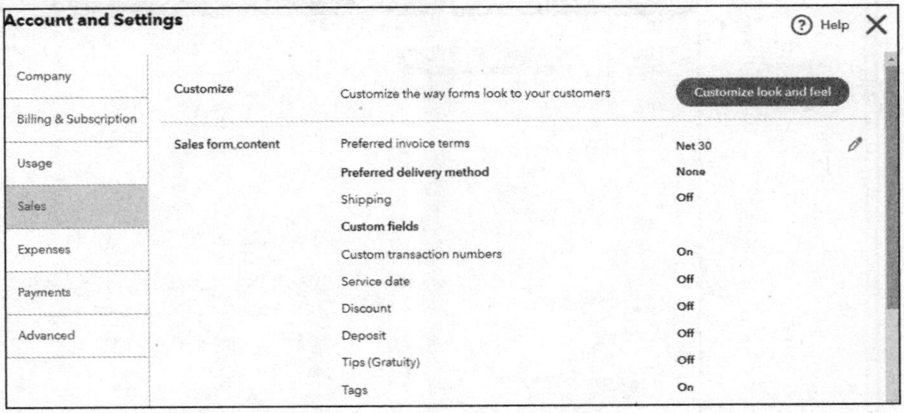

FIGURE 3-18: The Sales page of the Account and Settings dialog box.

To change a sales form, click Settings⇨Account and Settings⇨Sales. Click the Customize Look and Feel button in the Customize section at the top of the page. The Custom Form Styles page displays (see Figure 3-19).

The Custom Form Styles page lists any form styles you have already created. By default, QBO creates one Standard form style for you when you sign up; this style is used by default for invoices, estimates, and sales receipts.

FIGURE 3-19:
Use this page to edit an existing form style or set up a new form style.

If you're satisfied with the appearance of the majority of the form style, you can edit it instead of creating a form style. Alternatively, you can create separate customized forms for invoices, estimates, and sales receipts. To do so, click New Style in the top-right corner of the Custom Form Styles page, and choose (from the drop-down menu) the type of form you want to create. For this example, when I chose Invoice, QBO displayed the page shown in Figure 3-20, which varies only slightly if you opt to edit a different form. In particular, if you opt to create a form style, the page displays a form name for the form you're creating.

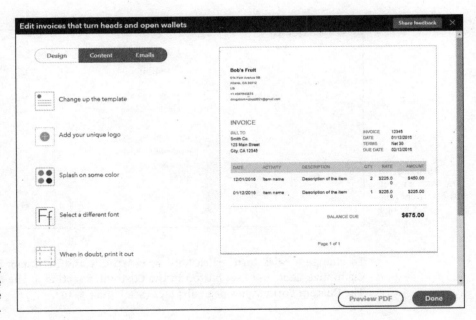

FIGURE 3-20:
The page you use to customize sales forms.

You use the tabs in the top-left corner to establish form style settings:

>> **Design:** On the Design tab, shown in Figure 3-20, you click Change Up the Template to select a style for the form: Airy New, Airy Classic, Modern, Fresh, Bold, or Friendly. The preview shown in Figure 3-20 is the Airy New form style.

You also can modify the appearance and placement of your logo, set the form's font, and try different colors.

>> **Content:** On the Content tab, you can edit the form directly. Just click the pencil icon in the top-right corner of a form section, and make changes in the boxes that appear on the left side of the page.

>> **Emails:** On the Emails tab, shown in Figure 3-21, you can edit the standard and reminder email messages your customers receive with each new or reminder form you send them. You make changes on the left side of the page; the right side of the page shows a preview of what customers receive.

>> If you've enabled Payments in QBO, you can use the Payments tab (not shown) to choose whether you want to give your customers the option to pay online and, if so, by which methods: bank transfers, credit card (fees apply), or both. Note that you need to finish setting up your payments profile before customers can pay you online.

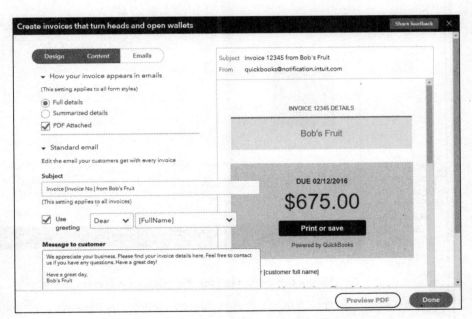

FIGURE 3-21:
Make changes in the emails your customers receive with their forms.

You can click the Preview PDF button in the bottom-right corner of the screen to preview your invoice in PDF format.

Click the Done button in the bottom-right corner to save the changes you make in the appearance of your forms.

Taking Advantage of QuickBooks Labs

From time to time QuickBooks makes new features available in QuickBooks Labs. This is a way to keep tabs on features that are almost ready for prime time, such as QuickBooks Themes which will enable you to activate dark mode in QuickBooks.

Here's how you turn on a QuickBooks Lab feature:

1. **Choose Settings ⇨ QuickBooks Labs.**

   As shown in Figure 3-22, the QuickBooks Labs window appears.

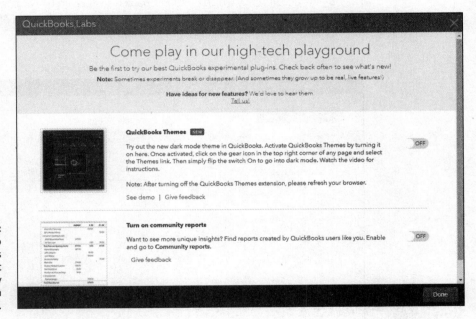

FIGURE 3-22:
Use this page to turn on features that aren't yet available by default in QuickBooks.

2. **Toggle the Off button for the features you want to try.**

   The Off button changes to an On button. You can always turn features off again if you don't like the effect or simply change your mind.

TIP

   Click Give Feedback on any feature to share your thoughts on any QuickBooks Labs feature. You can also click the Tell Us link to suggest new features that you'd like to see added to QuickBooks.

3. **Click Done when you've enabled or disabled any features.**

   Your QBO company reappears, with the features you selected enabled.

REMEMBER

You may need to refresh the browser page to see the new features you chose to make available. Click your browser's Refresh button or press F5 on your keyboard.

Working with Multiple Currencies

If you have an Essentials subscription or higher you can use multiple currencies, whereas Simple Start subscribers are only allowed a single home currency. Typically, you need the Multicurrency feature if you sell products and services to customers or buy products and services from vendors whose base currency is different from your home currency. If you don't need to record transactions in multiple currencies, don't turn this feature on, because you can't turn it off again. As an added bonus you can stop reading here and move on to the next chapter.

WARNING

The Multicurrency feature doesn't support customer- or currency-specific pricing. Take a look at QuickBooks Desktop if you need this functionality.

DO I NEED THE MULTICURRENCY FEATURE?

You need the Multicurrency feature only if you work with customers or vendors whose base currency is different from your base currency. Suppose that your home country doesn't use U.S. dollars, and you buy and sell only in your home country's currency. In this case, you work in a single currency, and you don't need the Multicurrency feature. Instead, you need to use the International version of QBO and set your home currency to the proper denomination.

If you turn on the Multicurrency feature, you can't change your home currency. If your home currency isn't the U.S. dollar, you can't use many U.S.-based services, such as Payroll and Payments.

Because you can assign only one currency to each account, customer, or vendor, you need to add new asset and liability accounts, customers, and vendors for each currency that you'll use in transactions. As you create these new elements in QBO, you assign to them the currency you want to use. Be aware that after you've posted a transaction to an account, a vendor, or a customer, you can't change the currency for the account, vendor, or customer.

Income and expense accounts continue to use your home currency — the currency of the country where your business is physically located.

If you've decided to use the Multicurrency feature, follow these steps:

1. **Choose your home currency.**

2. **Turn on the Multicurrency feature on the Advanced tab of the Accounts and Settings page.**

3. **Set up the currencies you intend to use.**

4. **Add customers, vendors, and asset and liability accounts for each currency you expect to use.**

   Note that QBO automatically creates accounts receivable (A/R) and accounts payable (A/P) accounts in the foreign currency after you create one foreign sales and one foreign purchasing transaction, so you don't need to set up those accounts.

5. **Enter transactions.**

Seeing how the Multicurrency feature changes QBO

After you turn on the Multicurrency feature, you see new fields in QBO. Specifically, you'll see changes on these screens:

>> When you open the Settings menu, you'll see the Currencies option at the bottom of the Lists column. You use the Currencies list to establish the foreign currency you want to use, along with the exchange rate.

>> When you view the chart of accounts, you'll find a Currency column that shows the currency assigned to each account. You'll also find a new account: an Other Expense account called Exchange Gain or Loss.

>> When you view bank and credit card registers, the currency of each transaction appears in parentheses in the Payment, Deposit (Charge in Credit Card registers), Sales Tax, and Balance Due columns. You'll also see a Foreign Currency Exchange Rate column in these registers.

>> Sales and purchase forms use both your home currency and the foreign currency; QBO does all the conversions for you onscreen.

>> On QuickBooks reports, you find that QBO converts all foreign-currency amounts to home-currency amounts, automatically reflecting exchange rates.

Changing your home currency

You can change your home currency from the same place that you enable the Multicurrency feature. Follow these steps:

WARNING

After you turn on the Multicurrency feature, you can't change your home currency. And you can't turn off the Multicurrency feature because it affects many accounts and balances in QBO.

1. **Choose Settings ⇨ Account and Settings.**

The Account and Settings dialog box appears.

2. **Click Advanced.**

3. **Scroll down to the Currency section.**

4. **Set your home currency by clicking the Home Currency list box.**

Choose the currency of your country. If you're not in the United States, don't set the United States as your home currency.

5. **Activate Multicurrency by clicking the green toggle button (see Figure 3-23).**

After you turn on the Multicurrency feature, QBO warns you that

(a) You can't turn it off.

(b) You can't change your home currency.

6. **Select the check box titled I Understand I Can't Undo Multicurrency.**

7. **Click Save.**

8. **Click Done.**

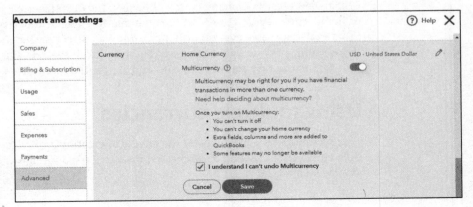

FIGURE 3-23: Turning on Multicurrency.

Setting up currencies

After enabling the Multicurrency option, you'll find an option to display the Currencies list if you click the Settings button; the Currencies option appears at the bottom of the Lists section on the Settings menu. Follow these steps to set up the currencies you need to use:

1. **Choose Settings ⇨ Currencies.**

   QBO displays the Currencies page (see Figure 3-24).

FIGURE 3-24:
The Currencies
page.

2. **In the top-right corner of the page, click Add Currency.**

   QBO displays a drop-down list.

3. **Choose the currency you want to use.**

4. **Click Add.**

   QBO redisplays the Currencies page with the new currency added.

QBO always records exchange rates, shown on the Currencies page, as the number of home-currency units needed to equal one foreign-currency unit. QBO downloads exchange rates every four hours from Wall Street on Demand, but you can, if you want, provide your own exchange rate. Click the Edit Currency Exchange link next to the rate you want to edit, and supply the rate you want to use.

Using multiple currencies

This section takes a brief look at the effects of creating an invoice that uses multiple currencies. Creating a purchase transaction for a foreign vendor works in a similar fashion.

REMEMBER

At this time, QuickBooks doesn't support letting either your employees or contractors record time entries (by using either the Weekly Time sheet or the Single Time Activity) associated with a foreign-currency customer.

Suppose that you have a customer whose base currency is the Canadian dollar and your home currency is the U.S. dollar. In this example, when I refer to the "foreign currency," I mean the Canadian dollar. Here's how to establish a foreign currency for a customer:

1. **Choose Sales ⇨ Customers (Sales & Expenses ⇨ >Customers) from the navigation bar.**

   The Customer page appears.

2. **Click New Customer if you need to add a customer; otherwise, click the customer name on the list, and then click the Edit button at the top of the customer's page.**

   If you're adding a new customer, fill in the fields in the usual fashion (see Chapter 4).

3. **Activate the Payment and Billing tab.**

4. **Select the customer's currency from the This Customer Pays Me With field.**

   In Figure 3-25, the customer, uninspiringly named Foreign Currency, uses the Canadian dollar.

   You'll find a similar setting available when you create a new vendor.

TIP

5. **Click Save.**

You'll see the foreign currency listed in the Currency column of your customer list. Your home-currency customers display your home currency.

Next, in the Invoice window, select your foreign-currency customer. QBO automatically displays, below the customer's name, the two currencies (first the foreign currency and then your home currency) associated with the transaction (see Figure 3-26).

When you add products or services to the invoice, the amounts for each line appear in the foreign currency, and totals appear in both currencies, as shown in Figure 3-27. The balance due on the transaction appears in the foreign currency so that your customer knows how much to pay.

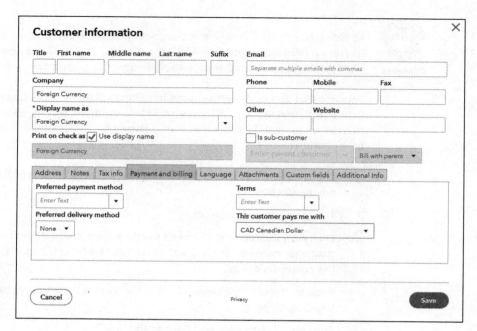

FIGURE 3-25:
Assigning a
foreign currency
to a new
customer.

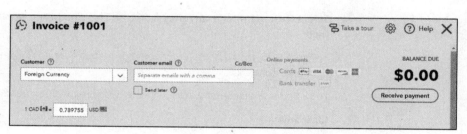

FIGURE 3-26:
Creating an
invoice for a
customer who
uses a foreign
currency.

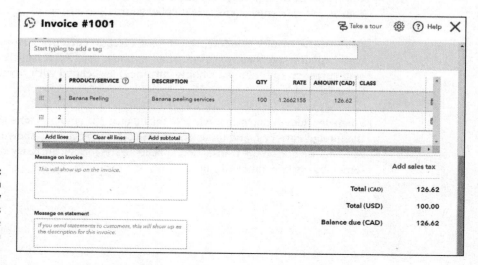

FIGURE 3-27:
An invoice for a
foreign-currency
customer shows
values in both the
home and foreign
currencies.

REMEMBER

Saving your first sales or purchase document for a customer or vendor who uses a foreign currency causes QuickBooks to automatically establish foreign-currency-related Accounts Receivable (A/R) and Accounts Payable (A/P) accounts.

QuickBooks reports show values in your home currency, such as the A/R Aging Summary in Figure 3-28. The customer who uses a foreign currency is at the bottom of the screen.

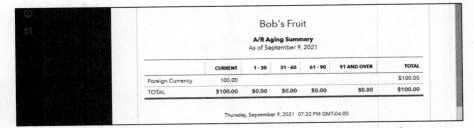

FIGURE 3-28:
Values in reports appear in your home currency.

Bob's Fruit

A/R Aging Summary
As of September 9, 2021

	CURRENT	1 - 30	31 - 60	61 - 90	91 AND OVER	TOTAL
Foreign Currency	100.00					$100.00
TOTAL	$100.00	$0.00	$0.00	$0.00	$0.00	$100.00

Thursday, September 9, 2021 07:32 PM GMT-04:00

Figure 3-29 shows the multiple A/R accounts that QBO uses when you've enabled the Multicurrency feature and created a sales transaction in a foreign currency. The values in the report appear in the home currency.

FIGURE 3-29:
QuickBooks establishes separate A/R accounts for transactions involving foreign-currency customers.

Bob's Fruit

Balance Sheet Detail
As of September 9, 2021

DATE	TRANSACTION TYPE	NUM	NAME	SPLIT	DEBIT	CREDIT	AMOUNT
ASSETS							
Accounts Receivable (A/R)							
09/09/2021	Invoice	1002	Lilian Milburn	Services	$375.00		375.00
Total for Accounts Receivable (A/R)							$375.00
Accounts Receivable (A/R) - CAD							
09/09/2021	Invoice	1001	Foreign Currency	Services	$100.00		100.00
Total for Accounts Receivable (A/R) - CAD							$100.00
TOTAL ASSETS							$475.00
LIABILITIES AND EQUITY							
Equity							
Retained Earnings							
Net Income							$475.00
Total Equity							$475.00
Total Liabilities and Equity							$475.00

Thursday, September 9, 2021 07:40 PM GMT-04:00

Chapter **4**

Managing List Information

I n this chapter, I cover the information you need to set up items or services you sell or buy and the lists of customers and vendors you sell to or buy from. You'll see how you can import these records from a spreadsheet or create new records manually. I also discuss creating bundles of items to streamline your sales process. Finally, at the end of the chapter, you find out where to find other lists you might need, such as terms, locations, and payment methods.

Importing Customers and Vendors

You can spend less time getting up and running with QuickBooks by importing your customers and vendors. If you're migrating from QuickBooks Desktop to QuickBooks Online, you can bring over all your records, or choose to selectively import only some lists if you want to start with a clean slate. For instance, it's easy to import customers and vendors, as well as inventory items for products and services that you offer.

REMEMBER

Importing lists isn't the same thing as importing a QuickBooks Desktop company. For details on importing a company, see Chapter 13.

Most accounting and contact management platforms allow you to export the customer and vendor information you've saved to a Microsoft Excel workbook or a comma-separated-values (.csv) file. Then you can use Excel or Google Sheets to access the exported data. Open the export file in the spreadsheet of your choice to review the information. If you happen to make any edits, be sure to save your file. You'll be able to import your list into QuickBooks.

Figure 4-1 shows the screen for importing vendors. The process for importing customers works the same way.

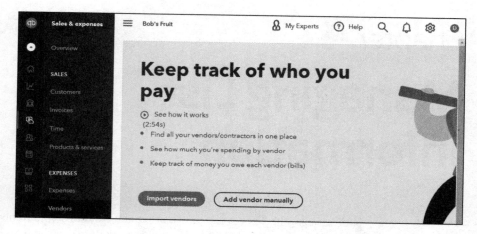

FIGURE 4-1:
It's easy to import vendors.

REMEMBER

The navigation bar you see in this book may differ from what you see in your QuickBooks company. QuickBooks defaults to Business View, but I find that Accountant View is easier to navigate because it puts more commands at the top level. Click Settings (the gear icon) in the top-right corner of the screen and choose Accountant View from the drop-down menu to change from Business View, or vice versa. Advanced subscribers also have some commands that aren't available in the other subscription levels.

TIP

The steps that follow assume that you've installed Excel on your computer. If you don't own a copy of Excel, you can use Google Sheets (http://sheets.google.com) and then choose File⇨Import to open an Excel workbook in Sheets. QuickBooks allows you to import directly from Sheets, so you won't have to save the file back to your computer.

TIP

If you don't already have a vendors list to import, you can download a sample file that illustrates what each import file should look like, such as for vendors. Follow these steps to review the sample file for the information you need for a newly created file:

1. **Choose Expenses ⇨ Vendors (Sales & Expenses ⇨ Vendors).**

2. **Click the Import Vendors button.**

If you don't see an Import Vendors button, click the arrow next to New Vendor to make the button display.

The Import Vendors page appears, as shown in Figure 4-2.

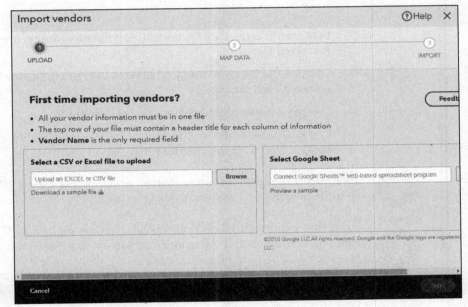

FIGURE 4-2:
The Import
Vendors page.

3. **Click the Download a Sample File link.**

The sample file appears in the downloads bar of most browsers. Otherwise, you can find it in your Downloads folder.

4. **Open the sample file by clicking it on the downloads bar of your browser window or double-clicking the file in your Downloads folder.**

The sample file opens in Excel (see Figure 4-3).

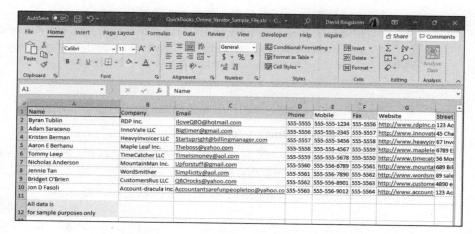

FIGURE 4-3:
A file showing the
format you need
to import list
information
successfully.

5. In Microsoft Excel, click **Enable Editing** if the spreadsheet opens in Protected View.

6. Examine the file's content by scrolling to the right to see the information stored in each column.

7. Create your own file, modeling it on the sample file.

If you also use QuickBooks Desktop, you can export lists to CSV or Excel files; see QuickBooks Desktop Help for details.

REMEMBER

Your import file can't contain more than 1,000 rows or exceed 2MB. You can save your file as either an Excel workbook or a CSV file.

TIP

Dates that you import into BO must be in *yyyy-mm-dd* format. If you have a date entered in cell A1 of an Excel worksheet, you can use this formula to transform a date such as 2/23/2022 into 2022-02-23:

```
=TEXT(A1, "yyyy-mm-dd")
```

THE SAMPLE IMPORT FILE'S LAYOUT

You'll see that information in the sample file is in a table format, where each row in the spreadsheet contains all the information about a single customer or vendor (each row is referred to as a *record*), and each column contains the same type of information for all customers and vendors (each column is referred to as one *field* in a record). In Figure 4-3, all the information about Aaron E Berhanu appears in row 5, and all vendor email addresses appear in column C. Also note that row 1 contains a label that identifies the type of information found in each column; you must include identifying labels in the first row of your data file.

Then you can copy the formulas and choose Home ⇨ Paste ⇨ Paste Special to convert the formulas to static values in the *yyyy-mm-dd* format.

Here's how to import a vendor list (and the steps are similar for importing any other list into QuickBooks):

1. **Make sure that your spreadsheet or CSV file is closed.**

2. **Navigate to the corresponding list page, such as Vendors (refer to Figure 4-1).**

3. **Click the Import or (in this case) Import Vendors button.**

4. **Click the Browse button for an Excel or CSV file or Connect for a Google Sheet (refer to Figure 4-2).**

5. **Navigate to the folder where you saved the file containing your list information.**

6. **Select the file and click Open for an Excel or CSV file, as shown in Figure 4-4 or Select for a Google Sheet.**

   The Import page displays the name of the file you selected.

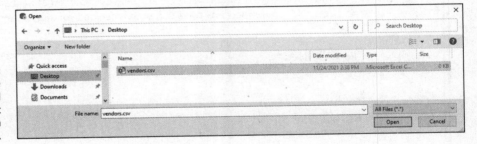

FIGURE 4-4:
A file showing the format you need to import list information successfully.

7. **Click Next.**

   Your file is uploaded.

8. **Make sure that the fields in your data file match the corresponding QuickBooks fields.**

   Use the Your Field drop-down lists (see Figure 4-5) to match the columns in your file with the import files.

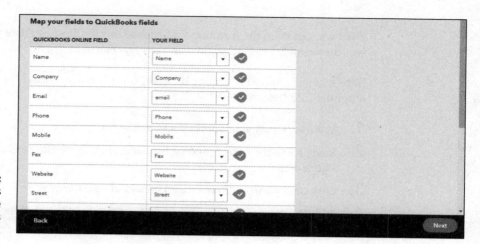

Map your fields to QuickBooks fields

QUICKBOOKS ONLINE FIELD	YOUR FIELD	
Name	Name	✓
Company	Company	✓
Email	email	✓
Phone	Phone	✓
Mobile	Mobile	✓
Fax	Fax	✓
Website	Website	✓
Street	Street	✓

Back
Next

FIGURE 4-5:
Match the fields in your data file with QuickBooks fields.

9. **Click the Next button.**

   As shown in Figure 4-6, a confirmation screen reports the records to be imported. You can widen the columns as needed.

10. **Review the records to make sure that the information is correct.**

   You can change the information in any field by clicking that field and typing. You also can deselect any rows that you've decided you don't want to import.

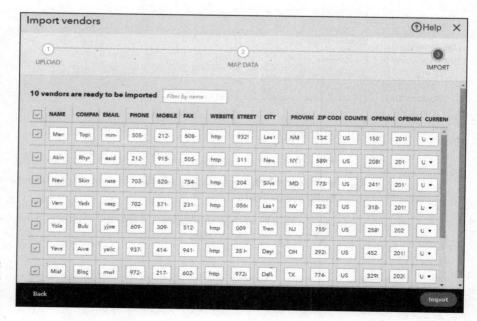

FIGURE 4-6:
The records imported from your data file.

11. When you're satisfied that the information is correct, click the Import button (refer to Figure 4-6).

As shown in Figure 4-7, QuickBooks displays a status message that tells you how many records were imported. During my test, two records wouldn't import because I had opening balance dates that were in *mm-dd-yyyy* format instead of *yyyy-mm-dd*.

WARNING

If the Import button is unavailable, some portion of the data can't be imported. Look for a field highlighted in red to identify information that can't be imported. If the problem isn't apparent, contact Intuit support for help, or set up the records manually.

FIGURE 4-7:
QuickBooks imports as many records as it can and shows you any records it couldn't import.

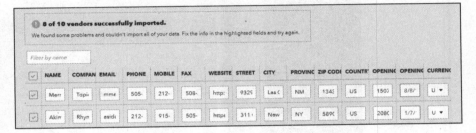

Adding New Records to a List

The steps are basically the same to do manual setup for a new customer, vendor, employee, or contractor. You start by clicking the appropriate link on the navigation bar: Sales for customers, Expenses for vendors, and Payroll for employees and contractors.

Creating a new customer

Customers have the most options you can establish, such as subcustomers and customer types.

REMEMBER

If you've determined that your company needs to use the Multicurrency feature, turn it on before you start creating new records so that you can assign the proper currency at the appropriate time. See Chapter 3 for details on the Multicurrency feature.

To set up a new vendor, employee, or contractor, follow these steps:

1. **Choose Sales ⇨ Customers (Sales & Expenses ⇨ Customers) to display the Customers page, shown in Figure 4-8.**

2. **Click the New Customer button in the top-right corner of the page.**

    The Customer Information dialog box appears (see Figure 4-9).

FIGURE 4-8:
The Customers page allows you to manage existing customers and add new ones.

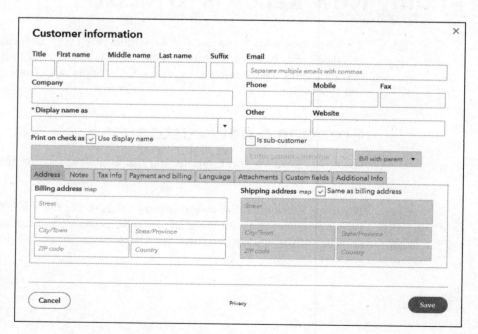

FIGURE 4-9:
Use this dialog box to enter information for a new customer.

3. Type the requested information.

For details on creating and assigning customer types on the Additional Info tab, see the next section, "Using customer types." If you need to set up a subcustomer, see the section "Adding subcustomers."

4. Click the Save button.

You also can view and edit the details you just established for the customer if you click the customer's name within the customer list. To redisplay the complete list of Customers, choose Sales ➪ Customers (Get Paid & Pay ➪ Customers).

TIP You can mark any customer, vendor, or contractor inactive — as long as the associated record has a $0 balance — by clicking the Action arrow at the right edge of the record and then choosing Make Inactive from the drop-down menu.

Using customer types

You can create customer types to group otherwise-unrelated customers, such as those to whom perhaps you offer special discounts at certain times of the year. To create customer types, click the Customer Types button in the top-right corner of the Customers page (refer to Figure 4-8). On the page that appears, select New Customer Type, complete the New Customer Type field, and then click Save.

To assign a customer type to a customer, click the Edit button to the right of the customer's name on the Customers page or on the Customer Details tab to display the dialog box shown in Figure 4-9. Select the Additional Info tab to assign a customer type to the customer.

REMEMBER QuickBooks often allows you to add new items on the fly to a drop-down list, such as new customers and vendors, but you can only choose from existing customer types on the Additional Info tab.

TIP You can simultaneously assign customer types to multiple customers. See the section "Working with a batch of records" later in this chapter.

QuickBooks offers three reports that allow you to view transactions or customers by type:

>> Sales by Customer Type

>> Sales by Customer

>> Customer Contact List

The first report doesn't require any modifications, but you need to group the Sales by Customer report by Customer Type. You also need to enable the Customer Type column on the Customer Contact List.

You can read more about running reports in Chapter 10.

Adding subcustomers

Identifying subcustomers enables you to create a hierarchy for customers that you can use pretty much any way you want. An architect, for example, might use sub-customers to represent jobs or projects for a particular client (called the *parent customer* in QuickBooks), and an attorney could use subcustomers to represent different legal matters being handled for a given client. If you have a Plus sub-scription or higher, see Chapter 6 to find out about projects before you embark on creating subcustomers because projects may give you better control and reporting.

If you do set up subcustomers, you can choose to bill either the parent or the sub-customer. Subcustomers' balances are included in the parent customer's balance. Transactions for subcustomers appear in the subcustomer's register as well as the parent customer's register. You can create as many subcustomers as you want, but, for any given customer, you can assign subcustomers only up five levels deep, including the parent customer.

WARNING

If you're considering using the Projects feature, which I discuss in Chapter 6, be aware that you can easily convert first-level subcustomers to projects if you establish the billing for the subcustomer separately from the parent customer. In other words, when you set up the subcustomer, enable the Bill This Customer option if you think you might want to convert the subcustomer to a project.

To create a subcustomer, follow the steps in "Creating a new customer" earlier in this chapter, and check the Is Sub-Customer box (below the Other field) of the Customer Information dialog box (refer to Figure 4-9).

Working with Records

Most lists will enable you to sort, export, and perform group actions, particularly the customer, vendor, and employees lists. There's always an exception to the rule, though. For instance, you can only search or prepare Form 1099s from the contractors list. However, you can print a basic report for any list by clicking the Print List button, which is shown in the margin and is just above the Action column.

Searching lists

To search for a particular record, type some characters that match the person or company name in the Search box that appears above the list, as shown in Figure 4-10, and then click on the name when it appears on the list.

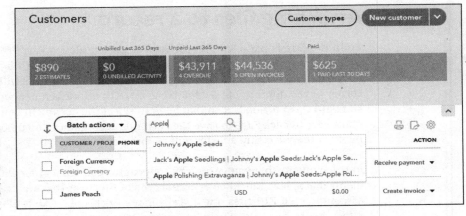

FIGURE 4-10:
To find a particular record in a list, use the Search box that appears above the list.

A page of related information appears. The page may have multiple tabs. In Figure 4-11, you see the Transaction List tab, the Projects tab, the Customer Details tab, and the Late Fees tab.

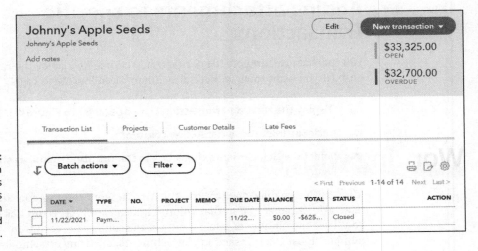

FIGURE 4-11:
The Transaction List tab shows transactions associated with the selected record.

TIP

The Project tab appears only if you've enabled the Projects feature in your company. You can read more about projects in Chapter 6.

Click the Edit button on any tab to edit information about that record. Click the New Transaction button to add a transaction associated with that record.

Attaching files to a record

From the details page of a record, you can attach files to keep track of important financial information. You can attach any almost any type of file up to 20MB. To do so, simply drag and drop the file to the Attachments box in the bottom-left corner of the appropriate details page, or click the Attachments box to display a standard Open dialog box so that you can select the document you want to attach. Make sure to click Save to save the customer record once you upload your attachments; otherwise, any uploads will be discarded.

Any documents that you've attached appear in sequential order within the Attachments dialog box. QuickBooks notifies you of file types that are unacceptable, such as compressed ZIP files and Excel Binary workbooks (.xlsb files). To be clear, attachments can collectively exceed 20 MB, but any single attachment cannot exceed 20MB in size. You can remove attachments by clicking the X to the right of the file name in the Attachments field, but be aware that QuickBooks does not ask you to confirm. If you click the X, the attachment vanishes immediately.

Adding attachments to specific transactions

You can add attachments to specific transactions. To display the Attachments column (if you want to view these attachments), follow these steps:

1. **Display the record's Transaction List page (refer to Figure 4-11).**

2. **Click Settings above the Action column.**

3. **Select the Attachments check box in the resulting menu, as shown in Figure 4-12.**

After you've enabled the feature, the Attachments column appears as part of the table grid. A paper clip in that column indicates that a record has an attachment. You'll see the number of attachments in the column for each transaction. Click the number to list the transaction's attachments; click any attachment to open it.

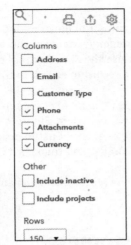

FIGURE 4-12:
Enabling the
Attachments
column on the
Transaction List.

Switching from record to record

When you finish working with one record, you can easily switch to another in that list by using the list's Split View pane.

You can click the Split View icon, which looks like an arrow pointing to the right toward three stripes, to display a pane that shows the records stored in the list (see Figure 4-13).

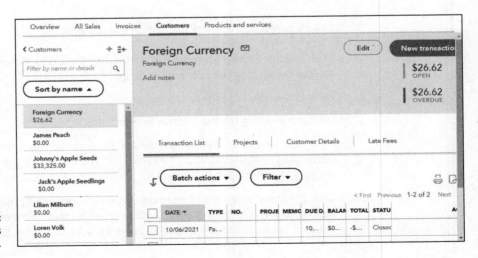

FIGURE 4-13:
Displaying a list's
Split View.

While working in the Split View pane, you can scroll down to find a record, or you can type a few letters of the person's or company's name in the Search box at the top of the list to find that record. You can use the Sort By drop-down list to sort the list by name or by open balance. Click a record to switch to that page.

To add a new record to the list, click the plus (+) symbol at the top of the list in the Split View pane to see the dialog box shown earlier in Figure 4-9. To return to the Customers page shown earlier in Figure 4-8, click Customers at the top of the Split View list or click Sales on the navigation bar and then click Customers.

 To close Split View, click the Close Split View button, which is an arrow pointing left toward three stripes.

Sorting a list on the Customers or Vendors page

You can sort the lists on the Customers and Vendors page by name or open balance. By default, the entries on these pages are sorted alphabetically by name in ascending order.

TIP

You can sort employees in alphabetical order and reverse alphabetical order, by pay method, or by status (active or inactive). The contractors list always appears in alphabetical order and can't be sorted. I talk more about employees and contractors in Chapter 9.

To sort a customers or vendors list, follow these steps:

1. Click Sales or Expenses on the navigation bar; then click Customers or Vendors to display the appropriate page.

For this example, I use the Customers page.

2. Click the heading for the column by which you want to sort.

If you click the Customer/Company column heading, the customers appear in descending alphabetical order. If you click the Open Balance column heading, the list appears in Open Balance order, from lowest to highest.

3. Click the column again to sort in reverse order and display balances from highest to lowest (which I'm sure will be of much more interest to you because we all like to see the big numbers first).

Exporting a list to Excel or Google Sheets

You can export QuickBooks lists to Excel or Google Sheets by doing the following:

1. **Open a blank worksheet in your spreadsheet program.**

2. **Choose File ➪ Import, and follow the onscreen prompts.**

3. **Click the appropriate link on the navigation bar, such as Expenses (Sales & Expenses) to display a list.**

   For this exercise, click Vendors.

4. **Click the middle button in the resulting page to export the list to an Excel file.**

   A button for the file typically appears on the status bar, as shown in Figure 4-14.

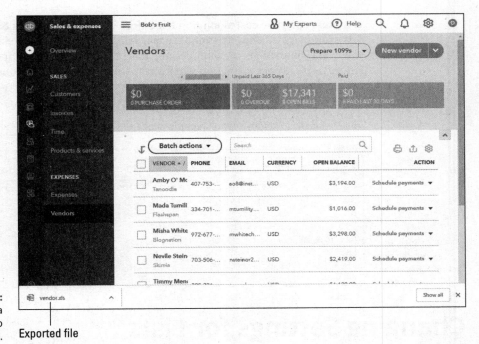

FIGURE 4-14:
Exporting a vendor list to Excel.

Exported file

5. Click the button at the bottom of the screen or look in your Downloads folder to open the file.

6. If you're using Microsoft Excel you may have to click Enable Editing to exit Protected View.

TIP

I talk about how to disable Protected View and to streamline opening Excel files exported from QuickBooks in Chapter 11.

If you're using Google Sheets instead of Excel, choose File ⇨ Import. Follow the prompts to upload your workbook, after which you can work with the spreadsheet in the usual way.

Working with a batch of records

Certain lists allow you carry out simultaneous actions for a group of records, such as sending emails, paying bills online, or making records inactive. You can also create and send customer statements and assign customer types in this fashion.

You must open the corresponding list before you can carry out a batch action. For this example, I used the Customers page. Select the check boxes next to the records you want to include in your action, and click the Batch Actions button (see Figure 4-15). Select the action you want to take, and follow the onscreen prompts to complete the action.

Click the boxes to modify several records at once.

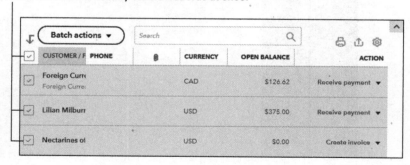

FIGURE 4-15: Performing an action for several customers.

Changing Settings for Lists

You can control the appearance of certain lists by determining which columns are displayed and whether to include inactive records. Here's how you do it:

1. **Display a list, such as Vendors, and then click the Settings button above the Action column, as shown in Figure 4-16.**

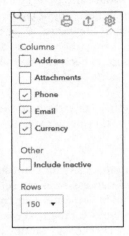

FIGURE 4-16:
The settings menu allows you to hide or display certain columns.

2. **Toggle check boxes as needed to display or hide columns in the list.**

3. **Click the Settings button again to close the menu.**

REMEMBER

The elements you can show or hide depend on the list you're using. You can show or hide address information in Customers and Vendors lists, for example, but not in Employees and Contractors lists.

To adjust the width of any column, hover over the right edge of any column heading, and drag the double-headed arrow to the left or right (see Figure 4-17). When you start to drag, the mouse pointer reverts to a pointer, and a vertical bar appears to guide you in resizing the column. Release the mouse button when you're satisfied with the column width.

Adjusting the column width

FIGURE 4-17:
Adjusting the width allotted to the vendor's name on the Vendors page.

TIP

QuickBooks remembers column width adjustments that you make in registers and on pages like Customers and Vendors, even after you sign out.

Setting Up Sales Taxes

You may be saying, "Why are you talking about sales taxes? This chapter is supposed to be about lists, and sales taxes aren't lists." Right you are, but setting up sales taxes *before* you set up items makes your life easier. Why? QuickBooks uses the sales tax information you supply as you set up items. If you don't set up sales taxes before you set up items, you'll have to go back and edit all your items for taxability. Who wants to do that?

QuickBooks offers a wizard that walks you through setting up sales taxes by asking you easy questions such as your address and whether you need to charge sales tax outside your state.

TIP

QuickBooks tracks and reports sales tax automatically for companies that operate on the accrual basis of accounting. You can't access sales tax setup if your company uses cash-basis accounting. What should you do if your company operates on cash-basis accounting? Temporarily set your company accounting method to Accrual before you set up sales taxes (choose Settings⇨Account and Settings⇨Advanced). Then set up sales tax and *then* change your accounting method back to Cash. Be aware that the Sales Tax Center will track your sales tax liability on the Accrual basis, but you can use the Sales Tax Liability reports to identify the correct amount of sales tax to pay. I talk about reporting and paying sales tax in Chapter 16.

REMEMBER

Six days before I submitted the last chapter of this book, I noticed that Intuit had made a late-breaking change regarding sales tax. Going forward, sales tax is calculated automatically based on a given customer's address, which means that you no longer have to set each customer's tax rate. But you need to fill in the customer address information before sales tax can be computed.

The first time you click Taxes on the navigation bar, QuickBooks prompts you to set up sales tax. Here's what you do:

1. **Click the Get Started button.**

   The wizard asks you to verify your address, after which you click Next.

2. **If you've imported your data from QuickBooks Desktop, the Bulk Matching screen enables you to assign one or more existing tax rates to an official agency name.**

   This screen appears only when applicable, so don't panic if you find yourself looking for a nonexistent Bulk Matching screen in your QuickBooks company.

WARNING

To riff off a classic movie line, the Bulk Matching screen related to sales tax will not be ignored, meaning that you can't advance through the sales setup process without assigning an official agency name to each of your existing sales tax rates.

3. **Click Next after you assign the sales tax agencies to display the Review Your Rates screen.**

4. **Click Change next to any tax rate to return to the Bulk Matching screen, or click Save to confirm your choices.**

A new screen reports You're All Set.

5. **Click Continue to see a short series of tax-related help screens that get you oriented.**

6. **Click Continue when prompted, and then click View Sales Tax Center.**

Whether or the Bulk Matching screen appeared in Step 2, a new screen asks How Often Do You File Sales Tax?

7. **Select the filing frequency for each agency and then click Next Agency if applicable; otherwise, click Save.**

At this point, the Sales Tax Center appears. Here, you can keep tabs on how much sales tax has been collected and when your next due dates are.

QuickBooks assumes that all customers are subject to sales tax, so you'll need to edit any tax-exempt customers (such as government agencies, schools, and charities) by following these steps:

1. **Choose Sales ⇨ Customers ⇨ Edit.**

2. **Deselect the This Customer is Taxable check box on the Tax Info tab of the Customer Details dialog box.**

3. **Supply exemption details, such as the reason why the customer is exempt from sales tax or the customer's exemption certificate ID.**

You could also attach a copy of the exemption certificate on the Customer Details tab.

REMEMBER

Because many small-business owners rely on their accountants to handle sales tax reporting, you can find more information about reporting and paying sales taxes in Chapter 16.

Working with Products and Services Items

 You can enable inventory tracking if you have a Plus or Advanced subscription. Choose Settings ⇨ Account and Settings. In the Account and Settings dialog box, click Sales; in the Products and Services section, click Track Inventory Quantity on Hand.

 Plus and Advanced subscribers can support basic inventory tracking capabilities, but if you're looking for inventory capabilities to support manufacturing, you'll be happier in QuickBooks Desktop Premier or Enterprise versions.

TIP

 To display the Products and Services list shown in Figure 4-18, choose Settings ⇨ Products and Services. To squeeze more records on the screen, click Settings and then select the Compact check box.

FIGURE 4-18:
The Products and Services list.

TAKING ADVANTAGE OF SKUs

You can control whether stock-keeping unit (SKU) information appears in the Products and Services list and on transaction forms from the Account and Settings dialog box. Choose Settings ⇨ Account and Settings ⇨ Sales. In the Products and Services section, toggle the Show SKU option, click Save, and then click Done. If you like, you can add the SKU to any custom invoice forms, which I discuss in Chapter 3.

You use the Products and Services list pretty much the same way you use the Customer and Vendor lists. You can search for an item by its name, SKU, or sales description, for example. You can identify the columns you can use to sort the list if you slide your mouse over the column heading; if the mouse pointer changes to a hand, you can click that column to sort the list using the information in that column.

REMEMBER

Enabling the Multicurrency feature (described in Chapter 3) has no effect on inventory item valuations; QuickBooks assesses and reports inventory item values in home currency units, regardless of the currency used by the vendor who sold you the items. For that reason, the Products and Services list shows no distinctions related to currency.

You can import and export items by using an Excel or CSV file, the same way that you import and export record information. See the sections "Importing Customers and Vendors" and "Exporting a list to Excel or Google Sheets" earlier in this chapter. The importing and exporting processes include information about the item's taxability.

Establishing categories

Categories are similar to subitems in QuickBooks Desktop but can't be used for items migrated from QuickBooks Desktop. Categories can help you organize what you sell and can group related items on various reports. Categories don't affect your accounting or your financial reports, and you can't assign categories to transactions. You can also use classes and/or locations to categorize related information. For instance, a construction company might have classes for Residential and Commercial activity. Or the Locations field would allow you to assign transactions to specific offices. See Chapter 3 for more information.

You can create new categories as you create items, or if you prefer, you can click the More button on the Products and Services list page and choose Manage Categories to create categories so that they're available as you create items. It's your call.

To set up one or more categories in advance, follow these steps:

1. **Click the Settings button and then choose All Lists.**

   The All Lists page appears.

2. **Click the Product Categories link, which appears in the first column just below Products and Services.**

   The Product Categories page appears, as shown in Figure 4-19.

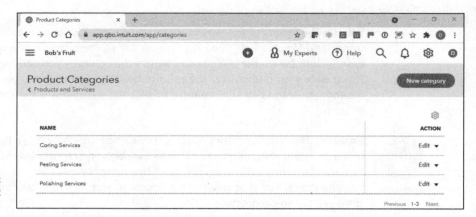

FIGURE 4-19:
The Product
Categories page.

3. **Click the New Category button on the Product Categories page to add a category.**

   The Category Information panel appears on the right side of your screen.

4. **Supply the category name.**

5. **If the category is a subcategory of an existing category, check the Is a Subcategory box, and select the name of the existing category.**

6. **Click Save at the bottom of the panel to set up your category.**

TIP

You can create subcategories up to four levels deep. That is, you can create a category called Clothing and then create a subcategory of Clothing called Shoes. For the Shoes subcategory, you can create a subcategory called Women's Shoes, and for the Women's Shoes category, you can create one last subcategory called Sneakers. You can't create a subcategory for Sneakers because it's the fourth level down, but you can create another subcategory for Women's Shoes, which is three levels down, called Dress Shoes.

To edit a category, open the category's Action drop-down menu in the table on the Product Categories page (refer to Figure 4-19) and choose Edit. The Category Information panel appears, displaying the category's current information. Make any changes and click Save; alternatively, click Remove at the bottom of the Category Information panel to delete a category. You can also click the arrow adjacent to the Edit link and choose Remove.

REMEMBER

The effect on items of removing a category depends on whether you remove a subcategory or a category. If you remove a subcategory, QuickBooks moves the items assigned to it up one level. If you remove a category (with no subcategories), QuickBooks reclassifies the items as uncategorized.

Adding service and noninventory items

You can create inventory, noninventory, and service items by following these steps:

1. **To display the Products and Services list, choose Settings ⇨ Products and Services.**

Alternatively, choose Sales ⇨ Products and Services.

2. **Click the New button.**

The Product/Service Information panel appears on the right side of your screen, as shown in Figure 4-20.

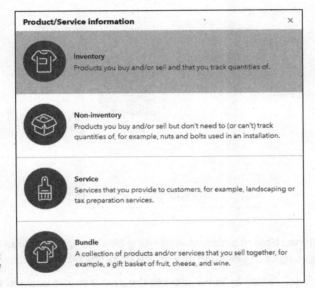

FIGURE 4-20:
Select a type of
item to create.

3. **Click a type to select it: inventory item, noninventory item, service, or bundle.**

You can read more about inventory items and bundles later in this chapter in the "Working with bundles" section.

For this example, I chose Noninventory item. You create a service item the same way you create a noninventory item, supplying the same kind of information shown in these steps. See the next section, "Creating an inventory item," for details on the additional information you supply when creating an inventory item, and see the section "Working with bundles" for details on creating bundles.

The panel appears for the type of item you chose. Figure 4-21 shows the Noninventory panel.

4. **Supply a name for the item and, if appropriate, an SKU.**

   You can also select the item's category.

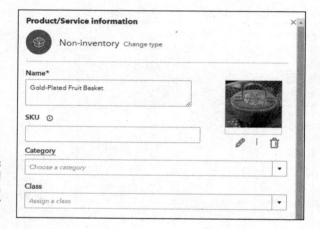

FIGURE 4-21:
Use this panel
to create a
noninventory
item.

5. **(Optional) Upload a picture of the item by clicking the Upload button and navigating to the location where you store the picture.**

6. **(Optional) Assign a default class to the item if you've enabled the Class feature.**

   I discuss classes in more detail in Chapter 3.

7. **In the Description section (see Figure 4-22), you can do the following:**

   (a) *Select the I Sell This Product/Service to My Customers check box, and supply a default description.*

   (b) *Supply the price you charge when you sell this item.*

   (c) *Select the income account associated with the item; if necessary, you can establish a new account.*

   QuickBooks uses this information when you select this item in sales transactions.

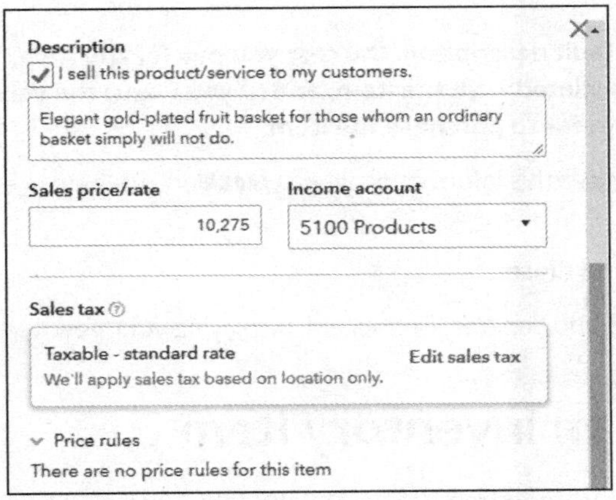

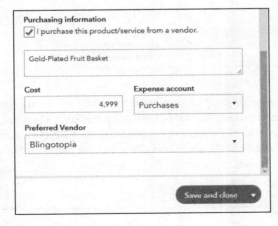

FIGURE 4-22:
You can indicate if you sell an item, and if so set a description and price.

8. **Click Edit Sales Tax to verify the sales tax settings, if applicable.**

   QuickBooks asks you to specify the type of product or service so that sales tax can be calculated correctly. If your item is nontaxable, scroll down and click the Still Don't See What You're Looking For link and then choose Non-Taxable. Regardless, click the Done button to save your changes.

9. **To display the Purchasing Information section (see Figure 4-23), select the check box titled I Purchase This Product/Service From a Vendor and then, if necessary, click the Show More link at the bottom of the window.**

FIGURE 4-23:
Add purchasing information for the item.

10. **Supply a default description, the cost you pay for the item, the expense account associated with the item, and (if you want) the vendor from which you prefer to purchase the item.**

QuickBooks uses this information when you select this item in expense transactions.

11. **Click Save and Close.**

The Products and Services list appears, displaying your new item.

Creating an inventory item

Creating inventory items requires a QuickBooks Plus or Advanced subscription. The steps are almost the same as I just described in the "Adding Service and Non-inventory Items" section above. When you add inventory items, you are required to provide a few additional types of information, as shown in Figure 4-24.

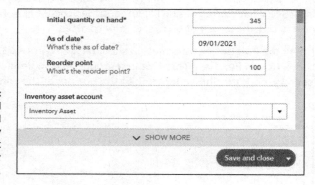

FIGURE 4-24:
Supply Initial Quantity on Hand and Inventory Asset Account information for inventory items.

REMEMBER

You must enable inventory tracking before you add inventory items. QuickBooks will ask whether you want to enable inventory tracking when you attempt to add your first inventory item. Or you can choose Settings ⇨ Account and Setting ⇨ Sales; in the Products and Services section of the resulting page, toggle on Track Inventory Quantity on Hand, as shown in Figure 4-25.

FIGURE 4-25:
The Track Inventory Quantity On Hand setting enables Plus and Advanced subscribers to track inventory quantities in real time.

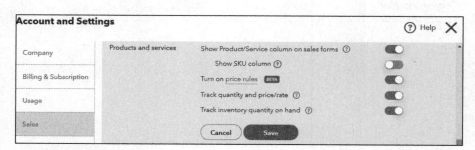

Enter your quantity on hand and the date on which you determined the quantity on hand by using the date picker or typing the date. You must supply an As Of date; if you don't, QuickBooks won't let you save the item. If you intend to enter historical transactions that use the item you're setting up, make sure that you enter an As Of date early enough to accommodate those transactions — typically, the beginning of your fiscal year.

REMEMBER

QuickBooks won't allow you to sell items that you don't own. If you have an order for five items but have only three on hand, for example, QuickBooks allows you to sell only three. After you replenish your stock, you can sell the other two items.

You can also specify a reorder point, which is the minimum quantity you want to have on hand at any given point in time. When the quantity on hand falls equal to or below the established reorder point, QuickBooks reminds you to order more by displaying Low Stock and Out of Stock graphic indicators above your inventory list, as shown in Figure 4-26.

TIP

You can set or adjust a reorder point after you create an inventory item. Find the item in the Products and Services list, click Edit in its Action column, enter the reorder point, and click Save and Close.

You also can use the Products and Services list to see reorder points for items that are low or out of stock. At the top of the list (see Figure 4-26), click Low Stock to show only items that have either a quantity below the reorder point you set, or an on hand quantity of 1. Click Out of Stock to view items that have an on-hand quantity of zero or a negative inventory quantity.

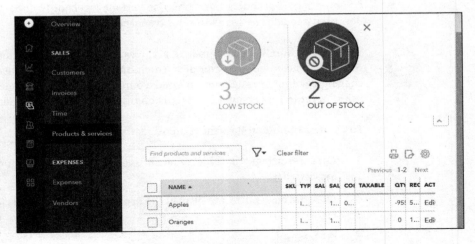

FIGURE 4-26:
You can filter the Products and Services list to show only Low Stock or only Out of Stock items for which you've specified a reorder point.

To order a low-stock or out-of-stock item, click the arrow in its Action column and choose Reorder from the drop-down menu that appears. A purchase order opens, with the item's information filled in. Complete the purchase order, and send it to the supplier. Be aware that QuickBooks creates only one purchase order for the items you select. To send purchase orders to multiple vendors, select the items to reorder for a single vendor, click Batch Actions (which appears above the Action column after you select an item), and then choose Reorder. Repeat the process for items to reorder from a different vendor.

You can easily cancel the filter for Low Stock or Out of Stock items. After you select one of these filters, an X appears in the top-right corner of the filter graphic. Click that X to display the complete Products and Services list.

Working with bundles

If you have an Essentials, Plus, or Advanced subscription, you can create bundles to group items that you often sell together. If you're a former QuickBooks Desktop user, bundles are known as *group items* in that program.

REMEMBER

A bundle is *not* an assembly. QuickBooks neither creates a bill of materials for a bundle nor tracks a bundle as a separate item with a quantity and separate cost. So QuickBooks doesn't track quantity on hand for bundles.

In general, think of a bundle as being a collection of items — products and/or services — that a customer buys from you in a single transaction. Suppose that your company sells fruit baskets. You can create one or more bundles that offer a combination of products that comprise various levels of fruit baskets so that you don't have to add the items to sales transactions one by one.

TIP

You can use bundles on estimates, invoices, credit memos, sales receipts, refund receipts, delayed credits, and delayed charges. Bundles aren't available for purchasing documents, and you can't add a bundle to a price rule. (See "Using pricing rules" later in this chapter for details on pricing rules.)

To create a bundle, follow these steps:

1. **Choose Settings ⇨ Products and Services to display the Products and Services list.**

2. **Click the New button to display the Product/Service panel (refer to Figure 4-20).**

3. **Click Bundle.**

   The Bundle panel appears, as shown in Figure 4-27.

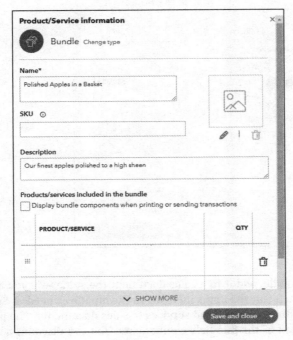

FIGURE 4-27:
The panel where
you establish a
bundle.

4. **Provide a name, an SKU if appropriate, and a description to appear on sales forms for the bundle.**

5. **In the Products/Services Included in the Bundle section, select the check box titled Display Bundle Components When Printing or Sending Transactions if you want to list the components of the bundle in sales documents.**

6. **Use the table at the bottom of the panel (see Figure 4-28) to identify the products included in the bundle:**

   (a) Click Show More to expand the panel so that you can add items to the bundle.

   (b) Click in the first row of the Product/Service column to display a list box you can use to select an item to include in the bundle.

   (c) Supply a quantity for the item.

   (d) Repeat Steps b and c for each item you want to include in the bundle.

   A bundle can include up to 50 items. You can reorder the items in the bundle by dragging the waffle button icon (the one that looks like nine dots) to the left of each item up or down within the list.

   (e) When you finish adding items to the bundle, click Save and Close.

REMEMBER

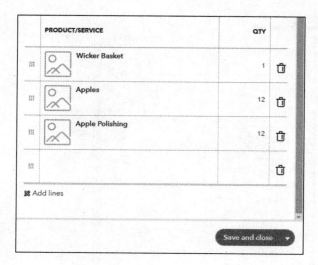

FIGURE 4-28:
Choosing the
items to include
in a bundle.

To use the bundle, add it to a sales document the same way you add any product or service. Then edit the items included in the bundle as needed. See Chapter 6 for details on adding products and services to sales documents. The price of a bundle equals the sum of the bundle's components. You can discount a bundle, but you can't mark up a bundle or track quantity on hand for a bundle.

REMEMBER

A bundle isn't an assembly; it's a shortcut for choosing two or more items at the same time.

You can search for bundles the same way that you search for any product or service. Use the Search box at the top of the Products and Services list to search by name or SKU.

Changing item types

You can change a service or noninventory item's type individually. In certain cases, you can select several items and change their item types simultaneously. Follow these steps to change any single item's type:

1. **Edit the item by clicking Edit in the Action column of the Products and Services list.**

   The item in the Product/Service information panel appears (refer to Figure 4-21).

2. **Click the Change Type link at the top of the panel above the item's name.**

   A panel very similar to the one shown in Figure 4-20 earlier in this chapter appears. The only differences you'll notice are that Bundle isn't an option and that the current item type contains a check.

3. Click the new item type to redisplay the Product/Service Information panel with the new item type.

4. Make any other necessary change.

5. Click Save and Close.

Changing the type of a single item by using this method works well when you need to change just one or two items or when you're designating a product as an Inventory item. Alternatively, use these steps to toggle two or more items between Service and Noninventory.

1. On the Products and Services page, select the check box that appears to the left of each item you want to change.

Make sure that you select either Service items or Noninventory items, but not both.

As shown in Figure 4-29, two buttons appear above the table of items.

2. Click the Batch Actions drop-down menu, and choose the new type for the selected items.

The Products and Services list reflects the new item types for the items you selected in Step 1.

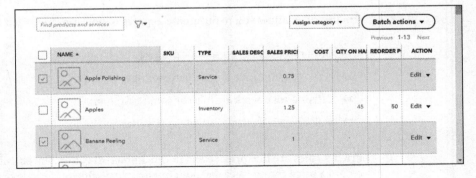

FIGURE 4-29:
Changing the type of multiple items simultaneously.

TIP

Note the Assign Category drop-down menu at the top of the Products and Services list. This menu appears when you select multiple items, and you can use it to assign the same category to multiple items simultaneously.

TYPES OF CHANGES YOU CAN MAKE

Be aware that you can change item types with some limitations. Specifically, you can't change Inventory items to any other item types. You can make the following types of changes:

- Noninventory and Service items to Inventory items
- Service items to Noninventory items
- Noninventory items to Service items

You can change several items at the same time only if you're changing Noninventory items to Service items or Service items to Noninventory items. If you need to change a Service item or a Noninventory item to an Inventory item, you can make the change only one item at a time.

You can't change a bundle to any other item type because a bundle is a collection of previously defined items. If you change the type of an item that's included in a bundle, the bundle reflects the new information.

Using pricing rules

Pricing rules allow you to automate aspects of your pricing, such as

- ❯❯ Offering discounts on specific products
- ❯❯ Increasing the price of specified products
- ❯❯ Offering special pricing to all or some customers
- ❯❯ Making special pricing available for a specified period

Pricing rules are like price levels in QuickBooks Desktop. Specifically, QBO doesn't record a price change as a discount but as an override of the sale price. This feature seems to be in perpetual beta testing, but rest assured that it's safe to enable for your company.

REMEMBER

You can't add a bundle to a price rule, but you can work around this issue if you add items included in a bundle to a price rule. Later, when you add the bundle to a sales document, the bundle will reflect the price-rule pricing.

To use pricing rules, turn the feature on by choosing Settings ⇨ Account and Settings ⇨ Sales and editing the Products and Services section to turn on price rules. After you enable the feature, Price Rules appears below Products and Services on the All Lists page.

TIP

You need to click Save in the Products and Services section of the Sales page of your Account and Settings area after toggling the Turn on Price Rules option. Depending on your screen resolution, you may have to scroll down slightly to see the Save button, which is separate from the Done button at the bottom of the screen. If you skip the Save button, QBO asks whether you want to leave without saving, which can be confusing if you didn't see the Save button in the first place.

You can establish as many price rules as you want, but fewer than 10,000 works best. To create a pricing rule, follow these steps:

1. **Choose Settings ⇨ Lists ⇨ All Lists.**

2. **On the page that appears, click Price Rules and then click Create a Rule.**

   The Create a Price Rule page appears, as shown in Figure 4-30.

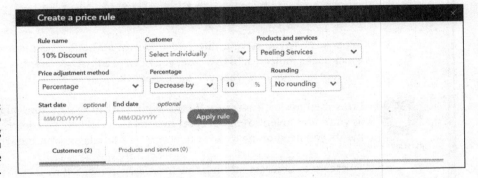

FIGURE 4-30: Use this page to create a pricing rule after you enable the feature.

3. **Supply a name for the rule, the start and end dates for the rule, the customers who qualify, and the products or services to which QuickBooks should apply the rule.**

4. **Use the Price Adjustment Method drop-down menu to specify how to adjust the price (by using a percentage, a fixed amount, or a custom price).**

5. **Indicate whether the rule is a price increase or decrease and how you want QuickBooks to handle rounding.**

6. **Click the Apply Rule button.**

7. **(Optional) At the bottom of the screen, use the Customers or Products and Services tab to select the customers and/or products to which you want to apply the rule.**

8. **When you finish, click Save or Save and Close.**

   When you create a sales transaction, any applicable price rules are applied to the transactions.

Adjusting inventory item information

On occasion, you may need to adjust inventory item information. Specifically, you may need to correct a typo in the description or to adjust inventory item quantities on hand or starting values, particularly after performing a physical inventory count.

TIP

You can edit descriptive information for any item by clicking the Edit link in the Action column next to the item's name on the Products and Services page. In this section, I'm talking about adjusting inventory item information, which encompasses more than editing descriptive information.

Adjusting inventory quantities

Suppose that you have a different quantity on hand of an inventory item than QuickBooks indicates. In this case, you need to adjust the quantity in your accounting records to match what you have in stock.

REMEMBER

Print the Physical Inventory Worksheet report to record item quantities on hand as you count inventory. The report information can help you determine the adjustments you need to make. See Chapter 10 for details on working with reports.

To create an adjustment for a few inventory items, follow these steps:

1. **Choose New ⇨ Inventory Qty Adjustment (see Figure 4-31).**

   Click Show More if you don't see the Inventory Adjustment command. The Inventory Quantity Adjustment window appears, as shown in Figure 4-32.

2. **If necessary, change the adjustment date and the inventory adjustment account.**

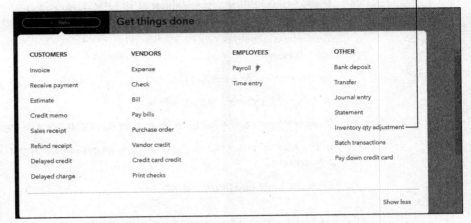

FIGURE 4-31:
Starting an inventory item adjustment transaction.

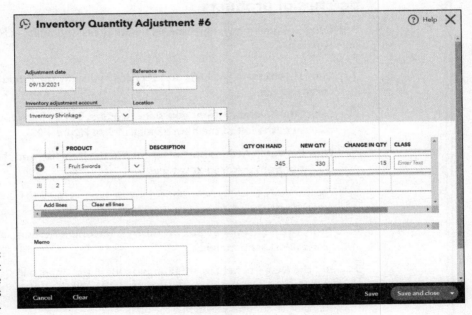

FIGURE 4-32:
You can adjust one or more inventory items at a time.

3. **In the table, click the arrow in the Product field, and choose an inventory item from the drop-down menu.**

Information about the item appears, and the Qty on Hand value is suggested as the New Qty value.

If you've enabled class and location tracking, you can supply information for those fields as you complete the Inventory Quantity Adjustment window.

REMEMBER

4. **Enter a new quantity or a change in quantity.**

   Suppose that the Qty on Hand field indicates that you own 345 units of your item, and you need to reduce the quantity you own by 15. You can do either of the following:

   (a) Enter 330 in the New Qty field.

   (b) Enter –15 in the Change in Qty field.

5. **Repeat Steps 3 and 4 for each inventory item you need to adjust.**

6. **In the Memo field, enter a description that explains why you made this adjustment.**

7. **Click the Save and Close button.**

Adjusting inventory quantities for batches of products

Depending on how many adjustments you may need to make, a batch action may save you time:

1. **Choose Settings ⇨ Products and Services to display the Products and Services page.**

2. **Select the inventory items you want to adjust by placing a check in the column to the left of the item name (refer to Figure 4-29).**

3. **Click the Batch Actions button just above the item list, and choose Adjust Quantity from the drop-down menu.**

   The Inventory Quantity Adjustment window appears (refer to Figure 4-30), prefilled with the information about the inventory items you selected.

4. **Verify the Adjustment Date, Inventory Adjustment Account, and if applicable, Location fields.**

5. **Edit the New Qty field or enter an amount in the Change in Qty field for each item.**

   Changing either field will update the other field.

6. **(Optional) Click Add Lines if you decide that you want to adjust quantities for other items.**

   You can click in the Product field of any row to select an inventory item.

WARNING

   The Clear All Lines button next to Add Lines completely erases the Inventory Quantity Adjustment screen without asking you to confirm. To guard against accidentally clicking this button, you can click the Save button at the bottom of the screen to save your work in progress. Conversely the Cancel and Clear buttons at the bottom of the screen provide a confirmation prompt.

7. **(Optional) Scroll to the bottom of the screen and fill in the Memo field.**

   Your accountant, or perhaps your future self, will thank you for your diligence in documenting why the adjustments were made.

8. **Click Save and Close to save your work and close the Inventory Quantity Adjustment screen.**

Editing an inventory quantity adjustment

Follow these steps if you need to adjust an inventory adjustment (hey, we're all human here!):

1. **Choose New ⇨ Inventory Qty Adjustment (refer to Figure 4-31) to display the Inventory Quantity Adjustment window.**

2. **Click the Recent Transactions button in the top-left corner of the window.**

   Recent inventory adjustment transactions are displayed (see Figure 4-33).

> ⟳ **Inventory Quantity Adjustment #7**   ⑦ Help ✕
>
> Recent Transactions
>
> Inventory Qty Adjust No.6   09/13/2021   Fruit Swords
>
> View More

3. **Choose an adjustment from the list, or click the View More link.**

   View More displays the Search page, where you can expand your search for the transaction, such as by modifying the date range.

4. **Make the necessary changes or delete the transaction.**

   You can remove a line from an adjustment by clicking its Delete button at the right edge of the row. You can delete the entire transaction by clicking the Delete button at the bottom of the screen.

5. **Click Save and Close in the bottom-right corner of the window.**

Adjusting an inventory item's starting value

Suppose that you made a mistake when you set up the starting value for an inventory item. You can edit the item's starting value as long as you created the inventory item after November 2015.

WARNING

Changing an item's starting value can have wide-ranging effects, and a note to this effect appears when it appears that you're trying to edit an inventory item's starting value. If you're not sure what you're doing, ask your accountant. Please. They won't mind.

To adjust an inventory item's starting value, follow these steps:

1. **Choose Settings ⇨ Products and Services.**

2. **As shown in Figure 4-34, click the arrow in the Action column for the inventory item you want to adjust and then choose Adjust Starting Value from the drop-down menu.**

   A warning appears, explaining that changing an inventory item's starting value may affect the initial value of your inventory.

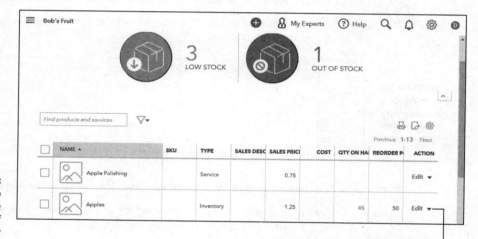

FIGURE 4-34: Getting ready to adjust the starting value of an inventory item.

Click and choose Adjust Starting Value.

3. **Assuming that you heeded the preceding warning and know what you're doing, click "Got It!".**

   The Inventory Starting Value window appears, as shown in Figure 4-35.

TIP

   If you've enabled class and location tracking, note that you can supply information for those fields along with other fields that affect the inventory item's starting value.

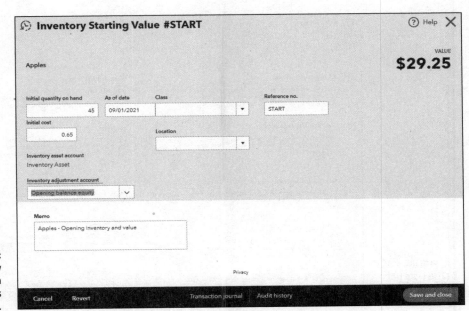

FIGURE 4-35:
Use this window
to adjust an
inventory item's
starting values.

4. Make the necessary changes.

REMEMBER

You can't change an item's inventory asset account in the Inventory Starting Value window. To change the item's inventory asset account, display the Products and Services page and click the Edit link for the item to display the item's information in the Product/Services Information panel (refer to Figure 4-23).

5. Click the Save and Close button.

Accessing Other Lists

QuickBooks lists range beyond just customers, vendors, employees, and items. Some examples include Payment Methods, Recurring Transactions, Attachments, and more. To access these lists, click the Settings icon on the toolbar at the top of the page, and on the menu that appears, choose All Lists (second column from the left). The Lists page appears, as shown in Figure 4-36.

Click any list to open and work with it. You can add entries, select and edit entries, and select and delete entries that have never been used. The steps for creating new list elements are pretty much the same as the steps discussed in this chapter for creating records, items, and product categories.

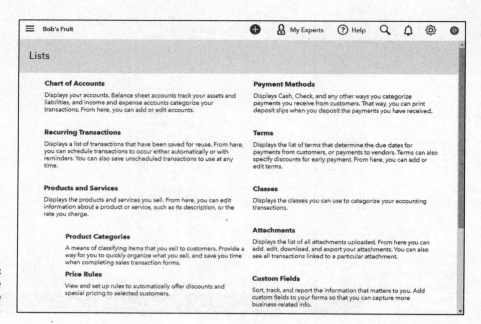

Bob's Fruit · My Experts · Help

Lists

Chart of Accounts

Displays your accounts. Balance sheet accounts track your assets and liabilities, and income and expense accounts categorize your transactions. From here, you can add or edit accounts.

Recurring Transactions

Displays a list of transactions that have been saved for reuse. From here, you can schedule transactions to occur either automatically or with reminders. You can also save unscheduled transactions to use at any time.

Products and Services

Displays the products and services you sell. From here, you can edit information about a product or service, such as its description, or the rate you charge.

Product Categories

A means of classifying items that you sell to customers. Provide a way for you to quickly organize what you sell, and save you time when completing sales transaction forms.

Price Rules

View and set up rules to automatically offer discounts and special pricing to selected customers.

Payment Methods

Displays Cash, Check, and any other ways you categorize payments you receive from customers. That way, you can print deposit slips when you deposit the payments you have received.

Terms

Displays the list of terms that determine the due dates for payments from customers, or payments to vendors. Terms can also specify discounts for early payment. From here, you can add or edit terms.

Classes

Displays the classes you can use to categorize your accounting transactions.

Attachments

Displays the list of all attachments uploaded. From here you can add, edit, download, and export your attachments. You can also see all transactions linked to a particular attachment.

Custom Fields

Sort, track, and report the information that matters to you. Add custom fields to your forms so that you can capture more business-related info.

FIGURE 4-36:
The Lists page contains links to all available lists.

» **Entering expenses**

» **Using purchase orders**

» **Entering and paying bills**

Chapter **5**

Dealing with the Outflow of Money

I t's always more fun to record money coming in than going out, but paying bills is part of life — unless you're a penguin and you eat with your one bill, but I digress. This chapter explores the transactions you use in QuickBooks to meet your financial obligations.

Getting Up and Running

Let's review some ground rules before you start entering bills:

>> If you recorded an opening bank account balance in Chapter 3, be sure to enter into QuickBooks the checks you wrote subsequent to that date that haven't cleared your bank yet.

>> If you didn't record an opening bank account balance in Chapter 3, or if you recorded a bank account balance as of December 31 of last year, be sure to enter all the checks you've written this year, even if they've cleared the bank.

» If you connect your bank account to your financial institution as described in Chapter 8, use the techniques described for the transactions in this chapter to review each transaction and make sure that it's assigned properly.

When recording an outflow for your business, you'll typically choose Expenses or Sales & Expenses on the navigation bar to display the Expense Transactions page, shown in Figure 5-1. Click the New Transaction button to select a transaction type.

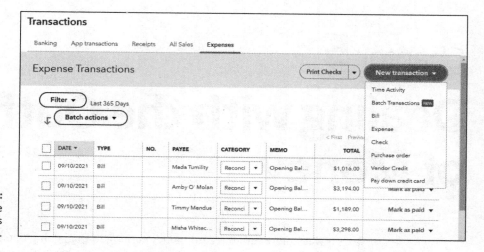

FIGURE 5-1: The Expense Transactions page.

TIP

QuickBooks Advanced subscribers can use a new Batch Transactions capability to enter multiple transactions on a single screen. You can also import transactions by way of a CSV format that you can create in Excel or Google Sheets. Click the New button and then choose Batch Transactions in the Other column. On the Batch Transactions screen, click Import CSV for documentation and a sample import file format.

If the transaction type you want to record isn't available, click the New button on the navigation bar (see Figure 5-2), and choose the type of transaction you want to record from the drop-down menu that appears. Expense-related transactions show up in the Vendors column.

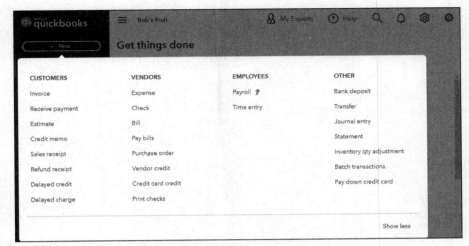

FIGURE 5-2:
Expense
transactions also
appear in the
Vendors column
of the New menu.

Writing a Check

Typically, you enter a check transaction when you need to print a check to pay for an expense. You can print checks on the spot, such as when the window washer is waiting to get paid, or enter checks that you print later as a batch.

Assigning a check to accounts or items

QuickBooks is moving away from a longstanding convention of accounting software with regard to posting activity to accounts. You're going to see the word *category* instead of *accounts*. Categories are intended to be those that you'd use in your income tax return. Thus, when you write a check, you can assign it to one or more categories and/or use the same check to buy one or more items.

Follow these steps to designate where a check should be assigned:

1. **Click the New Transaction button on the Expense Transactions page (refer to Figure 5-1).**

2. **Choose Check from the New Transaction list.**

   The Check window appears, displaying four sections:

   - *Header:* This section (shown in Figure 5-3) displays the balance in the selected checking account, the selected payee and the payee's mailing address, the payment date, and the check amount and number, and it gives the option to print the check later. If you opt to print the check later, the check number changes to To Print.

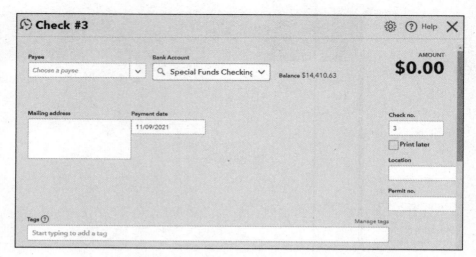

FIGURE 5-3:
The Header
section of the
Check window.

- *Category Details:* You use this section (shown in Figure 5-4) when the expense isn't related to an item you've defined.

- *Item Details:* Plus and Advanced subscribers can use this section (shown to Figure 5-4) when writing a check to pay for a product or service you purchased. If you don't see the table, its preference isn't enabled. To display the table, choose Account and Settings ➪ Expenses ➪ Bills and Expenses, and enable the Show Items Table on Expense and Purchase Forms option.

REMEMBER

You typically write a check by using either the Category Details section or the Item Details section, but sometimes, you need to use both. If you won't be using a section, you can hide it by clicking the down arrow next to the section's name.

- *Footer:* Not named onscreen, the Footer section contains the check total, the Memo box, and the box you use to attach an electronic document to the check.

3. From the Payee drop-down list (refer to Figure 5-3), choose a payee; also, from the Bank Account drop-down list, confirm the account from which to make the payment.

Along with the payee's address information, QuickBooks displays information from previously entered transactions unless you haven't entered any transactions for that payee yet or you've disabled the setting to display previously entered transaction information in Account and Settings.

TIP

If a payee has one or more outstanding see the next section, "Writing a check for an outstanding bill" to learn about the Add to Check pane, otherwise you can hide or ignore this Add to Check Pane.

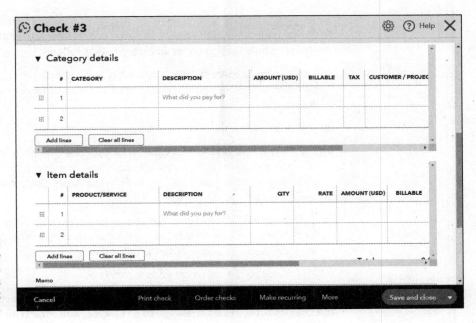

FIGURE 5-4:
The Category
Details and Item
Details sections
of the Check
window.

4. **Double-check the payment date and check number, and click Print Later, if appropriate.**

5. **Assign part or all of the check to an expense account or an item, using the Category Details section or the Item Details section (refer to Figure 5-4).**

   To assign a portion to an expense account, do the following:

   (a) Click the Category column, and select an appropriate expense account for the check you're recording. You can type characters that appear in the account name to filter the list of accounts.

   (b) In the Description column, describe the expense you're paying.

   (c) In the Amount column, supply the amount of the check that you want to apply to the selected account.

   (d) If you incurred the expense on behalf of a customer and want to bill the customer for the expense, check the Billable box — and, if appropriate, the Tax box — and select the customer's name in the Customer column.

   (e) Repeat Steps a–d to add more lines to the check.

6. **To assign part or all of the check to items or services you've defined, use the Item Details section (refer to Figure 5-4) as follows:**

(a) Click the Product/Service column, and select an appropriate item for the check you're recording. You can type characters in the Product/Service column to filter the item list.

(b) (Optional) Edit the Description column for the selected item.

(c) Use the Qty, Rate, and Amount columns to supply the quantity of the selected item you're purchasing, the rate you're paying for each item, and the amount you're paying. When you supply any two of these values, QuickBooks calculates the third value.

(d) If you purchased the item on behalf of a customer and want to bill the customer for the item, check the Billable box — and, if appropriate, the Tax box — and select the customer's name in the Customer column.

(e) Repeat Steps a–d to add more items to the check.

7. **(Optional) Scroll down in the Check window to the Footer section to view the check's total, type a message to the payee, and attach an electronic document (such as the payee's invoice) to the check.**

To attach an electronic document to the check, click in the Attachments box shown in Figure 5-5; a standard Open dialog box appears that you can use to navigate to the document. Alternatively, you can drag and drop the electronic copy into the Attachments box.

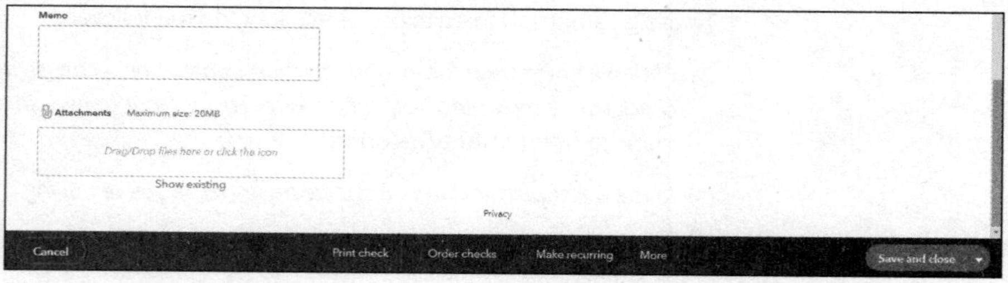

FIGURE 5-5: Click the Attachments box to display an Open dialog box for selecting a file, or drag a file into the box.

8. **At the bottom of the window, you can do the following:**

- Cancel your action, or clear the window and start again.

- Click Print Check to print the check. The first time you print checks, QuickBooks walks you through the process of selecting the type of checks to use and aligning them for your printer.

- Click Order Checks to visit the Intuit Marketplace and order check stock.

- Click Make Recurring to set up the check as a recurring payment you intend to make on a schedule you specify. (See "Managing recurring transactions" later in this chapter for details on recurring transactions.)

- Click More to see additional actions, such as voiding the check or viewing its audit history.

- Click the arrow next to the Save button and choose Save and New from the drop-down menu to save the check and redisplay the Check window so that you can write another check.

REMEMBER

The Save and New button is a sticky preference. If you click the arrow to the right of the button and choose Save and Close, the next time you open the window to write a check, the default button will be the Save and Close button.

Writing a check for an outstanding bill

You can use the Check window to write a check to pay a bill you previously entered — something that you can't do in the QuickBooks Desktop product. Note that you shouldn't use the Check transaction if you're planning to pay several bills; instead, see "Paying bills" at the end of this chapter.

If you select a payee for which an outstanding bill exists, a task pane on the right side of the Check window (see Figure 5-6) shows all transactions linked to the selected payee; each transaction appears as a separate entry. If nothing in the pane applies to your transaction, you can hide it by clicking the button shown in Figure 5-6.

Click here to close the pane.

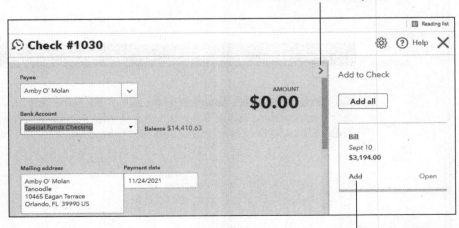

FIGURE 5-6:
If you select a payee for which you previously entered a bill, the outstanding bill appears in the pane on the right side of the Check window.

Click here to use the check to pay an outstanding bill.

If you're writing the check to pay a bill that appears in the pane, click Add in the Bill transaction you want to pay. That way, QuickBooks appropriately applies the check you're writing to the outstanding bill and correctly reduces your outstanding obligations.

WARNING

If you write a check to pay a bill and *don't* apply the check to the bill, your reports show that you continue to owe the bill amount to the payee, which means that you could end up paying the bill twice.

When you click Add, the bill is added to the check, and the screen switches to the Pay Bills window, essentially converting the check to a bill-payment transaction. In Figure 5-7, you see the Pay Bills window after I added an outstanding bill to a check in the Check window. If you compare Figures 5-6 and 5-7, you'll notice that the original check number was 1030, and it's still 1030 in the Pay Bills window.

FIGURE 5-7:
The Pay Bills window.

You complete the bill-payment transaction the same way that you complete a Check transaction; follow Steps 7 and 8 in the preceding section. If you add the wrong bill to a check, you can cancel the transaction without saving it.

Creating an Expense

You use an Expense transaction when you're trying to record an expense-related transaction without printing a check. You record an Expense transaction to account for a payment you make with a credit or debit card, for example. You also can use an Expense transaction if you manually wrote a check that you need to record without printing.

The major difference between the Expense transaction window and the Check transaction window is the lack of any tools to help you print an Expense transaction; compare Figure 5-4 and Figure 5-8.

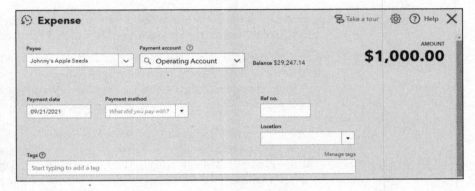

FIGURE 5-8: You can use the Expense transaction window to record making a payment without writing a check.

The Expense transaction window also contains a Payment Method drop-down list that you don't find in the Check transaction window. Other than those two differences, the windows look and function the same way.

CREDIT CARD TRANSACTION CONSIDERATIONS

By default, QuickBooks treats credit card transactions as cash transactions, a conservative approach that recognizes expenses as they occur. To account for credit card transactions, set up your credit card company as a vendor, and in your chart of accounts, set up a Credit Card account for the credit card. Then use Expense transactions to record credit card purchases for the credit card vendor. In the Header section, select the credit card vendor and credit card account. On the detail lines, assign each credit card transaction to the appropriate account or item for that purchase. If you use your credit card to buy office supplies, for example, select your Office Supplies account in the

(continued)

(continued)

Category Details section for that purchase. If you need to record a credit card return, use a Credit Card Credit transaction. Chapter 8 explains how you can download credit card transaction information into QuickBooks.

When the credit card bill arrives, you can pay it in several ways, but I'll focus on the easiest approaches:

- Use the Pay Down Credit Card transaction, select your credit card from the list, optionally specify your credit card company as the payee, specify the amount and date of your payment, and then choose a bank account. The option to indicate that you made the payment with a check appears; if you click the check box, you can fill in the check number or click Print Later.

- To pay by check, use the Check transaction; select your credit card company as the vendor; and, in the Category Details section, select your credit card account.

- To pay the bill while reconciling the credit card account, follow the steps in Chapter 8 to reconcile the account. When you click Finish, you'll be given the option to write a check to pay the amount due, enter a bill to pay the bill later, or do nothing about paying the bill now (and later, on your own, enter a check or a bill for the amount due).

If you want to recognize credit card expenses when you pay your credit card bill (rather than when you make a purchase with your credit card), *do* set up a vendor for your credit card company, but *don't* set up a credit card account in the chart of accounts, and don't enter Expense transactions or Credit Card Credit transactions in QuickBooks as they occur. Instead, when you receive your credit card statement, enter a Bill transaction for the credit card vendor (as described in the "Entering and Paying Bills" section of this chapter), and allocate each line on the credit card statement to the appropriate account or item on the bill; record credit card refunds as negative lines on the Bill transaction. QuickBooks treats your credit card account as an Accounts Payable vendor. When you're ready to pay the credit card bill, you can write a check, transfer funds, or use the Pay Bills page to pay the credit card statement. This approach to tracking credit card expenses is a conservative one; if you're a heavy user of your credit card, do yourself a favor and use the first approach so that you can manage your credit card spending effectively.

Entering a Purchase Order

Businesses that order lots of stuff from vendors often use purchase orders to keep track of the items on order. The purchase-order feature is available only to Plus and Advanced subscribers; it isn't available if you have a Simple Start or Essentials subscription.

Purchase orders don't affect any of your accounts; they simply help you keep track of what you have ordered. When the order arrives, you can compare the goods that come in the door with the ones listed on the purchase order to make sure that they match.

If you plan to use purchase orders, your ordering process typically happens in the following way:

1. Place an order with a vendor and then enter a purchase order in QuickBooks that matches the order you placed.

2. Receive the items you ordered, typically along with a bill for the items; then match the items you receive with the purchase order and enter a bill for the items. Note that sometimes, you may receive the bill without the items or the items without the bill.

3. Pay the vendor's bill.

Turning on the purchase-order feature

You won't be able to create purchase orders until you enable the purchase-order feature. To do so, choose Settings ⇨ Account and Settings, click Expenses on the left side of the Account and Settings dialog box, and enable the Use Purchase Orders option. You also can customize the default message that's added to purchase orders, as shown in Figure 5-9.

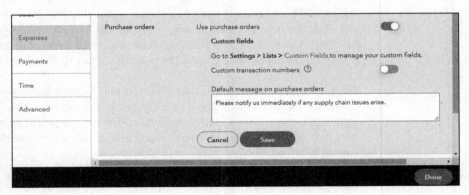

FIGURE 5-9:
Turn on the purchase-orders feature and set up a customized message to include in purchase orders to your vendors.

TIP

You can use custom purchase-order numbers if you choose. Choose Settings ⇨ Account and Settings ⇨ Expenses, and click the Purchase Orders section to edit the settings. Select the Custom Transaction Numbers check box, and then click Save. You also can convert Estimate transactions to Purchase Order transactions; see Chapter 6 for details.

Creating a purchase order

You enter purchase orders in the Purchase Order transaction window, which you can open from the New Transaction drop-down menu on the Expense Transactions page (refer to Figure 5-1), the New menu (refer to Figure 5-2), or Projects Center (for details on projects, see Chapter 6). The header area of a typical purchase order looks like the one shown in Figure 5-10.

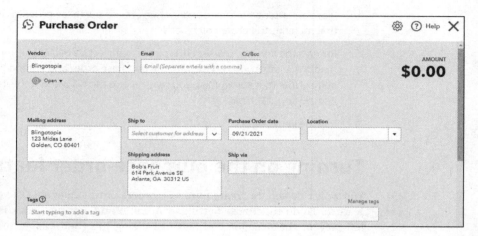

FIGURE 5-10: The header area of the Purchase Order window.

As you fill in the Purchase Order transaction window, QuickBooks assigns a status of Open to the purchase order; the status appears just below the vendor's name in the top-left corner of the window. When you complete the purchase order, you can click the arrow on the green button in the bottom-right corner and choose Save and Close, Save and New, or Save and Send from the drop-down menu. (Choosing Save and Send emails the purchase order to your vendor.)

When you receive the goods, the vendor's bill, or both for a particular purchase order, you could record a check as described in the next section, "Receiving items against purchase orders." Alternatively, you can record a bill, an expense transaction, or a credit card charge, as described later in this chapter in the "Entering and Paying Bills" section.

When you select a vendor that has open purchase orders for any of these types of transactions, an Add to Check pane appears on the right side of the window, showing available purchase orders. You add a purchase order to the transaction the same way that you add a bill to a Check transaction: by clicking the individual Add button for a given purchase order. In Figure 5-11, I've opened a Check transaction and selected a vendor that has open purchase orders.

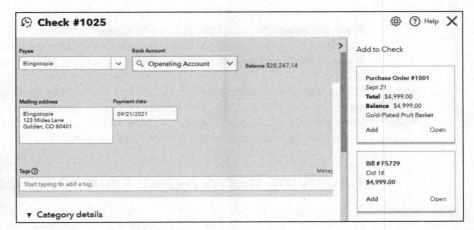

FIGURE 5-11:
The Check
window, with a
selected vendor
that has open
purchase orders.

When I click Add to add the purchase order to my transaction, QuickBooks adds
the purchase-order lines to the first available line in the Item Details section of
my Check transaction page. QuickBooks also indicates, immediately above the
vendor name, that the Check transaction has "1 linked Purchase Order," as shown
in Figure 5-12.

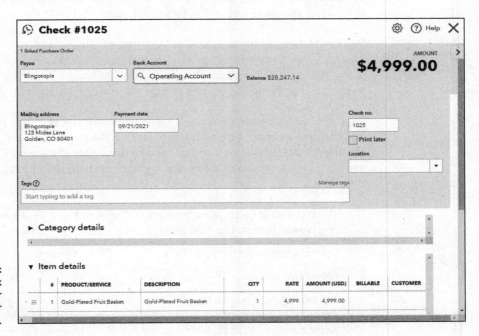

FIGURE 5-12:
A Check
transaction after
a purchase order
is added to it.

If you save the Check transaction and then reopen the purchase order, you find that QuickBooks has changed the purchase order's status from Open to Closed so that you don't accidentally add the purchase order to another transaction.

TIP

If you add the wrong purchase order to a transaction, you can remove the purchase-order line in the Item Details section by clicking the trash can icon at the right edge of the line. Depending upon your screen resolution, you may have to scroll to the right to see this; it's not visible in Figure 5-12.

Receiving items against purchase orders

Suppose that you receive only part of an order or that you want to pay for only part of an order. No problem. You can add part of a purchase order to a Bill, Check, or Expense transaction and later add more to another transaction, and continue in this way until you use the entire purchase order. QuickBooks links multiple transactions to the purchase order and automatically closes the purchase order when you've linked all lines on the purchase order to any combination of Bill, Check, or Expense transactions. If you determine that you're not going to receive some line on the purchase order, you can close that line without linking it to some other transaction. To do so, click the line you want to close on the purchase order and then select the check box in the Closed column.

TIP

You can close an entire purchase order if you no longer need it. To edit a purchase order, choose Expenses ➪ Expenses, and choose Purchase Orders from the Filter menu. Then open the purchase order, click the down arrow below the vendor's name (refer to Figure 5-10), and change the status from Open to Closed.

Suppose that you have a purchase order similar to the one shown in Figure 5-13 and that you've receive items for two lines on the purchase order, but you're still waiting for the third item. You can create a transaction to pay for only those items you've received and leave the remaining item open on the purchase order. Follow these steps:

1. **Open the New menu, and choose Bill, Check, or Expense, depending on the type of transaction you want to use.**

For this example, I'm using a check.

2. **Select the vendor.**

Available purchase orders for the selected vendor appear in the panel on the right side of the screen, where you can see some of the lines on the purchase order as well as its original amount and current balance (see Figure 5-14).

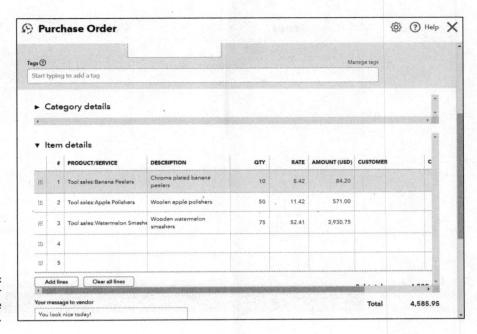

FIGURE 5-13:
A purchase order with multiple lines.

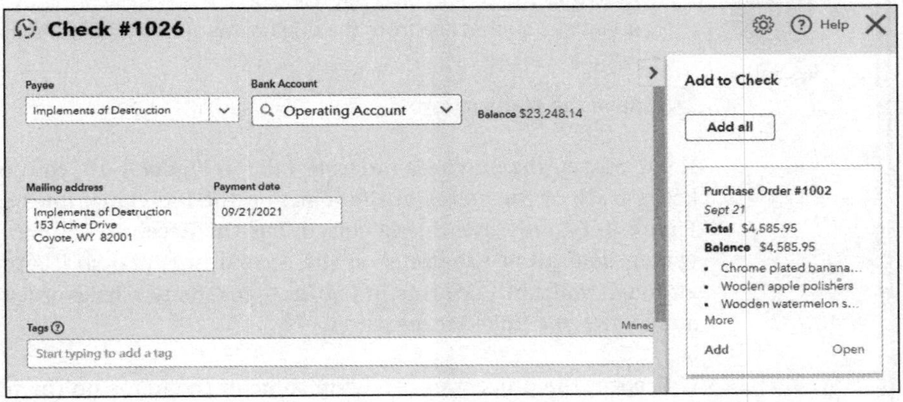

FIGURE 5-14:
A check showing an available purchase order with multiple lines for the selected vendor.

3. Click Add on the purchase order in the panel.

This action adds all the lines on the purchase order to the Item Details or Category Details section, starting at the first available line in the appropriate section.

4. Edit the quantity or amount for each line to reflect the portion you want to record as partially received or paid.

In Figure 5-15, I set the quantities on the first and last lines to zero to indicate that I haven't received those items yet and am not paying for them. I also set the second line to fully receive the ordered item.

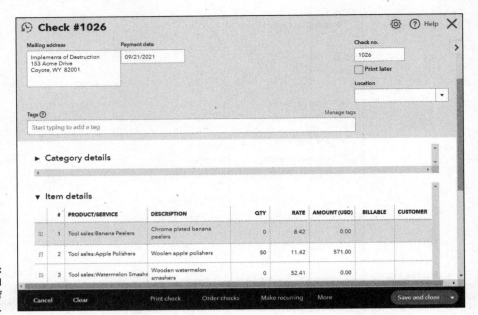

FIGURE 5-15:
Receiving and paying for part of a purchase order.

REMEMBER

Note that you can partially pay a line on the purchase order by changing the quantities on that line from the original number on the purchase order to the number you receive.

5. Save the transaction.

If you reopen the purchase order, as I did in Figure 5-16, you see that QuickBooks keeps track of the status of the items on the individual lines of the purchase. In Figure 5-15, only one line is closed, but the Received column indicates that the vendor sent all of the items on the second line, and so it's marked closed. And although you can't see this in Figure 5-16, the purchase order itself is still open and shows one linked transaction.

If I repeat the process of receiving some of the items on the purchase order, the purchase order in the side pane indicates that the total value and the current remaining balance are not the same, implying that a portion of the purchase order has been received. After I identify additional received items and save the transaction, the original purchase order shows two linked transactions and, if appropriate, additional closed lines.

TIP

Clicking Linked Transactions below the purchase order's status in the top-right corner of the Purchase Order window displays any linked transaction types. Click the linked transaction prompt to display the related transaction(s).

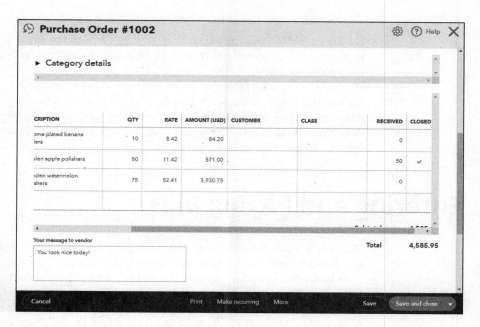

FIGURE 5-16:
Reviewing a
purchase order
after receiving
some of the
items on it.

When you're wondering how to determine how much of a particular purchase order you've received or paid and how much is still outstanding, use the Open Purchase Orders Detail report, shown in Figure 5-17. To do so, choose Reports (Business Overview ⇨ Reports) and start entering **Open Purchase Orders** in the search field. Click the report name from the resulting list.

Bob's Fruit
Open Purchase Orders Detail
September 1-21, 2021

DATE	NUM	VENDOR	PRODUCT/SERVICE	ACCOUNT	QTY	RECEIVED QTY
▾ Tool sales						
▾ Banana Peelers						
09/21/2021	1002	Implements of Destruction	Tool sales:Banana Peelers	Purchases	10.00	0.00
Total for Banana Peelers					10.00	0.00
▾ Watermelon Smashers						
09/21/2021	1002	Implements of Destruction	Tool sales:Watermelon Smashers	Purchases	75.00	0.00
Total for Watermelon Smashers					75.00	0.00
Total for Tool sales					85.00	0.00
TOTAL					85.00	0.00

Tuesday, September 21, 2021 05:24 PM GMT-04:00

FIGURE 5-17:
The Open
Purchase Orders
Detail report.

TIP

(In Figure 5-16, I hid the navigation pane by clicking the collapse/expand button in the top-left corner of the QuickBooks window; I wanted to give the report more screen real estate.)

To run the Open Purchase Orders Detail report, click Reports in the navigation pane; then type **Open Purchase** in the Search box. Click the report title in the search results to display the report. You also can use the Open Purchase Order List report. For more on reports, see Chapter 10.

Entering and Paying Bills

You create a Bill transaction to enter a bill from a vendor that you don't want to pay immediately. QuickBooks tracks the bill as a *payable*, which is a liability of your business — money you owe but haven't yet paid. Most companies that enter Bill transactions do so because they receive a fair number of bills and want to sit down and pay them at the same time, but they don't want to lose track of the bills they receive. They also want to be able to easily determine how much they owe. If you enter Bill transactions, you can print the A/P Aging Summary and Details reports to find that information.

If Bill transactions aren't included in your QuickBooks subscription, you can pay your bills by using Check or Expense transactions.

REMEMBER

Entering a bill

To enter a bill that you receive from a vendor, you create a Bill transaction by following these steps:

1. **Click the New button near the top of the navigation bar and choose Bill from the Vendors column from the window that appears.**

   The Bill transaction window appears, as shown in Figure 5-18.

2. **Select the vendor from which you received the bill.**

   The vendor's mailing address information appears.

3. **Check and, if necessary, change the bill date and the due date.**

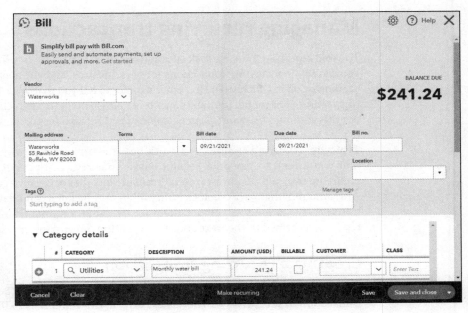

FIGURE 5-18:
The Bill transaction window.

4. **Use the Category Details section, the Item Details section, or both to record information about the bill.**

   See "Writing a Check" earlier in this chapter for details on filling out the Category Details and Item Details sections. I hid the Item Details section in Figure 5-18 so that you can see the information in the Category Details section.

REMEMBER

   If you're using the Projects feature in QuickBooks, you can use the Customer/Project field in the Category Details or Item Details section to assign the project name.

5. **(Optional) Scroll down to the Footer section (not shown in Figure 5-18) to enter information in the Memo field and attach electronic documents to the bill.**

6. **Click the down arrow next to the Save button, and choose Save and Close, Save and New, or Save and Schedule from the drop-down menu.**

   Save and Schedule is part of QuickBooks' Online Bill Payment option, which I discuss in "Paying bills" later in this chapter.

If you regularly pay a certain bill, such as rent or insurance, it might be a candidate to be a recurring bill, as discussed in the next section, "Managing recurring transactions."

Managing recurring transactions

To avoid repeating the same task over and over, you can set up recurring transactions. You can set up recurring transactions for bills, invoices, and just about any other type of transaction in QuickBooks. In fact, it's easier to tell you that you *can't* set up recurring transactions for bill payments, customer payments, and time activities. Throughout this section, I use a bill as an example of setting up a recurring transaction.

Typically, recurring transactions work best for transactions with static amounts that you intend to pay on a regular basis; your rent is a perfect candidate for a recurring transaction. Be aware that transactions that occur on a regular basis, but with amounts that vary (such as utility bills) may be good candidates for recurring transactions as long as you set them up by using Reminder for the transaction type, as described in the next section, "Creating a recurring transaction."

Creating a recurring transaction

In QuickBooks Essentials subscriptions and higher, you can create a recurring transaction in several ways. The easiest way, in my opinion, is to fill out the transaction the usual way and then click Make Recurring at the bottom of the transaction window (refer to Figure 5-18).

When you click Make Recurring, you're prompted to create a recurring transaction by using a template, as shown in Figure 5-19. The template serves as a model for the transaction and describes the way you want to pay the bill.

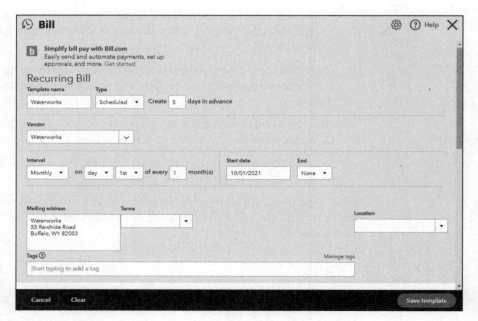

FIGURE 5-19: Setting up a recurring transaction.

To create a recurring transaction, follow these steps:

1. **From the Type drop-down list, choose one of the following:**

   - *Scheduled:* If you choose this type, QuickBooks automatically creates and enters the transaction. That is, if you set up a scheduled recurring bill to be entered on the first of each month, QuickBooks automatically enters the bill on the first of each month without any intervention from you.

REMEMBER

     For some recurring transactions, such as invoices, you have the option to send emails automatically. If you select this option, QuickBooks creates the transaction and emails it automatically.

   - *Reminder:* If you choose this type, QuickBooks displays a reminder for you to process the transaction. This option gives you more control of when and how recurring transactions are entered.

TIP

     This type is useful if you want to set up a recurring transaction for a bill, such as a utility bill, in which the amount changes but the due date doesn't. You can edit the transaction before entering it.

   - *Unscheduled:* If you choose this type, QuickBooks won't schedule the transaction or remind you that it's time to use the transaction; the template is simply available to use when you need it.

REMEMBER

     For this example, I chose Reminder because it has the same options as Scheduled except that I can control its entry into QuickBooks. For an Unscheduled transaction type, you don't establish the interval, start date, and end date.

2. **Fill in the number of days before the transaction date that you want to be reminded (or schedule the transaction).**

WARNING

   Be aware that QuickBooks sets the date on the scheduled transaction by using the scheduled date, not the date you enter the transaction. But a recurring transaction charges a customer's credit card or Automated Clearing House (ACH) payment on the day you record the recurring transaction. So the charge gets processed on the day it's recorded, but the transaction date could be a future date.

3. **Ensure that the vendor is correct.**

4. **In the Interval section, select the frequency with which you pay the bill, along with the time frame:**

   - For daily transactions, select the interval in days to pay the bill. You can opt to pay the bill every ten days, for example.

   - For weekly transactions, select the interval in weeks and the day of the week to pay the bill. You can pay a bill every three weeks on Thursday, for example.

- For monthly transactions, select the interval in months and the day of the month to pay the bill. You can pay a bill every month on the last day of the month, for example.

- For yearly transactions, select the month and day of the year to pay the bill.

- In the Start Date field, specify the first date on which you want QuickBooks to enter the bill and, if appropriate, the last date to enter the bill. You might set an ending date for a rent bill to coincide with the end of your lease.

5. **Confirm that the mailing date and terms are correct, scroll down the page to confirm that the detail section of the transaction is correct, and add any memo information or attachments to the transaction.**

   Any lines in the detail section that have a value of $0 won't be saved.

6. **Click Save Template in the bottom-right corner of the window.**

Making changes in recurring transactions

To work with existing recurring transactions, choose Settings ⇨ Recurring Transactions to display the Recurring Transactions list (see Figure 5-20).

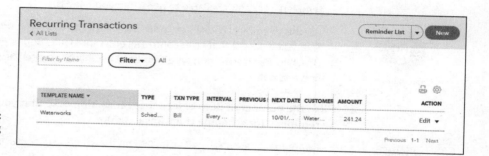

FIGURE 5-20:
The Recurring Transactions list.

To change an existing transaction, click Edit in the Action column to display the transaction (refer to Figure 5-19). Any changes you make in recurring-transaction templates aren't retroactive; you must manually change transactions that have already been entered to correct them.

REMEMBER

If you make customer or vendor changes that will affect an existing recurring transaction — when you change address information, for example — when you save those changes, QuickBooks tells you that the related recurring transaction templates will be updated.

If you click the down arrow next to Edit in the Action column, you see the options for a recurring transaction:

>> **Use:** Enter transactions with types of Reminder or Unscheduled. You don't need to enter transactions with a type of Scheduled because QuickBooks does that for you automatically.

>> **Duplicate:** Create additional recurring-transaction templates from existing recurring transaction templates. You might use the template for your rent to create another template to pay monthly insurance, for example.

>> **Delete:** Choose this option to remove a recurring-transaction template that you no longer need.

Finally, you can print a report of your existing recurring-transaction templates. Choose Reports on the navigation bar, type **recu** in the Search box (that's all you need to type to find the Recurring Template List report), and click it to display a report like the one shown in Figure 5-21.

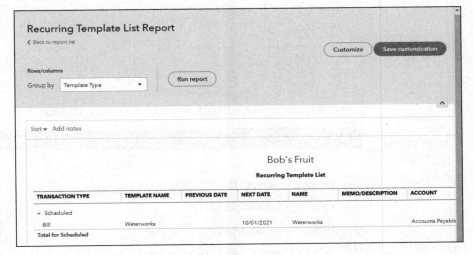

FIGURE 5-21:
The Recurring Template List report.

Recording a vendor credit

You enter a vendor credit to record returns to vendors or refunds from vendors. A vendor might supply you a credit document indicating that you no longer owe the amount stated on the document, or the vendor might issue a refund check to you.

If a vendor issues a credit document, you enter a vendor credit that you apply when you pay a bill for that vendor. If a vendor issues a refund check to you, you enter a vendor credit along with a deposit and then link the deposit to the vendor credit.

Follow these steps to enter a vendor credit:

1. Choose New ⇨ Vendor Credit.

The Vendor Credit window appears, as shown in Figure 5-22.

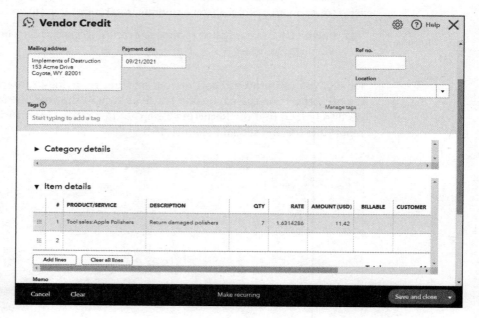

FIGURE 5-22:
The Vendor
Credit window.

2. Select the vendor that issued the credit.

3. Enter the date of the credit.

4. Enter the credit amount.

5. In the Category Details section, select the account used on the original bill.

If you received the credit because you returned items to the vendor, select the items you returned in the Item Details section.

6. (Optional) Scroll down to attach a digital copy of the credit to the Vendor Credit transaction.

7. Click the down arrow next to Save and New in the bottom-right corner of the window, and choose Save and Close from the drop-down menu.

RECORDING A REFUND TO A CARD CREDIT

If a vendor issues a credit to your credit card, the way you handle it depends on how you track credit cards in QuickBooks.

If you haven't set up a credit card account, and you wait to enter credit card transactions when you receive and record the credit card vendor's bill, enter a line on the Bill transaction, using the account associated with the refund, and make the amount negative.

If you *have* set up a credit card account, however, record a Credit Card Credit transaction, whether you record Expense transactions manually or download them. When you record a Credit Card Credit transaction, QuickBooks lets you post it to any of your available credit cards. In the Category Details section, select the account associated with the refund. Note that when you download transactions, you'll be able to match both Expense transactions and Credit Card Credit transactions to downloaded information.

If the vendor issued only a credit document, read "Paying bills" later in this chapter to see how to use the vendor credit to reduce the amount you owe the vendor when you pay the vendor's bill.

Handling a refund check from a vendor

If the vendor issues a refund check to you, you need to complete the steps in "Recording a vendor credit" earlier in this chapter to enter a vendor credit. Then follow these steps to enter a deposit to record the refund check in your bank account and link it to the vendor credit:

1. **Click New on the navigation bar, and in the Other section of the menu that appears, choose Bank Deposit.**

The Bank Deposit transaction window appears, as shown in Figure 5-23.

2. **In the Add Funds to This Deposit section at the bottom of the window, enter the following information:**

- In the Received From column, select the vendor that issued the check.

- In the Account column, select the Accounts Payable account.

WARNING

   Be sure to select Accounts Payable as the account; otherwise, you won't be able to apply the vendor credit against the check.

- In the Amount column (you may have to scroll to the right to see it), enter the amount of the check.

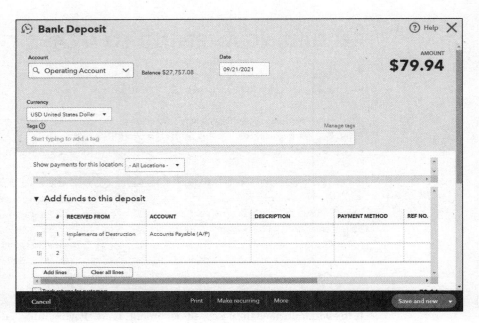

Bank Deposit   ⑦ Help ✕

Account
🔍 Operating Account ∨   Balance $27,757.08

Date
09/21/2021

AMOUNT
$79.94

Currency
USD United States Dollar ▾

Tags ⑦   Manage tags
Start typing to add a tag

Show payments for this location: - All Locations - ▾

▼ Add funds to this deposit

#	RECEIVED FROM	ACCOUNT	DESCRIPTION	PAYMENT METHOD	REF NO.
1	Implements of Destruction	Accounts Payable (A/P)			
2					

Add lines   Clear all lines

Cancel   Print | Make recurring | More   Save and new ▾

FIGURE 5-23:
The Bank Deposit
transaction
window.

3. **Click the arrow next to Save and New in the bottom-right corner of the window, and choose Save and Close from the drop-down menu.**

   The page you were viewing when you started the bank deposit reappears.

4. **Click New on the navigation bar, and on the menu that appears, choose Expense from the Vendors column.**

5. **Select the vendor whose refund check you deposited.**

   Available deposits, credits, and bills are displayed on the right side of the window, as shown in Figure 5-24.

6. **Click Add to apply the Deposit transaction; then click Add to apply the Vendor Credit transaction.**

   When you add these two transactions to the Expense transaction in this order, QuickBooks creates a Bill Payment transaction with a net value of $0 because the deposit is applied to the vendor credit. Figure 5-25 focuses on the Details section of the transaction.

7. **Click the arrow next to Save and New in the bottom-right corner of the window, and choose Save and Close from the drop-down menu.**

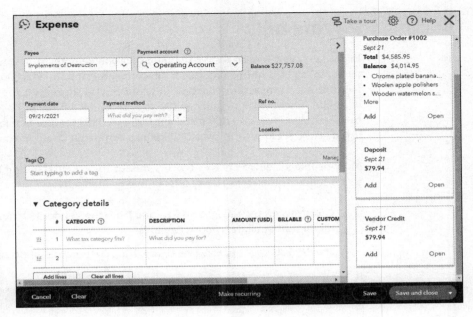

FIGURE 5-24:
Open transactions for the selected vendor.

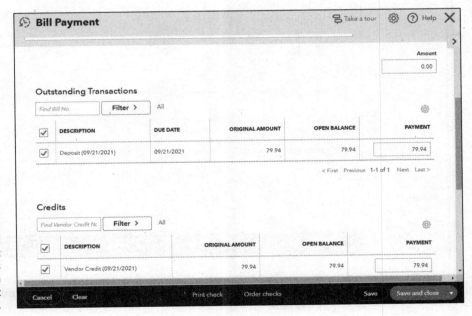

FIGURE 5-25:
Adding the vendor credit and the bank deposit of the vendor's check results in a $0 Bill Payment transaction.

Paying bills

Eventually, you'll need to pay the bills that you've entered in QuickBooks. In the past, paying bills online required a Bill.com subscription, which entails a monthly fee and per-transaction charges. Bill.com is still an option for managing bills online in QuickBooks, or you can use the embedded online bill payment available to Essentials, Plus, and Advanced subscribers. This feature is relatively new, and if it doesn't yet appear in your QuickBooks company, it will in coming months.

Most people sit down once or twice a month to pay outstanding bills. Generally, you'll follow these steps to pay bills online or manually:

1. **Click New on the navigation bar, and from the Vendors section of the menu that appears, choose Pay Bills.**

   The Pay Bills page appears (see Figure 5-26). Overdue bills display a red flag.

FIGURE 5-26: The Pay Bills page lists bills you owe but haven't yet paid.

2. **From the Payment Account drop-down list, choose an account to use to pay the bills.**

   For this example, I assume that you use a Checking account to pay your bills.

TIP

If you find yourself short on cash, you can use the QuickBooks Capital app, a free app available in the Intuit App Center, to apply for a loan. QuickBooks Capital uses your QuickBooks data to complete the loan application, and if approved, you can receive a short-term working capital from Intuit Financing, Inc. or one of its lending partners. Most applicants receive a decision within one to two days. The app adds a Capital tab to the navigation bar that you can use to track the loan.

3. **Provide a payment date at the top of the screen.**

4. **Enter the number of the first check you'll use to pay bills.**

REMEMBER

You can select the Print Later check box to identify bills to pay and schedule them to print later; when you print the checks, you can establish the starting check number. If you opt to print checks later, you can print those checks by choosing New ⇨ Print Checks. (The Print Checks option appears in the Vendor column of the Create menu.)

5. **(Optional) From the Filter list, choose an option to specify the outstanding bills you want to consider paying.**

By default, QuickBooks displays unpaid bills for the past year, but you can limit what appears onscreen by a variety of dates and selected payees.

WARNING

Be careful: Limiting what you see might mean missing a bill you need to pay.

By clicking the appropriate column heading, you can opt to sort the listed bills by Payee, Reference Number, Due Date, or Open Balance.

6. **Select the check box in the column to the left of each bill you want to pay.**

As you select bills to pay, QuickBooks updates the Payment and Total Amount columns using the bill amount as the default payment amount (see Figure 5-27). You can change the payment amount of any bill by typing in the Payment column.

REMEMBER

If a vendor credit exists, QuickBooks assumes that you want to apply outstanding vendor credits to reduce the amount you owe a particular vendor.

7. **In the bottom-right corner of the window, click Schedule Payments Online to use QuickBooks' free online bill payment service, or click the arrow and choose Save, Save and Print, or Save and Close from the drop-down menu.**

If you choose Schedule Payments Online, you'll walk through a process to connect your bank or credit card account. Payments through your bank account are free, whereas paying bills with a credit card incurs a 2.9 percent transaction fee. Alternatively, choose Save or Save and Close to mark the bills paid without printing any checks. Click Save and Print to print checks and mark the bills paid.

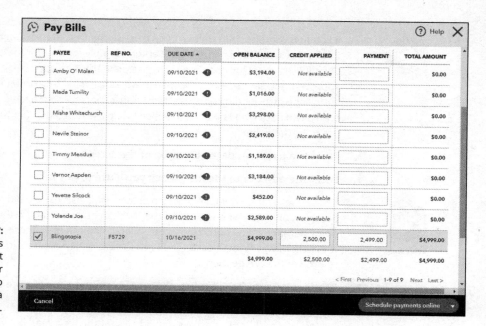

	PAYEE	REF NO.	DUE DATE ▲	OPEN BALANCE	CREDIT APPLIED	PAYMENT	TOTAL AMOUNT
☐	Amby O' Molan		09/10/2021 ❗	$3,194.00	Not available		$0.00
☐	Mada Tumility		09/10/2021 ❗	$1,016.00	Not available		$0.00
☐	Misha Whitechurch		09/10/2021 ❗	$3,298.00	Not available		$0.00
☐	Nevile Steinor		09/10/2021 ❗	$2,419.00	Not available		$0.00
☐	Timmy Mendus		09/10/2021 ❗	$1,189.00	Not available		$0.00
☐	Vernor Aspden		09/10/2021 ❗	$3,184.00	Not available		$0.00
☐	Yevette Silcock		09/10/2021 ❗	$452.00	Not available		$0.00
☐	Yolande Joe		09/10/2021 ❗	$2,589.00	Not available		$0.00
☑	Blingotopia	F5729	10/16/2021	$4,999.00	2,500.00	2,499.00	$4,999.00
				$4,999.00	$2,500.00	$2,499.00	$4,999.00

< First   Previous   1-9 of 9   Next   Last >

Cancel   Schedule payments online ▼

FIGURE 5-27:
QuickBooks uses
the bill amount
less any vendor
credits to
calculate a
payment amount.

TIP

If you choose to pay the bills by using a credit card rather than a bank account, the window looks the same, but as you'd expect, no options related to printing checks appear.

Chapter **6**

Managing the Inflow of Money

D o you remember the movie *Jerry Maguire* and the catchphrase "Show me the money!"? In this chapter, I show you how to handle the money coming into your business — in other words, invoicing your customers and recording their payments. But wait — there's more; I also cover estimates, credit memos, and projects.

Getting Started with Sales Transactions

When you're using new software, it always helps to be able to carry out actions a few times. If you have any unpaid invoices for your customers, for example, recording them in QuickBooks now will help reinforce what you read here. You'll also want to record all bank deposits that you've made since the starting date that you've chosen for using QuickBooks.

TIP

The navigation bar in QuickBooks has two modes: Business View and Accountant View. Even if you're not an accountant, you'll find it easier to navigate QuickBooks if you choose Settings⇨ Switch to Accountant View. You can't access the Sales Transactions page shown in Figure 6-1 if you're in Business View, for example, because QuickBooks hides the command.

Click here to start a new sales transaction.

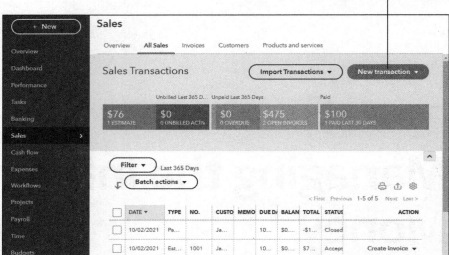

FIGURE 6-1: The Sales Transactions page.

You can choose Sales on the navigation bar to display the Sales Transactions screen (refer to Figure 6-1) and create almost every sales-related transaction. There's always an exception, so if you're looking to create a Refund Receipt, then click the New button and make a choice from the Customers column shown in Figure 6-2.

Preparing an invoice

Invoices are in effect written requests for payment for any goods and/or services that you've provided to your customers. An effective invoice makes it clear what value was provided. If you try to save a minute up front by creating a streamlined invoice, you could end up solving one problem but creating a new problem. The result could be delayed payment because the customer might table the invoice to pay later or ask questions about what the invoice covers.

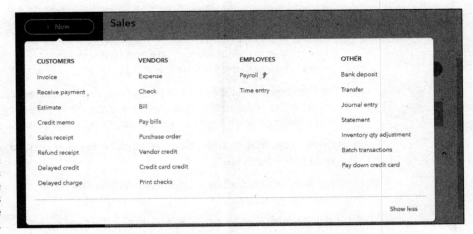

FIGURE 6-2:
Sales transactions
appear in the
Customers
column of the
New menu.

Follow these steps to create an invoice:

1. **Choose New ⇨ Invoice from the Navigation pane.**

   A new invoice window opens, as shown in Figure 6-3.

   REMEMBER

   If you're working with a project and need to associate the invoice with a particular project, you can choose Projects on the Navigation pane, select the project, and then click Add to Project. Later in the chapter, I discuss projects.

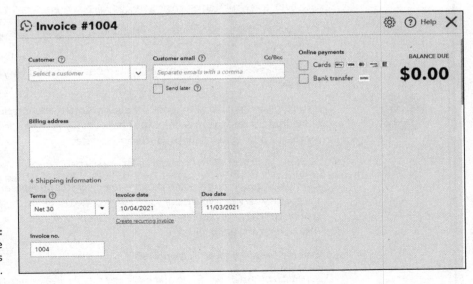

FIGURE 6-3:
A blank invoice
window awaits
your input.

2. Choose a customer.

The customer's mailing address, payment terms, invoice date, and due date appear, along with the Send Later option.

TIP

Any pending estimates or billable time entries appear in a transaction pane on the right side of the screen. I talk about this pane in the "Preparing an estimate" and "Creating Billable Time Entries" sections later in this chapter.

3. Confirm the Invoice Date, Due Date, and Terms, and optionally click the Send Later check box.

The Send Later check box allows you to indicate that you want to email an invoice at a future date.

4. You can set email preferences by clicking the Settings button on the Dashboard page and choosing Account and Settings.

Set up your company's email address on the Company page. Set up message preferences in the same Account and Settings dialog box; click Sales and edit the Messages section. In addition to editing the actual message, you can provide email addresses to which you want to send copies — regular and blind — of all sales documents.

5. Enter products and/or services.

QuickBooks Online requires you to provide an item name in the Product/Service field for each row of your invoice. If you try skipping the Product/Service field, a generic item such as Services will be entered for you.

(a) Click the Product/Service column (see Figure 6-4), and select an item for the invoice you're creating.

QuickBooks displays a list of matching items as you type a few characters in this field.

TIP

If you type an item name that doesn't exist, you can click Add New at the top of the list to create the new item. See Chapter 4 if you're not clear on the process of adding items for products and services.

(b) (Optional) Edit the Description column for the selected item.

(c) Fill in the Qty, Rate, and Amount columns to provide the quantity and price of the goods or services provided. If you fill in these two columns, the Amount column will calculate automatically. Or fill in Quantity and Amount, and the Rate column will autopopulate.

(d) Click the Tax box if sales tax is applicable.

(e) Repeat Steps a–d as needed to add more items to the invoice, as shown in Figure 6-4.

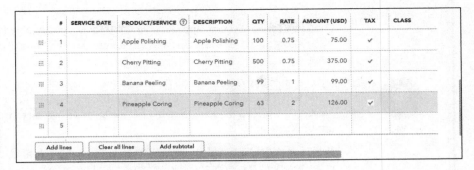

FIGURE 6-4:
Add as many line
items as needed
to your invoice.

TIP

Click the Add Subtotal button at the bottom of the screen if you want to subtotal two or more items on an invoice. QuickBooks allows you to subtotal a single item if you want, but doing that would be like wearing both a belt and suspenders. In the "Configuring automatic subtotals" section, I discuss enabling automatic subtotals on your sales forms.

6. **(Optional) Specify discount amount or percentage or override the location based sales tax with a custom rate (see Figure 6-5).**

The Discount field is hidden by default. To enable this field, click Settings in the top-right corner of the invoice screen, and click the Total Discount check box on the panel that appears.

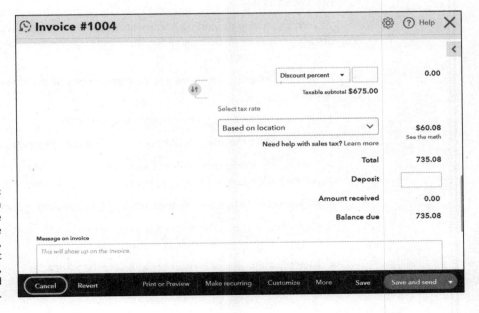

FIGURE 6-5:
Use the bottom
of the Invoice
window to handle
sales tax,
discount
information,
messages, and
attachments.

The Sales Tax Rate option appears on invoices only if you enabled Sales Taxes by choosing Sales Tax ➪ Set Up Sales Tax Rates. Chapter 4 has all the gory details.

TIP

If you enable both sales tax and discounts, you can use the switch that appears to the left of these fields to control whether discounts are pretax or after-tax. Position the discount above sales tax for pretax or below sales tax for an after-tax discount.

The Deposit field is hidden by default as well. To enable this field, click Settings in the top-right corner of the invoice screen, and click the Deposit check box on the panel that appears. If you turn on the preference to display the Deposit box at the bottom of the invoice, you can use it to reduce the amount of the invoice by a deposit amount paid by the customer.

7. **(Optional) Enter an invoice and/or statement message (refer to Figure 6-5).**

The bottom portion of the invoice screen allows you to include messages for your customer by typing an invoice and/or statement message. Statement messages are the description for an invoice when you send customer statements.

8. **To attach an electronic document to the invoice, click the Attachments box and navigate to the document, or drag the electronic copy into the Attachments box.**

You can attach any supporting documents to the invoice, such as pictures of your work, Aunt Mabel's pie recipe, a shipping confirmation, or anything else you want to include.

9. **At the bottom of the window, you can choose any of the following options:**

- Cancel to discard the invoice and close the window

- Clear to erase the invoice but keep the invoice window open

- Print or Preview to choose Print Later, see a print preview of the invoice, or print a packing slip

- Make Recurring to schedule the transaction as a recurring invoice

- Customize to choose or create a customized invoice form, as described in Chapter 3

- Save to assign an invoice number and save the transaction

- Save and Send to assign an invoice number, save the invoice, and email a copy to the customer

You can write an email message or edit the standard message and see a preview of the invoice. The email time and date-stamp information appears in the header of invoices that you send. Invoice emails are mobile-friendly and include invoice details so that customers see everything at a glance.

TIP

The arrow next to Save and Send allows you to choose Save and New to save the invoice and start a new one or Save and Close to save the invoice and close the Invoice window. Alternatively, choose Save and Share Link to copy and paste a link to the invoice, such as for insertion into a text or external email. The option you choose becomes the default behavior for invoices, but you can change this behavior at any time.

Printing invoices and packing slips

You can print the invoice and, if appropriate, a packing slip. Packing slips are basically an invoice that doesn't show any prices — kind of like certain menus in fancy restaurants. To an invoice click the Print or Preview button at the bottom of the Invoice window (refer to Figure 6-5), and then click Print or Preview again. For packing slips click the Print or Preview button and then choose Print Packing Slip. A preview version of your document should appear onscreen.

In either case, click Print or right-click the preview to print the document. If your browser can't render a preview, you'll see a screen with an Open button in the middle, or your screen may look like Figure 6-5, in which case you can click Download to create a PDF file or Print to send the document to a printer or the PDF print driver of your choice. If you're using Google Chrome, the downloaded PDF file is represented by the icon that appears in the bottom-left corner of Figure 6-6. You can click the PDF document shown in your browser's downloads bar to display it in the PDF viewer stored on your computer. Figure 6-7 shows the PDF document in Chrome.

TIP

If your browser can't display PDFs, free options for PDF viewers include Acrobat Reader and Nitro Reader.

REMEMBER

You can dismiss the Print Preview window by clicking the X in the top-right corner of the screen or the Close button in the bottom-left corner of the Print Preview window.

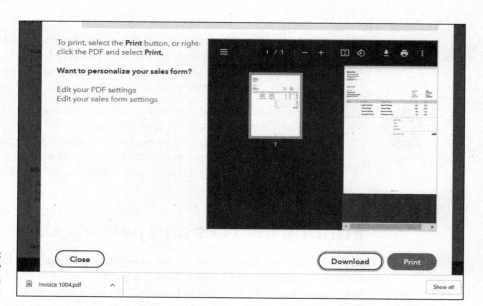

FIGURE 6-6:
The Print Preview window for an invoice.

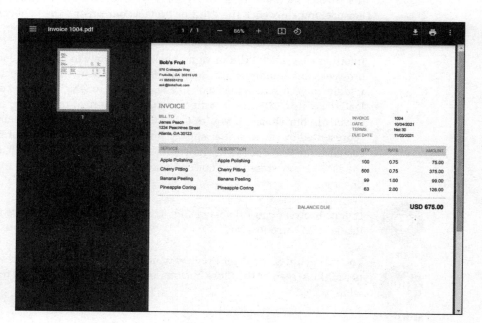

FIGURE 6-7:
The PDF version of an invoice.

QUICKBOOKS ONLINE AND GOOGLE CALENDAR

If you record work that you perform in Google Calendar, you can use the Invoice with the Google Calendar app to pull event details into an invoice. This app is free if you have a Gmail account or a Google Workplace subscription (formerly known as G Suite).

When the app is installed, you can click the Google Calendar icon that appears on the invoice form. A panel enables to you set search parameters, such as choosing a Google Calendar, specifying a time frame, and entering any keywords to search on. You can choose events to add to the invoice from the search results, which will record the title, description, hours worked, and date from Google Calendar — a great way to eliminate duplicate data entry.

If you thought the previous Print Packing Slip command was hard to find, wait until I show you the other way that you can generate such documents:

1. **Choose Sales ⇨ Customers (Sales & Expenses ⇨ Customers) from the navigation bar.**

   Your customer list appears.

2. **Click on a customer's name to display their transaction list.**

   Each customer's name becomes a clickable link when you hover over it.

3. **Within the transaction list, click the check box adjacent to each invoice or sales receipt for which you want to generate a packing slip.**

4. **Click the Batch Actions button and then choose Packing Slip.**

5. **A different version of the Print Preview window appears, from which you can print or download the packing slip.**

Configuring automatic subtotals

You can use the Add Subtotal button on Sales Transaction forms to add a subtotal manually to any set of items on a form. Or you can take subtotals to the next level by enabling QuickBooks to subtotal your items automatically by customizing your forms.

Certain actions, such as customizing forms, can't be performed in the iOS and Android mobile apps, but you can customize your forms in a web browser and then use your customized form in a mobile app. See `https://intuit.me/3qs5MOH` for details on what you can and can't do in mobile apps. Depending on your screen resolution, you may be able use your web browser on your mobile device to carry out these actions.

You can add subtotals to invoices, estimates, and sales receipts. In the following steps, you're enabling subtotals in an invoice:

1. **Choose Settings ➪ Custom Form Styles.**

   The Custom Form Styles page displays any form styles you've set up.

   I discuss customizing forms in detail in Chapter 3. If you don't already have a custom form to choose, select a form type, such as Invoice.

2. **Select a form to customize and then click Edit in the Action column.**

   The Customize Form Style page contains three buttons in the top-left corner: Design, Content, and Emails.

3. **Click Content (see Figure 6-8).**

   The Content page appears, with all sections disabled.

4. **Click the Table section.**

   The Table section is where you see column titles such as Date, Product/Service, and Description. As shown in Figure 6-8, the section is available to edit.

5. **Scroll down the page, and click Show More Activity Options in the bottom-left corner.**

   Additional options for the Table section appear, as shown in Figure 6-9.

6. **Click the Group Activity By check box, and make a choice from the drop-down list.**

   You can group items by day, week, month, or type. For this example, choose Type.

7. **(Optional) Click Subtotal Groups.**

   Choose this option if you want to subtotal related activities in your form automatically.

   You can always create ad hoc subtotals by clicking the Add Subtotal button when creating a sales transaction.

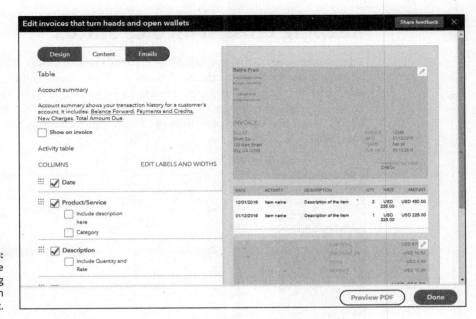

FIGURE 6-8:
The Content page after choosing the Table section to edit.

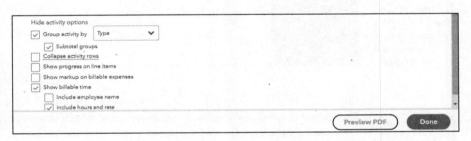

FIGURE 6-9:
Turning on the setting to enable grouping in the selected sales forms.

TIP

If you send progress invoices to customers, click the Show Progress on Line Items check box to add an Estimate Summary and a Due column to invoices. The Estimate Summary shows the estimate number and amount, invoices previously created for the estimate, and total amount you've invoiced to date. The Due column shows the amount still due for each line item.

8. **Click Done in the bottom-right corner of the window to save the settings, or click Preview PDF if you want to see what your customized form looks like.**

REMEMBER

You need to repeat the preceding steps to include subtotals for estimates and sales receipts if you want a consistent look and feel across all the forms you use.

Keeping tabs on invoice status

The Invoices page helps you track the status of your invoices. This page appears when you choose Sales on the Navigation pane and then click Invoices. Graphics show you at a glance the dollar amount of your unpaid and paid invoices. The unpaid invoices bar divides the total into Overdue and Not Due Yet. As shown in Figure 6-10, the bar for paid invoices breaks the total into Not Deposited and Deposited.

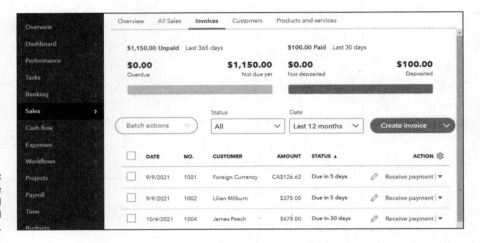

FIGURE 6-10: Determining the amounts of paid and unpaid invoices.

Click the Status column for any transaction to see the underlying details. Figure 6-11 shows the status of an invoice for which payment has not yet been deposited. Displaying the details shows you the payment dates and amounts. Click the Status column for the transaction again to hide the details.

A status of Deposited means exactly what you think: You received a payment, and you deposited it. Partially paid invoices show an amount in the Balance column that differs from the total, helping you keep track of how much is still due.

The Status column (refer to Figure 6-10) can provide additional information on invoices that are coming due as well as on overdue invoices. Overdue amounts appear onscreen in orange.

Unfortunately the status window won't show you if you have an invoice that hasn't been sent. Here's what to do instead:

1. Choose Sales (Bookkeeping ⇨ Transactions) from the navigation bar.

2. Activate the All Sales tab.

Invoice 1002 ✕

Due in 5 days (Not sent)

Total due

$ 375 00

Invoice date
9/9/2021

Due date
10/9/2021

Lilian Milburn   >

Invoice activity   ⌄

● **Opened**
9/9/2021

○ Sent

○ Viewed

More actions ⌄   Edit invoice

FIGURE 6-11:
Click anywhere in the Status column to see the details for the specific transaction.

3. **Click the Filter menu and then choose Send Later for the Delivery Status.**

   Any unsent invoices appear onscreen.

4. **Select the check boxes for any invoices you wish to send, or click the Mark All check box at the top of the list.**

5. **Click Batch Actions and then choose Send Transactions.**

TIP

You can use these same steps to print invoices that you marked Print Later; simply change the Delivery Status to Print Later.

Recording a customer payment

Alrighty, things are coming together. Your customer has paid your invoice, and now you're ready to record it in QuickBooks. Although some aspects of accounting may feel like drudgery, I have to say that I never get tired of recording payments from customers, and I'll bet you don't either. You can display the Receive Payment window in the following ways:

» Click Receive Payment in the Action column of the sales-transaction list (refer to Figure 6-10).

» Click the New Transaction button on the Sales Transactions page, and choose Payment.

>> Choose New ⇨ Receive Payment.

>> Select the project on the Projects page, and click Add to Project.

I discuss using projects in QuickBooks later in this chapter in the "Managing Projects" section.

The first method in the preceding list displays the Receive Payment window, pre-filled with the information for the invoice you selected as well as a default payment amount. The second and third methods display an unfilled Receive Payment window. When you select a customer, any unpaid invoices appear in the Outstanding Transactions section, shown in Figure 6-12.

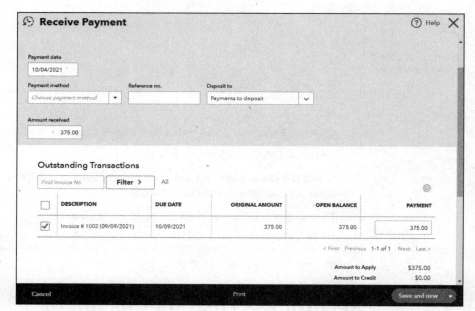

FIGURE 6-12:
The Receive Payment window after selecting a customer with unpaid invoices.

And now — the moment you've been waiting for — instructions for how to post a customer payment:

1. **Confirm the payment date.**

   Make sure that the payment date matches the date you're depositing the funds to make reconciling your bank account easier.

2. **Choose a payment method.**

   Default methods include Cash, Check, and Credit Card, but you can add others as needed.

3. **Enter a reference number.**

   This number is the check number if your customer paid by check. You can leave the reference field blank for cash for electronic deposits or add use it as a note field.

4. **Specify the account in which you want to deposit the payment.**

   If you're posting a transaction for which no fees are deducted, you can choose your bank account from the drop-down list. If you're depositing two or more checks in your bank on the same day, choose Payments to Deposit or Undeposited Funds, depending on which option appears in your company.

5. **Select the invoice(s) being paid.**

   Adjust the Payment field as needed for each invoice to apply a partial payment.

   If your customer has paid you via an online payment service such as Stripe or PayPal, see "Recording electronic transaction fees" later in this chapter.

   TIP

6. **Click Save and Close or Save and New.**

   The Save button is a sticky preference, meaning you can click it and change the default behavior for future transactions.

Using the Payments to Deposit account

Older QuickBooks companies may still have an Undeposited Funds account, which could feel like an oxymoron. You're going to deposit those funds pronto, of course! QuickBooks now refers to this as the Payments to Deposit account. If your bank deposits are always comprised of a single check, you can skip this section. But if you take two or more deposits to the bank, or if you receive electronic payments (such as credit card receipts) from more than one customer on a given day, a Payments to Deposit account makes your bank-reconciliation process much easier.

The goal of the Payments to Deposits account is to enable QuickBooks to mirror what will post to your bank statement. If you deposit five checks on a single deposit ticket, your bank will post one lump amount to your account. You want QuickBooks to post one lump amount to your bank account as well, which is the purpose of the Payments to Deposit account. This account is a holding area where you can accumulate customer payments and then batch them into amounts that match what the bank will post to your account. Then your bank-reconciliation process sails along, because you're not trying to play trying to play Tetris by figuring out which combination of individual payments aligns with the amount that the bank posted. I give you the lowdown on preparing bank deposits and reconciling bank statements in Chapter 8.

Recording bank deposits

It's important to remember to post your bank deposits in QuickBooks so that the money doesn't end up in purgatory within your Payments to Deposit account (refer to "Using the Payments to Deposit account" earlier in this chapter). This account should always have a zero balance after you've recorded any current bank deposits. Here's how to post a bank deposit:

1. **Record the customer payment as described in "Recording a customer payment" earlier in this chapter.**

    Make sure to apply the payment to your Payments to Deposit or Undeposited Funds account.

2. **As shown in Figure 6-13, select the payment(s) you want to deposit.**

    Click the check box next to each payment that you're including in this deposit.

3. **Scroll down to confirm the deposit total.**

    This total should match the sum of the checks that you're taking to the bank.

4. **Click Save and Close or Save and New.**

    Click the arrow on the Save button if you want to toggle to a different option.

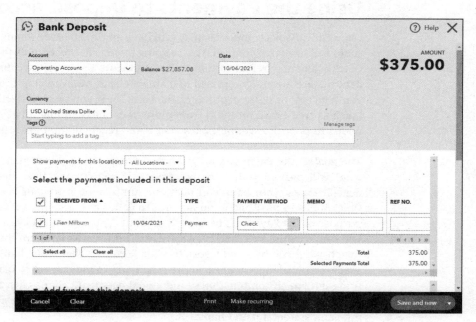

FIGURE 6-13: A bank deposit for payments made by check.

Recording electronic transaction fees

If you accept payments through an online payment processor such as Stripe or PayPal, the deposit amount that posts to your account may be net of a fee, typically in the range of 2 percent to 3 percent of the deposit amount. For instance, if a customer pays you $1,000, then $970 might post to your bank account. The difference is a processing fee retained by company processing the payment on your behalf.

I'm going to show you two ways to record these transactions. The first way shows you what to do when a customer pays an invoice through an online payment processor. The second approach, which appears in "Entering a sales receipt" later in this chapter, allows you to record ad hoc amounts that you receive through an online payment system — amounts that you don't create an invoice for in advance.

Kudos to you if you surmised that I'm going to show you how to record electronic transaction fees:

1. **Record the customer payment as described in "Recording a customer payment" section in this chapter.**

Make sure to apply the payment to your Payments to Deposit or Undeposited Funds account.

2. **As shown in Figure 6-14, select the payment(s) you want to deposit.**

Click the check box next to each payment that you're including in this deposit.

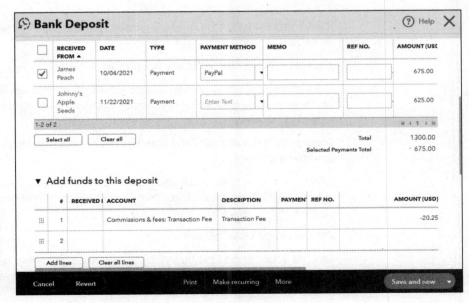

FIGURE 6-14: A bank deposit for payments that incur a transaction fee, such as a credit card discount.

3. **Enter a value in the Received From field of the Add Funds to This Deposit section.**

   Typically, this value is the same value as that of the payment method, such as Stripe or PayPal. If the name of the payment platform doesn't exist, type it the field and then click Add New. Change the type to Vendor and then click Save.

4. **Choose an account to post the transaction fee to, such as Transaction Fees.**

   You may need to create this account the first time around if you don't see it in the list:

   (a) *Click See, and choose Add More Categories.*

   (b) *Click New.*

   (c) *Enter a category name, such as Transaction Fee.*

   (d) *Click Select Category, choose Expenses, and then click Next.*

   (e) *Choose Commissions & Fees, and click Save.*

   (f) *(Optional) Enter a description and/or account number, and click Save.*

5. **(Optional) Enter a description, such as Transaction Fee.**

   This description will help you understand the deduction in both your bank account and the expense account.

6. **Choose the same payment method that you chose for the original deposit.**

   If you chose PayPal on the Receive Payment screen, choose PayPal here as well.

7. **Enter a negative number in the Amount field.**

   The error message `This Value is Out of Range` will flash on the screen briefly when you type a minus sign. Disregard this warning, and enter the amount, such as –20.25.

8. **Confirm that the deposit total matches the net amount that will post to your bank account.**

   I didn't have room to show you this total in Figure 6-14, but if I deposit $675 and post –$20.75 in the Add Funds to this Account section, the net deposit will be $654.75.

9. **Click Save and Close or Save and New.**

   Click the arrow on the Save button to toggle between those two settings. Your choice will then become the default for future transactions.

WARNING

Make sure to enter a negative amount in the Add Funds to this Deposit section; otherwise, you'll overstate your deposit by *adding* the transaction fees to the deposit amount instead of *deducting* the fees. Always check the total deposit amount so that you don't create other problems for yourself by artificially inflating your bank account balance within QuickBooks.

TIP

You can sign up for QuickBooks Payments to enable your customers to pay you by Automated Clearing House (ACH) or credit card payments. This service integrates with QuickBooks Online in such a way that customer payments and fees post to your books automatically. See `https://quickbooks.intuit.com/payments` or contact Intuit for details.

Entering a sales receipt

Invoices are useful for notifying your customers of what they owe and then tracking the unpaid amounts. Sometimes, though, you'll be given cash on the barrelhead, so to speak, paid at the time you provide goods or render services. Rather than entering an invoice and then immediately receiving a payment against it, you can use a sales receipt. You can also print a packing list based on the sales receipt; this list shows the quantities of the items the customer purchased without price information. This approach also works well when you receive payments that you didn't invoice in advance via an electronic payment platform such as Stripe or PayPal.

To create a sales receipt, choose New ⇨ Sales Receipt, or choose New Transaction ⇨ Sales Receipt on the Sales Transactions page to display the window shown in Figure 6-15.

The sales receipt form closely resembles other sales forms you see in this chapter; think of it as being a mashup of the Invoice and Receive Payment screens. Fill out the form in much the same way that you do an invoice; provide the payment-specific details, such as payment method and reference number, and select the account where the funds should go. See "Using the Payments to Deposit account" earlier in this chapter for information on selecting an account from the Deposit To list.

You fill out the rest of the Sales Receipt transaction the same way that you fill out an invoice transaction. If you scroll down in the window, you'll find the same fields at the bottom of the Sales Receipt window as the ones that appear at the bottom of the Invoice window.

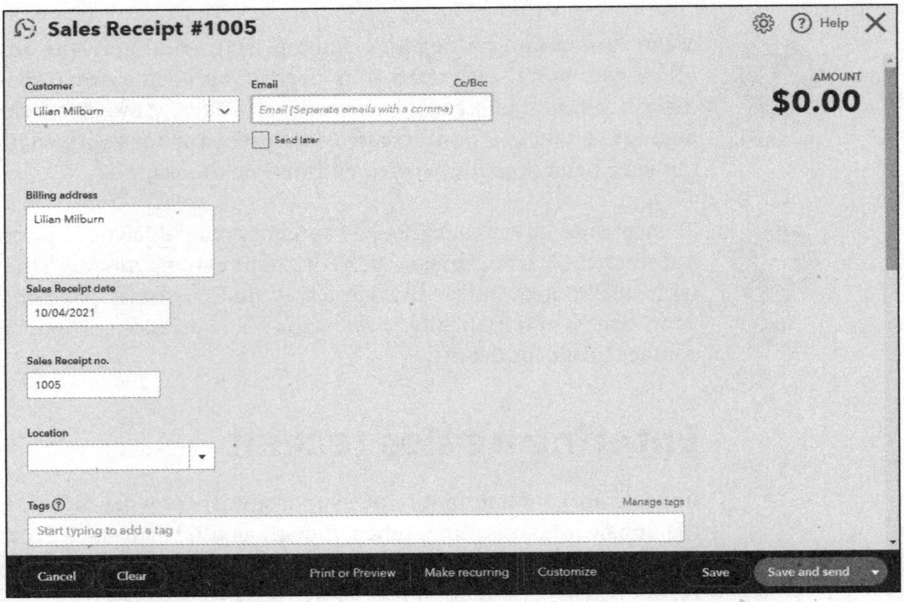

FIGURE 6-15:
A sales receipt.

HANDLING OVERPAYMENTS

From time to time, a customer might pay you more than you're expecting. You can choose to give your customer credit for this overpayment or keep the excess as a gratuity. Either way, you must first instruct QuickBooks to apply credits automatically. Choose Settings ⇨ Account and Settings and then click Advanced on the left side of the Account and Settings dialog box. In the Automation section, toggle Automatically Apply Credits on and then click Save. Going forward, QuickBooks will create credit transactions for overpayments automatically.

You'll receive payment as described earlier in this chapter, but include the overpayment when you fill in the Amount Received field. You can choose among three scenarios:

- **Apply the overpayment to an existing invoice.** Select the invoice(s) you want to apply the payment against in the Outstanding Transactions section of the Receive Payment window. Most likely, this option will result in partial payment for at least one invoice and possibly payment in full for other invoices.

- **Apply the overpayment to a new invoice.** Choose an invoice to apply the overpayment to in the Outstanding Transactions section of the Receive Payment window. If the invoice is $100, but you received $120, show the amount paid as $120. QuickBooks will create a credit transaction for $20 when you click Save and Close. This credit will be applied automatically to the next invoice you create for this customer.

- **Keep the overpayment as income.** Add a Gratuity income account to your chart of accounts and a Gratuity service item assigned to the Gratuity income account. Create a new invoice for the customer, using the Gratuity item and the overpayment amount. QuickBooks automatically marks the invoice paid because it uses the overpayment credit that it created from the overpaid invoice.

If you need to post an electronic payment net of a transaction fee, such as one assessed by Stripe or PayPal, add a row for the transaction fee. In this case, you need to create a Service or Non-Inventory item labeled Transaction Fee or something along those lines. Choose the Transaction Fee item, and record a negative amount. QuickBooks briefly flashes a warning that the negative amount is out of range, but disregard this warning. The net amount of the sales receipt should match the net deposit that will post to your bank account.

Giving Money Back to a Customer

Occasionally, you need to return money you've received from a customer. It's a bummer, but it happens.

You have two options for returning money to customers: Issue a credit memo that the customer can apply against a future invoice, or issue a refund receipt when you need to return the funds immediately.

You can think of a Credit Memo transaction as being the opposite of an Invoice transaction and a Refund Receipt transaction as being the opposite of a Sales Receipt transaction. A Credit Memo transaction is similar to an Invoice transaction but has the opposite effect. Similarly, a Refund Receipt transaction is similar to a Sales Receipt transaction but has the opposite effect.

Recording a credit memo

Credit memos allow you reduce the outstanding or future balance for your customer when warranted.

By default, credit memos are applied automatically to outstanding or future invoices. If you want to change that behavior, open the Account and Settings dialog box (choose Settings ⇨ Account and Settings), and click Advanced on the left side of the dialog box. Scroll down to the Automation section, toggle off the Automatically Apply Credits option, click Save, and then click Close.

You enter a Credit Memo transaction pretty much the same way that you enter an invoice. To display the Credit Memo window shown in Figure 6-16, you can choose New ⇨ Credit Memo, or on the Sales Transactions page, you can click the New Transaction button and choose Credit Memo.

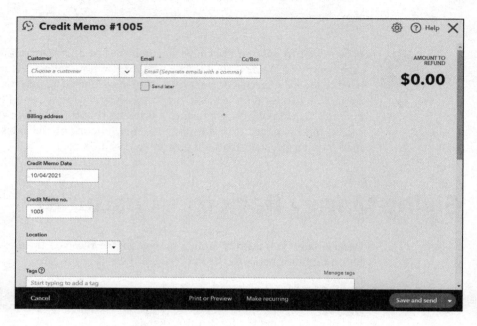

Select the customer, fill in the products or services for which you're issuing a credit memo, fill in the bottom of the Credit Memo window with appropriate information, and save the transaction. This transaction window is similar to the Invoice transaction window; refer to "Preparing an invoice" earlier in this chapter for details.

You can enter a credit memo for a customer even if that customer currently has no outstanding invoices; when you enter the customer's next invoice, the credit memo will be applied to the invoice automatically unless you've disabled that option. Conversely, credit memos are applied automatically to outstanding invoices. If you view the Sales Transactions list for that particular invoice, you'll notice that its status is partially paid, as shown in Figure 6-17.

If you click the invoice to view it, you'll see a link just below the outstanding balance indicating that a payment was made (and the amount of the payment). And if you scroll to the bottom of the invoice, you'll see the credit amount on the Amount Received line at the bottom of the invoice (see Figure 6-18).

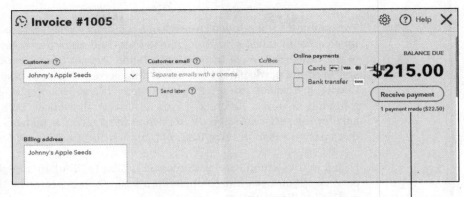

FIGURE 6-17:
An invoice to which a credit memo has been applied.

Indicates a payment has been made for this invoice

Invoice #1005 ⚙ ? Help ✕

Subtotal	237.50
Discount percent ▼	0.00
Taxable subtotal $0.00	
Select tax rate	
Based on location ⌄	$0.00
	See the math
Need help with sales tax? Learn more	
Total	237.50
Deposit	
Amount received	22.50
Balance due	215.00

Message on invoice

This will show up on the invoice.

Cancel   Print or Preview   Make recurring   Customize   More   Save   Save and close ▼

FIGURE 6-18:
Credit memos are applied against outstanding invoices unless you decide otherwise.

Credit amount

Issuing a refund to a customer

Create a Refund Receipt transaction if you need to refund money to a customer instead of reducing an outstanding or future balance. In this example, you're going to issue a refund check to a customer, which will deduct the amount of the refund from a bank account and reduce an income account. The customer didn't return any items.

TIP

To account for refunds you issue when a customer doesn't return an item, first set up an account called something like Returns and Allowances. Assign this account to the Category Type of Income and a Detail Type of Discounts/Refunds Given. If you need the particulars, I discuss adding accounts to your chart of accounts in Chapter 3. Next set up a service on the Products and Services list, and call it something like Customer Refunds or even Returns & Allowances. Do *not* select Is Taxable for the service. Assign the service to the Returns & Allowances account, and don't assign a default Price/Rate. I discuss creating services in Chapter 4.

Filling in the Refund Receipt window is similar to filling in the Sales Receipt window, so if you need more details than I supply here, refer to "Entering a sales receipt" earlier in this chapter. Follow these steps to display and fill in the Refund Receipt window shown in Figure 6-19:

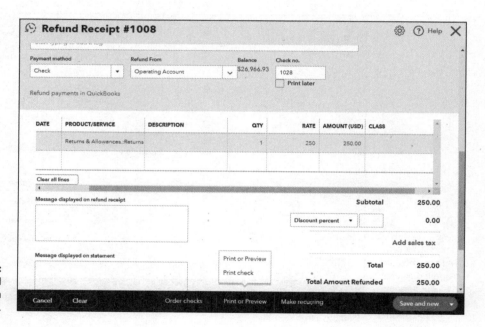

FIGURE 6-19:
Issuing a refund check by way of a Refund Receipt.

1. **Choose New ⇨ Refund Receipt.**

2. **Select a customer to fill in related information.**

3. **Select a payment method and make a choice from the Refund From drop-down list.**

   If you select a bank account, the current balance and the next check number associated with the account appear.

4. **(Optional) Select the Print Later check box.**

   The Print Later check box doesn't appear onscreen until you make a choice from the Refund From drop-down list.

5. **If your customer is returning items, select the item that the customer is returning in exchange for the refund in the Product/Service column, and don't select the Returns & Allowances item shown in Figure 6-19.**

   In this example, the customer isn't returning any items, so I selected the Refunds & Allowances item.

6. **(Optional) Scroll down to the bottom of the window, and fill in the information (the same as the information at the bottom of an invoice).**

7. **Either click Print or Preview at the bottom of the screen and then choose Print Check if you want to print a check or make a choice from the Save button.**

   The transaction is saved when you print the check, or you simply save the transaction if you want to print it later. The Save button allows you to choose between Save and New, Save and Send, or Save and Close. The Print or Preview button allows you simply print the check as well.

REMEMBER

If you are using QB Payments, you can only refund credit card charges processed through your payment account. You cannot refund ACH payments electronically. You'll have to kick it old school and print a paper check or facilitate an electronic transaction outside of QuickBooks.

Working with Estimates

You can use estimates — also known as quotes or bids — to prepare documents that forecast what you'll charge a client to complete a project. Estimates don't affect your general ledger or financial statements but do enable you to keep track of proposals you make to customers. If necessary, you can convert an estimate to a purchase order to facilitate ordering the items needed to complete the job. You also can convert an estimate to an invoice when it's time to bill your customer, which eliminates redundant typing.

WARNING

You can convert Pending estimates only to purchase orders or invoices. Converting an estimate to an invoice sets its status to Closed, so convert estimates to purchase orders first if you need both.

NONPOSTING TRANSACTIONS

Estimates and purchase orders are two examples of nonposting transactions. Nonposting transactions don't affect your accounting records in any way, but they're helpful because they enable you to track potential transaction information you don't want to forget. Other nonposting transactions include Delayed Charges and Delayed Credits.

Delayed Charges transactions record potential future revenue, much like estimates. In fact, you convert a Delayed Charge to an invoice in the same way that you convert an estimate to an invoice. For details, see "Converting an estimate to an invoice" later in this chapter.

Conversely, if you want to stage a credit memo to be posted against an invoice later, you can create a Delayed Credit transaction. Credit Memo transactions affect your books upon entry, but Delayed Credit transactions affect your books only when they're included in an invoice. This is helpful for situations where you want to post a credit to a customer's account in a contingent basis, such as the credit will only apply if they actually place another order in the future.

Creating either transaction is much like creating an invoice. Refer to "Preparing an invoice" earlier in this chapter for details on creating invoices.

Preparing an estimate

Creating an estimate is pretty much identical to creating an invoice. Choose New ⇨ Estimate to display the Estimate page, shown in Figure 6-20. Alternatively, choose Sales ⇨ All Sales on the navigation bar, click the New Transaction button, and click Estimate. From there, all the steps are exactly the same as those for creating an invoice, so refer to "Preparing an invoice" earlier in this chapter if you're unclear about the process.

REMEMBER

Estimates don't affect your financial reports. If you enter an estimate for $10,000, you won't see that $10,000 in your Profit & Loss report until you convert the estimate to an invoice, as I explain in the nearby "Nonposting transactions" sidebar. You could consider an estimate to be a preinvoice, if you will.

TIP

If you are working with a project, you can choose Business Overview ⇨ Projects, select the project, and click Add to Project. Doing so gives you the ability to see all transactions related to a project in one place. I discuss projects in more detail later in this chapter.

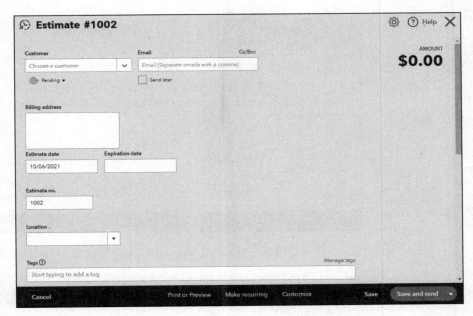

FIGURE 6-20:
The Estimate
page.

Invoices have a status of Unpaid or Paid, whereas estimates have a status of Pending or Closed. An estimate's status remains Pending as long as the estimate is open and has not expired or been converted to an invoice. The status appears just above the customer's billing address.

If you scroll down the Estimate page, you see the additional fields shown in Figure 6-21. Depending on the preferences you've set, you can select a sales tax rate, as well as apply a discount percentage or dollar amount to the estimate. I walk you through the process of enabling these fields in the "Getting Started with Sales Transactions" section. As with invoices, you can type a message to the customer; write a memo about the invoice; and attach supporting documentation, such as the spreadsheet you used to build the estimate, pictures of the job site, or anything else that you'll want to be able to reference easily later. To do so, click the Attachments box and navigate to the document, or drag the file into the Attachments box.

At the bottom of the page, you can do the following:

>> Click Cancel to discard the estimate before you've saved it or to cancel any changes after you've saved it.

>> Click Revert to undo any changes you've made in a saved estimate. This button appears only after you've saved the estimate.

>> Click Print or Preview to print the document now or mark it to print later.

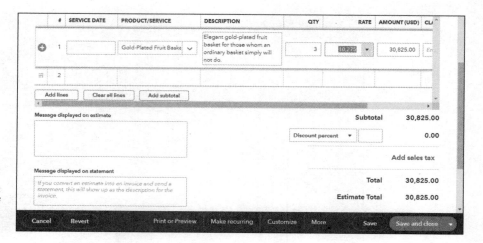

FIGURE 6-21:
The bottom of the Estimate page.

>> Click Make Recurring to schedule the transaction as a recurring estimate.

>> Click Customize to choose or create a customized estimate form, as described in Chapter 3.

>> Click More to copy or delete the estimate, as well as view its audit trail. This button appears only after you've saved the estimate.

>> Click Save to assign a number to the estimate and save the transaction.

>> Click Save and Send to assign a number to the estimate, save it, and email a copy to the customer. After you send your estimate, the email time- and date-stamp information appears in the header.

TIP

You can click the arrow next to Save and Send and then choose Save and New to save the estimate and start a new one, or choose Save and Close to save the estimate and close the Estimate page.

QUICKBOOKS ONLINE AND DOCUSIGN

QuickBooks Online Advanced users can subscribe to the DocuSign app to integrate managing the paper trail of estimates. DocuSign enables you to send documents that your clients sign and return electronically. If you're using QuickBooks Essentials or Pro, you can use DocuSign as a stand-alone app from https://docusign.com; Advanced users have the option of built-in integration. At this writing, DocuSign offers a discount on the first year's subscription.

Managing estimate statuses

When you close the estimate window in QuickBooks, you may find yourself wondering how to get back to estimates that you've created. One approach is to choose New ⇨ Estimates and click the clock icon to the left of the estimate number in the top-left corner of the screen to see a list of recent estimates. You can also click the Search button at the top of the screen to search for the estimate. Select Advanced Search, change the transaction type to Estimates, optionally enter a search term, and click Search. If you omit the search terms QuickBooks will display all your invoices, but you can add one or more filters if that list is overwhelming. Yet another alternative is to use the Estimates by Customer Report by choosing Reports, type **Estimates By** in the Search box, and then click the report title.

When you have your estimate on the screen, you can change the status of the estimate from Pending to any of the following:

» Accepted, meaning that the estimate is approved

» Closed, indicating that the job is complete

» Rejected, recording the fact that your customer declined your offer

You can customize the Estimates by Customer report to provide a list of estimates based on a variety of statuses, including Pending, Accepted, Closed, and Not Rejected.

Copying an estimate to a purchase order

Good news! Your customer wants to purchase based on the quote you provided. In this case, you may want to use the estimate information to prepare a purchase order for a vendor. Plus and Advanced subscribers can convert an estimate with a status of Pending or Accepted to a purchase order; these versions turn on this feature by default.

WARNING

Converting an estimate to an invoice automatically changes the estimate's status to Closed. You can convert Pending or Accepted estimates only to purchase orders, so make sure that you create purchases orders before invoices if you're using both types of documents.

In Chapter 4, I discuss creating inventory items, and how to set the I Purchase This Product/Service from a Vendor option for products and services that you set up. Purchase orders are created only for such items. Conversely, all items in an estimate appear in invoices. If you discover that an item isn't appearing on a purchase order as expected, edit the inventory item to turn on the purchase option.

You can convert any estimate with Pending or Accepted status to a purchase order by following these steps:

1. **Create and save a new estimate (following the steps in "Preparing an estimate" earlier in this chapter), or open an existing pending estimate.**

   To open an existing estimate, choose New ⇨ Estimates, and click the clock icon to the left of the estimate number in the top-left corner of the screen to see a list of recent estimates.

2. **Click the arrow next to the Create Invoice button and choose Copy to Purchase Order from the drop-down menu, as shown in Figure 6-22.**

   You may see a message that some items on the estimate won't carry over to the purchase order. This situation occurs when one or more items in the estimate don't have the I Purchase This Product/Service from a Vendor option enabled within your item list.

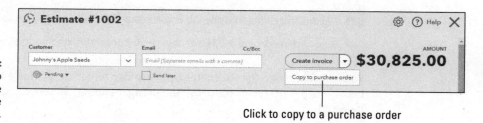

FIGURE 6-22: Getting ready to copy an estimate to a purchase order.

Click to copy to a purchase order

3. **Click OK if a prompt indicates that some items may not carry over to a purchase order.**

   As shown in Figure 6-23, a purchase order displays.

4. **Edit the purchase order as necessary, selecting a vendor and adding any more items to the purchase order.**

5. **Save the purchase order.**

Converting an estimate to an invoice

You've finished the project or delivered the goods, so it's time to send your customer an invoice. You're most of the way there; you simply need to convert the estimate to an invoice. You can make adjustments to the invoice by adding or removing lines as needed. You have several ways to create an invoice from an estimate.

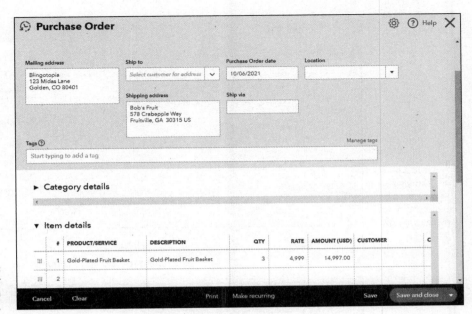

FIGURE 6-23:
A purchase order created from an estimate.

REMEMBER

Converting an estimate to an invoice changes the status to Closed, which means that you can no longer convert the estimate to a purchase order. (Always copy estimates to purchase orders first.)

Use one of these options to create an invoice from an estimate:

>> Open the Invoice window, and select a customer with the open estimate. As shown in Figure 6-24, you see a list of available documents you can link to the invoice, including any estimates. Click the Add button below an estimate to add the line items to your invoice.

>> Filter a customer's Sales Transactions page to display only open estimates, and click the Create Invoice link in the Action column next to the estimate you want to convert, as shown in Figure 6-25. This action creates a new invoice based on the estimate.

>> On a customer's Sales Transactions page, open the estimate, and click the Create Invoice button. This button is available when the estimate status is Pending or Accepted. You can't create invoices from Closed or Rejected estimates.

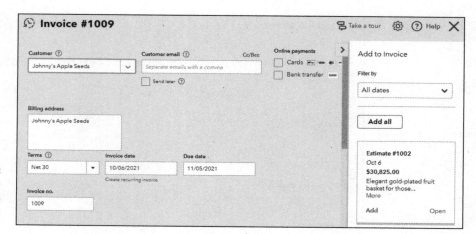

FIGURE 6-24:
Copying an estimate to an invoice from the Invoice window.

Filtering to view only estimates

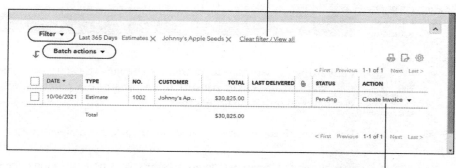

FIGURE 6-25:
Click the Create Invoice link to use estimate information in an invoice.

Click to create an invoice based on the estimate.

TIP

No matter which route you take, creating an invoice from an estimate changes the status of the estimate to Closed, even if you don't invoice the customer for all lines on the estimate. You can change an estimate's status from Closed to Pending or Accepted (or even Rejected), but doing so makes *all* lines on the estimate available for invoicing, which means that you could accidentally invoice your customer twice for the same items. If you need to create a partial invoice, it's best to first make a copy of the invoice that has only the pending items in it and then close the original estimate.

TIP

If you frequently need to send an invoice for only a portion of an estimate, progress billing may be a better fit for you. Read more in "Creating a progress invoice for an estimate" later in this chapter.

Copying an existing estimate

Copying an estimate enables you to make an exact duplicate, which is helpful if you want to send a partial invoice or another customer wants the same set of items. Open an existing estimate from a customer's Sales Transactions list, or choose New⇨Estimates and click the clock icon to the left of the estimate number. Figure 6-26 shows an estimate with a status of Closed.

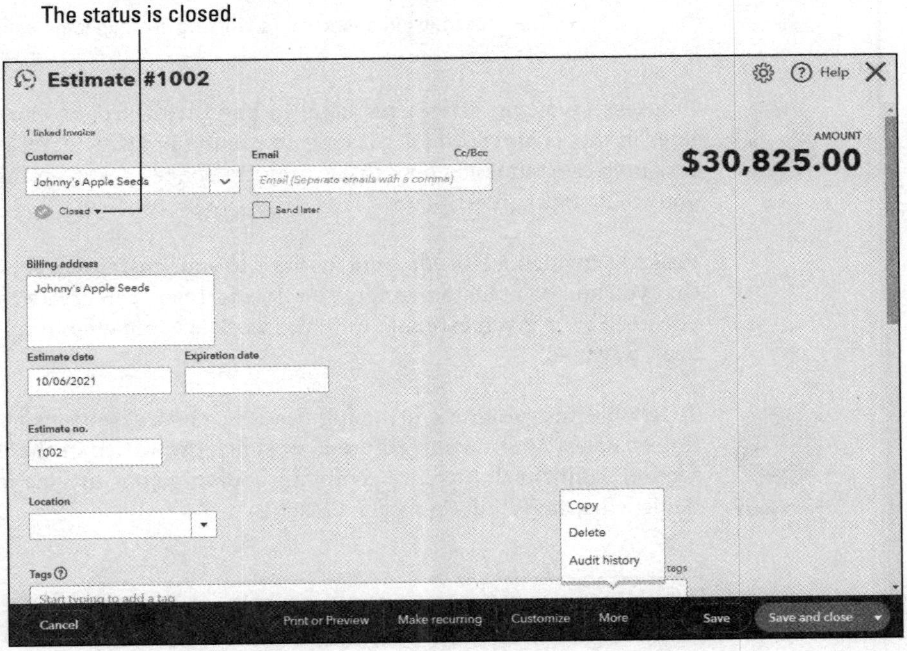

The status is closed.

FIGURE 6-26:
Choose Copy to
duplicate an
estimate, even if
it's closed or
rejected.

Click the More button at the bottom of the screen and choose Copy from the pop-up menu. A copy of the estimate appears, along with a message explaining that you're viewing a copy of an estimate, as shown in Figure 6-27. You might change the customer, for example, or add, delete, or modify the pricing. Click Save or Save and Send in the bottom-right corner of the window, as appropriate.

Creating a progress invoice for an estimate

Suppose that your business requires your work for a customer to stretch out over a lengthy period — say, six months, a year, or longer. If you have to wait until you complete the work to collect any money, you'd have a hard time staying in business, because you wouldn't have the money to pay your bills. Accordingly, you work out arrangements with your customers so that you're paid at various intervals, often known as *progress invoicing*.

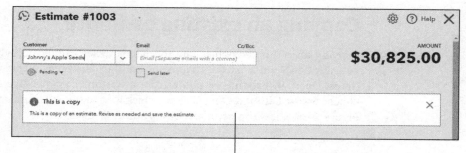

FIGURE 6-27:
Edit and then
save the
duplicated
estimate.

This message indicates you're working in a duplicate estimate.

TIP

Progress invoicing often goes hand in hand with project work, which I discuss later in this chapter. You don't have to use the Projects feature to generate progress invoices, but if you plan to use projects, make sure to set the project up before you create even an estimate.

Progress invoicing lets you send invoices to your customers at periodic milestones that you and your customer agree on. In short, you can create as many invoices as you need for a given estimate until the work is completed in full or all goods have been provided.

REMEMBER

To enable the progress invoicing feature, choose Settings ⇨ Account and Settings ⇨ Sales. As shown in Figure 6-28, click the switch in the Progress Invoicing section, confirm that you're cool with updating your invoice form with the new fields, click Save, and then click Close.

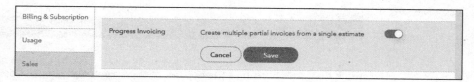

FIGURE 6-28:
Turn on the
option to create
partial invoices.

Next, create an estimate in the usual fashion, as described earlier in this chapter. When you're ready to invoice a portion of the estimate, create an invoice, which displays the window shown in Figure 6-29.

Based on the choice you make in this window, an invoice is created with the appropriate values filled. If you opt to create an invoice with custom amounts for each line, an invoice is created with no amounts filled in so that you can supply them. You create additional progress invoices for the estimate as appropriate until the estimate is closed out.

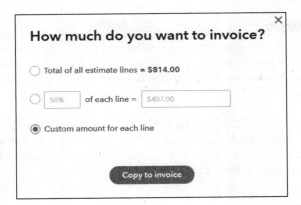

How much do you want to invoice?

○ Total of all estimate lines = $814.00

○ [50%] of each line = [$407.00]

⦿ Custom amount for each line

Copy to invoice

FIGURE 6-29:
Use this window
to establish the
amount of a
progress invoice.

Creating Billable Time Entries

Your employees may complete activities required to run your company (such as preparing customer invoices or entering accounting information), and they may also perform work related directly to your customers. In the latter case, you may need to track the time employees spend on client-related projects so you can bill your customers for your employees' time. This section focuses on the time-tracking tools that are native to QuickBooks Online.

TIP

If your business has time-tracking needs that go beyond the default offerings, consider using the QuickBooks Time app (formerly known as TSheets), one of several timekeeping apps that fully integrate with QuickBooks Online to enable your employees to track time on their mobile devices. Any time they record syncs automatically with your books, with all the appropriate customer, job, and employee information. For more information, visit the Intuit App Center (`https://quickbooks.intuit.com/app/apps/home`), and search for *QuickBooks Time.* To track time using tools available within QuickBooks Online, make sure that you turn on Time Tracking options. Choose Settings ➪ Account and Settings ➪ Advanced (see Figure 6-30). Then, in the Time Tracking section, enable these two options:

» Add Service Field to Timesheets

» Make Single-Time Activity Billable to Customer

FIGURE 6-30:
Enabling the
built-in Time
Tracking options.

You use either the Time Activity window or the Weekly Timesheet window. Regardless of the window you use, QuickBooks tracks the time entered and corresponding billable amounts, if applicable. QuickBooks prompts you to add the time entries the next time you create an invoice for a given customer that has billable time.

In this section, you enter time by using both the Time Activity window and the Weekly Timesheet window, and you see how you're prompted to include the billable time in a customer's invoice. Note that a time entry that you can bill back to a customer is called (cleverly) *billable time*.

Entering a single time activity

A single time activity is a bit of work that you want to record for payroll and/or billing purposes. For instance, you might want to record two hours that you worked on a consulting project. QuickBooks distinguishes single time activities from weekly timesheets that allow you to log multiple time entries. To open the Time Activity window, follow these steps:

1. **Click the New button.**

   If you're working with a project, you can choose Projects (Business Overview ⇨ Projects), select the project, and click Add to Project.

REMEMBER

2. **In the Employees column, click Single Time Activity.**

   The Time Activity window appears (see Figure 6-31) when you click the Stick with Basic Time button the first time you access the Time screen.

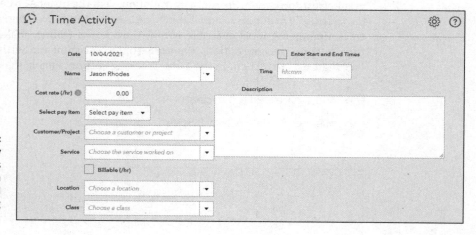

FIGURE 6-31:
The Time Activity window allows you to record an event for payroll and/or billing purposes.

3. **Click Add Time on the Overview or Time Entries screen.**

4. **If you're prompted to do so, click Add Employee to add an employee.**

TIP

Perhaps Mercury was in retrograde the day I wrote this chapter, but when I clicked Add Employee, my QuickBooks screen went dark, and I was unable to add an employee. As you can see, the chapter continues because there's an alternative: I clicked Add Employee in the Shortcuts area of the Overview page, and away I went.

5. **From the Name list, select the employee or vendor who performed the work.**

6. **Choose the date when the work was performed.**

7. **Click Add Work Details.**

The Add Work Details pane opens, as shown in Figure 6-32.

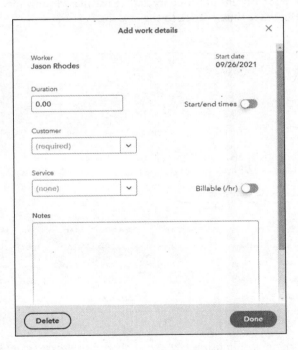

Add work details   ×

Worker   Start date
Jason Rhodes   09/26/2021

Duration
0.00   Start/end times ⬤

Customer
(required)   ⌄

Service
(none)   ⌄   Billable (/hr) ⬤

Notes

Delete   Done

FIGURE 6-32:
The Add Work
Details pane.

8. **Enter a time amount in the Duration field.**

You can enter start and end times by toggling the Start/End Times option.

9. **Select the customer for which the work was performed.**

10. **Select the service that was performed.**

11. Toggle the Billable (/hr) option if applicable.

12. Enter any notes, such as a description of the work.

You can change the description after adding the time entry to the invoice.

13. Click Done to save the entry, or click Delete to discard the entry.

Adding a billable expense to an invoice

You can add billable expense entries, including billable time entries, to an invoice in a couple of ways. First, you can click Sales ⇨ Customers (Sales & Expenses ⇨ Customers) in the navigation bar to display the Customers page. Click any customer's name to display a list of transactions, as shown in Figure 6-33. The Action column displays Create Invoice for any Time Charge transactions that have not been invoiced yet. If you have multiple time charges you want to invoice, simply click Create Invoice for any one of the charges. The Invoice window that appears enables you to add the other time entries to the invoice.

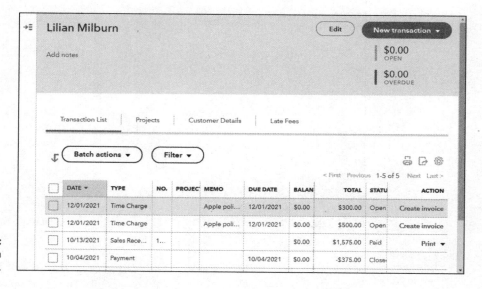

FIGURE 6-33:
Viewing a
customer's page.

REMEMBER

If you're working with a project, you can choose Projects, select the project, and click Transactions to view available billable expenses.

But you don't need to go looking for billable time entries; QuickBooks prompts you to add them to any invoice you create for a customer for which billable entries exist. Start an invoice (choose New ⇨ Invoice), and select a customer. If the customer has billable expense entries, they appear in the pane on the right side of the screen (see Figure 6-34).

Click to filter the time entries displayed.

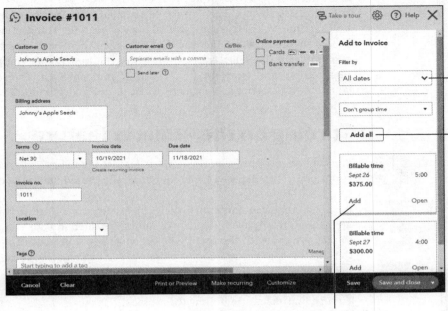

FIGURE 6-34:
Creating an
invoice for a
customer with
billable time
entries.

Click to add a single entry to the invoice.

Click to add all entries to the invoice.

Use the Filter options to limit the billable time entries that appear. Then click the Add button in each billable time entry that you want to add to the invoice. Or, to add all the entries, click the Add All button at the top of the pane. Each billable time entry's information is added to the invoice as a line with the service, description, quantity, rate, and total amount filled in. By default, time entries appear individually in the invoice, but you can opt to group time entries by service type. You can edit any information as needed. Fill in the rest of the invoice as described in "Preparing an invoice" earlier in this chapter, adding other lines that may not pertain to time entries.

Don't forget that you can add a subtotal for time entries, if you choose. See the "Configuring automatic subtotals" section of this chapter for details.

Managing Projects

If your business completes projects for your customers, the Projects feature helps you organize, in one centralized location, all the pieces — that is, associated transactions, time spent, and necessary reports — that make up . . . well, a project.

Also, the reports included in the Projects feature help you determine each project's profitability and keep on top of unbilled time and expenses as well as non-billable time. You'll still complete all the various sales transaction forms described in this chapter in the same way that I describe them, with one change: Instead of starting from the Sales Transaction list or the New menu, you'll be able (but not required) to start from the Project tab. If you enable the Projects feature before you enter transactions, your picture of a project's profitability will be clearer.

Turning on the Projects feature

REMEMBER

You can take advantage of the Projects feature if you have a Plus or Advanced subscription in Canada, the United Kingdom, the United States, or Australia.

WARNING

Be aware that you can't turn the Projects feature off after you turn it on. You aren't required to use it, but it will remain enabled in your company. If you want to play around with the feature before enabling it in your company, try it out in the QuickBooks Online sample company. You can read about the sample company in Chapter 12.

To turn on the feature, follow these steps:

1. **Choose Settings ➪ Account and Settings ➪ Advanced.**

2. **In the Projects section, click the Organize All Job-Related Activity in One Place option to turn on the Projects feature, as shown in Figure 6-35.**

FIGURE 6-35:
Enabling projects
in QuickBooks.

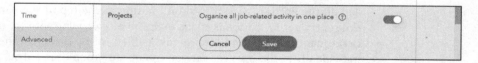

3. **Click Done to close the dialog box.**

   A new option, Projects, appears on the Accountant View navigation bar (see Figure 6-36). If you're using Business View choose Business View ➪ Projects. You'll be prompted to start your first project when you choose that option.

TIP

The navigation bar at the left has two primary configurations: Accountant View and Business View. Click the Settings button and then click the view link that appears at the bottom right-hand corner to toggle between the views.

But before you jump in and start creating projects, read on.

FIGURE 6-36:
Starting a new
project.

Enabling projects in Customer lists

Before you set up any new projects, you need to complete one housekeeping chore for the Projects feature to work properly. Choose Sales ⇨ Customers to display the Customers page. In the table portion of the page, just above the Action column, click the Table Settings icon. Then select the Include Projects check box (see Figure 6-37). You'll be able to see projects on the Customers page and in list boxes on transactions, as well as on the Projects Center page.

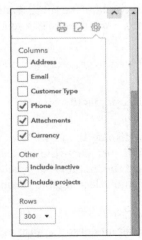

FIGURE 6-37:
Enable the
Include Projects
check box.

Converting subcustomers to projects

You can use subcustomers to act as projects, and you may have been using them up until now. So is the line blurring between subcustomers and projects? Not really. If you use the Projects feature, you'll notice that projects appear in the Project Center. You can use this window to track employee time, see labor costs by projects, and monitor your profit margin by project. When you click on a project name you can view window with four tabs:

>> Overview gives a bird's-eye view of income and costs.

>> Transactions shows every transaction assigned to the job.

>> Time Activity enables you to view activity by time period and then employee or service.

>> Project Reports lets you choose from three reports.

Conversely subcustomers remain only in the Customers list, which means you can't access all the details previously described.

The benefit of using the Projects feature lies in the fact that the Project Center keeps the information for each project in one place. Subcustomers don't offer this centralization — unless you convert them to projects.

Before you start adding projects, you may want to consider whether you've created subcustomers that you want to convert to projects. Be aware of the following:

>> You can convert subcustomers to projects only if the subcustomers are set up to be billed with the parent customer. You may need to edit your subcustomers to make this change.

>> You don't need to convert all subcustomers to projects simultaneously; you can make individual selections.

>> You can't undo the conversion of a subcustomer to a project.

To convert a subcustomer to a project, display the Customers list by choosing Sales ⇨ Customers. On the Customers page, just above the table of transactions, a message asks whether you want to convert the first level of subcustomers to projects. Click Convert Now in the message, and select eligible subcustomers to convert (see Figure 6-38).

TIP

If the Convert Subcustomers to Projects prompt doesn't appear on your Customers screen, choose Projects on the navigation bar, click the arrow next to New Project, and choose Convert from Subcustomer from the drop-down menu.

FIGURE 6-38: Converting a subcustomer to a project.

After you click Convert (not shown in Figure 6-38), a message explains that you're about to convert a subcustomer to a project — and that there's no going back. If you're sure you want to do this, click Continue to convert the subcustomer(s), set the status of the project(s) to "in progress," and then decide whether you want to go to the Projects Center or redisplay the Customer list.

Setting up a project

Now you're ready to set up a project. Click Projects on the navigation bar, and if you didn't convert any subcustomers to projects, the Start a Project button appears on the Projects Center page. If you did convert one or more subcustomers to projects, those projects appear on the Projects Center page.

To start a new project, click New Project on the Projects Center page. A panel appears on the right side of the screen; in the pane, supply a project name, which can be anything you want and should be something you'll easily recognize. Also supply the customer associated with the project and, if you want, any notes about the project. When you finish, click Save, and look for a message to let you know that the project is set up. When you click OK to dismiss the message, a page like the one shown in Figure 6-39 appears.

REMEMBER

Even though you select a customer when you create a new project, existing transactions for the customer don't appear on the Projects page. Newly created projects have no transactions; therefore, logically, the Transactions page is empty, and reports contain no information. But converted subcustomers are a different story. When a subcustomer is converted to a project, previous activity *does* appear in the Projects page.

WARNING

If you're thinking about changing the customer name in existing transactions to pull those transactions into the project, be careful. Changing the customer can have repercussions throughout QuickBooks. If you try to change the customer assigned to a payment transaction that you've deposited, for example, you'll be warned that you must remove the transaction from the deposit before you can change the customer name, which will mess up your deposit unless you remember to add the payment to the deposit again. So you see, things can get complicated very quickly. Even though there's a connection between a customer and subcustomer or project, entries in the Customers list are unique list elements. QuickBooks Desktop works the same way in this regard.

FIGURE 6-39:
The Project Reports page for a project.

Adding transactions to a project

There's no special, secret way to add transactions to a project. (It isn't like double secret probation in *Animal House.*) In fact, you have two choices. You can use the techniques described throughout this chapter for the various types of transactions; just make sure that you choose the project name from the Customer dropdown list rather than choosing the customer name itself, as shown in Figure 6-40.

Or you can start many (but not all) your transactions from the Projects Center. Starting your transaction from the Projects Center by clicking the Add to Project button has one added advantage: The project name is prefilled in the transaction. Note that you can't create a sales receipt from the Projects page; use the New menu or the Sales page instead.

REMEMBER

If you can't add a transaction for a project from the Projects Center, simply select the project in the transaction when you create it from either the New menu or the Customers list page.

Make sure to select the project, not the customer.

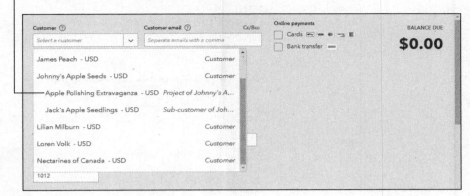

FIGURE 6-40:
Creating a new
transaction for a
project.

Reporting on projects

The power of projects becomes apparent once a project accumulates some activity, such as invoices, time charges, expenses, and so on. The Projects Center allows you to list your transactions on the Transactions and Time Activity tabs, while the Project Reports tab offers three reports:

>> Project Profitability is essentially a Profit & Loss report for the project, as shown in Figure 6-41.

>> Time Cost by Employee or Vendor reflects the labor and external service fees posted to the job.

>> Unbilled Time and Expenses shows you time and costs assigned to the project but not yet billed.

The Overview tab of the Projects Center enables you to manage the status of projects. When you create a new job, the status defaults to In Progress, but you can click the Options button for a given project to change the status to Not Started, Completed, or Canceled. The Options menu also enables you to delete a project if no transactions have been assigned to it.

FIGURE 6-41:
A sample Project
Profitability
report.

Chapter **7**

Working in Registers

I n Chapters 5 and 6, I show you how to use transaction screens for entering checks, sales receipts, invoices, customer payments, and more. I also show how you can search and filter existing transactions. In this chapter, I show how to use registers to carry out these actions. Another way registers are helpful is for accessing a bird's-eye view of transactions that affect certain accounts in your books.

Understanding Registers

Registers allow you to see every transaction that affects a particular account. In short, *registers* are chronological lists of transactions that were maintained on paper before the advent of computers, but now appear onscreen.

To view the register for a particular account, choose Settings ➪ Accounting ➪ Chart of Accounts in the Your Company column. Next, click the View Register link in the Action column to display the register for the account of your choice, as shown in Figure 7-1.

TIP

If you haven't accessed the Chart of Accounts page previously, you may need to click the See Your Chart of Accounts button to display your chart of accounts.

Click to view a register.

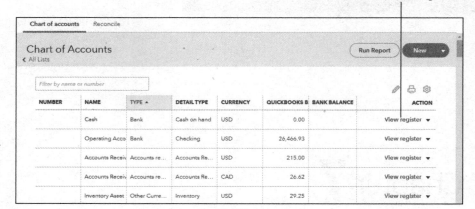

FIGURE 7-1:
Use the Chart of Accounts page to open a particular account's register.

Figure 7-2 shows a checking account register. If you've connected your bank account to QuickBooks, the bank balance appears alongside the bank account name; the book balance always appears in the top-right corner of the register. Differences between the two represent transactions that you've recorded but that haven't cleared the bank yet.

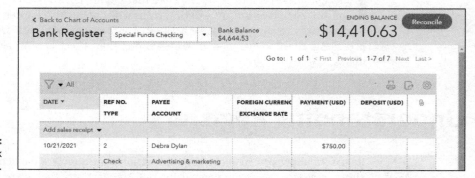

FIGURE 7-2:
A typical bank account register.

TIP

By default, transactions appear in reverse chronological order — from newest to oldest. Later in this section, I show how you to change the way that the register displays information.

Only asset, liability, and most equity accounts, such as the following, have registers in QuickBooks:

- » Bank
- » Accounts Receivable
- » Other Current Assets
- » Fixed Assets
- » Other Assets

- » Accounts Payable
- » Credit Card
- » Other Current Liabilities
- » Long-Term Liabilities
- » Equity

Retained earnings, income, and expense accounts don't have registers. But you can run reports that show the transactions within these accounts, which is fairly close to having a register.

TIP

If you use account numbers, a typical numbering scheme is for all asset accounts to begin with 1, such as 1000 or 10000, all liability accounts to begin with 2, and all equity accounts to begin with 3. This numbering scheme isn't carved in stone, but most accountants recommend that you follow these guidelines when you assign numbers to the accounts in your chart of accounts.

Within the register, column headings identify the information contained in each column for every transaction, and at the right edge of a register page, you see a running balance for the account. All the transactions in a bank account register affect a bank account — along with some other account, as dictated by the rules of accounting. *Double-entry bookkeeping,* a founding principle of accounting, means that every transaction affects at least two accounts. At the right edge of a register page is the Balance column, which has the running balance for the account as long as the register is sorted by date.

WARNING

Accountants typically find the register to be a useful area within QuickBooks to make various changes efficiently. Keep in mind that working in the actual transaction windows is much safer because it minimizes the chances that you inadvertently edit the wrong transaction. Registers are a great way to get a bird's-eye view of your transactions, but tread carefully if you feel inclined to make adjustments within your registers.

Customizing the Register View

By default, the most recent transactions appear at the top of the register, but you can click the Date column heading to sort the transactions from oldest to newest instead. Another approach is to turn on Paper Ledger mode, shown in Figure 7-3. In a paper register, transactions are entered as they occur, so the earliest transactions appear at the top of the register, and the latest transactions appear at the bottom of the register. You can still click the Date column to change the sort order in Paper Ledger mode.

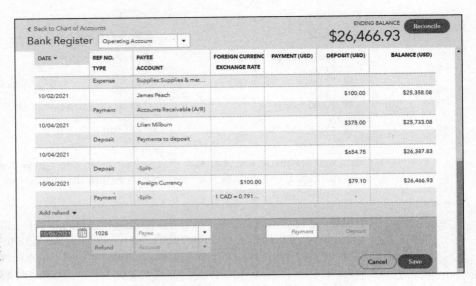

FIGURE 7-3:
A bank account register in Paper Ledger mode.

To switch to Paper Ledger mode, follow these steps:

1. **Click the Settings icon above the Balance column.**

2. **In the Settings menu, click the check box for Paper Ledger mode.**

   The transactions appear in date order from oldest to newest.

You can turn off Paper Ledger mode by clearing the check box in Step 2. Any setting changes you make in one register, such as changing the display to Paper Ledger mode, or any of the other adjustments I discuss in this chapter, apply to all ledgers automatically.

REMEMBER

As shown in Figure 7-3, a space for entering new transactions appears at the bottom of certain registers when you activate Paper Ledger mode. You can't add a transaction directly to the Accounts Receivable or Accounts Payable registers, for example, but you can for most other registers.

In addition to using Paper Ledger mode, you can control the appearance of a register in a few other ways:

» Changing the sizes of columns

» Controlling the number of rows on a page

» Reducing each register entry to a single line

To change the size of any column, slide the mouse pointer into the column-heading area on the right boundary of the column. In Figure 7-4, I'm resizing the Payee Account column. Drag the double-headed arrow mouse pointer to the left to make the column narrower or to the right to make the column wider, just like in a spreadsheet. As you drag, a solid vertical line helps you determine the size of the column. Release the mouse button when the column reaches the size you want.

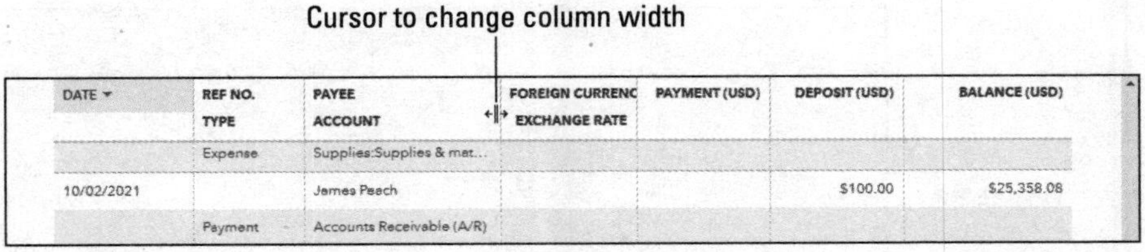

Cursor to change column width

DATE ▾	REF NO. TYPE	PAYEE ACCOUNT	FOREIGN CURRENC EXCHANGE RATE	PAYMENT (USD)	DEPOSIT (USD)	BALANCE (USD)
	Expense	Supplies:Supplies & mat...				
10/02/2021		James Peach			$100.00	$25,358.06
	Payment	Accounts Receivable (A/R)				

FIGURE 7-4: Resizing a column.

You can also show or hide columns in most registers. Click the Settings button above the Balance column on the right edge of the page. If a Columns section appears, as shown in Figure 7-5, toggle the check marks for any columns you want to show or hide.

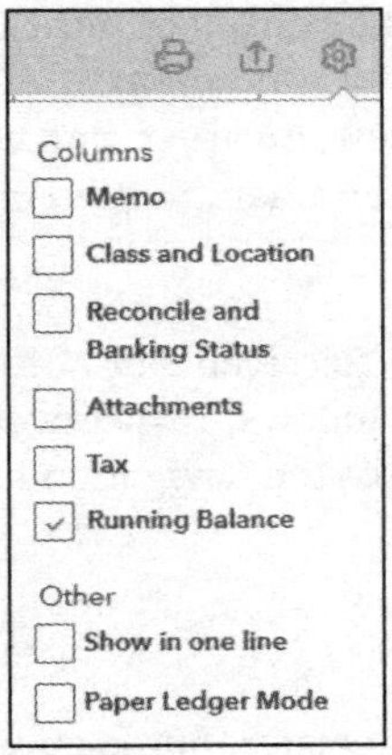

Columns

- Memo
- Class and Location
- Reconcile and Banking Status
- Attachments
- Tax
- ✓ Running Balance

Other

- Show in one line
- Paper Ledger Mode

FIGURE 7-5: Toggle on the columns you want to show.

You can control how many rows appear on a single page of your registers. Click the Settings button above the Balance column, and choose 50, 75, 100, 150, or 300 in the Rows section of the Settings menu. To move from one page of transactions to the next or to a previous page, click the Next and Previous links at the bottom of the register.

Typically, a QuickBooks register displays transactions in two-line format, but Figure 7-6 shows that you can collapse this format to a single line for each transaction. To do so, click the Settings button above the Balance column, and select the Show in One Line check box. This action may hide the Memo, Reconcile, and Banking Status columns in certain registers. You can turn these fields back on clearing the Show in One Line check box on the Settings menu.

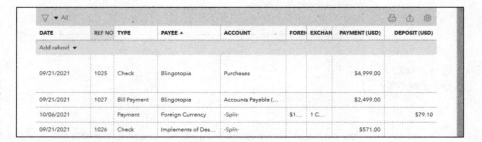

FIGURE 7-6:
A register displaying one line for each transaction.

DATE	REF NO	TYPE	PAYEE ▲	ACCOUNT	FOREI	EXCHAN	PAYMENT (USD)	DEPOSIT (USD)
Add refund ▼								
09/21/2021	1025	Check	Blingotopia	Purchases			$4,999.00	
09/21/2021	1027	Bill Payment	Blingotopia	Accounts Payable (...			$2,499.00	
10/06/2021		Payment	Foreign Currency	-Split-	$1...	1 C...		$79.10
09/21/2021	1026	Check	Implements of Des...	-Split-			$571.00	

Entering and Editing Transactions

The transaction entry area that appears at the bottom of most QuickBooks registers (refer to Figure 7-4) offers a quick, easy way to enter simple transactions. This area limits you to a single transaction row, however, and you can't reference inventory items here. But if you need to enter a handwritten check quickly, then this is the place.

REMEMBER

You can't enter transactions in the Accounts Receivable or Accounts Payable registers. Use the Invoice or Bill transaction windows, respectively, which you can access by clicking the New button at the top of the navigation bar.

Entering a transaction

You can enter a variety of transactions in a register, but keep in mind that you'll be limited to a single row. If you need to divide a transaction among multiple accounts or reference inventory items, you need to click the New button at the top of the navigation bar. QuickBooks allows you to create the following transactions in some (but not all) registers:

>> Check

>> Deposit

>> Sales Receipt

>> Receive Payment

>> Bill Payment

>> Refund

>> Expense

>> Transfer

>> Journal Entry

QuickBooks suggests a default transaction type for a given register or remembers the last type of transaction that you entered in that register. If you want to change the transaction type, click the Add button to choose any of the transaction types in the preceding list. The Add button for transactions appears at the top of the register unless you activate Paper Ledger mode, in which case the Add button moves to the bottom. Keep in mind that you'll be working blindly if you add certain transactions types, such as Receive Payment or Bill Payment. The transaction window in the register screen doesn't show you open invoices or bills, so amounts you entered will be applied arbitrarily by QuickBooks.

To add a transaction to a register, follow these steps:

1. **Click the down arrow next to the Add button.**

As shown in Figure 7-7, a list of available transaction types appears.

REMEMBER

You see only transactions that are appropriate for a given account type. Bank accounts display the most options; other accounts may offer fewer options or none.

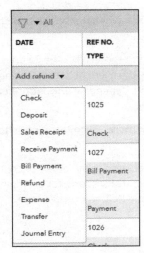

FIGURE 7-7:
Choose the type of transaction you want to enter.

2. **Choose a transaction type.**

Today's date is filled in, and fields related to the transaction appear. Remember that you're limited to a single row when working within the register.

3. **Change the transaction date, if necessary.**

4. **(Optional) Enter a reference number.**

The Ref No. Type column (see Figure 7-8) is disabled for certain types of transactions, such as deposits, transfers, and refunds.

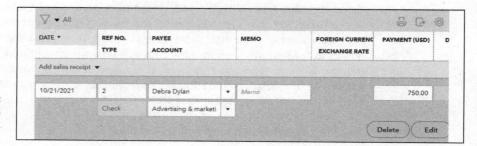

FIGURE 7-8:
Entering a sales receipt in a bank account register.

5. **If permitted, enter a payee name.**

You can choose existing names from the list or add a new name on the fly.

6. **If permitted, choose an account.**

You won't be able to choose an account for certain transactions, such as sales receipts, bill payments, and refunds.

7. **(Optional) Fill in the Memo field, if it's available for the transaction type you chose.**

If the Memo column isn't shown in your register, click the Settings button above the Balance column, and toggle the check box. You can enable the Class and Location fields in the same fashion, depending on your preferences and QuickBooks Online subscription level.

8. **Enter an amount in the Decrease or Increase column (not shown in Figure 7-8).**

QuickBooks sometimes disables one column or the other. Decrease is disabled for Sales Receipts and Receive Payment transactions, for example, whereas Increase is disabled for Bill Payment and Refund transactions.

9. **(Optional, not recommended) Modify Reconcile Status, if applicable.**

The Reconcile and Banking Status column may be hidden in your register, but you can enable it as discussed earlier in this chapter. This column displays a character representing the status of the transaction: C for Cleared or R for Reconciled. When the column is blank, the transaction is neither cleared nor reconciled. Although you can set the reconciliation status of a transaction here, doing so is one of those "not that you should, but you could" situations. You should modify the reconciliation status of a transaction only through the Reconcile screen in QuickBooks, as I discuss in Chapter 8.

If the account is connected electronically to your financial institution, the Reconcile and Banking Status column indicates whether transactions were added or matched when transactions were downloaded via the account's bank feed.

WARNING

I'm so nice that I'll say it twice: Don't be tempted to adjust the reconciliation status of a transaction from this screen. Doing so adjusts the account's reconciled balance in a way that won't show up in reconciliation reports. You can quickly have a mess on your hands if you modify the reconciliation status outside the reconciliation process.

10. **(Optional) Click Edit and then use the Attachments area if you want to link one or more electronic documents.**

If shown, the Attachments column displays the number of attachments linked to a given document. You cannot add attachments directly in a register, but you can always add attachments via the transaction screens.

11. **Click the Save button.**

The transaction is saved and replaced by a blank transaction screen of the same type.

WARNING

You can't change the sales account for a sales receipt when entering a transaction directly in the checking register. You can edit transactions through the respective transaction form, however, which would enable you to change the account if necessary.

Editing a transaction

You can edit a transaction in the register by clicking the transaction and then making changes. Alternatively, you can edit a transaction from a given transaction window, as discussed in Chapter 5.

REMEMBER

You can't add or view attachments directly within a register, but you can enable the Attachments column (identified by a paper clip icon at the top, as shown in Figure 7-2) to display the number of attachments associated with each transac-tion. To view attachments, click a transaction in the register and then click the Edit button that appears just below the transaction to display the associated transaction entry screen.

Other Things You Can Do in a Register

It's pretty useful to be able to add and edit transactions in a register, but wait, there's more! You can also sort and filter your transactions, create a printout of the register, or export the printout to a spreadsheet that you can access in Micro-soft Excel or Google Sheets.

Sorting transactions

Looking for a transaction by skimming the register — eyeballing it — can be a nonproductive way of finding a transaction. Instead, sorting the register based on any column can help you zero in on a particular transaction.

Click any column heading to sort the register in that order. Figure 7-9 shows transactions in the default order of newest to oldest.

Click a column heading to sort by that column.

DATE ▼	REF NO. TYPE	PAYEE ACCOUNT	FOREIGN CURRENC EXCHANGE RATE	PAYMENT (USD)	DEPOSIT (USD)	BALANCE (USD)
Add sales receipt ▼						
10/06/2021	1007	Loren Volk			$500.00	$26,966.93
	Sales Receipt	Services				
10/06/2021		Foreign Currency	$100.00		$79.10	$26,466.93
	Payment	-Split-	1 CAD = 0.791...			
10/04/2021					$654.75	$26,387.83
	Deposit	-Split-				
10/04/2021		Lilian Milburn			$375.00	$25,733.08
	Deposit	Payments to deposit				
10/02/2021		James Peach			$100.00	$25,358.08
	Payment	Accounts Receivable (A/R)				
09/21/2021		Johnny's Apple Seeds		$1,000.00		$25,258.08

FIGURE 7-9: Transactions are displayed from newest to oldest unless you change the sort order.

Note the down arrow in the Date column heading. Click the Date column heading to reverse the order of the transactions. Now the arrow next to the column heading's name changes direction, pointing up.

Alternatively, you can click the Payee column heading to sort transactions in alphabetical order by payee, and you can click the column heading a second time to sort in reverse alphabetical order.

WARNING

You can sort by any column heading except Account, Foreign Currency Exchange Rate, Balance, Memo, and Attachment. Sorting on any column other than Date causes the Balance column to display n/a because the balances can't be computed in that order.

Filtering transactions

Very often, filtering is a more effective means of sifting through a sea of transactions than sorting. To do so, click the Filter button that appears above the Date column to display the menu shown in Figure 7-10.

Click the Filter button to view filter options.

Currently selected filter

The current filter criteria appear to the right of the Filter button. The word `All` appears when no filter criteria have been set.

Here are some examples of filter criteria:

>> Enter **1234** in the Find field to display all transactions with 1234 in the memo or reference field.

>> Enter **$5000** or **5000** in the Find field to display all transactions that have a total of $5,000; don't enter commas for the thousands position.

>> Enter **<$25** or **< 25** in the Find field to display all transactions with amounts less than $25.

You can fill any or all of the fields shown in Figure 7-10, which means that you could search for the Not Reconciled checks written to a particular vendor in a specific period.

REMEMBER

Unfortunately, you can't search for transactions between $500 and $1,000. QuickBooks accepts only a single criterion in the Find field and doesn't support <= or >=. Use <500.01 if you want to search for transactions that are less than or equal to 500. Invalid search criteria turn red within the filter field, almost as though they're radioactive.

Any transactions that meet the criteria you specify in the Filter window appear in the register after you click Apply. As shown in Figure 7-11, the filter criteria appear beside the Filter button. Click the Clear Filter/View All link to clear the filter and redisplay all transactions in the register.

Click to export the register to a spreadsheet.

FIGURE 7-11:
A list of transactions based on criteria specified in the Filter window.

DATE ▾	REF NO. TYPE	PAYEE ACCOUNT	FOREIGN CURRENC EXCHANGE RATE	PAYMENT (USD)	DEPOSIT (USD)	BALANCE (USD)
Add sales receipt ▾						
10/06/2021		Foreign Currency	$100.00		$79.10	(Only displayed with date/reconcile status sort)
	Payment	-Split-	1 CAD = 0.791...			
10/04/2021		Lilian Milburn			$375.00	n/a
	Deposit	Payments to deposit				
10/02/2021		James Peach			$100.00	n/a
	Payment	Accounts Receivable (A/R)				
09/21/2021		Implements of Destruction			$79.94	n/a
	Deposit	Accounts Payable (A/P)				

Printing a register

You can always generate an old-school paper copy of your register when necessary. To do so, click the Print button beside the register's Table Settings button above the Balance column. As shown in Figure 7-12, a Print tab appears, offering a preview of your report.

On the right side of the tab, select the printer you want to use, and make any other necessary selections, such as pages to print, number of copies, and orientation. When you finish selecting settings, click Print. When the report finishes printing, you can close the Print tab to return to your electronic register.

TIP

You aren't restricted to printing to paper. You can choose Save As PDF or Microsoft Print to PDF on the Print tab to send your register to a PDF document. You can even choose Save to Google Docs if you sign in to Google Cloud Print.

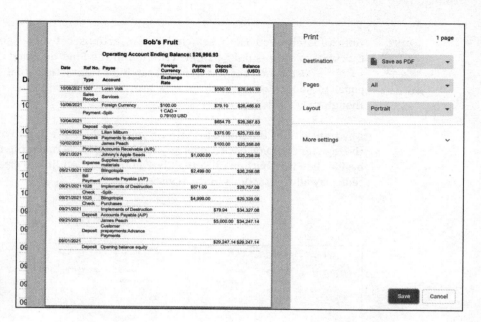

FIGURE 7-12:
Printing a
register.

Exporting a register

The Export to Excel button next to the Settings button (refer to Figure 7-11) allows you to export the register to an Excel spreadsheet. You can open the resulting file in Microsoft Excel or Google Docs and then use the more robust filtering tools available in that platform to perform more-granular searches than are possible in QuickBooks Online. In Chapter 11, I discuss ways to analyze QuickBooks data in Excel, and in Chapter 17, I show you how automate Excel analysis with Power Query.

Chapter **8**

Handling Bank and Credit Card Transactions

lthough the chapter is titled "Handling Bank and Credit Card Transactions," that tried-and-true infomercial line "But wait, there's more!" applies here. In this chapter, I show you not only how to enter bank and credit card transactions but also how to enable automation by connecting QuickBooks to your financial institutions. You'll see how to reconcile bank accounts and use tagging in QuickBooks, which offers another dimension in threading related transactions together.

Setting Up a Bank or Credit Card Account

In Chapter 3, I show you how to create a new Bank account, but in that chapter, I don't connect the account to a financial institution because opportunities to build suspense in a book about accounting software are few and far between, and

I wanted to keep you on the edge of your seat. I'm going to extend my moment here by still not showing you how to connect your bank account. Instead, I'll walk you through connecting a credit card account, but the steps are exactly the same for connecting your bank account, so you get a two-for-one here.

WARNING

QuickBooks exuberantly encourages you to connect your new Bank or Credit Card account to your financial institution. This decision isn't one to be made lightly, as you can see in the "Don't let this happen to you" sidebar later in the chapter. I recommend that you read "Connecting QuickBooks Accounts to Financial Institutions" later in this chapter so that you can make an informed decision.

Follow these steps to set up a Credit Card account:

1. Click Settings, and on the left side of the menu that appears, choose Chart of Accounts in the Your Company column.

The Chart of Accounts page appears.

2. Click the New button on the Chart of Accounts page to open the Account dialog box (see Figure 8-1).

FIGURE 8-1:
The dialog box you use to create an account.

3. Choose Credit Card from the Account Type drop-down list.

Detail Type is prefilled for you.

4. Provide a name for the account.

5. (Optional) In the Number field, enter a general ledger account number for the new account if your chart of accounts has account numbers.

WARNING

Don't enter your credit card number in this field. The word *Number* that describes the field refers to the general ledger account number, not the number on the face of your credit card.

6. (Optional) Provide a description.

7. (Optional) Specify a currency, if you have multicurrency enabled in your QuickBooks company.

8. (Optional) If applicable, select the Is Sub-Account check box, and then select a parent account.

I can't see this applying to bank accounts, but some businesses have a master credit card account with individual subaccounts. The Is Subaccount option would give you the ability to mirror that structure inside QuickBooks.

9. (Optional) Enter your account's balance as it appears on the last statement.

WARNING

If you enter a balance, QuickBooks updates both the account balance and the Opening Balance Equity account, and your accountant probably won't be happy with you for creating a discrepancy with last year's income tax return, or maybe they'll relish the job security. I suggest that you not enter a balance.

10. Click Save and Close.

The Chart of Accounts page displays your new account in the list.

REMEMBER

You'll need to enter expense and credit card credit transactions that have occurred since you received the last statement for this credit card, which you can do by entering the transactions manually, as I discuss in Chapter 5, or connecting your QuickBooks account to your financial institution.

Making a Bank Deposit

In Chapter 6, I show you how to record payments from customers, and I strongly recommend that you use the Payments to Deposit (or Undeposited Funds) account as you record Receive Payment transactions. As you may surmise from the name,

Payments to Deposit is simply a stopover along the way to your bank account. To create a bank deposit transaction, follow these steps:

1. **Click the New button, and select Bank Deposit in the Other column.**

The Bank Deposit transaction window appears (see Figure 8-2). Existing payment transactions appear in the Select the Payments Included in This Deposit section. You can use the lines in the Add Funds to This Deposit section shown in Figure 8-3 to add new payment transactions that aren't associated with an outstanding invoice, such as refund checks, reimbursement payments, and so on.

FIGURE 8-2:
Use the Bank Deposit window to select payment transactions to deposit.

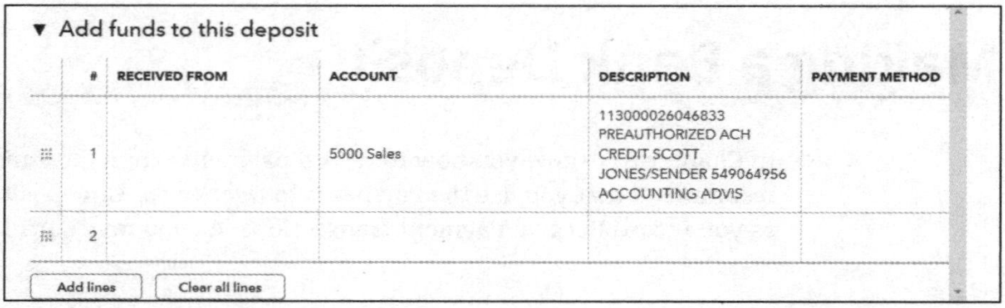

FIGURE 8-3:
Record payment amounts that are unrelated to customer invoices in the Add Funds to This Deposit section.

WARNING

Don't try to record a payment from a customer for an outstanding invoice in the Add Funds to This Deposit section. Doing so won't mark an outstanding invoice as paid, so you may end up trying to collect it again. Instead, create a Receive Payment, which will appear in the Select the Payments Included in This Deposit section of the Bank Deposit transaction window.

2. **From the Account drop-down list at the top of the window, choose the account into which you plan to deposit the payments.**

3. **In the Select the Payments Included in This Deposit section, click the check box beside each transaction you want to include in the deposit.**

4. **Select the payment method for each transaction you intend to deposit.**

TIP

Intuit Payments automatically posts deposits in a QB Payments section, which is collapsed by default for the benefit of users who don't rely on that service. If you have your own merchant account, credit card transaction receipts may get deposited in your bank account as often as daily. Make sure to record a separate deposit for each day so that the amounts mirror what's hitting your physical bank account. Then create a separate deposit to group any checks and cash payments into a bank deposit.

5. **(Optional) Enter a memo and a reference number.**

   The total of the selected payments — and the amount you intend to deposit unless you add entries in the Add Funds to This Deposit section — appears below the Select the Payments Included in This Deposit list.

6. **(Optional) Scroll down the window, and add any or all of the following:**

   - Memo for the deposit transaction itself, which is an additional level of documentation you can add apart from the memo field available on each line of the transaction.

   - Cash-back amount, account, and memo

   - Electronic document, such as a scanned copy of the paper deposit ticket

TIP

To attach an electronic document to the deposit, click in the Attachments box and navigate to the document, or drag the electronic copy into the Attachments box.

7. **Click Save and Close.**

   Any amounts from the Payments to Deposit account are moved to the account you selected in Step 2; other deposits post directly to your Bank account.

All that's left to do is take a trip to the bank. Or if you're mobile-savvy, ask your banker whether you can deposit checks remotely via your mobile device. If you receive a significant number of paper checks, you may be able to sign up for a remote check scanner that eliminates a significant amount of drudgery from making bank deposits.

Reconciling a Bank Account

Most people's least-favorite task is reconciling the bank statement, but I like knowing that my books are aligned with my bank; it's a great way to avoid surprises. Fortunately, if you're diligent about entering transactions in QuickBooks and recording bank deposits as described in the preceding section, reconciling your bank statement should be a fairly easy process. Grab your most recent bank statement, and follow these steps:

1. **Click Settings, and choose Reconcile from the Tools section.**

Make sure that you click Settings, and not the New transaction button.

2. **Select the account you want to reconcile, as shown in Figure 8-4.**

Note that you can and should reconcile credit card statements as well.

TIP

You may see a Get Started button that you can click to see a summary, road map–style, of the reconciliation process. At the end of the wizard, click Let's Do It to continue and display the page shown in Figure 8-4.

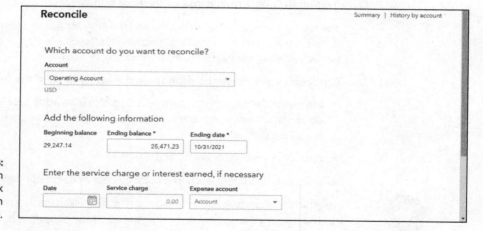

Reconcile   Summary | History by account

Which account do you want to reconcile?

Account

Operating Account   ▼

USD

Add the following information

Beginning balance	Ending balance *	Ending date *
29,247.14	25,471.23	10/31/2021

Enter the service charge or interest earned, if necessary

Date	Service charge	Expense account
📅	0.00	Account ▼

FIGURE 8-4:
Enter information from your bank statement on this page.

3. **Enter the ending date and balance from your bank statement, and click Start Reconciling (not shown in Figure 8-4).**

The Reconcile page shown in Figure 8-5 appears.

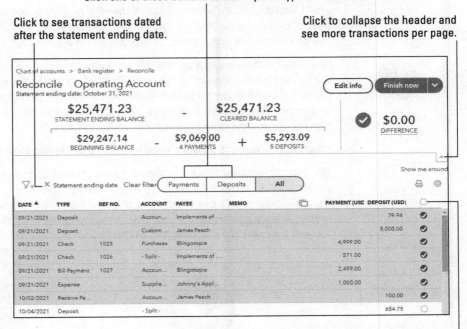

Click one of these buttons to filter by that type of transaction.

Click to see transactions dated after the statement ending date.

Click to collapse the header and see more transactions per page.

Click transactions in this column to mark them as cleared.

FIGURE 8-5:
Match transactions from your bank statement with those shown on the Reconcile page.

4. **Select each transaction that appears in your bank statement and on the Reconcile page by clicking the rightmost column.**

TIP

Paychecks divided between two bank accounts show up as two distinct transactions in QuickBooks, so they should be easy to match during reconciliation.

By selecting a transaction, you're marking it as having cleared the bank. Your goal is to have the Difference amount at the top right-hand corner of the Reconcile page equal $0. If your account is connected to your bank, many transactions might already display a check mark in the rightmost column because the transaction has been downloaded from the bank and matched with your accounting records.

By default, the Reconciliation page displays all uncleared transactions dated before the statement ending date, but you can click Payments or Deposits to filter by either of those options, similar to the way most bank statements are organized. Any transactions with dates later than the statement ending date are hidden by default. If, after you select all the transactions you see, the Difference amount isn't $0, click the X next to Statement Ending Date to look for additional transactions to mark as cleared. You also can take advantage of the Filter icon (which looks like a funnel) to limit the transactions in a way that works best for you. Be sure to compare the total payments and deposits with the corresponding numbers on the bank statement. This comparison can help you determine whether deposits and/or payments are missing.

TIP

You can click the Bank Register link in the top-left corner of the page to view the register for the account you're reconciling. When you finish viewing the register, click the Reconcile button in the top-right corner of the register page (not shown). If you'd like to see more transactions on the reconciliation page, click the upward-pointing arrow to collapse the header.

5. **When the Difference amount equals $0, click the Finish Now button.**

The Success message shown in Figure 8-6 gives you the opportunity to view the Reconciliation report by clicking the View Reconciliation Report link. The Reconciliation report looks like the one shown in Figure 8-7. The report is broken into a summary section that you can see in Figure 8-7 and a detail section (not entirely visible) that lists all checks and deposits you cleared.

FIGURE 8-6:
QuickBooks offers confirmation that you successfully reconciled your bank account.

You reconciled this account

To see a report of this reconciliation, click View reconciliation report. Otherwise, you're done!

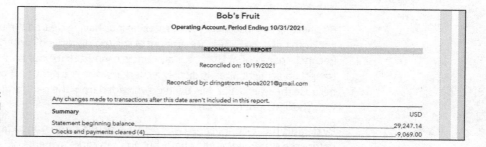

FIGURE 8-7:
A typical Reconciliation report.

Bob's Fruit
Operating Account, Period Ending 10/31/2021

RECONCILIATION REPORT

Reconciled on: 10/19/2021

Reconciled by: dringstrom+qboa2021@gmail.com

Any changes made to transactions after this date aren't included in this report.

Summary	USD
Statement beginning balance	29,247.14
Checks and payments cleared (4)	-9,069.00

REMEMBER

You don't have to finish your reconciliation in a single sitting. Click the drop-down arrow on the Finish Now button and then choose Save for Later if you get interrupted or simply can't get the reconciliation to zero out. Returning with a fresh eye can often make discrepancies jump off the screen. You can also choose Close Without Saving if you want to abandon the entire process.

WHEN THE OPENING BALANCE DOESN'T MATCH THE STATEMENT

It happens sometimes. You go to reconcile an account, and its opening balance doesn't match the ending balance of the previous reconciliation period. You need to fix the beginning balance before you can reconcile the account.

Good news: QuickBooks provides a tool that helps you fix the problem. This tool is in the form of a Reconciliation Discrepancy report, which lists transactions associated with the erroneous beginning balance. When you select an account to reconcile that has a beginning-balance problem, a prompt identifies the amount by which the account beginning balance is off and offers a Let's Resolve This Discrepancy link. Click the link to display a Reconciliation Discrepancy report that lists the transactions affecting the erroneous beginning balance. Typically, the report contains transactions that were changed after they were reconciled or that weren't reconciled when they should have been. The Reconciliation Discrepancy report also contains a Difference amount, and your goal is to make that amount $0. You accomplish that task by handling the transactions in the Reconciliation Discrepancy report.

If you want to explore what happened to the listed transactions that caused the discrepancy, click the View link of the transaction (it appears in the right column of the report) to display an Audit report for the transaction, detailing the changes that were made in the transaction.

To correct a transaction, click it in the report to see ways to correct it. When you correct the transaction in the Reconciliation Discrepancy report, the account is ready to reconcile.

 You can click any transaction in the report to view it in the window where you created it. To produce a paper copy of the report, click the Print button in the top-right corner of the report window.

You can view the Reconciliation report at any time. Just redisplay the Reconcile page shown in Figure 8-5 (by choosing Settings ⇨ Reconcile). After you reconciled an account, a History by Account link appears in the top-right corner of the page. When you click the link, the History by Account page appears, listing earlier reconciliations for an individual account (see Figure 8-8). Click the View Report link beside any reconciliation on this page to see its Reconciliation report.

To view reconciliations for other accounts, choose a different account from the Account drop-down list.

FIGURE 8-8:
Earlier
Reconciliation
reports that you
can view.

Connecting QuickBooks Accounts to Financial Institutions

What does it mean to connect your QuickBooks accounts to a financial institution? It means that activity that posts to a bank or credit card can get synchronized with your books, which can simplify your reconciliation process. QuickBooks offers a "choose your adventure" approach:

>> Connecting directly

>> Using QuickBooks Web Connect

>> Importing transactions stored in a Microsoft Excel file

>> Not connecting at all

If the fourth option appeals to you, skip the connection sections in this chapter, and look for the sections on organizing your dashboard and tagging transactions. But let's say you're ready to connect or are shyly considering doing so. I'll give you the lowdown in a moment, but first, please read the cautionary tale in the nearby sidebar.

Connecting . . . or not connecting

As you can see from the cautionary tale in the sidebar, a paraphrased version of Hamlet's famous quote applies here: "To connect or not to connect, that is the question." Connecting requires commitment on your part to not let the transactions pile up or hang out on the side. Also, you may not be able to connect Quick-Books Bank and Credit Card accounts to their counterparts at financial institutions. Although a direct connection streamlines the process for you, two semimanual alternatives still make things easier.

DON'T LET THIS HAPPEN TO YOU

My friend Stephanie Miller learned a tough lesson about connecting bank accounts to QuickBooks. A couple of years ago, she started to connect her bank account to QuickBooks and downloaded a significant number of transactions into QuickBooks. Life got in the way, and the transactions didn't get reviewed; they sat in the For Review list, which I discuss in the "Managing Downloaded Activity" section later in this chapter. A temporary bookkeeper found that the bank account had been disconnected, and during the reconnection process, they unwittingly downloaded the original transactions again, plus all subsequent transactions. None of this was an actual problem until the bookkeeper selected all the transactions and clicked Accept. The result was that Stephanie had to decide whether to find and delete the duplicate transactions one at a time or start a new set of books.

Connecting your books to your financial institution isn't something you can kinda, sorta do. Either fully embrace the concept and follow through by reviewing and accepting the transactions each time you connect or import, or run the risk of compromising your accounting records at some point in the future. The download and import processes that I'm about to share with you bring in new sets of transactions each time; they don't overwrite existing transactions in the For Review list. If you can't act on downloaded transactions immediately, it's best to select all transactions and choose Exclude, because you can undo the exclusion later without setting up a potential accounting nightmare for yourself.

Before I dive into connecting, it's important to explain that *you don't have to connect.* You can work quite happily in QuickBooks without ever connecting to an account in a financial institution. You simply enter transactions that affect the appropriate account and reconcile the accounts monthly.

Also, you can also disconnect your accounts at any time, so no actions in this section are irreversible. That said, connecting allows you to electronically verify the transactions recorded in QuickBooks with the transactions your financial institution has on file. In short, connecting is a matter of convenience.

REMEMBER

See Chapters 5 and 6 for details on entering transactions that affect a Bank account. You typically use an Expense transaction to record credit card purchases and a Credit Card Credit transaction to record refunds to a credit card. You also use a Credit Card Credit transaction to record a payment you make to reduce your credit card's balance.

Your transactions have to have a place to go, so make sure that you set up your Bank and Credit Card accounts in QuickBooks before attempting any sort of connection.

Directly connecting a Bank or Credit Card account

The Banking page in QuickBooks lists accounts that you've connected to a financial institution. Before you connect any accounts, the page houses a big green Connect button, which you click to connect your first account to a financial institution. Thereafter, the Banking page becomes more meaningful, as you'll see when you finish the steps in this section. To connect subsequent accounts, you click the Add Account button that appears in the top-left corner of the Banking page.

No one likes a pop quiz, so before you click that Connect button, make sure that you have your online banking credentials handy, meaning your user ID and password. Also, you'll have an easier time if you add Bank or Credit Card accounts to your chart of accounts (as described in "Setting Up a Bank or Credit Card Account" earlier in this chapter) before connecting. If you haven't set up an account before trying to connect, setting up the account becomes part of the connection process, which can be confusing. That said, connect an account by following these steps:

1. **Set up the account as described in "Setting Up a Bank or Credit Card Account" earlier in this chapter.**

2. **Choose Banking (Bookkeeping ⇨ Banking) on the navigation bar.**

   The Banking page appears.

   If the first command on your navigation bar is Get Things Done, then you're using the Business View. If you click the Banking command below that, you'll be shunted into a marketing area rather than your banking page. Your banking page is in the Bookkeeping section of the navigation bar. Conversely, if the first command on your navigation bar is Overview, you're using the Accountant view, and the Banking command on the navigation bar will get you directly to your banking page.

3. **Click Connect Account or Add Account.**

   A wizard appears to help you connect to a financial institution.

4. **On the first wizard page, shown in Figure 8-9, search for the name of your financial institution; then confirm the selection by making a choice from the list or click the logo for your bank if it appears below the Search box.**

   To search for financial institutions, type a name in the Search box.

FIGURE 8-9:
Identify your
financial
institution.

5. **On the next page, enter your user ID and password, and click the Continue button.**

You may be directed to go to your bank's website and sign in, after which you'll be returned to the connection process.

You may have to prove your "nonrobotness" by way of a reCAPTCHA. Who doesn't like looking for stoplights in grainy photos? Fortunately, this method is falling out of favor, so you may be prompted instead to authorize an OAuth connection. Just follow the onscreen prompts.

If all goes as expected, a new page displays the accounts you have at the financial institution and lets you choose which ones you want to connect to QuickBooks, as shown in Figure 8-10.

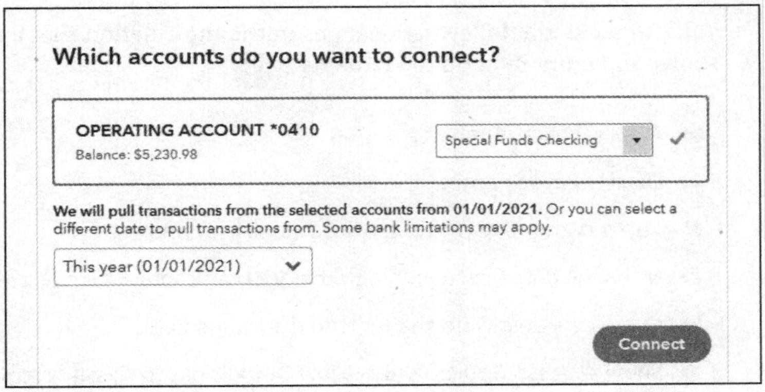

Which accounts do you want to connect?

OPERATING ACCOUNT *0410
Balance: $5,230.98

Special Funds Checking ▾ ✓

We will pull transactions from the selected accounts from 01/01/2021. Or you can select a different date to pull transactions from. Some bank limitations may apply.

This year (01/01/2021) ▾

Connect

FIGURE 8-10:
Select the
accounts you
want to connect
and their types.

6. **Choose the accounts you want to connect.**

For each account you choose, QuickBooks asks you to choose an existing Bank or Credit Card account or allows you to create a new account. QuickBooks also asks you how far in the past you want to pull transactions for the account. Depending on your bank, options may include Today, This Month, This Year, or Last Year, or you may be able to specify a custom range.

7. **Click Connect.**

8. **Follow any additional onscreen prompts you see to finish setting up the account.**

After you connect your first account to a financial institution, QuickBooks changes the appearance of the Banking page to display a list of connected accounts and their related information as downloaded from the bank (see Figure 8-11). In most cases, QuickBooks automatically downloads activity from your financial institution nightly, but your mileage may vary.

FIGURE 8-11:
After you connect an account, the Banking page displays connected accounts.

REMEMBER

The automatic download of transactions is only the first phase of the process, you must still review and accept the transactions.

You can make the following changes in the information that appears in the table shown in Figure 8-12 on the Banking page:

» Display check numbers.

» Display Payee names.

» Turn on grouping to group transactions by month.

» Make the date field editable so that you can change it if necessary.

» Copy bank detail information into the Memo field.

» Show suggested rules (which allow QuickBooks to classify accounting transactions automatically).

» Remember category selection.

» Display detailed information about a transaction provided by the bank.

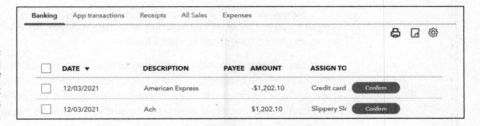

FIGURE 8-12:
You can control
the amount of
information that
appears in this
table.

 To make a change in the page's table, click Settings just above the Action column, and add or remove check marks to display or hide columns. You can also adjust the column widths; QuickBooks remembers any column-width adjustments you make, even after you sign out and then back in. If you need to display the Memo field in an individual bank register, see Chapter 7 for directions.

Troubleshooting connections to financial institutions

In some cases, you can't connect your financial institution to an account in Quick-Books, or you can connect, but transactions don't download. All is not lost. You can still update a Bank or Credit Card account with financial institution information by using either QuickBooks Web Connect or by importing an Excel file.

Using Web Connect

QuickBooks Desktop users may have used Web Connect, which has long been part of QuickBooks. This feature allows you to download transactions from your financial institution's website to your computer and then upload the transactions from your computer. The process isn't as automated as a direct connection, but the result is the same.

WARNING

Don't use a public computer to download information via Web Connect, because the files aren't encrypted.

Follow these steps to use Web Connect:

1. **Make sure that your Bank or Credit Card account is established in your chart of accounts.**

I cover the steps in "Setting Up a Bank or Credit Card Account" earlier in this chapter, or you can refer to Chapter 3 if you want more details.

2. **Log in to your financial institution's website, and look for a link that enables you to download to QuickBooks.**

Some banks have a Download button associated with each account, whereas others offer Download to QuickBooks or QuickBooks Web Connect links. If you can't find a link, odds are that your financial institution doesn't offer this functionality. But don't take no for an answer; ask for help. Sometimes, what you're looking for is hiding in plain sight.

3. **Using the link you found in Step 2, select any of the following file formats:**

- .qbo (QuickBooks)

- .qfx (Quicken)

- .ofx (Microsoft Money)

- Any file format that references QuickBooks or QuickBooks Online

Your bank controls the file formats you see.

TIP

In the next section, "Importing transactions via Excel," I explain how to use the .csv format so that you have an additional avenue to consider.

4. **Select the dates for the transactions you want to download.**

The account's opening balance will change if you download transactions with dates that precede the opening balance, so double-check the dates you choose here.

5. **Save the file to a location on your computer where you'll be able to find it later.**

Many people download to the Downloads folder or to their computer's desktop.

6. **To upload the file, log in to QuickBooks, and choose Banking (Transactions ⇨ Banking) on the navigation bar.**

The Bank and Credit Cards page appears.

- If you've connected other accounts, you see the Link Account and Update buttons on the right side of the page, as shown in Figure 8-13.

- If you haven't connected accounts, you see the Connect button and (to the right of it) the Upload Transactions button.

7. **Click the Upload Transactions button, or click the arrow next to the Link Account button on the right side of the page and choose Upload from File from the drop-down list (see Figure 8-13).**

The Import Bank Transactions Wizard appears (see Figure 8-14).

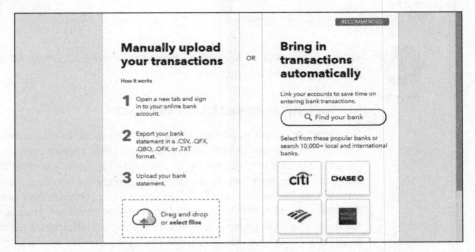

8. **Click the Select Files link, navigate to the location where you saved the transactions you downloaded in Step 5, and select the downloaded file.**

9. **Click Next in the bottom-right corner (not shown in Figure 8-14).**

10. **On the next page, select the Bank or Credit Card account where the transactions should appear and then click Continue (see Figure 8-15).**

   QuickBooks uploads the transactions, which could take a few minutes, depending on the speed of your internet connection and the number of transactions you're importing.

11. **Click Let's Go when you see the confirmation screen that explains your next step (to accept your transactions).**

   Importing the transactions is only the first phase of the process; you must also review and accept the transactions. Follow the instructions in "Managing Downloaded Activity" later in this chapter.

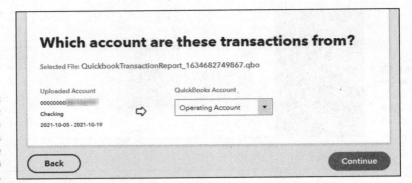

Which account are these transactions from?

Selected File: QuickbookTransactionReport_1634682749867.qbo

Uploaded Account

00000000 ▓▓▓▓▓▓

Checking

2021-10-05 - 2021-10-19

QuickBooks Account

Operating Account ▼

Back   Continue

FIGURE 8-15: Select the account where QuickBooks should place the transactions from your bank.

WARNING

Always delete Web Connect files, because they're not encrypted and contain your financial account information.

Importing transactions via Excel

If your bank supports downloading transactions to CSV (comma-separated values) format, which can be read by Excel and other spreadsheet programs, you can download your banking activity to a CSV file and then import it into QuickBooks. First, log in to your bank's website, and save your banking transactions in CSV format. QuickBooks accepts CSV files formatted in three or four columns, as shown in Table 8-1 and Table 8-2. Keep in mind that these columns are the minimum required. The CSV file from your bank may include additional columns that QuickBooks can ignore, so you don't need to make the file conform to either of these formats as long as the columns needed are present in any order in the CSV file.

TABLE 8-1 **An Acceptable Three-Column Format**

Date	Description	Amount
1/1/2022	Example payment	–100.00
1/1/2022	Example deposit	200.00

TABLE 8-2 **An Acceptable Four-Column Format**

Date	Description	Credit	Debit
1/1/2022	Example payment	100.00	
1/1/2022	Example deposit		200.00

Open your CSV file in a spreadsheet program, and make sure that it includes all of the columns from either of these formats. If necessary, edit the file, but feel free to leave any extraneous columns in place in the CSV file. Save and close the CSV file, and then follow these steps to import the transactions:

1. **Make sure that your Bank or Credit Card account is established in your chart of accounts.**

    Review the steps in the "Setting Up a Bank or Credit Card Account" section earlier in this chapter, or refer to Chapter 3 if you want more details.

2. **Choose Banking (Transactions ⇨ Banking) on the navigation bar.**

3. **Click the arrow next to the Link Account button, and choose Upload from File from the drop-down menu.**

    The Import Bank Transactions page appears (refer to Figure 8-14).

4. **Click the Select Files link, select the CSV file you downloaded from your bank's website, and click Continue in the bottom-right corner.**

    Depending on your screen resolution, you may need to scroll down to find the Continue button.

5. **Use the Select an Account page to specify the account into which you want to import transactions, and click Continue in the bottom-right corner.**

6. **Choose Yes or No from the first drop-down menu to indicate whether the first row of your file is a header (see Figure 8-16).**

    Headers are column names, such as Date and Amount.

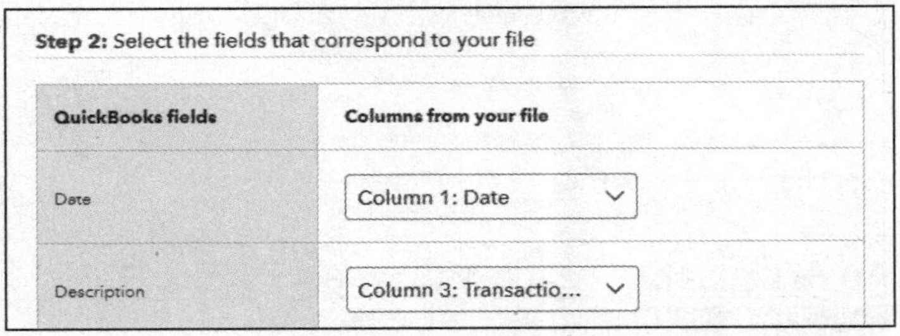

Step 2: Select the fields that correspond to your file

QuickBooks fields	Columns from your file
Date	Column 1: Date
Description	Column 3: Transactio...

FIGURE 8-16:
Match QuickBooks fields with the fields in your CSV file.

7. **Choose One Column or Two Columns from the second drop-down menu to indicate how many columns show amounts.**

    QuickBooks makes an educated guess, but you can change the setting if necessary.

8. **Choose a date format from the third drop-down menu that matches how the dates look in your file.**

   Formats include mm/dd/yyyy, mm-dd-yyy, dd/mm/yyyy, and dd-mm-yyyy.

9. **Scroll down to the Step 2 section, and confirm the mapping.**

   Typically, you confirm the date, transaction description, and amount columns. QuickBooks makes an educated guess, but you can override the defaults if necessary.

10. **Click Continue.**

    The Which Transactions Do You Want to Add? page appears, as shown in Figure 8-17.

WARNING

You may not be able to import transactions from a CSV file if the date field contains both the date and time of the transaction. The Which Transactions Do You Want to Add? page will inform you of any transactions that cannot be imported. If you open the CSV file in Excel, you can use a formula to remove the time portion. Let's say a date/time value is in cell A1. The formula =ROUND(A1,0) would return only the date portion. You can copy that formula to the clipboard and then paste as values over the original date/time value. Save your CSV file and then you should be able to import the file into QuickBooks.

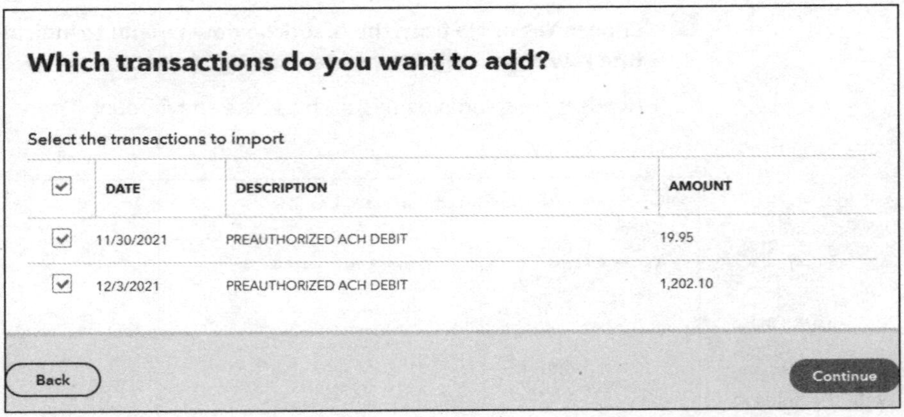

Which transactions do you want to add?

Select the transactions to import

☑	DATE	DESCRIPTION	AMOUNT
☑	11/30/2021	PREAUTHORIZED ACH DEBIT	19.95
☑	12/3/2021	PREAUTHORIZED ACH DEBIT	1,202.10

Back   Continue

FIGURE 8-17: Match QuickBooks fields with the fields in your CSV file.

---

11. **Confirm the transactions to import.**

    Click the check box to the left of the Date heading to select all transactions, or click the check boxes for individual transactions.

12. **Click Continue.**

    QuickBooks displays the number of transactions it will import and asks whether you want to import the transactions.

13. **Click Yes.**

A confirmation screen appears when the import process is finished.

14. **Click Done.**

QuickBooks redisplays the Banking page referenced in Step 2.

15. **Follow the instructions in "Managing Downloaded Activity" later in this chapter to review and accept the transactions.**

WARNING

When you import transactions from a CSV file, the bank balance in QuickBooks may be reported as zero. Don't panic! This report simply means that the balance amount isn't available in the CSV file. Refer to "Reconciling a Bank Account" earlier in this chapter for the steps to take to reconcile your QuickBooks account with your bank.

Managing Downloaded Activity

Getting transactions from a financial institution imported into QuickBooks is only the first part of the process. Regardless of the download method you use, you need to evaluate each transaction and, as appropriate, update your accounting records with the downloaded transactions. The Bank and Credit Cards page allows you to match, exclude, or add transactions downloaded from a financial institution.

REMEMBER

Don't worry if you make a mistake; you can fix it, as described in the later section titled (what else?) "Fixing mistakes."

Choose Banking on the navigation pane; then click Banking to display the Bank and Credit Cards page (see Figure 8-18). If necessary, select an account by clicking it at the top of the page. Note that you match transactions the same way for Bank accounts and for Credit Card accounts.

You see three transaction status tabs just below your bank account(s):

>> **For Review:** Transactions that you've downloaded but haven't yet specified how you want to handle

>> **Categorized:** Transactions that you've reviewed and added

>> **Excluded:** Transactions that you've reviewed and decided not to include

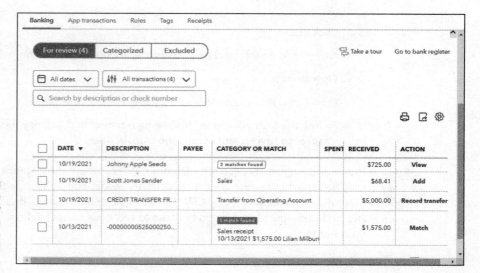

FIGURE 8-18:
Use this page to specify how QuickBooks should handle each downloaded transaction.

For Review (see Figure 8-18) serves as a to-do list for processing the transactions you downloaded. To work through the transactions quickly, click the All Transactions filter button, and choose one of the following options:

>> **Recognized:** View transactions that have been recognized (you updated the category manually).

>> **Matched:** See transactions in which a match was made between the transaction downloaded from your financial institution and your accounting records.

>> **Transferred:** See transactions that are deemed to be a transfer between accounts, such as a credit card payment, or a transfer of funds between two Bank accounts.

>> **Rule Applied:** View transactions that are automatically updated by a rule, which I discuss later in the "Establishing rules to accept transactions" section.

>> **Missing Payee/Customer:** See a list of transactions for which the payee or customer couldn't be identified.

>> **Unassigned:** View a list of transactions that have a status other than Add and haven't been processed yet.

TIP

Transactions can correspond to more than one filter. A transaction can be Recognized, Matched, and Unassigned at the same time, for example.

In the Category or Match column, QuickBooks suggests a way to assign each transaction. Using information from other businesses like yours and your past behavior, QuickBooks tries to identify downloaded transactions that potentially match transactions you entered previously. If you previously accepted a transaction from a vendor, QuickBooks assumes that you want to assign the same category to subsequent transactions for that vendor. And if you change the payee on a transaction, QuickBooks suggests that change the next time a transaction appears for that payee.

TIP

Although the suggestions are helpful, after a while, you may find yourself wishing that QuickBooks would stop suggesting and just record the transaction. You can use rules to accomplish that behavior. See "Establishing rules to accept transactions" later in this chapter for details.

QuickBooks tags transactions for review in one of four ways, all of which are shown in the Action column of Figure 8-15:

>> *Add* indicates that the Category or Match field reflects QuickBooks' best guess.

>> *Match* signifies transactions for which QuickBooks found an exact counterpart in your books.

>> *View* means that two or more transactions in your books potentially match the banking transaction. The number of matches are shown in the Category or Match column.

>> *Record Transfer* marks transactions that appear to be a transfer between bank accounts or a payment on a liability account such as a credit card.

The Category or Match column displays the best guess as to where a transaction should be posted. To accept the match, click the Add button in the Action column. QuickBooks moves the transaction to the Categorized tab. If you want to change the category or other information about the transaction, click the transaction to display the form shown in Figure 8-19, which you use to do the following things:

>> Choose the Categorize radio button to change the vendor/customer, category, location, class, tags (which I discuss in "Tagging Transactions" later in this chapter), or memo.

>> Choose the Find Match radio button to view potential matches or search for other matches.

>> Choose the Record As Transfer radio button to select an offsetting account for the transfer.

>> Add an attachment, such as a PDF copy of a receipt.

>> Create a rule (which I discuss in the "Establishing rules to accept transactions" section).

>> Exclude a transaction so that it doesn't post to your books.

>> View the categorization history for similar transactions when you choose the Categorize option.

>> Split a transaction that you're categorizing among two or more categories.

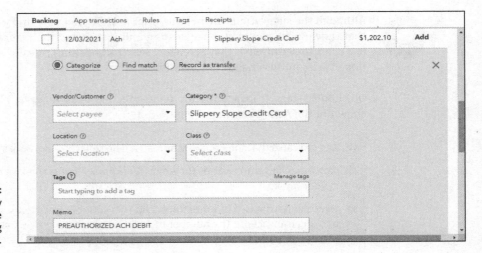

FIGURE 8-19:
Click any transaction to see the underlying details.

To the left of the Date column is the Select All check box, which you can select to display buttons that allow you to accept, update, or exclude all transactions shown onscreen. Accept, Update, and Exclude buttons appear when you select the Select All check box.

Excluding transactions

Typically, you won't need to exclude transactions, but doing so can be a helpful way to recover from certain situations, such as importing transactions for a given period more than once. To exclude a transaction, follow these steps:

1. **On the For Review tab (refer to Figure 8-18), select the check box to the left of each transaction you intend to exclude.**

2. **Click Exclude on the Batch Actions bar that appears (see Figure 8-20).**

   The selected transactions move to the Excluded tab of the Bank and Credit Cards page.

4 money out transactions: -$3,868.90
7 money in transactions: $4,984.55

Accept   Update   Exclude

TIP

When you select one or more transactions, you can choose Undo or Delete to move the transactions back to the For Review tab or remove the transactions from QuickBooks. This prompt appears only when you choose one or more transactions, so at first glance, it may seem that you can't delete excluded transactions.

Including transactions

The remaining transactions fall into two categories: those that don't have an obvious matching transaction and those that do, based upon the command that appears in the Action column. If you see *Add* in the Action column (refer to Figure 8-18), QuickBooks couldn't find an obvious matching transaction; if you see *Match, Record Transfer,* or *View* in the Action column, QuickBooks did find one or more potentially matching transactions. QuickBooks makes its best guess about adding and matching transactions, but it isn't perfect.

Confirming correct guesses

If QuickBooks guesses correctly, you need to confirm each transaction before you include it in your books. If the listed transaction information is correct, follow the steps in the preceding section, but choose Accept in Step 2. You can select two or more transactions and click Update on the Batch Actions bar that appears if you need to make the same changes in each transaction.

Changing incorrect guesses

QuickBooks may not know how to handle a transaction, or it may guess incorrectly. In these cases, you need to edit the transaction before you accept it. You can easily identify a transaction that QuickBooks isn't sure how to handle if the Add command is in the Action column along with the words Uncategorized Expense or Uncategorized Income in the Category or Match column.

Click one of these transactions to expand the information so you can edit it, as shown in Figure 8-21.

FIGURE 8-21:
Click any transaction and choose the Categorize or Record As Transfer radio button to assign the transaction to an appropriate category.

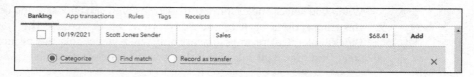

You can use the radio buttons above the transaction information to specify whether you want to categorize the transaction, search for a matching transaction, or transfer the transaction information to another account. You can also click the Split button in the bottom-right corner to distribute the transaction among multiple categories when you choose the Categorize option.

If you're working with a bank account transaction, be aware that you can change the check number if necessary.

If you change the transaction's category, QuickBooks assumes that all future transactions for the selected vendor should be assigned to the category you choose. You can change this behavior by clicking the Create a Rule link just below the memo to create a custom rule; I talk about rules in "Establishing rules to accept transactions" later in this chapter.

You can add attachments to any transaction by clicking the Add Attachment link at the bottom of the expanded transaction-information page. After you make your changes, click Add to save the transaction to your books.

Examining transactions QuickBooks thinks it can match

You can easily identify these types of transactions; a Match link appears beside them in the Action column. When you click a downloaded transaction that QuickBooks suggests you match with an existing transaction, a different set of details appears, as shown in Figure 8-22.

FIGURE 8-22:
The transaction
details appear
when you click a
downloaded or
imported
transaction that
you plan to match
to an existing
QuickBooks
transaction.

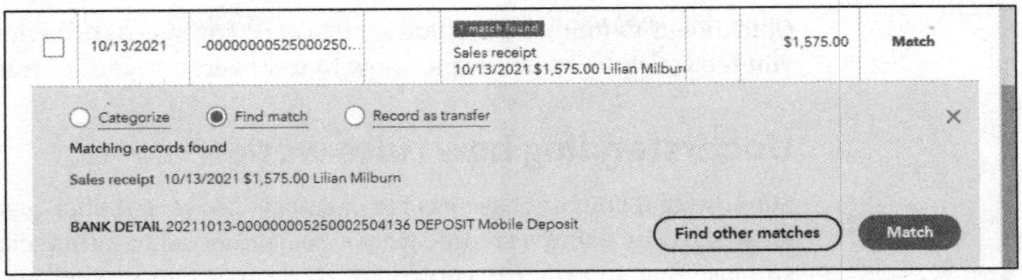

On this page, you can do the following things:

>> **Select the correct matching transaction.** In the Matching Records Found section, click a link next to any possible match to display the transaction in its transaction window, where you can identify the category to which that possible match was assigned. If that category is appropriate for the transaction QuickBooks downloaded, cancel the transaction window to return to the Banking page, select the correct match in the Records Found section, and click the Match button.

>> **Search for other matching transactions.** If none of the possible matches is applied in the way you want to apply the downloaded transaction, click the Find Other Matches button to search for additional matches.

>> **Add the transaction and supply account information for it.** If you can't find a similar transaction already recorded in QuickBooks, you can click the Categorize radio button and then add the transaction.

>> **Transfer the transaction to a different account.** Click the Record As Transfer or Record Credit Card Payment radio button, select a new account for the transaction, and then click the Transfer button (which replaces the Match button shown in Figure 8-22).

Repeat the process of adding and matching until you've handled all downloaded transactions. Each transaction you add or match disappears from the For Review tab of the Bank and Credit Cards page and appears on the Reviewed tab. See "Fixing mistakes" later in this chapter for more information on using the In QuickBooks tab.

Establishing rules to accept transactions

I've already established that QuickBooks tries to learn your habits as you review downloaded transactions; you can help the process along by establishing rules for

QuickBooks to follow. When you set up rules, you speed the review process because you tell QuickBooks in advance how to treat certain types of transactions.

Understanding how rules work

Suppose that you purchase gas for business-use cars at Shell gas stations, and you always pay by using a credit card you've connected to a financial institution. Also suppose that you want to categorize all transactions at Shell stations to your Fuel Expense account. You can assign the category to one of these transactions manually and wait for QuickBooks to learn your preference, or you can set up a rule for QuickBooks to follow.

When you establish a rule, you stipulate information such as the accounts and the types of transactions (money in or money out) to which the rule should apply. Note that you can create rules that affect all accounts or rules that affect specific accounts.

Then you identify criteria that individual transactions should meet before Quick-Books acts on the transactions. Finally, you specify the information QuickBooks should assign to transactions that meet the criteria. You can specify a transaction type and/or a category, for example, as well as modify other fields.

THE HIERARCHY OF RULES

The sequence of the rules you establish matters. QuickBooks processes your rules in the order in which they appear on the Rules page and applies only one rule to any particular transaction. To ensure that QuickBooks applies the correct rule to a transaction, you may need to reorder the rules. Drag the icon that looks like a grid of nine dots to the left of the rule on the Rules page.

Suppose that you set up two rules in the following order:

- **Rule 1:** Categorize all transactions of less than $10 as Miscellaneous Expenses.
- **Rule 2:** Categorize all Shake Shack transactions as Meals & Entertainment.

If a $12 dollar transaction from Shake Shack appears, Rule 2 applies. But if a $7.50 transaction from Shake Shack appears, Rule 1 applies.

The rules you establish can work in one of two ways:

>> Your rule can apply suggested changes to downloaded transactions that you review and approve.

This approach lists affected transactions on the For Review tab of the Bank and Credit Cards page. These transactions display a Rule icon in the Category or Match column.

Different icons identify transactions matched by rules but not yet added to your company and transactions added automatically by rules. You can read more about these icons in "Fixing mistakes" later in this chapter.

>> You can have the rule apply automatically to all transactions that meet the criteria and then add the transactions to QuickBooks.

This approach may seem to be risky, but it really isn't, because you can still change transactions that QuickBooks accepts automatically.

Creating a rule

You follow the same steps to set up either type of rule: a rule that suggests changes for your review, or a rule that automatically updates and adds transactions. Only one step lets you do things differently, and I'll point it out when it comes around.

To create a rule, follow these steps:

1. **Choose Banking (Transactions ⇨ Banking) on the navigation pane.**

The Bank and Credit Cards page appears.

2. **Click Rules above the list of bank and credit cards.**

The Rules page appears (see Figure 8-23).

3. **Click the New Rule button.**

The Create Rule panel appears (see Figure 8-24).

4. **Assign the rule a name — one that will be meaningful to you.**

You can't use special characters like the apostrophe (') in a rule name.

5. **Specify whether the rule applies to money coming in or money going out, and select the accounts to which you want the rule to apply.**

FIGURE 8-23:
The Rules page.

Create rule

Rules only apply to unreviewed transactions.

What do you want to call this rule? *

Office Supplies

Apply this to transactions that are

Money out ∨   in   All bank accounts ∨

and include the following: All ∨

Description ∨   Contains ∨   Office Supplies

+ Add a condition

FIGURE 8-24:
The Create
Rule panel,
where you set the
information you
want to apply to
transactions that
use the rule.

6. **Use the drop-down lists in the Include the Following section to set criteria to use in determining whether to apply the rule.**

You can set multiple criteria by clicking the Add a Condition link, and you can specify that a transaction should meet all or any of the criteria. Specifying All is more stringent and makes QuickBooks more selective about applying the rule.

TIP

The first list box in the section enables you to specify whether QuickBooks should compare the transaction description, the bank text, or the transaction amount with a condition you set. For those inquiring minds out there, Description (the transaction description) refers to the text that appears in the Description column of the Bank and Credit Cards page. The Bank Text option refers to the Bank Detail description the bank downloads; you can view the Bank Detail description if you click any downloaded transaction. The Bank Detail description appears in the bottom-left corner of the transactions being edited.

7. **At the bottom of the Create Rule panel, set the information you want to apply to transactions that meet the rule's criteria (see Figure 8-25).**

   You can do one or more of the following:

   (a) *Select the transaction type to assign to the transaction.*

   (b) *Select the category and (optional) split to use for classifying the transaction. Splits can be based on percentages or dollar amounts.*

   (c) *Select the payee to apply the transactions that meet the rule's conditions.*

   (d) *Specify one or more tags for grouping related transactions.*

   (e) *(Optional) Click Assign More to add a memo to each transaction that meets the rule's conditions. For more on ways to use the Memo field, see the nearby sidebar "The Memo field and transaction rules."*

   (f) *Toggle on the Automatically Confirm Transactions This Rule Applies To if you want to automatically add transactions that meet the rule's conditions to your company.*

   REMEMBER

   This step is the "different" one I referred to earlier in this section. If you select this check box, you don't need to approve transactions to which QuickBooks applies this rule. But you can always change transactions that are added automatically.

8. **Click Save in the bottom-right corner of the Create Rule panel.**

FIGURE 8-25:
Provide the changes to be made to transactions that meet the rule's criteria.

After you create a rule or rules, you can use the Actions column of the Rules page (refer to Figure 8-23) to copy them (so that you don't have to create similar rules from scratch) and to delete rules you no longer want. If you need to edit a rule, click the Edit link in the Actions column to reopen the Rule dialog box and make changes.

TIP

Accountants can streamline processes by creating a set of rules in one company and then exporting and importing rules into other QuickBooks companies. See Chapter 13 for details.

Fixing mistakes

On the Bank and Credit Cards page, you can easily identify transactions to which QuickBooks has applied rules, because in the Added or Match column, QuickBooks uses different labels to identify transactions added by rules and transactions added automatically by rules. You can see how QuickBooks handles each down-loaded transaction in your company when you click the Categorized tab of the Banking page (see Figure 8-26).

Suppose that you accidentally include a transaction that you meant to exclude. Or suppose that QuickBooks assigned the wrong category to a transaction. You can easily correct these mistakes by using the Categorized tab of the Bank and Credit Cards page.

REMEMBER

The method used to match and add a transaction — manually, through a rule, or automatically through a rule — doesn't matter. You can change any downloaded transaction. Be aware, though, that QuickBooks treats downloaded transactions as having cleared your bank, so if you edit a downloaded transaction in the register, QuickBooks will ask you whether you're sure.

FIGURE 8-26:
Use the Categorized tab to find transactions you've accepted in QuickBooks.

If you include a transaction that contains mistakes — such as one that was added automatically by a rule, but to the wrong category — you can undo the action. Undoing an accepted transaction removes it from the register and places it back on the For Review tab, where you can make changes and accept it again, as described in "Excluding transactions" and "Including transactions" earlier in this chapter.

To undo an accepted transaction, follow these steps:

1. **Click the Categorized tab on the Bank and Credit Cards page.**

2. **Find the transaction, and click the Undo link in the Action column.**

   A message appears, telling you that the undo was successful.

3. **Switch to the For Review tab, find the transaction, edit it, and accept it again.**

   Alternatively, you can exclude it, as described in "Excluding transactions" earlier in this chapter.

Converting Paper Receipts to Electronic Transactions

QuickBooks enables you to convert paper or electronic receipts or bills to transactions without having to key in all the details. To get started, choose Banking ⇨ Receipts (Transactions ⇨ Banking ⇨ Receipts). You can capture receipts in four ways (see Figure 8-27):

» Upload files from your computer.

» Upload files from Google Drive.

» Forward from email, which means establishing a special @qbodocs.com email address. The benefit is that you can establish a filter in your email to automatically forward receipts that you receive by email for automatic posting to QuickBooks.

» Take pictures of receipts on screen or on paper with the QuickBooks Online mobile app (not shown in Figure 8-27).

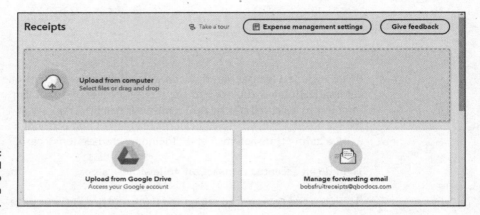

FIGURE 8-27:
You can send receipts or bills to QuickBooks in several ways.

TIP

To create an email address, click Manage Forwarding Email on the Receipts page. You'll be prompted to create a special @qbodocs.com email address (see Figure 8-28) that has a maximum of 25 letters to the left of the @ symbol. Click Next, Looks Good, and then Done to create the email address. Now you can email receipts to that address to have the activity appear in QuickBooks. Keep in mind that you can send receipts only from registered accounts. Click the Manage Forwarding Email button and add new users in the Manage Receipt Senders section. You can choose only users who have credentials for your QuickBooks company.

FIGURE 8-28:
You can establish an @qbodocs.com email address that you forward receipts and bills to for automatic posting into QuickBooks.

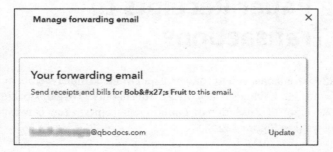

No matter which route you take, receipts appear in the For Review section shown at the bottom of Figure 8-29.

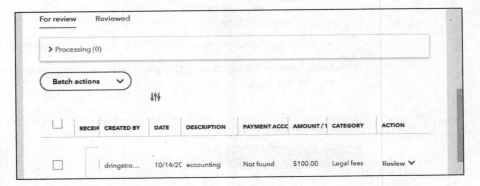

FIGURE 8-29:
A receipt to be
reviewed.

After you click the Review link, you'll be prompted to review the following information, as shown in Figure 8-30. Here's how:

1. **Specify a document type.**

   Choose Receipt or Bill.

2. **(Optional) Specify a payee, or leave the setting blank.**

3. **Choose a Bank or Credit Card account.**

4. **Confirm the payment date.**

   The date from your receipt or bill should appear, but you can override this setting if necessary.

5. **Confirm the account and/or category.**

   QuickBooks attempts to classify the transaction for you, but you can change the default value if necessary.

6. **Edit the description.**

   You can override the default description if necessary.

7. **Confirm the amount in the field titled Total Amount (Inclusive of Tax).**

   QuickBooks attempts to capture this amount for you, but you can correct the amount if necessary.

8. **(Optional) Enter a memo (not shown in Figure 8-30).**

   This field allows you to write a paragraph or more about the transaction if you'd like.

9. **(Optional) Set the following options:**

- Click Make Expense and Items Billable if you plan to be reimbursed by a customer.

- Choose a customer from a drop-down list.

- Add a reference number, such as a receipt or invoice number.

10. **Click Save and Next to post the transaction and review the next transaction in the queue.**

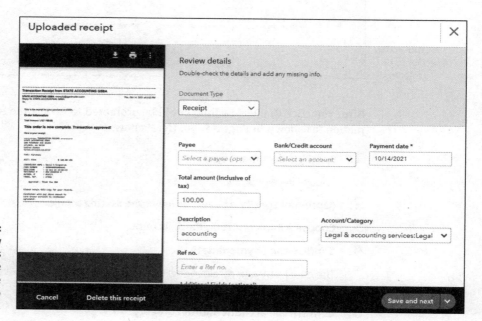

FIGURE 8-30: You can review uploaded receipts or bills before you commit the transaction to your books.

Controlling the Appearance of Bank Accounts

All Bank accounts (and Credit Card accounts) appear on the Business Overview tab of the Dashboard page, and connected accounts also appear on the Banking page. As you'll see, connected accounts are direct links between QuickBooks and your financial institution. You can control the order in which your accounts appear on these pages. Perhaps you'd like your accounts to appear in alphabetical order, or maybe you'd like them to appear in most-used order — whatever works for you.

On the Business Overview tab of the Dashboard page, click the pencil that appears to the right of Bank Accounts if you have two or more accounts. Using the icon that appears to the left of an account (nine small dots forming a square), drag up or down to move the account. When the accounts appear in the order you want, click Save — the pencil shown in Figure 8-31 toggles to a Save command. Changes you make appear on the Dashboard page and, if you have connected accounts, on the Banking page.

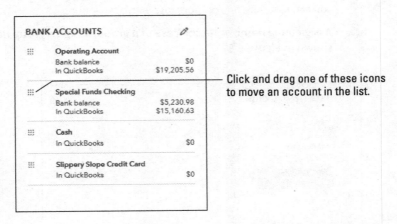

Click and drag one of these icons to move an account in the list.

FIGURE 8-31: Drag accounts to place them in the order you want.

In addition to changing the order of accounts, you can control (to some extent) the information for connected accounts that appears in the table on the Banking page. Earlier in the chapter, in the "Connecting QuickBooks Accounts to Financial Institutions" I show you how to connect accounts, which makes the Banking page more meaningful.

Tagging Transactions

Tags offer an additional dimension for categorizing and reporting on related transactions. You must assign an account or category to each line item in a transaction, but QuickBooks allows you to assign transactions to classes, locations, and even tags. All three categories work similarly by enabling classes or locations in the Advanced Settings area of the Settings dialog box. Unlike classes or locations, tags are already turned on in QuickBooks, so you can populate the tag field in any transaction. Tags, classes, and locations are three ways of categorizing transactions in groups that are meaningful to you beyond the chart of accounts.

Normally, QuickBooks allows you to do a "quick add" of a new vendor, customer, account, and so on, but you must set up tags before you start tagging transactions. To do so, follow these steps:

1. **Choose Banking ⇨ Tags (Transactions ⇨ Tags).**

2. **Click the New button, and choose Tag Group or Tag.**

    Think of a tag group as being a parent tag and a tag as being a subtag, in that you can associate one or more tags with a tag group.

3. **Assign a tag name or (in the case of a group) assign a group name, as shown in Figure 8-32.**

FIGURE 8-32:
The Create New Group task pane enables you to establish new tag groups.

4. **(Optional) Assign a color.**

5. **(Optional) Enter a tag name in the Add Tags to This Group section and then click Add.**

Tag groups and tags correlate to accounts and subaccounts on your chart of accounts, as well as customers and subcustomers in your customer list. Tag groups are the parent level label, while tags are a child level label.

When you have at least one tag or group created, you can start tagging transactions. Figure 8-33 shows two tags added to a tag group.

FIGURE 8-33:
Two tags have
been added to
the Marketing
Expenses tag
group.

TIP

The number of tag groups you can create depends on your subscription level. Simple Start, Essentials, and Plus users can create 40 tag groups, whereas Advanced users have unlimited tag groups. The tag groups can collectively contain up to 300 tags. Alternatively, you can have unlimited ungrouped tags, which QuickBooks refers to as "flat" tags. Tags that are not within a group cannot be viewed in reports, but you can use them for searches to return lists of transactions that have that tag.

Follow these steps to add a tag to a transaction:

1. **Choose Transactions ⇨ Tags (Banking ⇨ Tags).**

2. **Click Start Tagging Transactions in the Money In or Money Out section.**

   A list of your transactions appears.

3. **As shown in Figure 8-34, select one or more transactions that you want to tag.**

   You can use the Filter button to select transactions, if you like.

4. **Click Update Tags and then choose Add Tags.**

   You can also choose Remove Tags if you want to untag transactions.

5. **Choose or type the name of the tag, and click Apply.**

   Tags appear in the new Tags column.

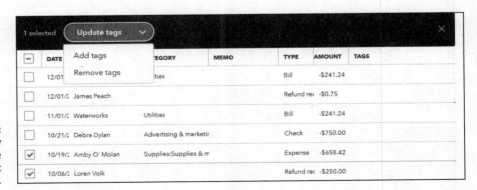

FIGURE 8-34:
You can apply
tags to multiple
transactions at
once.

WARNING

The ability to tag transactions en masse is available only when you first click Start Tagging Transactions in the Money In or Money Out section. As soon as you leave this screen, you can't return to it, although you can still edit and tag individual transactions through the normal transaction screens. If you want to apply tags widely across your transactions, make sure that you allow enough time to complete this work in a single sitting if you want to use the batch tools that are initially available.

Chapter **9**

Paying Employees and Contractors

A s an employer, you have a responsibility to pay both your employees and any contractors who work for you. In this chapter, I explore both responsibilities.

In the past, QuickBooks Online users could prepare payroll in one of two ways: using QuickBooks with Self Service Payroll or using QuickBooks with Full Service Payroll. Intuit has revised its offerings to blur the lines between these two methods. All QuickBooks Payroll plans now offer automated tax deposits and tax forms. All three plans also offer Auto Payroll, which, if enabled, instructs QuickBooks to process payroll automatically as well. Among Auto Payroll, automated tax deposits, and automated payroll return findings, much of your payroll process can be set-and-forget.

WARNING

If you subscribe to QuickBooks Payroll, you're giving up the option to deposit your payroll taxes and file your payroll tax forms on your own. Some folks will shout "Sign me up now!" whereas others may feel trepidation over ceding control of compliance tasks. Do note that when you start completing the payroll tax screens, Intuit automatically verifies the information you enter with governmental websites, so don't embark on setting up payroll unless you're sure that you want Intuit making automated tax deposits and payroll filings on your behalf.

At the end of this chapter, I explore the ways that QuickBooks users typically pay — and report on paying — contractors, who are vendors who perform work for a company but don't qualify as employees.

If you're wondering about Intuit Online Payroll, all accounts have been migrated to QuickBooks Payroll, and that offering is no longer available.

Understanding the Employee Payroll Process

Running payroll is more than just issuing paychecks to your employees. After you've prepared paychecks, you need to remit amounts withheld for deductions and benefits to the appropriate parties. QuickBooks Payroll handles the tax deposits and file payroll tax returns with the appropriate taxing authorities for you.

Getting Started with QuickBooks Payroll

When you prepare payroll, the process involves doing setup work so that you can calculate payroll checks accurately. You must also account for payroll taxes withheld from each employee's paycheck. The payroll service will remit federal, state, and (in some cases) local payroll taxes to the appropriate tax authorities. You remit to the appropriate institutions any required deductions and contributions that affect each employee's paycheck.

This section examines the payroll setup process and details differences in the process for new employers and established employers.

Turning on QuickBooks Payroll

The service uses a to-do list approach to walk you through the payroll setup process. You start by turning on payroll in QuickBooks Online. Then you complete tasks in the to-do list that walk you through setting up your company so that you can pay your employees.

ESTABLISHED EMPLOYERS ENTERING PAYROLL HISTORY

If you're an established employer using QuickBooks for Windows Desktop, you may want to import your company into QuickBooks Online, as described in Chapter 13. In that case, your employees will appear in QuickBooks. But assuming that you intend to use QuickBooks Payroll, you'll have some setup work to complete, much of which is similar to the work described in this chapter, and as you'll see, the Payroll Setup Wizard walks you through that work. Entering payroll history is different for new businesses, however, which don't have any payroll history to enter, so the treatment for entering payroll history is light.

Switching midyear can cause confusion. I recommend (and your accountant will agree) that you plan to switch at the start of a new year or, at the very least, at the start of a quarter. You can enter history as of the last day of the preceding quarter; the only additional information you need to enter is information that affects an annual form, such as the employee's W-2.

But for those who have been recording payroll in QuickBooks Desktop, you'll find the QuickBooks Desktop Payroll Summary report most useful, because it contains all the information the Payroll Setup Wizard requests to establish your payroll history information. Using the information on the Payroll Summary report, you enter, for each employee for the current year, total wages, deductions, and taxes for previous quarters. Using the same report, enter the same information for the Year-to-Date As of Today column presented by the Payroll Setup Wizard. Finally, established employers enter previous payrolls, totaled for all employees, once again using the Payroll Summary report from QuickBooks Desktop.

You enter the total payroll for each pay period in the current quarter. As you enter these numbers, you're entering information paid to *all* employees for the date, which makes the task less onerous because there's less data entry. Similarly, you enter total taxes paid by tax for that pay period.

And because you've been paying employees, you'll need to enter information about any payroll tax payments you made during the current payroll year to reconcile the payroll tax history.

You can use the details at https://intuit.me/3FJkdSX to complete your company's setup after you import it. This chapter also helps you set up payroll.

REMEMBER

You can set up employees without a payroll subscription. After you establish your subscription, you can enter previous payroll data back to your subscription date.

Click the Payroll link on the navigation bar to display the Employees page; then click the Get Started button. On the first page, shown in Figure 9-1, choose the options that appeal to you, or scroll down to choose among Core, Premium, and Elite payroll processing. All three plans include automated tax deposits and payroll tax form filing. If you click the Try Now button below the Premium Payroll option, the QuickBooks Online Employees page reappears; click the Get Started button to start the payroll setup process.

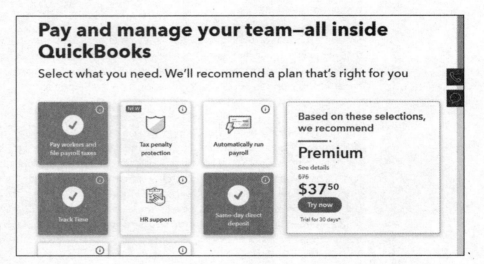

FIGURE 9-1:
Choosing an option for payroll.

WARNING

QuickBooks walks you through the payroll process. You can't progress through the to-do list without completing each task, so allow enough time to complete each section. Follow these steps to complete the process:

1. When the Get Ready for Payroll Wizard asks you whether you've paid any employees in the current year, select No, I'm Not Sure, or Yes and then click Next.

If you indicate that you've previously done payroll and are now switching to QuickBooks Payroll, the wizard displays additional questions for you to answer concerning the method you used to pay employees. Answer the questions and then click the Continue button in the bottom-right corner of the screen. If you indicate that you haven't previously paid employees, no additional questions appear, so click Next in the bottom-right corner of the screen.

2. **On the next screen, select a date for your next payday and then click Done.**

   QuickBooks displays the contact information you provided when you initially set up your company. Edit the fields if necessary.

3. **If you've been using QuickBooks Desktop to prepare payroll, enter payroll history information for each employee and each payroll, using information from the Payroll Summary report in the QuickBooks Desktop program.**

4. **Add employees on the screen shown in Figure 9-2.**

   In this case, the first employee is marked incomplete because he was added before QuickBooks Payroll was activated.

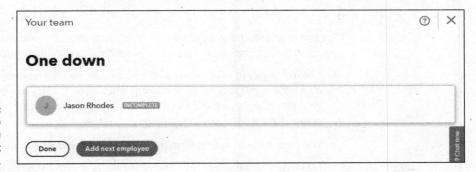

5. **Click Add Next Employee.**

   The wizard displays a fairly lengthy screen for you to complete.

6. **On the first part of the screen, shown in Figure 9-3, provide the employee's name, email address, and hire date.**

   Notice the option to allow the employee to enter their data directly in QuickBooks Workforce. You can deselect this option, but you may prefer to push the data entry work to your employees, which enables them to ensure that the information is entered correctly.

REMEMBER

   Form W-4 is the Internal Revenue Service form that employees complete to specify their withholding allowance. If you need to complete Form W-4 for any employee, visit www.irs.gov, and click the W-4 link in the Forms & Instructions or use this link: www.irs.gov/pub/irs-pdf/fw4.pdf.

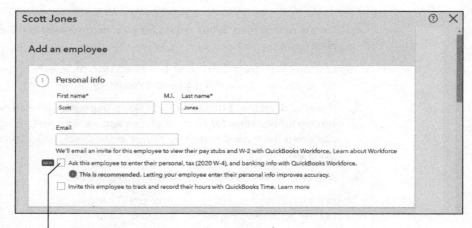

FIGURE 9-3:
Fill in the basic
information
about the
employee, and
decide whether
the employee
should add their
own information.

Click to allow the employee to enter their information.

For this example, I'm going to assume that you want to provide the information yourself. Scroll down the page, and fill in the following information:

- The frequency at which you pay the employee and the next expected pay date. When you supply pay-frequency information, a pay schedule is generated, and you can choose to apply it to subsequent employees you create. Figure 9-4 shows a typical pay schedule.

- The amount you pay the employee (hourly, salaried, or commission only).

WARNING

Make sure to pay close attention when working in the How Much Do You Want to Pay section. For hourly employees, QuickBooks makes it easy and intuitive to enter regular time. Make sure to scroll down on this page and enable any other types of pay that the employee could accrue, such as overtime, holiday pay, bonuses, and so on. If you don't enable the fields here, you won't be able to enter the amounts when you process payroll.

- Whether the employee has any deductions.

- Form W-4 withholding information, which includes the employee's address, Social Security number, tax filing status (single, married, head of household, etc.), and withholding amount (see Figure 9-5). State payroll tax information appears at the bottom of the screen and isn't shown in Figure 9-5. The requirements vary from state to state, but QuickBooks prompts you to supply information for the state in which your business operates.

TIP

To identify your state's payroll tax requirements, visit your state's website and search for *payroll taxes*.

- The method you want to use to pay the employee (such as paper check or direct deposit). If you choose direct deposit, specify the bank account information for the employee (account type, routing number, and account number).

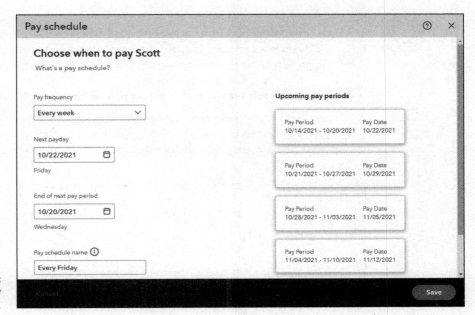

FIGURE 9-4:
A typical pay
schedule.

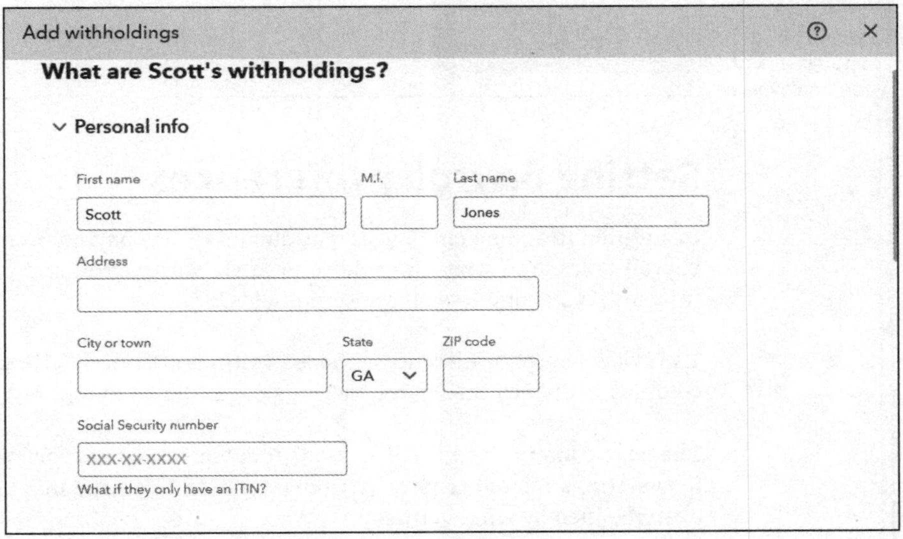

FIGURE 9-5:
Information
required to
complete a
federal Form W-4.

TIP

For direct-deposit checks, you can choose to deposit the paycheck in its entirety in a single account, deposit the check into two accounts, or deposit a portion of the check directly and pay the balance as a paper check.

7. **When you finish supplying the employee's information, click Done.**

QuickBooks displays the Your Team page, listing active employees (see Figure 9-6). On this page, you can edit employees, add employees, and start a payroll. At this point, you probably should add the rest of your employees.

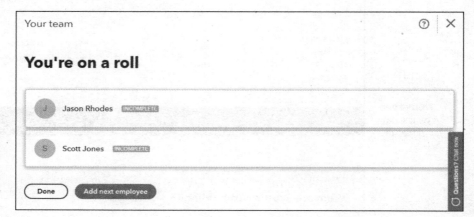

FIGURE 9-6:
The Your Team page enables you to monitor the setup status of your employees.

Setting payroll preferences

In addition to adding employees, you should review payroll preferences and set up payroll taxes. You won't be able to process your payroll and payroll tax returns fully until you complete all the setup fields.

To review payroll preferences, choose Settings ➪ Payroll Settings (Your Company column) to display the Payroll Settings page, shown in Figure 9-7.

The page contains a series of sections that you can use to review or establish various settings related to payroll. Understanding this page may make you feel less overwhelmed by what you see:

» General Tax allows you to edit your company type, filing name, and filing address, as well as change your first payroll date if necessary.

» Federal Tax allows you to indicate your Employer Identification Number (EIN), opt out of workers comp offers from Intuit partners, and specify a filing requirement and deposit schedule.

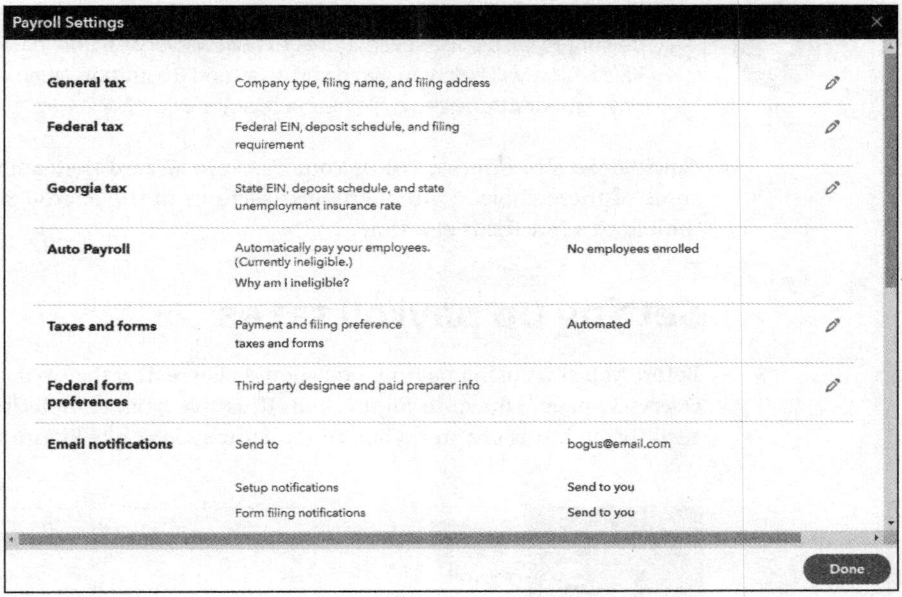

FIGURE 9-7:
The Payroll Settings page.

>> Special federal programs such as the CARES Act may appear here if payroll tax deferrals or other relief is available.

>> A state tax section allows you to specify your state EIN, payroll tax deposit schedule, and state unemployment rates.

>> Email notifications allow you to opt in or out of payroll-related email notifications.

>> Shared Data allows you to give your employees the option to import their W-2 data into TurboTax.

>> Bank Accounts requires you to connect your bank account to remit deductions, pay your employees via direct deposit, as well as e-file and e-pay your taxes.

>> Check Printing allows you to specify whether you want to print checks on plain paper (assuming that your printer allows you to use a MICR cartridge to generate the row of numbers at the bottom of a check) or on preprinted QuickBooks-compatible checks. This section also offers a link for ordering checks.

>> Accounting Preferences enables you to map payroll tax payments, expenses, and liabilities to your chart of accounts.

TIP

Be sure to set aside a few minutes to review every section in Payroll Settings. This review will help you avoid surprises and frustration when you make a tax payment or attempt to e-file near a deadline.

QuickBooks also offers a Fill In Your Tax Info Wizard that can walk you through some of these choices, although most sections in the Payroll Settings screen are limited to a few fields at a time.

Setting up payroll taxes

Before you start using payroll, you should also review the to-do list on the Payroll Overview page, shown in Figure 9-8. If you've been completing steps as you've read through this chapter, your To Do list may look like Figure 9-8.

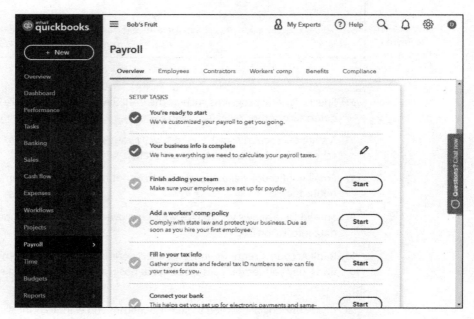

FIGURE 9-8:
The to-do list on the Payroll Overview page.

As shown in the figure, you can click Edit to edit any data that you've already entered, or you can click Start next to add a workers' comp policy. A wizard first asks you to choose between Yes, I'm Covered and No, I Don't Have It. If you choose No, QuickBooks offers to help you find a policy, or you can opt to do the work yourself. If you choose Yes, you'll be asked whether you want to connect your policy to QuickBooks. If you do, select the check box titled Help Me Add My Policy to QuickBooks and then click Next. If you skip the check box and click Next, you return to the To Do list.

At this point, you can use the Fill In Your Tax Info Wizard to set up your payroll by clicking Start. The wizard first asks you to confirm your general business info, such as your company's legal name and address, and company type. Click Next to continue to the next screen.

The next step in the list relates to workers' compensation insurance. If workers' compensation insurance is required in your state, QuickBooks asks you whether you're already covered or whether you'd like a quote on a policy that integrates with QuickBooks Payroll. You can connect your workers' compensation policy or simply click Next.

TIP

The date when you start using QuickBooks Payroll determines the "as of" date of historical information you need to collect, and determines that date to be the first day of the current quarter. Try to start using QuickBooks on January 1 of any year; that way, you don't need to enter any historical information. If you can't start using QuickBooks on January 1, try to start using it on the first day of an accounting period, either the first day of your company's fiscal year or the first day of a month. Historical payroll transactions can be summarized before that date but must be entered in detail after that date.

Next, you provide the legal name and address of your company, as well as federal and state tax information. After you complete the General screen, a single Federal and State Tax Details page appears if you indicated that you're a new employer. Existing employers see the more detailed Federal Tax Info screen, shown in Figure 9-9. Supply your federal EIN, and confirm the payroll tax form you use and how often you must remit payroll taxes. You should also specify whether your company is a federally recognized not-for-profit organization that isn't required to pay federal unemployment taxes. Also indicate whether you want to share your information for the purpose of getting workers' comp insurance offers. When you click Next, the State Tax Details form appears; provide your state tax ID number and unemployment information. I'm not showing you this page because when you complete the Federal Tax page, Intuit sends the information to the Internal Revenue Service, and I don't need any folks wearing dark suits and sunglasses knocking on my door. Click Done to complete this part of the To Do list.

WARNING

If you enter data in a field incorrectly, a payroll form can appear to be broken or frozen. Scroll back up to look for any fields marked in red. If you typed that someone works 40 hours a day or 8 days a week (instead of 8 hours a day and 5 days a week), for example, you won't be able to access other parts of the page until you clear up the issue.

The final task in the Payroll Setup to-do list is to link your bank account. This step is required because as of this writing, QuickBooks automatically deposits your payroll taxes for you and files your payroll tax forms.

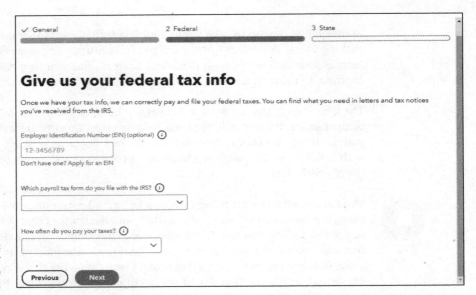

FIGURE 9-9:
The Give Us Your
Federal Tax Info
page.

In short, if you use QuickBooks Payroll, you can't deposit your payroll taxes or file your payroll returns on your own; the system does those things for you.

You can use the links on the Payroll Tax Center screen to change any of the settings you provided as you worked through the checklist.

Preparing Payroll

When you get past the setup work, you're ready to process payroll, which is essentially a three-step process:

1. Record paycheck information.

2. Review paycheck information.

3. Generate paychecks.

TIP

Mobile users: Consider trying the Intuit Online Payroll mobile app, which works with both QuickBooks Payroll and other Intuit payroll products. You can use it to pay your employees and your payroll taxes, file payroll tax forms electronically, and review employee information and paycheck history. Data syncs automatically between the mobile app and your Intuit payroll account. Download the mobile app from the Apple App Store or from the Google Play Store; it's free with a payroll subscription.

Recording payroll information

To start preparing paychecks, click the Payroll link on the navigation bar, click Employees to display the Employees page, and click the Run Payroll button in the top-right corner of the page. The Run Payroll Wizard displays the screen shown in Figure 9-10, which lists all your employees. If you use multiple pay schedules, you're prompted to choose a pay schedule before you see the screen in Figure 9-10.

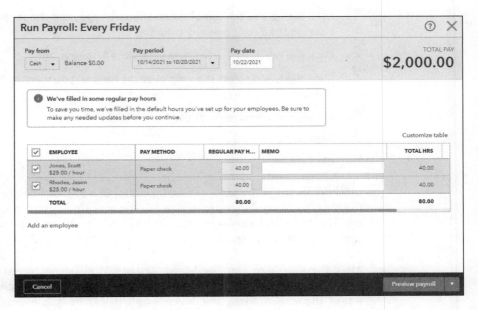

FIGURE 9-10:
Use this screen to enter payroll information for your employees.

At the top of the screen, verify the account from which you'll pay employees, and double-check the pay period and pay date. By default, a check mark appears to the left of each employee scheduled to be paid, but you can remove the check if appropriate. For each employee paid on an hourly basis, supply the hours worked during the pay period.

TIP

If you have a long list of employees, you can see more employees onscreen by clicking the Settings button in the top-right corner and choosing Compact to reduce the amount of screen real estate allotted to each employee.

Letting employees use time sheets

If you use QuickBooks Online Essentials or higher, you can set up time-tracking users who can log in with limited privileges that enable them to complete time sheets (and do nothing else). Alternatively, QuickBooks Payroll Premium or Elite includes the QuickBooks Time Tracker app (previously called Tsheets) in the payroll plan, which allows workers to use the free mobile app to log their time. Your employees and contractors are notified automatically when you provide their email addresses in the employee setup screens.

If you're not using QuickBooks Time Tracker and want to add a time-tracking user, follow these steps:

1. **Click Settings at the top of the Dashboard page, and choose Manage Users in the Your Company column.**

2. **Click the Add User button, and click Time Tracking Only.**

3. **Click Next, and select the employee (or vendor) you want to fill out time sheets.**

4. **Supply the employee's (or vendor's) email address.**

5. **Click Next.**

6. **Click Finish.**

QuickBooks sends the user an email containing a link that they click to complete the Time Tracking Only setup process. If the user already has a QuickBooks Online sign-in name and password, they can use it; otherwise, they need to create a sign-in name and password.

After the user signs in, the Single Activity Time Sheet screen appears; if the employee prefers to use the Weekly Time sheet screen, they can click the tab at the top of the screen. Many employers don't pay their employees based on hours reported on time sheets; they use time sheets to bill clients for time spent on client projects or to track labor costs associated with a project; see Chapter 6 for details on entering time.

If you have a QuickBooks Online Plus or Advanced subscription, you can use time sheets without using QuickBooks Payroll if you want to track time to be billed to clients or customers. You can view hours entered on time sheets by time-tracking employees. Before you start payroll, click the Create (+) button on the QuickBooks navigation bar, select Weekly Time Sheet, and select the employee. If you prefer, you can print information. Run a Time Activity by Employee report by clicking the Reports link on the navigation bar and then search for Time Activities by Employee Detail. Customize the report to display the payroll time frame. For information on reports, see Chapter 10.

Reviewing and generating payroll checks

When one of everyone's favorite days of the month, known as payday, has come around on the calendar it's time to process payroll:

1. **Choose Payroll from the navigation bar.**

The Payroll Overview page appears.

2. **Assuming that it's time to process payroll, click the Let's Go button beneath the large It's Time to Run Payroll banner.**

QuickBooks really doesn't want you to miss payday. Your employees don't either. The Run Payroll page appears to help you with the process.

3. **Enter regular pay hours and an optional memo.**

Your active employees appear on individual rows. If you need to override federal or state withholdings for a single paycheck, click Edit at the right-hand side of an employee's row.

REMEMBER

QuickBooks only shows you fields for pay types that you've enabled within each employee's record. Infrequent pay types, such as holiday pay or bonuses, can suddenly feel like a pop quiz when there's no place to enter the information. To enable additional pay types on the fly, click the employee's name on the Run Payroll page, and then scroll down to the How Much Do You Pay section. Within this page you'll see check boxes for enabling additional pay types.

4. **Click Preview Payroll (refer to Figure 9-10).**

If you need more time, click the arrow on the Preview Payroll button and choose Save for Later to save your work in progress rather than abandoning a payroll run completely.

5. **Use the Review and Submit page shown in Figure 9-11 to make sure everything looks in order.**

Click Edit next to each employee's Net Pay amount if you need to edit their check, or click the Compare to Last icon to display a chart that compares this paycheck to the employee's previous check.

WARNING

If you use the Compare to Last Payroll page, make sure that you click the Close (X) button in the upper-right hand corner. If you're like me and press the Escape key to close windows on your computer, you'll not only close the Compare to Last Payroll page, but you'll also cancel your payroll run as well.

6. **(Optional) Click Preview Payroll Details.**

A detailed report shows every aspect of your employees' compensation, withholdings and deductions, and any employer costs such as the employer portion of payroll taxes.

FIGURE 9-11:
Reviewing
paychecks before
generating them.

7. **Click Submit Payroll to finalize your payroll.**

If you have any issues you need to resolve before submitting your payroll, you can click the arrow beside Submit Payroll and choose Save for Later.

8. **The Payroll Is Done page appears.**

Hold your horses though; you might not be completely done yet. If you use direct deposit and don't need to print pay stubs, you can skip the next two steps. Otherwise, you still have some unfinished business to attend to.

9. **(Optional) Click Auto-Fill to assign check numbers, or manually enter check numbers if you use hand-written checks.**

If you happen to catch a last-minute issue, you can click an employee's pay amount to display a screen from which you can edit their check. Payroll isn't over until it's really over.

10. **(Optional) Click Print Pay Stubs to preview paychecks and stubs and print them, as shown in Figure 9-12.**

This report appears in an additional browser tab.

11. **(Optional) Click View Payroll Reports.**

The Your Payroll Reports Are Ready page allows you to pick the reports that you want to export to Excel. Each report is placed on a separate worksheet that you can open in Microsoft Excel or Google Sheets. Click OK to close this page.

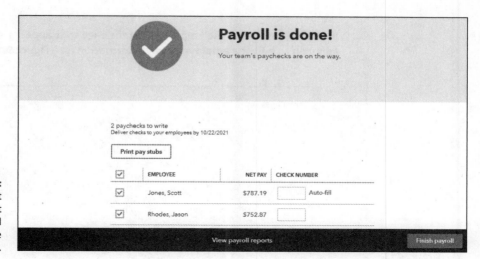

FIGURE 9-12:
When you don't direct-deposit paychecks, you'll see a page like this one.

WARNING

When you open your payroll report workbook, you could encounter a warning prompt in Excel that informs you that the file format and extension don't match, and that the file could be corrupted or damaged. You can safely click Yes to open the report. The geeky details are that the programmers at Intuit are generating a workbook that has an .xls file, but the workbook itself is in the modern .xlsx format. In short, there's nothing to see here. Click Yes and move along.

12. **Click Finish Payroll.**

Take a deep breath. Now, my friend, you are truly done with payroll.

TIP

You can click Edit at the right edge of the line for any employee to see the details associated with the employee's paycheck. If necessary, you can change certain paycheck details, such as hours worked and federal/state tax amounts.

If you pay your employees by direct deposit, expect next-day deposits for Payroll Core or same-day deposits for Premium or Elite for transactions initiated by 7 a.m. Pacific time.

Establishing or correcting payroll exemptions

Although it's unlikely you'll need to, you can establish payroll tax exemptions when necessary by following these steps:

1. Click Payroll on the navigation bar, click Employees, and elect the name of the employee whose status you need to change.

2. **In the Pay section of the Employee Details page that appears, click the Edit icon to edit the employee's pay information (see Figure 9-13).**

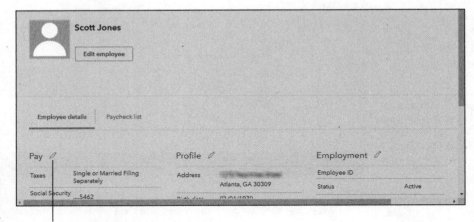

FIGURE 9-13:
Click the Edit icon in the Pay section to edit pay information.

Click to edit the employee's pay information.

3. **On the page that appears, click the Edit icon below What Are [Employee Name's] Withholdings?" (see Figure 9-14).**

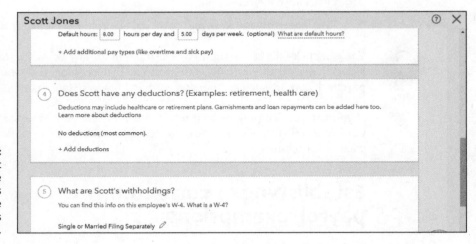

FIGURE 9-14:
Click the Edit icon in the withholdings section to edit the employee's withholdings.

4. **On the Payroll Taxes Setup and Compliance page that appears, scroll down, and expand Tax Exemptions (see Figure 9-15).**

TIP

At points in the past, QuickBooks users have been directed to contact a payroll specialist to establish an exemption. If that's the case for you, instructions on next steps appear.

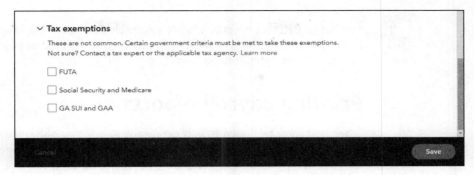

FIGURE 9-15:
Click Tax
Exemptions to
determine
whether you can
manage an
employee's
exemption on
your own.

As shown in Figure 9-16, the Employee Setup screen has the Pay tab, which I've walked you through, as well as two human resources-related tabs: Profile and Employment. The Profile tab allows you to store an employee's home address, email, and phone numbers, among other personal details. A free-form notes field allows you to enter about 90 characters. The Employment tab allows you to specify an internal employee ID and status. Other fields include Hire Date, Work Location (the drop-down list allows you to add new locations as needed), and Workers' Comp Class.

5. **Click Done when you finish editing.**

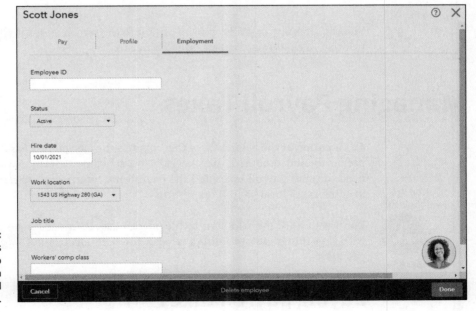

FIGURE 9-16:
QuickBooks
Payroll offers two
tabs of human
resource–related
information.

TIP

To void or delete a paycheck, click Paycheck List in the top-right corner of the Employee page, select a paycheck, and then click the Void or Delete button above the list. A series of questions helps you get the job done.

Printing payroll reports

When you complete payroll, you may want to print payroll-related reports. Click the Reports link on the navigation bar to display the Reports page. Scroll down to the payroll reports, shown in Figure 9-17. Along the way, you may see an Employees section that has reports related to time tracking.

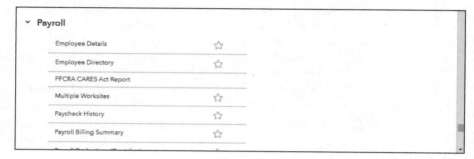

FIGURE 9-17:
Scroll down the Reports page to locate payroll reports.

You can click any payroll report to print it to the screen and, subsequently, to your printer. To customize reports, see Chapter 10.

Managing Payroll Taxes

As I mention at the beginning of this chapter, the payroll process doesn't end with preparing and producing paychecks. On a schedule determined by the IRS, you need to remit payroll taxes and file payroll tax returns, not to mention state and in some cases local payroll tax returns.

WARNING

Don't wait until the 11th hour to file payroll tax returns, because you may end up with late filings due to buffers needed for both electronic filing and electronic payments.

Paying payroll taxes

Using rules established by the IRS, most employers pay payroll taxes biweekly or monthly, depending on the amount you owe (called your *payroll tax liability*). All versions of QuickBooks Payroll now include automated tax deposits and forms, so your payroll tax compliance is automated. You must either let QuickBooks Payroll manage your payroll tax deposits and filings, or you must complete the forms by hand. You can't use QuickBooks Payroll to generate paper forms that you print. Payroll Premium and Elite handle local taxes where applicable.

You must make federal tax deposits by electronic funds transfer by connecting your bank account to QuickBooks Online. If you opt out of this service in Payroll Core, you need to make federal tax deposits using the Electronic Federal Tax Payment System (EFTPS; www.eftps.gov), a free service provided by the U.S. Department of the Treasury. QuickBooks Payroll doesn't use EFTPS; it pays directly on your behalf. For this reason, you need to complete and sign IRS Form 8655 (Reporting Agent Authorization) before your tax deposits and form can be filed on your behalf. You can't opt out of the EFTPS service in Payroll Premium or Elite.

To see your payroll taxes that will be paid, choose Taxes ⇨ Payroll Tax to display the Payroll Tax Center. Normally, I'd show you what this page looks like, but I didn't here because I'm not using a real company. I can tell you that once you've paid employees, the Payroll Tax Center displays taxes that are due, along with their due dates and e-payment cutoff dates. You can preview how much you owe by printing the Payroll Tax Liability report; click the View Your Tax Liability Report link on the Payroll Tax Center page.

Viewing payroll tax forms

Quarterly, you must complete and submit a federal payroll tax return by using Form 941, which identifies the total wages you paid, when you paid them, and the total taxes you withheld and deposited with appropriate taxing authorities throughout the quarter. The IRS permits you to file the form electronically or to mail the form. If you connect your bank account, QuickBooks Payroll automatically files these returns for you.

TIP

If you live in a state that imposes a personal income tax, you typically also must file a similar form for your state; check your state's website for the rules you need to follow for payroll tax reporting. Your state probably has a state unemployment form that you need to prepare and submit as well.

When you click Filings on the Payroll Tax Center page, QuickBooks displays the reports you need to prepare and submit. In my sample company, QuickBooks refused to show me any forms because I didn't have real employer identification numbers to enter, so I can't share an example with you here, as much as I'd like to.

Paying Contractors

Paying contractors is pretty much a straightforward experience. You can wait until you receive a bill from a contractor, enter it, and then pay it, as described in Chapter 5.

But to ensure that you can accurately report payments you made to contractors, you need to ensure that they're set up as vendors who will receive Form 1099-NEC. I'll call these folks *1099-eligible contractors* going forward.

TIP

The IRS has reactivated Form 1099-NEC as a reporting vehicle for compensation paid to contractors. Previously, nonemployee compensation was reported in Box 7 of Form 1099-MISC. Now you report these amounts on Form 1099-NEC.

REMEMBER

I use the term *1099-eligible* because if you hire someone as a contractor but don't pay that person at least $600 — the threshold established by the IRS — technically, you don't have to produce a 1099 for that contractor. Further, if you don't pay a contractor more than $600, QuickBooks doesn't show payments to that contractor on certain reports.

1099-eligible contractors are people who work for you but who aren't your employees. Specifically, the IRS distinguishes between 1099-eligible contractors and employees based on whether you, the employer, have the means and methods of accomplishing the work or simply have the right to control and direct the result of the work. If you have the means and methods to accomplish the work, the person who works for you is an employee, not an independent 1099-eligible contractor. If you're at all uncertain, ask your accountant.

In this section, I focus on setting up 1099-eligible contractors, paying them (without using direct deposit), reporting on 1099 payments you've made, and preparing 1099s for those of your contractors who need them.

TIP

If you use QuickBooks Payroll, you can pay contractors (as well as employees) via direct deposit. First, you must complete direct-deposit setup for your company's payroll subscription, which involves supplying the routing and bank-account information for paying contractors and employees. To set up a contractor as a direct-deposit recipient, choose Workers ➪ Contractors. On the page that appears, click the Check It Out button, and follow the onscreen directions to add a contractor's banking information and initiate payment the same way you would for employees if you're willing to pay a monthly fee on a per-contractor basis. Keep in mind that it may be far less expensive to add ACH capabilities to your bank account and pay contractors directly unless you only have one or two contractors that you'd like to pay this way.

Setting up 1099-eligible contractors

You can set up 1099-eligible contractors in two ways, with the same result:

» You can use the information in Chapter 4 to set up a new vendor. Make sure that you select the Track Payments for 1099 check box.

» You can use the Contractors page to set up a contractor. Any contractor you add from this page becomes a 1099-eligible contractor.

Because you saw how to set up new people in Chapter 4, here, I focus on using the Contractors page to create a new contractor. Follow these steps:

1. **Choose Workers ⇨ Contractors (Payroll ⇨ Contractors).**

The Contractors page appears.

2. **Click the Add Your First Contractor button.**

The dialog box shown in Figure 9-18 appears.

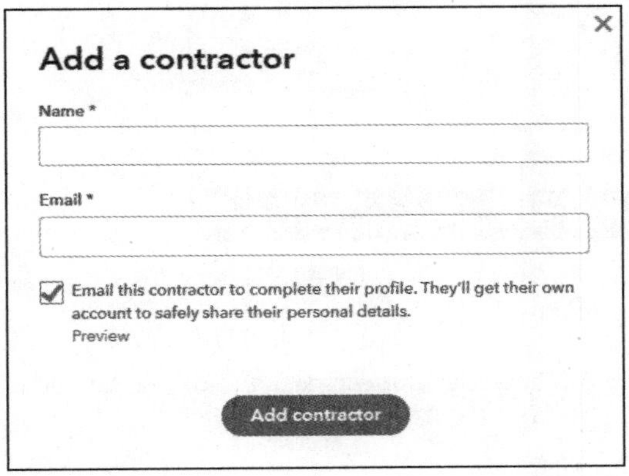

Add a contractor

Name *

Email *

☑ Email this contractor to complete their profile. They'll get their own account to safely share their personal details.
Preview

Add contractor

FIGURE 9-18: Setting up a new contractor.

3. **Provide the contractor's name, and if you want the contractor to complete their profile, enter their email address.**

TIP

If you provide the contractor's email address, Intuit contacts the contractor and gets their 1099 information for you, including the contractor's signature on the W-9 form that the IRS requires you to keep on file. Intuit uses the form information to populate the contractor's record and leaves a PDF of the W-9 form for you on the Contractors page (Documents section).

4. **Click Add Contractor.**

The contractor's details page appears.

5. **Click Add (or Waiting for Info if you opted to send the contractor an email) to provide details about the Contractor Type (see Figure 9-19).**

This information is used when you prepare 1099s for the year.

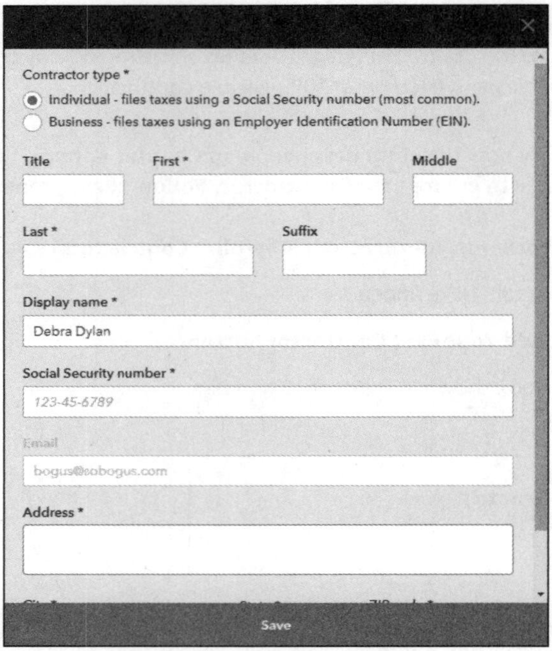

FIGURE 9-19:
Provide the
Contractor Type
information
needed for Form
1099 preparation.

6. **Click Save.**

The contractor's details page appears again, showing the details you just provided.

Paying contractors

You pay contractors the same way you pay any other vendors; see Chapter 5 for details on entering bills, expense transactions, and checks. If a contractor sends you a bill, you can enter it and pay it when appropriate.

Reporting on 1099 vendor payments

Here comes the tricky part. QuickBooks offers 1099 Contractor Summary and 1099 Contractor Detail reports, but both reports show information only on outstanding bills — *not* on bills you've paid. You can think of these reports as being accounts-payable reports for contractors.

To view payments you've made to 1099-eligible contractors, you need to do the following:

>> Make sure that you've set up your company to prepare 1099s.

>> Prepare the 1099 Transaction Detail report, which shows contractors whom you've paid more than $600, the IRS-specified threshold.

REMEMBER

The report excludes payments you make to contractors by using a credit card, because you aren't responsible for providing a 1099-NEC for credit card payments. Instead, the contractor's payment processor will provide the contractor a Form 1099-K.

QuickBooks e-files 1099s with the IRS on your behalf, e-delivers 1099s to your contractors, and prints and mails hard copies of 1099s to your contractors. I regret to inform you that you pay a fee for these services. As of this writing, here are the prices:

>> **1099s filed by January 15:** $12.99 for your first 3 forms, $2.99 for each additional form up to 20, and no charge for 1099s beyond the first 20. If you had 25 forms to file, your cost would be $63.82 ($12.99 + $2.99 * 17 + $0 x 5).

>> **1099s filed on or after January 16:** $14.99 for your first 3 forms, $3.99 for each additional form up to 20, and no charge for 1099s beyond the first 20. If you had 25 forms to file, your cost would be $82.82 ($14.99 + $3.99 * 17 + $0 x 5).

You can also order a 1099 kit that allows you to print your 1099s on paper. As of this writing, pricing starts at $58.99 for ten forms, so opting in to the e-filing method is cheaper and requires much less involvement on your part.

Because of the new e-filing automation in QuickBooks, you can't access the 1099 process whenever you like; you have to wait for certain time frames during the year to carry out these steps:

1. **Choose Workers ➪ Contractors (Payroll ➪ Contractors).**

   The Contractors page appears, listing the 1099-eligible contractors you have set up.

2. **Click the Prepare 1099s button in the middle of the page.**

   The resulting screen explains what happens as you go through the process.

3. **Click Let's Get Started.**

   Due to changes in QuickBooks, you may be able to process 1099s only during certain time frames. If you're outside one of those time frames, you'll see the dates when you can start preparing to file your 1099 forms. When you can click Let's Get Started, you're prompted to review and (if necessary) edit your company's name, address, and tax ID number.

TIP

   If you've partially completed the 1099 process, you'll see a Continue Your 1099s button instead of Let's Get Started.

4. **Click Next.**

   You're prompted to categorize payments you made to your contractors.

TIP

   In most cases, you'll check Box 7, Nonemployee Compensation, and then select an account from your Chart of Accounts list where you assigned your 1099-eligible contractor payments.

5. **Click Next.**

   On the next page, you can review information about the contractors you've set up. Only contractors who meet the $600 threshold appear on this page. You review the contractor's address, tax ID, and email address, and you can click Edit in the Action column if you need to make changes.

6. **When you finish reviewing contractor information, click Next.**

   The total payment you've made to each contractor appears for you to review; you can print the information shown on the page or view a report of the information.

   You've set up your company sufficiently to view reports on 1099 information.

7. **If you're not ready to prepare 1099 forms, click Save and Finish Later.**

You can print the 1099 Transaction Detail report at any time during the year. This report gives you detailed information about the amounts you've paid to 1099-eligible vendors who met the IRS's $600 threshold. Click Reports on the navigation bar, and enter **1099** in the Search box to locate the report.

REMEMBER

If you paid any of your 1099-eligible vendors by credit card, those payments won't appear in the 1099 Transaction Detail report because payments made by credit card are reported to the IRS by the credit card company.

Preparing 1099s

There's really not much to say here; you follow the steps in the preceding section except Step 7; click Finish Preparing 1099s and follow the onscreen instructions to print Form 1099s for you and for your contractors who qualify to receive them.

3 Reporting and Analysis

Examine how the business is performing.

Use Excel to analyze QuickBooks data.

Chapter **10**

Evaluating How the Business Is Doing

Quickbooks Online reports help you keep tabs on the pulse of your business, as well as do a deep dive into the details whenever warranted. This chapter provides an overview of the reporting capabilities QuickBooks offers and shows how you can export reports to Microsoft Excel, PDF files, or Google Sheets.

Reviewing Income and Expenses

When you click Reports (Business Overview ⇨ Reports) on the navigation bar, you see a page like the one shown in Figure 10-1.

Reports are typically organized into three tabs: Standard, Custom Reports, and Management Reports, but Advanced subscriptions have an additional Multi-Co Reporting tab. As you scroll down the Reports page, you'll find the Standard reports organized in the following categories:

» Favorites

» Business Overview

» Who Owes You

» Sales and Customers

» What You Owe

» Expenses and Vendors

» Sales Tax

» Employees

» For My Accountant

» Payroll

FIGURE 10-1:
The Reports page.

REMEMBER

The list of available payroll reports depends on whether you have a payroll subscription. If you don't have a payroll subscription, you see only an Employee Contact list and two reports related to time tracking. Also, you see Sales Tax listed only if you have the Sales Tax option enabled.

All QuickBooks users have the ability to customize the standard reports, which I talk about in "Customizing a report" later in this chapter. Advanced subscribers have access to a Smart Reporting option that uses the Fathom app (which I mention in the "Saving a customized report" section), along with a Custom Report Builder option that enables you to build reports from scratch. Advanced subscribers access the Custom Report Builder by clicking the Create New Report button (refer to Figure 10-1).

TIP

If the Reports menu feels overwhelming, click the down-pointing arrow next to a section heading, such as Favorites, to collapse that section of the page temporarily.

Finding the Report You Want

Reports in QuickBooks are organized in three or four categories:

>> Standard

>> Custom Reports

>> Management Reports

>> Multi-Co Reporting (requires an Advanced subscription)

Click the corresponding tab (refer to Figure 10-1) to access a particular set of reports.

Examining standard reports

The reports available to you on the Standard tab of the Reports page are based on your subscription level, the features you use, the preferences you've set, and the add-ons you've installed.

TIP

In Figure 10-2, I've scrolled down the Standard tab to show you many of the reports in the Business Overview section of that tab in QuickBooks Advanced. Your list of reports may differ if you have a different subscription.

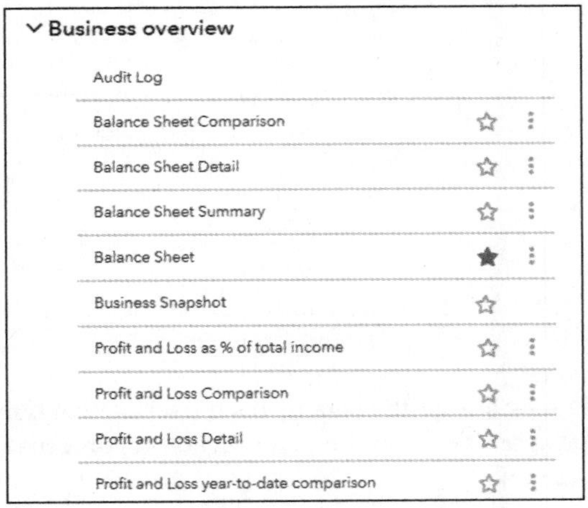

> ∨ Business overview
>
> Audit Log
>
> Balance Sheet Comparison ☆ ⋮
>
> Balance Sheet Detail ☆ ⋮
>
> Balance Sheet Summary ☆ ⋮
>
> Balance Sheet ★ ⋮
>
> Business Snapshot ☆
>
> Profit and Loss as % of total income ☆ ⋮
>
> Profit and Loss Comparison ☆ ⋮
>
> Profit and Loss Detail ☆ ⋮
>
> Profit and Loss year-to-date comparison ☆ ⋮

FIGURE 10-2:
Business
Overview reports.

If you're following along onscreen, note the star next to the Balance Sheet report; the star is green, but in this black-and-white book, it looks dark gray at best. Green stars indicate *favorite* reports. The Balance Sheet report appears in the Favorites section of the Standard tab in Figure 10-1 as well.

Click the star next to any report to place it in your favorites section. If a report falls out of favor with you, don't worry; I won't say a word. Simply click the star to remove it from your sight. Rest assured that the report will still appear in its typical section on the Reports page.

Finding customized reports

When you first click the Custom Reports tab, you may think, "Welp, nothing to see here!" Hang tight; I show you how to add reports to this tab in the upcoming "Saving a customized report" section. For now, know that the Custom Reports tab is a repository for reports that you've customized and saved to run again later. You can store report groups here as well. You may guess that report groups are a batch of related reports that you want to run in one fell swoop.

TIP

Saving a customized report in QuickBooks Online is the equivalent of memorizing a report in QuickBooks Desktop.

Reviewing management reports

The Management Reports tab, shown in Figure 10-3, lists three predefined management report packages that you can prepare and print by clicking the View link in the Action column.

NAME	CREATED BY	LAST MODIFIED	REPORT PERIOD	ACTION
Company Overview	QuickBooks		This Year ⌄	View ⌄
Sales Performance	QuickBooks		This Year ⌄	View ⌄
Expenses Performance	QuickBooks		This Year ⌄	View ⌄

FIGURE 10-3:
The Management Reports tab.

These report packages are quite elegant. Each package contains a professional-looking cover page, a table of contents, and several reports that correspond to the report package's name:

>> The Company Overview management report contains the Profit and Loss report and the Balance Sheet report.

>> The Sales Performance management report contains the Profit and Loss report, the A/R Aging Detail report, and the Sales by Customer Summary report.

>> The Expenses Performance management report contains the Profit and Loss report, the A/P Aging Detail report, and the Expenses by Vendor Summary report.

When you click View in the Action column of a management report, QuickBooks displays a Print Preview window, as shown in Figure 10-4. You can click Print, or if you move your mouse to the preview area, you can click the Download button on the toolbar to save the report in PDF format. Alternatively, if you click the View arrow in the Action column, you have some additional choices:

>> Edit allows you to add your logo to the cover page, add more reports to the package, include an executive summary, and add end notes to the package. Click the icons along the left side of the screen to modify each section of the report.

>> Send allows you to email the report package as a PDF file.

>> Export As PDF allows you to save your report package as a PDF file.

>> Export as DOCX saves your report package in a format compatible with Microsoft Word, Google Docs, and other word processing platforms.

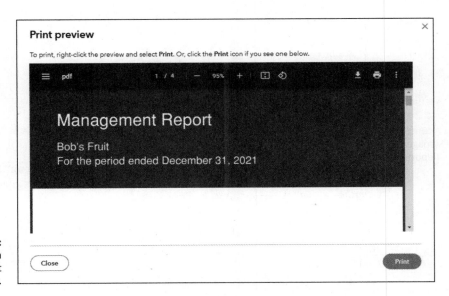

FIGURE 10-4: Print Preview of a management report.

>> Copy creates a new version of the report package while keeping the original intact. QuickBooks adds a number to the report name, such as Company Overview-1, but you can change the name if you want.

>> Delete appears only next to management reports that you've copied. You can't delete the three default report packages.

Contemplating Multi-Co Reporting

The new Multi-Co Reporting option in QuickBooks Advanced allows you to group two or more QuickBooks companies into a single consolidated financial report. You can also create custom key performance indicators (KPIs), which are metrics you can use to measure certain aspects of your businesses. This feature also allows you to set up performance targets and alerts for your group.

Searching for a report

You can enter part of a report name in the Find Report by Name Search box in the top-right corner of the Reports page. As shown in Figure 10-5, any report names that include the letters you type appear in a drop-down list. Click the report that you want to view, or enter a different combination of letters if the desired report doesn't appear.

FIGURE 10-5:
Searching for a report.

 You also can use the Search tool, adjacent to the Settings menu in the top-right corner of the screen, to search for a report from anywhere in QuickBooks.

Printing a Report

Click the report's title to display a report using its standard settings. On most reports, you can drill down to view the details behind the report's numbers. Click any Income or Expense account value in the Profit and Loss report, for example, to display the transactions that make up the number. I clicked the dollar amount for Reconciliation Differences to generate the Transaction report shown in Figure 10-6.

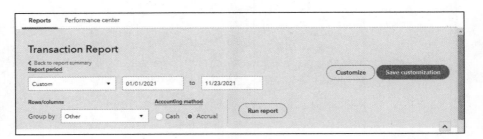

FIGURE 10-6:
The Transaction report that appears after you click an income account on the Profit and Loss report.

To redisplay the original report — in this case, the Profit and Loss Report — scroll up to display the top of the report, as shown in Figure 10-7, and click the Back to Report Summary link. Alternatively, click Reports (Business Over ⇨ Reports) on the navigation bar to return to the Reports listing.

FIGURE 10-7:
Scroll up on any report to change the configuration settings and to access the Back to Report Summary link when applicable.

REMEMBER

The Back to Report Summary link is only available when you're viewing a report that has been generated by clicking an amount to drill down into the details.

TIP

If you want to keep the original summary version of the report open and also view the details from drilling down, duplicate the browser tab that contains the summary version of the report before you drill down to view details. When you finish working with the details, you can close the second tab. To duplicate a tab in Google Chrome, right-click the tab and choose Duplicate from the shortcut menu. For all other browsers, consult the browser's Help menu for instructions on duplicating a tab.

Customizing a report

You can customize most reports, such as choosing between cash-basis and accrual-basis on accounting reports. Some reports allow you to change the date range; most reports allow you to control which columns appear. Click the Run Report button to refresh the report each time you make any changes in the report settings.

Suppose that you want to customize the Profit and Loss report, which appears by default in the Favorites section of your Reports page. Click the Customize button at the top of the report to open the Customize panel; the choices available may vary from report to report.

As shown in Figure 10-8, the Customize Report panel typically contains several sections. The General section, for example, may allow you to choose between cash and accrual accounting methods for a given report.

FIGURE 10-8:
The General section of the panel you use to customize a report in greater detail.

Click the right-pointing arrow next to a section name, such as Rows/Columns, to see the available options. If you click the Change Columns link shown in Figure 10-8, for example, you see the panel in Figure 10-9, where you can control the columns and rows that appear in the report and add a variety of comparison and percentage columns.

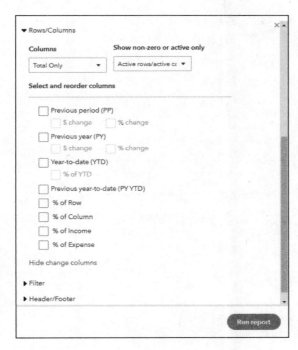

FIGURE 10-9:
Use these settings to control the rows and columns that appear in the report.

TIP

When you choose columns to add to your report, the field names move above the list of available columns below Select and Reorder Columns. This separate section lets you easily see the columns you've added. As shown in Figure 10-10, certain reports allow change the order the fields by using the waffle buttons adjacent to each column name.

You can use the Filter section, shown in Figure 10-11, to control the data that appears on some reports. For instance, you may be able to specify distribution accounts, either by type or by account name/number, or apply filters such as vendor, employee, product/service, and much more. The filters available can vary from one report to the next. Click the check box to apply a given filter, and then use the adjacent drop-down box to specify your filter criteria.

Drag to reorder the fields.

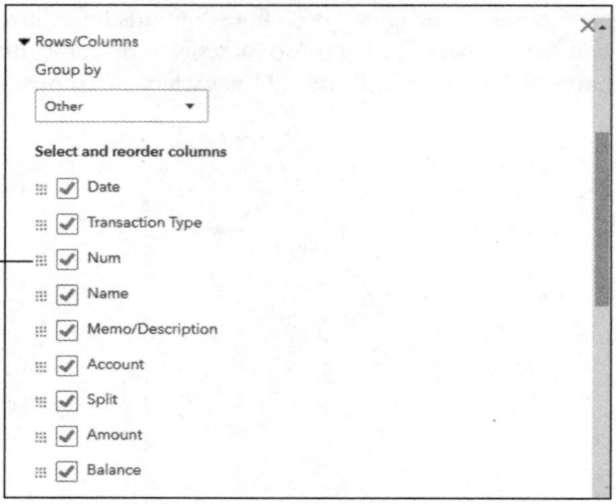

FIGURE 10-10:
Some reports
allow you change
the order of the
fields by dragging
the waffle
buttons to the left
of the columns.

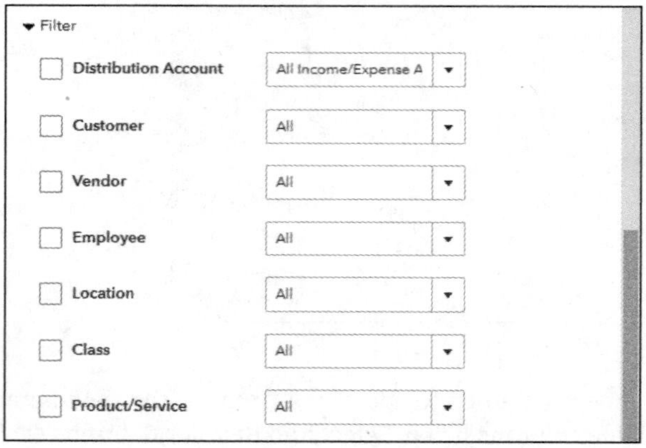

▼ Rows/Columns

Group by

| Other ▼ |

Select and reorder columns

⋮⋮ ☑ Date

⋮⋮ ☑ Transaction Type

⋮⋮ ☑ Num

⋮⋮ ☑ Name

⋮⋮ ☑ Memo/Description

⋮⋮ ☑ Account

⋮⋮ ☑ Split

⋮⋮ ☑ Amount

⋮⋮ ☑ Balance

FIGURE 10-11:
The filtering
options you can
control in the
Profit and Loss
report.

▼ Filter

☐ **Distribution Account** | All Income/Expense A ▼ |

☐ **Customer** | All ▼ |

☐ **Vendor** | All ▼ |

☐ **Employee** | All ▼ |

☐ **Location** | All ▼ |

☐ **Class** | All ▼ |

☐ **Product/Service** | All ▼ |

REMEMBER

Filters limit the amount of information included on the report. Use the Rows/ Columns section when available to control which fields appear on the report itself.

Figure 10-12 shows the settings you can control in the Header and Footer sections of the report. Use the check boxes to select the information you want to display in the header and footer of the reports. The Alignment section enables you control the alignment of the header and footer on the page, meaning left, right, or center.

FIGURE 10-12: The header and footer settings you can customize in the Profit and Loss report.

When you're finished customizing the report, click Run Report in the bottom-right corner of the Customize Report panel to display the report onscreen, using your customized settings (see Figure 10-13). Then you can click the Print button to print the report to paper or to a PDF file. Alternatively, you can click the Email button to email the report; you can also click the Export button to export the report to Excel, a PDF file, or (if you're an Advanced subscriber) to Google Sheets.

FIGURE 10-13: The report after customization to include % of Income and % of Expense columns.

Bob's Fruit

Profit and Loss
January 1 - September 16, 2021

		TOTAL	
	JAN 1 - SEP 16, 2021	% OF INCOME	% OF EXPENSE
▾ Income			
Services	475.00	100.00 %	
Total Income	$475.00	100.00 %	0.00%
▾ Cost of Goods Sold			
Inventory Shrinkage	0.00	0.00 %	
Total Cost of Goods Sold	$0.00	0.00 %	0.00%
GROSS PROFIT	$475.00	100.00 %	0.00%
Expenses			
Total Expenses		0.00%	0.00%
NET OPERATING INCOME	$475.00	100.00 %	0.00%
▾ Other Expenses			
Unrealized Gain or Loss	0.00	0.00 %	
Reconciliation Discrepancies	2,589.00	545.05 %	
Total Other Expenses	$2,589.00	545.05 %	0.00%

Saving a customized report

Now that you've tailored the report to your liking, click the Save Customization button at the top of the report page to display a panel like the one shown in Figure 10-14. Accept the default name for the report, or provide a more meaningful name that reminds you of the customizations you made.

You can add any report to a report group by clicking the Add New Group link, which displays the New Group Name box. Enter a name in the New Group Name box, and click the Add button. Going forward, when you want to add other reports to the group, you can select the group name from the Add This Report to a Group list box in the panel. Report groups make it easy to attach two or more reports to one email as well.

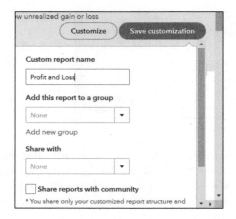

FIGURE 10-14:
Use this panel
to save a
customized
report.

You can choose to share the customized report with other QuickBooks users in your company, and accountants can share reports with users in their firm. Click the Share With list box and then select All, or select None to prevent others from seeing your customization. If you click Share with Community, other QuickBooks users will be able to use your customizations in their companies. Rest assured that Intuit shares only the report settings — never your data. Click Save to confirm your choices.

The saved report appears on the Custom Reports tab of the Reports page or within a report group. In Figure 10-15, my customized version of the Profit and Loss report appears in a group called (uninspiringly) Bob's Group.

	Standard	**Custom reports**	Management reports	Multi-Co Reporting new		
NAME		**CREATED**		**DATE RANGE**	**EMAIL**	**ACTION**
> Bob's Group					Unscheduled	Edit ∨
Profit and Loss		.com		This Year-to-date		Edit ∨

FIGURE 10-15:
The Custom
Reports page
after you create a
custom report.

Click the title to display the custom report. You also can take any of the following actions if you click the down arrow in the Action column for the report:

>> Create a PDF version of the report by clicking Export As PDF.

>> Export the report to Excel by clicking Export as Excel.

>> Delete the customized report by clicking Delete.

TIP

The Action list for Advanced subscribers doesn't offer an Export to Google Sheets option, but if you display the report onscreen, you can choose that option, as I discuss in more detail in the "Exporting to Google Sheets" section later in the chapter.

To change a custom report's name or group, click the Edit link in the Action column for the report. You can also use this link to set an email schedule for the report group, as shown in Figure 10-16. The email interval defaults to Daily, but you can change it to Weekly, Monthly, or Twice a Month. Note that every interval allows you to specify the frequency for emailing the reports, as well ending options. Fill in the Email information, making sure to separate email addresses with a comma (,). You can customize the subject of the report email. There wasn't space to show it in the figure, but if you scroll down you'll be able to click the Attach the Report as an Excel File check box at the bottom of the screen if you prefer that format to a PDF file.

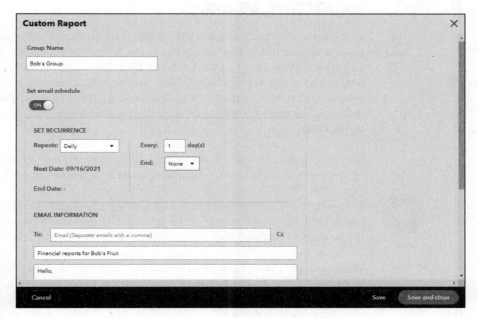

FIGURE 10-16: Set an email schedule for a report group.

For report groups, click the down arrow in the Action column of a report group to do the following:

» Export the group in PDF format.

» Delete the group.

WARNING

Be aware that deleting a group has more consequence than just removing a named group from the Custom Reports page. If you choose Delete from the Action drop-down menu for a report group, you delete the report group and all custom reports that the group contains.

TIP

QuickBooks Online Accountant (QB Accountant) users can access the Business Performance Dashboard, which enables accountants to tap in to metrics that show at a glance how a client is doing, as well as track trends. You can take this feature further by making industry comparisons. QB Accountant compares anonymized, aggregated data that offers peer comparisons based on comparable revenue. In addition, the Fathom add-on (www.fathomhq.com) for QuickBooks enables any user to track KPIs, trends, and other metrics. The Fathom app is included in Advanced subscriptions but can be added to other QuickBooks subscriptions for an additional monthly fee.

Exporting to Excel

To export a report to Excel, click the Export button shown in the margin. Exported reports appear in the downloads bar at the bottom of the screen in your browser and typically are saved to your Downloads folder. Alternatively, you can instruct your browser to ask you where to save your reports. (See your browser's help system for instructions on adjusting this setting.) Keep in mind that changing the download settings for your browser will affect all downloads, not just those from QuickBooks.

When the report has been downloaded, click the report's name to open it in Excel, or see the next section to see how to open Excel files in Google Sheets.

TIP

In most browsers, you can click the up arrow on the right side of the report's button in the bottom-left corner of the QuickBooks screen and choose Show in Folder if you want to navigate to the location where the report is stored.

When you open the downloaded report in Excel, the file is in Protected View, and you have to click Enable Editing to work with it. If you don't, you can't make any changes in the report, such as deleting rows or performing calculations on the side. Protected View may also present numbers in your report as zeros.

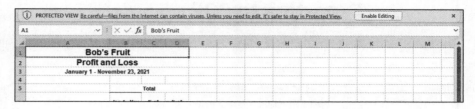

The Protected View feature in Excel perceives reports downloaded from the internet as being potential security threats. You should certainly be careful when opening unfamiliar email attachments or website downloads, but if clicking Enable Editing over and over again feels onerous, you can disable this feature, as follows:

1. **Choose File ⇨ Options in Excel.**

   The Options dialog box opens.

2. **Choose Trust Center in the left column and click the Trust Center Settings button on the right.**

   The Trust Center dialog box opens.

3. **Click Protected View in the left column, and clear the check box titled Enable Protected View for Files Originating From the internet.**

   Optionally, you can clear the check box titled Enable Protected View for Outlook Attachments as well, but be sure to leave the check box titled Enable Protected View for Files Located in Potentially Unsafe Locations turned on.

4. **Click OK twice to close the Trust Center and Options dialog boxes.**

Now you'll no longer have to click Enable Editing whenever you open a QuickBooks report in Excel. You streamline the export process by having files open automatically in Excel from QuickBooks. The next time you export a report to Excel, click the arrow along the right edge of the Report button in the downloads bar and then choose Open Files of This Type Automatically. You'll have a seamless integration between QuickBooks and Excel.

WARNING

Disabling Protected View will make it easier for you to access reports that you export from QuickBooks, but doing so can expose you to risk from spreadsheets that you download outside QuickBooks. Fortunately, you can enable Protected View on a case-by-case basis. In Excel, choose File ⇨ Open, click Browse in the Open dialog box, select the suspicious spreadsheet, click the arrow next to the Open button, and choose Open in Protected View.

Exporting to PDF

All versions of QuickBooks enable you to export to a PDF file. You can do this in three ways:

» Click the Email button in the top-right corner of the report to attach your report to a blank email as a PDF file.

» Click the Print button and then click Save as PDF.

» Click the Export button and then choose PDF.

TIP

You can open and edit many PDF files in Microsoft Word 2013 and later. Choose File ⇨ Open, click Browse in the Open dialog box, and then select your PDF file the same way you would a Word document. Some reports don't convert cleanly, so your mileage may vary. Google Docs extracts text from PDF files, so you may lose some of the look and feel of the report. You can explore add-ins for Google Drive that offer a better experience.

Exporting to Google Sheets

Advanced subscribers have the ability to export reports directly to Google Sheets. To do so, click the Export button (which looks like an up arrow in the top-right corner of the screen) and then choose Export to Google Sheets. In any other version of Quick-Books, follow these steps to export to Excel and then open the file in Google Sheets:

1. **Click the Export button and then choose Export to Excel.**

This step places the report in your Downloads folder unless you customized your browser to specify alternative download locations.

2. **In Google Sheets, choose File ⇨ Import and then click Upload.**

You must upload any files stored locally on your computer so that they can be accessible in Google Sheets.

3. **Drag a file into the window or click Select a File from Your Device.**

If you have a Windows Explorer or Apple Finder window open, you can drag a file from there into the upload window. Otherwise, use the Select a File from Your Device button to select the file.

4. **Confirm the Import Location and then click Import Data.**

Among other things, the Import Location list allows you to replace or insert sheets into an existing spreadsheet or create a new spreadsheet entirely.

Once your spreadsheet appears in Google Sheets then you can edit, save, or delete as you would spreadsheets that you've created from scratch. For more details see *Google Apps For Dummies* by Ryan Teeter and Karl Barksdale.

Chapter **11**

Analyzing QuickBooks Data in Excel

A longtime complaint that I've had about QuickBooks and other accounting programs is that it often feels that accounting records are literally trapped under glass. You may find, for example, that you can't quite get to the report format you want to see inside QuickBooks. In this chapter, I share some of my favorite tricks and techniques for unlocking your accounting data and viewing it the way you want to see it. If you don't have much experience in Excel, the book *Microsoft Excel For Dummies* by Greg Harvey will help you get up to speed.

For this chapter, I'm using the sample company available for QuickBooks Online, which you can access at `https://qbo.intuit.com/redir/testdrive`. I chose this example so that you have an easy way to generate reports that contain actual data, in case you haven't started using QuickBooks Online. You can and should follow along with your own data, of course, but it's always good to have options.

Also, I used the Microsoft 365 version of Microsoft Excel. Everything I discuss in this chapter can be carried out in older versions of Excel, but in some cases, menus or commands may differ slightly from what you see in this chapter.

Automatically Opening Excel Reports Exported from QuickBooks

First, you need to set up a seamless transition for reports that you export from QuickBooks to Excel. By default, you may have to overcome a couple of hurdles. Suppose that you decide to export a Profit & Loss report to Excel. Follow these steps:

1. **Choose Reports (Business Overview ⇨ Reports) on the navigation bar.**

   The Reports page appears.

2. **Choose Profit & Loss in the Favorites, Business Overview, or For My Accountant section.**

   One confusing aspect of QuickBooks is the fact that reports can appear in multiple sections. Choose whichever section is easiest for you to access, or click the star next to a report to add it to the Favorites section.

3. **Click the Export button and then choose Export to Excel.**

   See Chapter 10 for more information about running reports in QuickBooks.

4. **Click the report name's on your browser's downloads bar or in your Downloads folder.**

   Depending up on your browser of choice, files that you download may appear in a downloads bar across the bottom of your screen. If you close this bar or your browser doesn't offer this feature, you can generally choose Downloads from your browser's main menu to redisplay the bar, or you can navigate to the Downloads folder on your computer.

5. **Click Enable Editing on the message bar in Excel to see your report (see Figure 11-1).**

   Protected View is a sandbox environment in which you can open an Excel report to determine whether it's hazardous — something to consider if you're downloading an Excel template from an unknown website. Conversely, it can be a major speed bump if you're exporting reports to Excel multiple times a day.

FIGURE 11-1:
QuickBooks
reports that you
export to Excel
generally open in
Protected View,
which sometimes
hides the
amounts
temporarily.

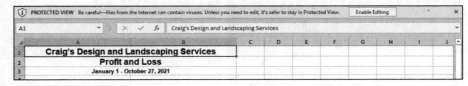

I can't do anything about Steps 1–3, but I can help you eliminate the last two steps if your downloads appear in a downloads bar within your browser. First, set your browser to open Excel files automatically by following these steps:

1. Carry out Steps 1–3 of the preceding list.

Make sure that you don't click the report name on the downloads bar this time.

2. Click the arrow to the right of the filename and choose Always Open Files of This Type from the pop-up menu (see Figure 11-2).

This command instructs your browser to automatically open files that you download in the associated program, eliminating the need to open the file manually.

3. Click the report name on the downloads bar one last time.

Going forward, your reports will open automatically in Excel, but you'll need to coax it there now.

4. If necessary, click Enable Editing to clear Protected View.

In Chapter 10, I show you how to eliminate repetitive work by turning off Protected View.

FIGURE 11-2:
Choose Always
Open Files of
This Type to
seamlessly open
Excel reports that
you export from
QuickBooks.

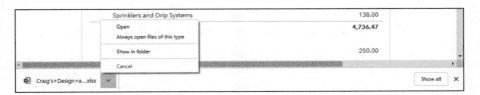

Sifting through Excel Reports

Now that I've helped you pave the way for faster exports from Excel, I'll show you how to transform QuickBooks data into meaningful reports. In this section, I use the Transaction List by Date report, shown in Figure 11-3. I like this report more than the Transaction Detail by Account Report shown in Figure 11-4; you can probably tell why. Notice that the Transaction List by Date report is a simple transaction listing, which gets very close to the optimal analytical report format in Excel because it has the following features:

>> Columns are contiguous, so there are no blank columns.

>> Rows are contiguous, so there are no blank rows.

>> The report doesn't have subtotal or total rows; you can use Excel to add them if necessary.

>> The report doesn't have headings within the data, such as the account headings shown in Figure 11-4.

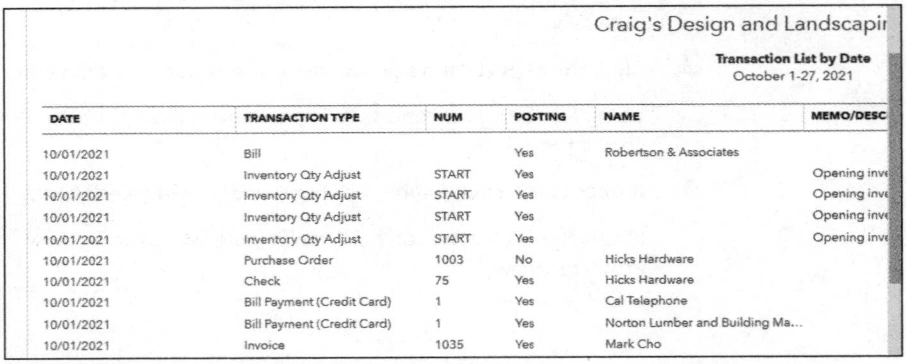

FIGURE 11-3:
The Transaction List by Date report is best suited for analyzing your data in Excel.

DATE	TRANSACTION TYPE	NUM	POSTING	NAME	MEMO/DESC
10/01/2021	Bill		Yes	Robertson & Associates	
10/01/2021	Inventory Qty Adjust	START	Yes		Opening inve
10/01/2021	Inventory Qty Adjust	START	Yes		Opening inve
10/01/2021	Inventory Qty Adjust	START	Yes		Opening inve
10/01/2021	Inventory Qty Adjust	START	Yes		Opening inve
10/01/2021	Purchase Order	1003	No	Hicks Hardware	
10/01/2021	Check	75	Yes	Hicks Hardware	
10/01/2021	Bill Payment (Credit Card)	1	Yes	Cal Telephone	
10/01/2021	Bill Payment (Credit Card)	1	Yes	Norton Lumber and Building Ma...	
10/01/2021	Invoice	1035	Yes	Mark Cho	

Craig's Design and Landscapir
Transaction List by Date
October 1-27, 2021

Here's what I recommend that you do to clean up the report:

1. Select rows 1–4 and then choose Home ⇨ Delete in Excel.

The report title rows use merged cells, which can stymie certain analytical activities in Excel.

2. Delete column A.

It's best to eliminate blank columns in spreadsheets whenever possible.

3. Scroll down and delete the date/time row at the bottom of the report.

This row also consists of merged cells. You'll thank me for eliminating this potential snag.

Craig's Design and Landscaping Service

Transaction Detail by Account
October 1-27, 2021

DATE	TRANSACTION TYPE	NUM	NAME	MEMO/DESCRIPTION
▾ Checking				
10/01/2021	Check	75	Hicks Hardware	
10/01/2021	Deposit			
10/01/2021	Expense	76	Pam Seitz	
10/04/2021	Cash Expense		Tania's Nursery	
10/15/2021	Credit Card Credit			
Total for Checking				
▾ Savings				
10/01/2021	Deposit			Money to savings
Total for Savings				
▾ Accounts Receivable (A/R)				
10/01/2021	Invoice	1035	Mark Cho	
10/01/2021	Invoice	1037	Sonnenschein Family Store	

FIGURE 11-4: Most transaction list reports have headings or subtotals that make Excel analysis more difficult.

TIP

At this point, I encourage you to save your Excel workbook so that you don't have to redo the cleanup as you try the various techniques that I'm about to walk you through.

TIP

In Chapter 17, I show how to automate cleanup of accounting reports by using an Excel feature known as Power Query. Instead of cleaning up a monthly report by hand over and over, you can use Power Query to prescribe a set of automated steps to be performed on the report. After you export the report from QuickBooks the first time, you can pull the data from the report into Power Query, and your cleaned up results appear in a second workbook. Going forward, you can save over the monthly report workbook as needed with new exports from QuickBooks, and then update the results workbook by clicking the Refresh button on the Data menu in Excel. This makes for a set-and-forget approach to reporting.

Filtering data

The Filter feature is one of my favorites in Excel because it enables me to get a bird's-eye view of data within a report. I can also collapse a report to see just the information that interests me. Follow these steps to use the Filter feature:

1. **Click any cell in your report and then choose Data ⇨ Filter or Home ⇨ Sort & Filter ⇨ Filter.**

You could also press Ctrl+Shift+L (⌘+Shift+L for Mac users).

2. **Click the filter arrow at the top of any column (see Figure 11-5).**

As shown in Figure 11-5, the resulting filter menu shows you one of each item in the column, ordered in alpha-numeric sequence, which makes for a nice overview of your data.

Click a Filter arrow next to a column title to sort or filter that column.

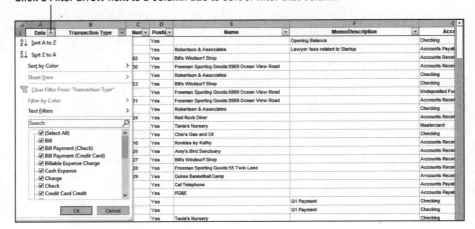

FIGURE 11-5:
The Filter feature adds an arrow to the top of each column of your data.

TIP

If you click the filter arrow in the Amount column, you'll see the smallest number in that column at the top of the list. Scroll down to the bottom of the list to see the largest number in the list. Most users resort to sorting reports to see information in this format. Filtering allows you to keep transactions in their original order.

3. **(Optional) Clear the Select All check box, choose the specific data that you want to see, and then click OK.**

You can filter in this fashion on as many columns as you want.

4. **(Optional) Choose Data ⇨ Clear or Home ⇨ >Sort & Filter ⇨ Clear to remove all the filters from a list.**

You can also clear filters for individual columns by clicking the filter arrow and then choosing the Clear command from the drop-down menu.

REMEMBER

When you filter data in Excel, information in any hidden rows is protected. If you color-code, delete, or otherwise alter anything in any of the visible rows, nothing in the hidden rows will be affected. Conversely, if you delete an entire column, the hidden rows will *not* be protected because the entire column will be removed.

TIP

I don't have enough room to talk about this function in any detail, but if you're using Microsoft 365 or Excel 2021, you can use the FILTER worksheet function to filter data with a worksheet function instead of manual commands. This technique enables you to filter a list by changing the criteria in an input cell.

Guarding against a tricky trap

The Transaction List by Date report has one tricky aspect that I want to bring to your attention because it can surface in other QuickBooks reports. Look closely at column A of Figure 11-6 which you can see is comprised of dates. To your eye, they may look like normal dates, but if you dig below the surface, you'll find that these dates are masquerading as text. This means that Excel treats them as words instead of dates. Click the filter arrow for column A and you'll see each date listed individually instead of automatically grouped by month. Follow these steps to transform the text-based dates into numeric dates that Excel will treat as such:

1. **Select column A, as shown in Figure 11-6.**

You do this by clicking the column letter on the worksheet frame to highlight the entire column.

FIGURE 11-6:
Text-based dates exported from QuickBooks sometimes masquerade as numeric dates.

	A	B	C	D	E	F	G
1	Date	Transaction Type	Num	Posting	Name	Location	Memo/Description
2	10/01/2021	Bill		Yes	Waterworks		
3	10/01/2021	Invoice	1003	Yes	James Peach		
4	10/02/2021	Estimate	1001	No	James Peach		
5	10/02/2021	Payment		Yes	James Peach		
6	10/04/2021	Invoice	1004	Yes	James Peach		
7	10/04/2021	Payment		Yes	Lilian Milburn		

2. **Choose Data ⇨ Text to Columns.**

The Text to Columns Wizard appears. Ostensibly, this feature allows you to take text in one column and split it into two or more columns. In this case, I'll use the feature to transform text-based dates to numeric values that Excel will see as dates instead of a group of characters that happen to look like a date.

3. **Click Finish.**

The Text to Columns Wizard has three steps, but you don't need to carry any of them out in this context. Simply click Finish, and your dates will be transformed into dates that Excel recognizes as such.

WARNING

At this point, you might encounter a prompt that says, in effect, "We can't do that to a merged cell." Exactly who is this *we,* Excel? Regardless, I warned you about this situation earlier in the chapter. If you skipped the step of removing the title rows at the start of the "Sifting through Excel Reports" section, you have one or more merged cells slowing your roll. You have two choices: Delete the title rows and then repeat the preceding steps, or select the cells that contain dates and then repeat the steps.

4. **Click the filter arrow in column A again, and then optionally pick one or more time periods.**

   You should see the dates grouped by month; if your report spans more than one year, they're grouped by year as well. You can expand any grouping to make a granular section.

5. **Your spreadsheet should only show you the rows that match the time period(s) that you selected.**

   You can filter on as many columns as needed, meaning that you can display sales from one or more customers for a specific time period or perhaps determine which customers bought one or more products.

TIP

Click the Filter arrow in a number column, such as quantity or total sales, choose Filter, and then Number Filter to reveal options such as greater than, less than, and Top 10. Top 10 would be better named Top *x* where *x* can be is whatever number you want it to be for filtering the largest or smallest amounts within a list.

Slicing your data

I'd like to bring the Slicer feature to your attention. I often describe Slicers as being a remote control for the Filter feature. A Slicer is a floating object that you can add to your worksheet that displays one of each item within a column of data. If you click an item within the Slicer, Excel filters the list for that item. You can hold down the Ctrl key and make multiple choices from a Slicer if you want to filter for multiple items. This saves you from having to click the Filter arrow in a column and make choices from the list. One of my favorite aspects of Slicers is that you can also easily determine which items are presently hidden within the list. Items that you've "sliced" (or more correctly filtered on) will have shading behind them within the Slicer, whereas hidden items will be disabled or have no shading, as shown in Figure 11-7.

You can apply the Filter feature to any range of cells that you wish in Excel, but you can only use the Slicer feature with lists that are formatted as a Table:

1. **Choose any cell in your data.**

   Sometimes, users think that they have to select all the cells in a report before carrying out an action in Excel. Selecting everything is necessary for applying formatting (such as colors, fonts, and number formats), but it's not necessary for performing data actions.

2. **Choose Insert ⇨ Table, and then click OK in the Table dialog box that appears.**

   The check box titled My Table Has Headers should be selected automatically, confirming that the first row of your list contains column titles.

3. **(Optional) Choose Table Design ⇨ Total Row.**

This command adds a total row to the bottom of your list. The last column is automatically summed or counted, depending on whether that column contains numbers or other content (such as dates or text). Click any other cell in the total row to display an arrow that looks similar to a filtering, but in this case is a menu from which you can choose a mathematical function such as sum, average, count, and so on. When you make a choice from the list, Excel adds the corresponding formula to the total row for that column. If you then filter or slice the table, the total row only tallies the visible rows.

4. **Choose Table Design ⇨ Insert Slicer to display the Insert Slicers dialog box.**

You can use slicers only with data that is formatted as a table or a pivot table. I show you how to create a pivot table in "Custom Reporting with Pivot Tables" later in this chapter.

5. **Choose one or more fields and then click OK.**

A slicer appears for each field that you choose. You can add as many slicers as you want, but keep in mind that it usually doesn't make sense to slice on columns that contain dates or numbers. Slicing works best for text-based cell contents in situations where items you want to slice on appear multiple times.

6. **Click any item in a Slicer.**

Your list gets filtered with one click, as shown in Figure 11-7.

TIP

Hold down the Ctrl key to select two or more items. The total row reflects the sum of only the visible rows.

FIGURE 11-7:
Slicers allow you to filter data in a table with a single click.

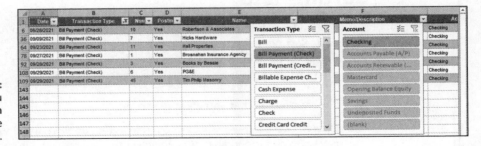

TIP

If you use two or more slicers, the second and later slicers reflect any matches based on choices made in the first slicer. In Figure 11-8, Bill Payment (Check) is selected, which means that the only account that has activity is the Checking account. All other accounts are disabled, with no activity in them.

To reset a slicer, click the Clear command, which looks like a funnel with an x.

You can make choices from as many slicers as you choose. As shown in Figure 11-7, any items on the slicer that are being displayed in the list have shading behind them. Items that do not have shading or that are disabled are either hidden or not available, respectively. Conversely, when you use the Filter feature, you don't have any visual cues as to what data has been hidden based upon your choices.

I could tell you much more about the Table feature because it's a fantastic automation opportunity in Excel. But this book is about QuickBooks, so I'll close this discussion with a few tips:

TIP

>> Expand the Quick Styles section of the Table Design menu and then click the first icon at top-left to remove the shading from the table or choose other colors.

>> Right-click a slicer and choose Remove from the shortcut menu if you change your mind about using the feature.

>> Choose Table Design ⇨ Convert to Range if you no longer want the data to be in a table. This command removes any slicers you have in place.

Sorting data

Sorting enables you to rearrange data sequentially, such as from A to Z or highest to lowest. Sort commands appear when you click a filter arrow. Sort commands also appear on the Home and Data menus. In Excel, you can sort on up to 64 columns. To sort data in Excel, follow these steps:

1. **Choose any cell that you want to sort on.**

Excel is always tracking what's referred to as the *current region,* the contiguous block of cells surrounding your cursor. For this reason, you don't need to select all your data in advance.

2. **Choose Data ⇨ Sort A-Z, Data ⇨ Sort Z-A, or Home ⇨ Sort & Filter.**

The names of these commands are Sort A to Z or Sort Z to A if your cursor is in a column of text, or Sort Smallest to Largest or Sort Largest to Smallest if your cursor is in a column of numbers.

3. **(Optional) Click the Sort button to display the Sort dialog box if you want to sort based on two or more columns.**

You can also use the Sort dialog box to sort based on color or conditional formatting. If you dig deep enough, you'll find that you can sort on custom lists or even sort lists sideways, meaning sorting columns from left to right or right to left versus sorting rows up and down the spreadsheet.

TIP

Here I go again: If you're using Microsoft 365 or Excel 2021, you can use the SORT or SORTBY worksheet functions to sort data with a worksheet function instead of using manual commands. Any changes you made in the original data will be reflected by the worksheet functions.

Custom Reporting with Pivot Tables

Many users are intimidated by pivot tables. The name itself can be intimidating. Rest assured, however, that pivot tables are among the easiest features to use in Excel. Pivot tables allow you to transform a list of data in Excel into meaningful reports simply by clicking check boxes or dragging field names. Even better, nothing you do in a pivot table affects the original data. and you'll unlock a drill-down capability that's similar to drilling down into reports within QuickBooks.

Understanding pivot table requirements

Although Excel is forgiving when it comes to how your data is laid out, when it comes to pivot tables, you must conform to the rules I laid out earlier in the "Sifting through Excel Reports" section for creating analysis-ready formats in Excel. Every column must have a unique heading, for example.

Although doing so isn't required, for best results you should make your data into a table, as shown earlier in the "Slicing your data" section of this chapter. When you do, a Summarize with PivotTable command appears on the Table Design menu. This command is important if you have reports to which you want to add data, such as a year-to-date report to which you add a new month of data after each accounting period. The Table feature enables a pivot table to "see" any data that you add. If you don't use the Table feature, there's a good chance that the new data you add to your list will be left off your pivot table report. In the "Removing Fields" section, I show you how to manually resize your pivot table source data manually if you choose not to use the Table feature.

Follow these steps to create a pivot table:

1. **Select any cell in your list.**

   Make sure that you've cleaned up your data as described earlier in the "Understanding pivot table requirements" section of the chapter.

2. **Choose Insert ⇨ PivotTable.**

   The Create PivotTable dialog box appears.

3. **Accept the default settings by clicking OK.**

   A blank pivot table canvas appears on a new worksheet in your workbook, along with a PivotTable Fields task pane. You'll also see two new tabs in the Excel Ribbon: PivotTable Analyze and Design.

REMEMBER

The PivotTable Analyze and Design tabs, as well as the PivotTable Fields task pane, are context-sensitive. If you move your cursor to any cell outside the pivot table canvas, the menus and task pane disappear; they reappear when you click inside the pivot table canvas again. This behavior can be a bit disconcerting if you're new to the feature.

Adding fields

At this point, you're ready to add fields to your pivot table. You have two choices:

» Select the check box for any field. Text or date fields appear in the Rows quadrant of the PivotTable Fields task pane; these fields will be displayed as rows in the report. Number-based fields appear in the Values section as new columns in the report.

» Drag fields from the field list into any of the quadrants.

In Figure 11-8, I added Account to the Rows quadrant, Date to the Columns quadrant, and Amount to the Amount quadrant. In Excel 2019 and later, when you add dates to a pivot table, they should group by month and/or year automatically. I didn't apply any number formatting to the numbers in Figure 11-8 so that you can see the raw format that first appears. You can change the formatting in a pivot table in the same fashion as any other cells in Excel.

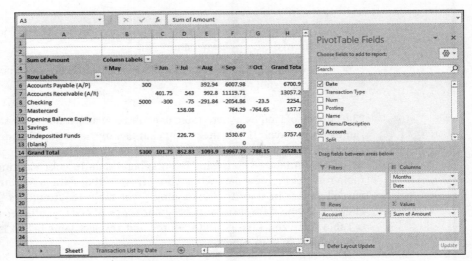

A3   ✕ ✓ f_x Sum of Amount

	A	B	C	D	E	F	G	H
1								
2								
3	Sum of Amount	Column Labels						
4		May	Jun	Jul	Aug	Sep	Oct	Grand Tota
5	Row Labels							
6	Accounts Payable (A/P)	300			392.94	6007.98		6700.9
7	Accounts Receivable (A/R)		401.75	543	992.8	11119.71		13057.2
8	Checking	5000	-300	-75	-291.84	-2054.86	-23.5	2254.
9	Mastercard			158.08		764.29	-764.65	157.7
10	Opening Balance Equity							
11	Savings					600		60
12	Undeposited Funds			226.75		3530.67		3757.4
13	(blank)					0		
14	Grand Total	5300	101.75	852.83	1093.9	19967.79	-788.15	26528.1

PivotTable Fields

Choose fields to add to report:

Search

- ☑ Date
- ☐ Transaction Type
- ☐ Num
- ☐ Posting
- ☐ Name
- ☐ Memo/Description
- ☑ Account
- ☐ Split

Drag fields between areas below:

▼ Filters	▥ Columns
	Months
	Date

▥ Rows	Σ Values
Account	Sum of Amount

☐ Defer Layout Update   Update

Sheet1   Transaction List by Date   ... ⊕

FIGURE 11-8:
Pivot tables allow you to create instant summaries of your data by dragging and dropping fields.

TIP

If you're using a current version of Excel and instead find all the individual dates listed, refer to the "Guarding against a tricky trap" section earlier in the chapter, because your dates are most likely being stored as text. To make your pivot table reflect your changes, right-click the pivot table and choose Refresh from the shortcut menu. At this point, however, you'll need to group your columns manually (which is also the case in older versions of Excel). Right-click a date, and choose Group from the shortcut menu. Choose Months and Years in the Grouping dialog box, and click OK to group your dates by month and year. If your data spans more than one year, and you don't see a total by year, right-click any date and choose Subtotal from the shortcut menu.

Removing fields

Excel can feel overwhelming because you often have three or four ways to carry out almost every task, such as removing fields from a pivot table. Rest assured that you don't need to commit all the options to memory. Instead, use the approach that makes the most sense to you:

>> Clear the check box for a field in the main area of the PivotTable Fields task pane to remove a field from your report.

>> Drag any field out of a quadrant and off the PivotTable Fields task pane. When you release your mouse button, the field is removed from the pivot table.

>> Click the arrow on the right side of any field in a quadrant and choose Remove Field from the drop-down menu.

>> Right-click the field within the pivot table itself and choose Remove from the shortcut menu.

WARNING

The data displayed by a pivot table doesn't recalculate automatically, the way formulas do in Excel. If you make any changes in the underlying data, you need to right-click the pivot table and choose Refresh from the shortcut menu, or choose PivotTable Analyze ⇨ Refresh. If you append data to your existing list, the pivot table reflects the new data when you refresh if that data is within a table, as discussed earlier in the "Understanding pivot table requirements" section of this chapter. If your data resides in a regular range of cells, you'll need to choose PivotTable Analyze ⇨ Change Data Source and reselect your list to include any new rows of data in your report.

If you find yourself repetitively cleaning up QuickBooks reports so that you can create a pivot table report from your data, see Chapter 17, which shows you how to automate this process by using Power Query in Excel. If you want to learn more about pivot tables see *Microsoft Excel Data Analysis For Dummies* by Paul McFedries.

4

Working in QuickBooks Online Accountant

Chapter **12**

Setting Up Shop in QuickBooks Online Accountant

art 1 of this book covers the details of QuickBooks Online, which allows you to maintain detailed accounting records for a business. If you're an accountant, however, you may be supporting multiple clients who use QuickBooks Online. Trying to keep track of multiple sets of credentials for multiple clients very quickly can feel like trying to herd cats. Also, you may carry out work for your clients that they don't want to touch, such as using journal entries to classify income or expenses correctly and to write off bad debts. That's where QuickBooks Online for Accountants (QB Accountant) joins the party. This free platform is designed to enable accountants to switch to any client's QuickBooks company easily on the fly. When you work with a client, you have access to the features for that client's subscription level: Simple Start, Self-Employed, Essentials, Plus, or Advanced.

As you see in this chapter, the interface for a client's QuickBooks company opened in QB Accountant varies slightly from the interface your client sees when they open the company.

REMEMBER

Registering for and Signing in to QuickBooks Online Accountant

Unlike QuickBooks Online, which offers a free trial for 30 days, a QuickBooks Online Accountant subscription is free for as long as you use it. You can register for the ProAdvisor Preferred Pricing program and receive discounted QuickBooks Online rates for each client subscription you manage. For more information on the program, see "Working with ProAdvisor Preferred Pricing" later in this chapter. Further, your free QuickBooks Online Accountant subscription entitles you to a free QuickBooks Online Advanced subscription, with which you can maintain your own set of books. Visit `https://quickbooks.intuit.com/accountant` and then click the Sign Up for Free button on the left side of the page.

If you try abbreviating the URL to qbo.intuit.com/accountant, you'll encounter a "page not found" error, so make sure to spell out QuickBooks when accessing that page.

TIP

After you click the Sign Up for Free button, the web page shown in Figure 12-1 appears. Provide the requested information, including a password, and then click the Continue button (not visible in Figure 12-1) at the bottom of the page.

On the page that appears, enter your accounting firm's name and zip code. Intuit uses the name you provide to create a free company you can use to manage the books for your own business. You can read more about this company in "Understanding and Using the Free QB Accountant Company" later in this chapter.

Click Finish to create your account, sign in, and start a short tour of the QB Accountant interface. When you complete the tour, your home page looks similar to the one shown in Figure 12-2. Before creating the figure, I added two clients; you won't have any clients in your list when you first sign in.

Just as you'd expect, by clicking the Finish button, you're agreeing to Intuit's terms of service, the end-user license agreement, and the privacy policy for QuickBooks Online Accountant.

REMEMBER

FIGURE 12-1:
Provide the
requested
information
to create a
QB Accountant
account.

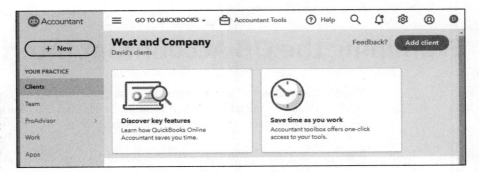

FIGURE 12-2:
A typical
QB Accountant
home page after
creating an
account.

TIP

In addition to the video tour, QuickBooks offers you some cards you can click to get more information about certain subjects, such as how to save time while you work in QB Accountant. If you don't want to see a particular card, click the X in its top-right corner.

After you add clients, they appear in a list on the home page. (See Chapter 13 for details on adding clients to QB Accountant.)

You use the same page to log in to QuickBooks Online Accountant that your client uses to log in to QuickBooks Online: `https://qbo.intuit.com` (see Figure 12-3).

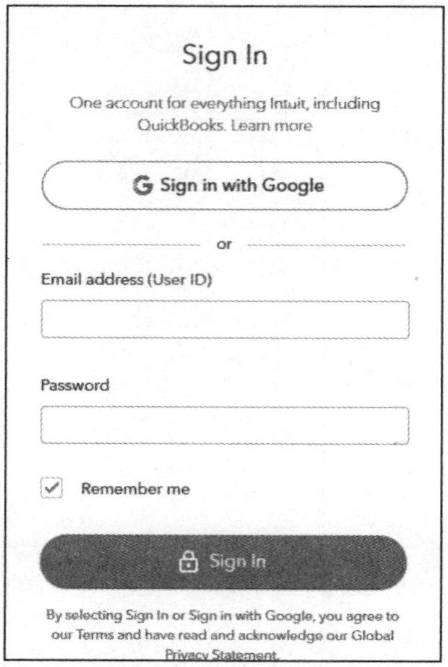

FIGURE 12-3:
The page you use
to sign in to
QB Accountant
after you set up
an account.

Examining the QB Accountant Interface

The QB Accountant interface focuses on giving accountants access to tools they need to manage multiple clients. Although the view in the interface depends on where you're working, two common elements appear:

>> The navigation bar runs down the left side of the page. The bar is gray when you're in your practice and dark gray when you access a client's books.

>> A QB Accountant toolbar runs across the top of the page.

You use the navigation bar to display the various pages in QB Accountant. The navigation bar contains two choices that display different views and affect the choices on the toolbar: the Your Practice and Your Books views. The following two sections explore the navigation bar and the QB Accountant toolbar in these views.

Working with Your Practice view

By default, when you log in to QB Accountant, the home page displays the Clients page of Your Practice view, as shown in Figure 12-4. The Clients page displays . . . well, a list of your clients. If you want to navigate to this page (because you viewed another portion of QB Accountant and now want to return to the list of your clients), click Clients in the Your Practice section of the QB Accountant navigation bar.

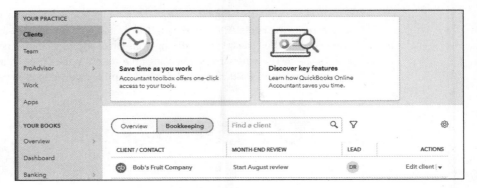

FIGURE 12-4:
The client listing
in QB Accountant.

On the Clients page, you can search for a client, see overview information about each client, and open a client's QuickBooks company. You can also control the appearance of the Clients page. See "Controlling the Appearance of the Client List" later in this chapter for details on working with the Clients page.

When you click Team on the navigation bar, you can set up the users in your firm who will have access to various client companies. For more information, see "Setting Up Your Team" later in this chapter.

When you click ProAdvisor, you see options for information about the benefits and training offered through the Intuit ProAdvisor program. If you weren't previously a member of the ProAdvisor program, a free Silver membership is established for you automatically. For details, visit `https://quickbooks.intuit.com/accountants/tools-proadvisor`.

When you click Work, you display the area of QB Accountant that provides practice-management support; see Chapter 16 for details on the tools available.

And when you click Apps, you visit the App Center, where you can search for apps that extend the capabilities of QuickBooks and QB Accountant. You can also view the apps you've already installed.

Across the top of the interface, you find a toolbar with the following elements, from left to right:

- **QB Accountant:** This button, which features the QuickBooks logo, offers you another way to display the client list shown in Figure 12-4.

- **Expand/Collapse:** This button, which has three horizontal lines, hides and displays the navigation bar in the same fashion as within QuickBooks.

- **Go to QuickBooks:** You can use this drop-down list to display a list of your clients; clicking a client name in the list opens the client's company.

>> **Accountant Tools:** Think of this button as being an accountant-specific version of the New button, offering quick links and tools that accountants frequently use when they're working on a client's books. (See Figure 12-5.) See Chapter 16 for details on these tools and on practice-management tools.

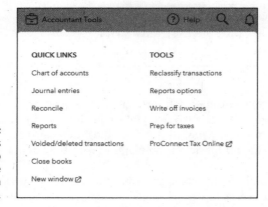

QUICK LINKS

Chart of accounts

Journal entries

Reconcile

Reports

Voided/deleted transactions

Close books

New window

TOOLS

Reclassify transactions

Reports options

Write off invoices

Prep for taxes

ProConnect Tax Online

FIGURE 12-5:
The tools available to accountants while working in a client company.

>> **Help:** This button displays help documentation for QuickBooks and QB Accountant.

>> **Search:** This feature works the same way that it does in QuickBooks, enabling you to find a list of recent transactions or reports.

>> **Notifications:** This feature displays messages from Intuit about new features in QuickBooks, webinars for accountants, and other information.

>> **Settings:** Click this button to display the Settings menu, which shows the settings you can establish for your own company, your client's company, and your QB Accountant account (see Figure 12-6).

You also can open the QuickBooks sample company from the Settings menu; read more about opening and working in the sample company in "Working with the Sample Company" later in this chapter.

REMEMBER

ProAdvisor Profile: This button, which looks like a person's head, allows you to view your ProAdvisor profile and any leads from potential clients. These features require you to complete the QuickBooks Online Certified ProAdvisor Certification program. As an added bonus, certified public accountants (CPAs) can earn continuing education credit for completing the program.

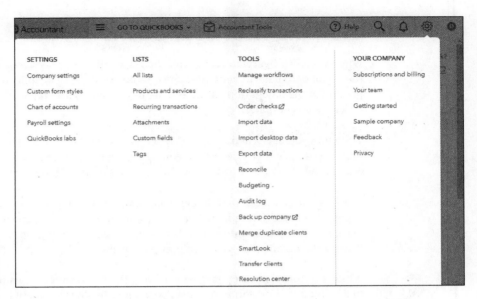

FIGURE 12-6:
The choices available on the Settings menu.

TIP

You can also attain Certified ProAdvisor Advanced Online, Payroll, and Desktop certifications. The ProAdvisor program also gives you access to marketing tools such as potential client leads from QuickBooks.

The navigation bar also has the following elements:

>> **New:** This button displays the New menu, which you use to create a client or a user from the home page. While working in a client's company or your own QuickBooks company, you use the New menu to create transactions.

>> **Clients:** This button, the first of several tools in the Your Practice section, enables you to display your client list.

>> **Team:** This button enables you to manage team members in your firm, as I discuss in "Setting Up Your Team" later in this chapter.

>> **ProAdvisor:** This button provides links to benefits and training offered by Intuit's ProAdvisor program.

>> **Work:** This button unlocks a to-do list of items to be completed in clients' accounting records. In addition, you can create client requests that post to your client's books, as well as create projects that are collections of tasks to be completed by your team.

>> **Apps:** This button provides access to the QuickBooks app store, which includes apps that may benefit your clients as well as your accounting firm.

Working with Your Books

When you click Overview in the Your Books section of the navigation bar, you open the Dashboard page of your own QuickBooks company. The links in the Your Books portion of the navigation bar match the links your client sees when they view their QuickBooks company.

The view you see when you open your own company's books in QB Accountant matches the view you see when you open any client's company; the only difference is the name of the company that appears on the QB Accountant toolbar.

The Dashboard screen of a QuickBooks company displays outstanding invoice and expense information, a list of your bank account balances, profit and loss information, and sales in interactive filters. Click part of any graphic on this page to display the details that make up that part of the graphic.

REMEMBER

While any company is open, you can click the Go to QuickBooks button to switch to a different client company. Also, you can redisplay the Clients page at any time by clicking the QB Accountant button on the toolbar.

Setting Up Your Team

If your accounting firm has more than one person who needs access to clients' QuickBooks companies, the person who creates the QB Accountant account becomes the master administrator and can set up as many other users as necessary. The other users get their own login credentials and access to clients specified by the master administrator; for those clients, the QB Accountant user can access the Accountant tools described in Chapter 16. The master administrator also specifies the user's level of access to the firm's information: basic, full, or custom.

TIP

Using separate login information helps maintain security in QB Accountant because a lot of financial information (product subscriptions and billing information, for example) is tied to the login information.

Here's the difference among basic, full, and custom access:

>> Users who have full access can open and work in the firm's books as well as in client QuickBooks companies. They can also access the Team page and change any user's privileges.

>> Users who have basic access can access only client QuickBooks companies.

>> Users who have custom access have basic or full access with at least one privilege set differently from the QB Accountant defaults.

To set up multiple users in a QB Accountant account, the master administrator or any firm member who has full access privileges sets up other members of the firm. During the process, an email is sent to the other firm members; I'll call them *invitees.* An invitee who accepts the invitation is prompted to establish their own QB Accountant login credentials. Follow these steps to set up a new user:

1. **Log in to QB Accountant.**

2. **Click Team on the navigation bar.**

   The Team page appears, as shown in Figure 12-7.

FIGURE 12-7:
View, edit,
and add
QB Accountant
team members.

3. **Click the Add User button.**

   The three-step Add User Wizard begins.

4. **On the first page of the Add User Wizard, fill in the name, email address, and (optional) title of the team member you want to add.**

5. **Click Next.**

   The second page of the Add User Wizard appears (see Figure 12-8). On this page, you identify the privileges related to your firm that you want to provide the team member. In this example, I set up a team member with custom access. This team member has access to the books of certain clients but doesn't have access to the firm's books or to firm-administration functions.

6. **Select the type of access you want to give to the team member.**

   You can assign Basic, Full, or Custom access; a description of each type of access appears on the right side of the page. Assign Full access to those team members who should have access to your company's books. Assign Basic access to give a team member access to client companies only.

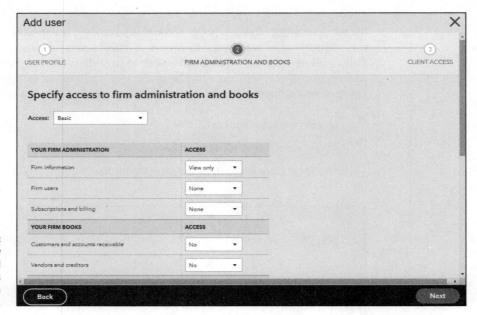

FIGURE 12-8:
Specify the new user's access level to your firm's administration and books.

TIP

If you change individual settings, the team member's access automatically changes to Custom.

7. **Click Next in the bottom-right corner of the page.**

   The last page of the Add User Wizard appears (see Figure 12-9). On this page, you identify the clients for whom the team member should be able to perform work.

8. **Deselect clients as necessary and then click Save.**

   The new user is added to your team and assigned a status of Invited. In addition, the Status column of the Team page indicates that an email invitation was sent to the user. After the user accepts the invitation, their status changes to Active.

When an invitee clicks the Accept Invite button in the email invitation, a page appears, showing the invitee's user ID or email address and prompting the invitee to establish a password and (if they're being granted full privileges) a security question and answer. When the invitee supplies the information and clicks Create Account, a Success message appears. The invitee can click Continue to log in. The home page of a team member who has no access to the firm's books looks like Figure 12-10.

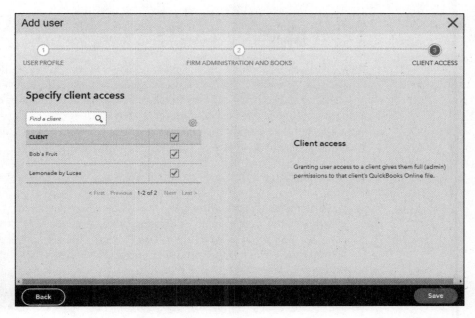

FIGURE 12-9:
You can give a team member access to your firm's clients on a selective basis.

FIGURE 12-10:
The home page of an invited team member who has limited privileges in QB Accountant.

Going forward, the team member navigates to `https://qbo.intuit.com` and supplies their login credentials to log in.

TIP

If the team member already has a QuickBooks or QB Accountant login, they click the Accept Invitation button in the invitation email. If the team member has no account, they click the Create Account button instead.

LEAD ACCOUNTANTS

As you'd expect, you add clients who use QuickBooks to your QB Accountant account so that you can work easily with their accounting data. (You can read about adding clients to your account in Chapter 13.) For most firms, managing clients involves establishing responsibility for various clients. To address this need, QB Accountant uses the Lead Accountant role, assigned to the firm member through whom a client provided access to a QuickBooks subscription.

QB Accountant assigns the Lead Accountant role when

- **A client invites an accountant.** The invited accountant goes through the process of accepting the client invitation and selecting the firm under which the client is assigned. After the accountant accepts the invitation, the accounting firm has access to the client, and the invited accountant — who is a member of the firm — is assigned the Lead Accountant role.

- **A firm member creates a client company.** The team member within the firm who creates a client company in QB Accountant becomes the Lead Accountant. Chapter 13 describes how to add clients to your QB Accountant account.

But things happen, and a team member with a Lead Accountant role for one or more clients might leave the firm. In this case, you can make the team member inactive. (You can't delete users in QB Accountant.) You'll be prompted to assign a new Lead Accountant to the client(s) associated with the (now-inactive) team member.

To make the team member inactive, navigate to the Team page (refer to Figure 12-7), and select the team member. The Edit User dialog box appears. Choose Inactive in the Status list box, and save your changes.

Controlling the Appearance of the Client List

You can use the Clients page to open any client's QuickBooks company, and you can control the appearance of the Clients page.

To open any client's company, click the QuickBooks logo in the Status column of the Client List page. Or, if you prefer, choose the company you want to open from the Go to QuickBooks drop-down list on the QB Accountant toolbar. Note that in Figure 12-11, the second company in the list can't be accessed because its subscription wasn't renewed. Live companies can be identified by the QuickBooks logo to the left of the client name.

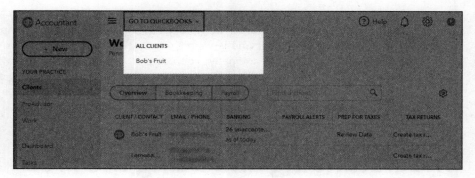

FIGURE 12-11:
Click a
QuickBooks logo
or use the Go to
QuickBooks
drop-down list to
open a client's
company.

REMEMBER

If you click a client's name rather than the QuickBooks logo, you don't open the client's company. Instead, you see overview details such as tasks to complete in the client's books, the account watch list, and payroll alerts.

You can control the appearance of the Client List page. You can use the list box above the table to filter the list to show all clients, for example, or only the QuickBooks Payroll clients in your list. You can also control the columns of information that appear on the page, and you can hide or display inactive clients. (For more information on making a client inactive, see "Removing clients from your ProAdvisor Preferred Pricing subscription" later in this chapter.) Click Settings just above the list of clients, and make choices from the Settings menu (see Figure 12-12).

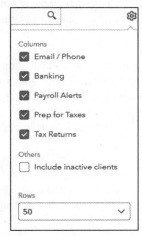

FIGURE 12-12:
Control the
appearance of
the Client List
page with the
Settings menu.

REMEMBER

QB Accountant contains multiple Settings menus. One of them appears on the QB Accountant toolbar and is visible on most QB Accountant pages, even while you work in a client's company; you use that Settings menu to provide information about your QB Accountant account, establish settings, view lists, and access tools. On the Clients page, the Settings menu appears above the list of clients; you use that menu to control the information that appears on the page.

Understanding and Using the Free QB Accountant Company

As I mention at the beginning of this chapter, QB Accountant users get one free QuickBooks Plus subscription to use for their own books. To open the company reserved for you, click — yep, you guessed it — any choice within the Your Books section of the navigation bar. If you click Your Books, you'll see the Overview page for your company. Alternatively, click Your Practice to display your team list. The interface you see when you open your company looks just like the interface you see when you open any client's company. This interface varies slightly from what a client sees.

You can use the free subscription to manage the books for your firm, including importing your data from QuickBooks Desktop if you've decided to migrate to the cloud. You can refer to the chapters in Part 1 of this book when you're ready to start entering transactions because QB Accountant users and QuickBooks users do so in the same fashion.

TIP

You can import QuickBooks Desktop information, or you can import list information. For details on importing lists, see Chapter 4. If you want to try importing a QuickBooks Desktop company, see Chapter 13 and the appendix, which describes the limitations associated with importing information. Please note that importing into a regular QuickBooks company has time limits, but importing into the QB Accountant free company doesn't.

REMEMBER

Be aware that the Your Books company is intended to house the firm's data, not a client's data or the data of some other business owned by the QB Accountant owner. The Your Books company ties into QB Accountant and updates as clients are added, so if you use it to store the wrong kind of data, that data will be messed up as you add other clients. Each client you add in QB Accountant, for example, is automatically set up as a customer in the Your Books company, although team members aren't set up as employees.

Working with the Sample Company

If you've been a QuickBooks Desktop user, you know that QuickBooks Desktop comes with a variety of sample companies that you can use to test company behavior. Like its desktop cousin, QuickBooks Online has a sample company. To open the sample company, follow these steps:

1. **Click Settings on the QB Accountant toolbar.**

   The Settings menu appears.

2. **In the Your Company section, click Sample Company.**

   A warning message informs you that you'll be logged out of QB Accountant if you continue.

3. **Click Continue.**

   You're signed out of your company and signed in to the sample company, Craig's Design and Landscaping Services (see Figure 12-13). The interface looks like the QB Accountant interface you see when you open a client's company. The Accountant button is in the top-left corner, for example, and the QB Accountant toolbar is to the right of the Accountant button. The toolbar contains the same tools you see while working in a client's company.

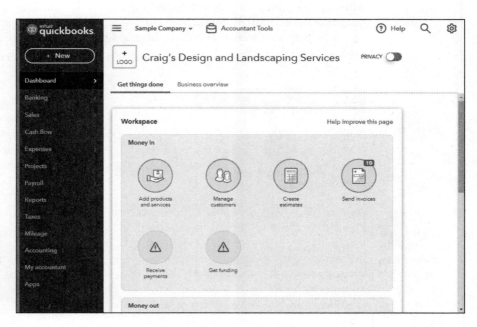

FIGURE 12-13: Craig's Design and Landscaping Services is the QuickBooks Online sample company.

TIP

To redisplay your QB Accountant interface (similar to the one shown in Figure 12-11 earlier in this chapter), click the Go QuickBooks button, which currently displays Sample Company, and then choose Back to Practice. You'll need to sign back in to your QB Accountant account.

If your clients would like to test drive QuickBooks Online Plus or Advanced you can direct them to https://intuit.me/3qd8eqC. This page contains links to both sample companies so that your clients can try before they buy.

Closing Companies in QB Accountant

When you finish working in a company, you don't close it in QB Accountant the way you might in QuickBooks Desktop. When you switch from one QuickBooks company to another, the first client's company is closed automatically.

TIP

To work in two QuickBooks companies simultaneously, you can use two different browsers, two instances of a single browser, or Chrome's Profile feature (if you're using Chrome). For more information on working with QuickBooks in multiple windows, see Chapter 15. For details on using Chrome, see Chapter 18.

Although you don't close QuickBooks companies while working in QB Accountant, you close QB Accountant by clicking the last button on the toolbar (most likely, it will have your first initial) and then clicking Sign Out on the pop-up window (see Figure 12-14).

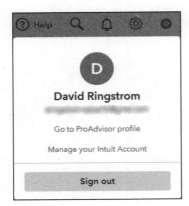

FIGURE 12-14:
Exit QB
Accountant by
signing out.

Working with ProAdvisor Preferred Pricing

As I mention in Chapter 2, if you're an accounting professional, you can sign up for the free ProAdvisor Preferred Pricing program. This offers an ongoing 30% discount on most QuickBooks products if you allow Intuit to charge your bank account or credit card automatically for your clients' subscriptions. QB Accountant offers invoice templates that you can in turn use to bill your clients. Intuit provides a monthly consolidated bill for all the QuickBooks subscriptions you manage. Conversely you can share a 30% discount that is good for 12 months when Intuit bills your clients directly. For all the latest details on these offerings visit https://quickbooks.intuit.com/accountants/products-solutions/pricing-promotions/papp/.

REMEMBER

You don't have to enroll clients as part of the ProAdvisor Preferred Pricing program, but if you do, you can pass the reduced subscription prices along to your clients, saving them money and making you a hero. This program was formerly referred to as both the Wholesale Pricing program and the Wholesale Billing program.

Signing up for ProAdvisor Preferred Pricing

Accounting professionals are automatically signed up for the free ProAdvisor Preferred Pricing program logging into QB Accountant for the first time. The program doesn't become active, however, until the accounting professional enters billing information in the Billing Profile in QB Accountant.

Follow these steps to enter information in the Billing Profile:

1. **Click Settings on the toolbar.**

2. **In the Your Company column, select Subscriptions and Billing.**

   The Subscriptions and Billing page appears, displaying two tabs:

   - The Your Subscriptions tab lists exactly what you'd expect: clients whose subscriptions you're managing, the QuickBooks product (Essentials, Plus, and so on), the subscription price, and the status.

   - Initially, the Billing Details tab displays payment information you can provide to subscribe to the ProAdvisor Preferred Pricing program. After you subscribe to the ProAdvisor Preferred Pricing program, the Billing Details tab provides key details, such as the total number of subscriptions, the amount you currently owe, and past monthly charges.

TIP

   If you subscribe to the ProAdvisor Preferred Pricing program, the Billing Details tab shows the details you need to bill clients who are part of your subscription for the portion they owe.

3. **Click the Billing Details tab.**

4. **Fill in all Payment Information fields.**

5. **Click Subscribe.**

    The Your Account page reappears, and ProAdvisor Preferred Pricing is activated.

Adding existing clients to your ProAdvisor Preferred Pricing subscription

As I discuss in Chapter 13, you can add clients to your QB Accountant account without using the consolidated billing option. That is, you can opt to add retail clients who manage their own subscriptions to your account. "Why," you ask, "would I have added clients to my account without adding them to my consolidated billing subscription?" Well, to name just two possible reasons,

» You might have added clients to your account before you joined the ProAdvisor Preferred Pricing program.

» You might have added clients to your account who wanted to manage their own subscriptions.

LIMITATIONS OF PROADVISOR PREFERRED PRICING

You don't have to administer your clients' subscriptions through the Pro Advisor Preferred Pricing subscription — you can still work with clients who pay for their own QuickBooks subscription directly. Administering a client's subscription can save your clients money, but it also makes you responsible for collecting subscription costs. Also, the program may not be right for all clients, including the following:

- Companies created through the ProAdvisor Preferred Pricing program can transfer master administrator rights. But *no* accountant can be removed from the company as long as that company is part of your consolidated billing, including an accountant who isn't associated with the firm housing the company in the ProAdvisor Preferred Pricing program.

- The free 30-day trial isn't available when an accounting professional creates a QuickBooks company through QB Accountant. Instead, subscription fees begin immediately.

Chapter 13 shows you how to add clients to your QB Accountant account as retail clients or as part of your consolidated billing subscription.

Before you can move an existing client to your consolidated billing subscription, you must enter billing information for your account, meaning a bank or credit card account.

Further, the client's subscription must be eligible for the ProAdvisor Preferred Pricing program. Use the following criteria to determine eligibility:

>> The client company's Next Payment Date must be within 33 days of the day you attempt to add the company to the ProAdvisor Preferred Pricing subscription. You can find this date in the client company by choosing Settings ⇨ Account and Settings ⇨ Subscriptions and Billing.

>> Clients must have an active monthly billing subscription and must be listed on your Clients page. See Chapter 13 for details on adding clients to your Clients page.

You can add only monthly QuickBooks subscriptions to the ProAdvisor Preferred Pricing program; annual subscriptions aren't eligible. Annual billing subscriptions can be changed to monthly billing subscriptions 30 days before the next annual billing date.

>> Clients must be in the region of QuickBooks that corresponds with your region of QB Accountant (United States, United Kingdom, Australia, France, or Canada).

>> QB Accountant users in the United States can add QuickBooks Self-Employed companies to ProAdvisor Preferred Pricing subscriptions if the client is subscribed to the stand-alone plan.

Note that ProAdvisor Preferred Pricing isn't available to QuickBooks Self-Employed/Turbo Tax bundle users, because QB Accountant has its own default tax software. Turnaround time for the client to be moved to ProAdvisor Preferred Pricing is 24 hours.

How do you go about adding a client to your consolidated billing subscription? First, you must add the client to your client list, as shown in Chapter 13. Then follow these steps:

1. **Click Clients on the navigation bar.**

2. **Click Settings on the toolbar.**

3. **In the Your Company section, choose Subscriptions and Billing from the drop-down list.**

   The Subscriptions and Billing page appears.

4. **In the Client-Billed Subscriptions section, click the Client Actions link in the Action column, and then choose Transfer Billing to Me.**

   Note: This button is available only if you've filled in the Billing Details tab.

5. **Review the charges in the Subscription Summary section, confirm or adjust your payment method, and then click Transfer Billing to Me.**

   The client will now appear on the Accountant-billed Subscriptions tab of your Subscriptions and Billing page.

Removing clients from your ProAdvisor Preferred Pricing subscription

Sometimes, you and a client need to part ways. If you previously added that client's QuickBooks company to your consolidated billing subscription and need to move on, you'll want to remove the client:

1. **Click Settings on the toolbar.**

2. **In the Your Company section, choose Subscriptions and Billing from the drop-down list.**

   The Subscriptions and Billing page appears.

WHY CAN'T I MIGRATE A CLIENT?

You may not be able to move a particular client to your Accountant-billed subscriptions for a variety of reasons. Here are a few:

- The client company's next payment date must be within 33 days of the day you attempt to add the company to your ProAdvisor Preferred Pricing subscription.

- Clients must have an active monthly billing subscription and be listed in your client list.

  You can change a yearly billing subscription to a monthly billing subscription, but only 30 days before the next annual billing date.

- The client's region must match your region.

- You can't add QuickBooks Self-Employed companies to a consolidated billing subscription.

3. **Find the company you want to remove from your consolidated billing subscription.**

4. **In the Actions column, select Transfer Billing to Client.**

   The Transfer Billing to Client confirmation page appears.

5. **Review information shown, and then click Confirm Transfer.**

The client no longer appears on your Accountant-billed subscriptions listing.

REMEMBER

When you remove a QuickBooks company from your consolidated billing subscription, that company is no longer eligible for the ProAdvisor Preferred Pricing discount, and all previous discounts are removed as well. The client will be billed the standard rate for their subscription as of the date the subscription is removed unless they establish a relationship with another QB Accountant user. In that case, the client regains the discounts starting from the ProAdvisor Preferred Pricing activation date.

Be aware that removing a client from your consolidated billing subscription doesn't remove the client from your client list. You can't delete QuickBooks clients, but you can make them inactive by following these steps:

1. **Click Clients to display your client list.**

2. **In the Actions column, click the down arrow next to the name of the client you want to make inactive, and choose Make Inactive from the drop-down list.**

   A prompt asks whether you're sure you want to make the client inactive.

3. **Click Yes.**

   The page shown in Figure 12-15 appears, and the client no longer appears in the client list.

FIGURE 12-15:
Click Edit Client to display a menu from which you can make a client inactive.

TIP

You can change the client's status back to Active if you opt to display inactive clients on the Clients page. Click Settings above the Actions column in the table on the Clients page, and select the Include Inactive option (refer to Figure 12-13). QB Accountant displays all your clients, both active and inactive. To make an inactive client active again, click the Make Active link in the Actions column next to the client's name.

Stopping consolidated billing

At some point, you may decide that you don't want to participate in the consolidated billing subscription or manage QuickBooks subscriptions for your clients. Although you can't cancel your ProAdvisor Preferred Pricing subscription, you can stop using it. Nothing prevents you from working with clients who manage their own QuickBooks subscriptions.

REMEMBER

You can't cancel your ProAdvisor Preferred Pricing subscription because that action would also cancel the QuickBooks subscriptions of the clients who are assigned to your consolidated billing subscription.

To stop using the consolidated billing subscription, you need to remove all the clients who are currently in your subscription. For details, refer to "Removing clients from your ProAdvisor Preferred Pricing subscription" earlier in this chapter.

After you remove all companies from your Billing Profile, Intuit will no longer bill you, because you won't have any clients in your consolidated billing subscription.

Chapter **13**

Adding Companies to the QB Accountant Client List

After getting established in QB Accountant, you need to populate the client list with QuickBooks clients, which can happen in a couple of ways. In addition, you may need to help a client set up a QuickBooks company by creating a new company or by importing information into the QuickBooks company. This chapter shows you how to add client companies to the Client list and how to import company information from the QuickBooks Desktop product.

TIP

Need to remove a client from your Client list? See Chapter 12 for details on making a client inactive.

Adding a Client's Company to the Client List

You can add a client company to the Client list in two ways:

>> By letting your client create a company and then invite you to access it

>> By creating a client's company for the client

If you participate in the ProAdvisor Preferred Program that I discuss in Chapter 12, you can opt to manage clients' subscription for them. In this case, Intuit bills you for clients' subscriptions, and then you bill your clients. Alternatively, your clients can opt to manage their own QuickBooks subscriptions but still give you access to their books. At the time this book was written, Intuit was running specials on QuickBooks through its main website. In addition, Intuit was offering discounts for QuickBooks companies managed by accountants using QB Accountant regardless of whether the accountant or the client created the client's QuickBooks company.

TIP

You're not bound by one choice or the other — that is, managing a client's subscription or not managing a client's subscription. You can change who manages the subscription at any time if you participate in the ProAdvisor Preferred Pricing Program.

REMEMBER

After you add a new client to the list, you'll likely want to start examining their books, and the Client Overview feature described in Chapter 14 can help you sort through the information.

When a client invites you to be the accountant user

When a client creates their own company, they accept the responsibility to pay for their company's QuickBooks subscription. Even so, your client can invite you to access the company by using the Invite Accountant process. You can manage any type of QuickBooks subscription in QB Accountant, including Schedule C and Pro-Connect Tax Online clients.

Your client should follow these steps:

1. Open your QuickBooks company, and click Settings.

The Settings menu appears, as shown in Figure 13-1.

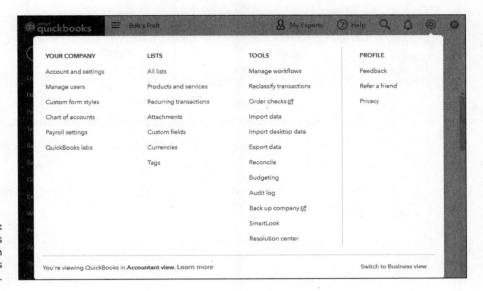

FIGURE 13-1:
The Settings
menu in
QuickBooks
Online.

2. **In the Your Company column, click Manage Users.**

   The Manage Users page appears. This page identifies the company's primary admin and enables you to add users to your QuickBooks subscription.

3. **Click the Accounting Firms tab (see Figure 13-2).**

   The window shown in Figure 13-3 appears.

4. **Provide an email address, and click Invite.**

   The Accounting Firms tab of the Manage Users page reappears, showing the accountant's email with a status of Invited. An email invites the accountant to sign in to your company. From this page, if necessary, you can resend the invitation.

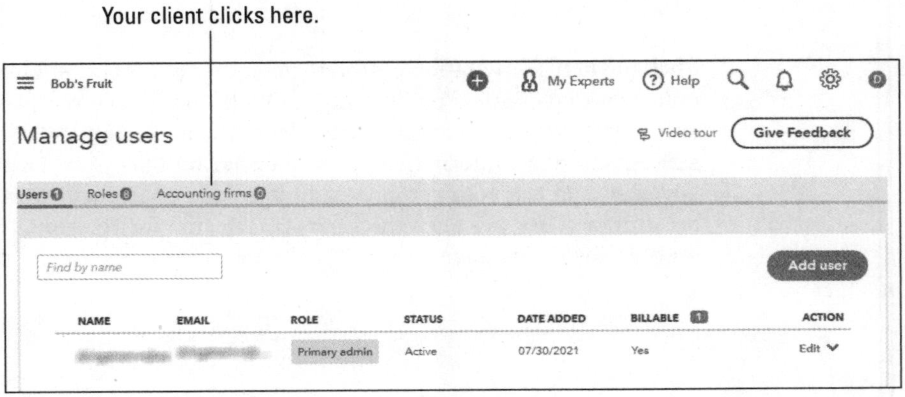

Your client clicks here.

FIGURE 13-2:
The Manage
Users page has
three tabs: Users,
Roles, and
Accounting Firms.

FIGURE 13-3:
The client fills in
the accountant's
email
information.

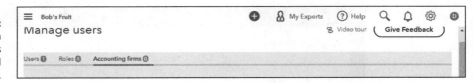

5. **Provide your cellphone number to generate a verification code.**

   You needs to enter a six-digit code that is texted to you before your invitation can be sent.

The email you receive from your client will look something like the one shown in Figure 13-4.

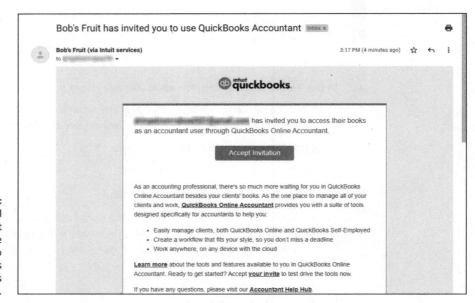

FIGURE 13-4:
A sample email
an accountant
might receive
when invited to
access a client's
QuickBooks
company.

Click the Accept Invitation button to open the QB Accountant login page. After you enter your credentials and log in, the Welcome Back screen appears. Choose the accounting firm you want to use to accept the invitation and click Continue on the subsequent page. Alternatively, if you click Don't See Your Firm? QuickBooks will advise you to ask your company admin to add you to your firm's QB Accountant account or allow you to create a new QB Accountant account. Then click Continue on the subsequent page.

Once you've fully accepted the invitation, QB Accountant opens, and the new client appears in your client list, as shown in Figure 13-5. By default, QB Accountant gives access to the team member invited by your client and to your primary admin. If you click the Edit Client link to the right of any client's name, you can use the Edit Client page to identify additional people in your firm who should have access to the client's QuickBooks Online books by way of the Team Access section.

FIGURE 13-5:
A Client List page after you accept an invitation from a client to be the accountant.

You'll also get an email telling you that the client has been added to your QB Accountant account.

When you invite a client to your practice

You don't have to wait for clients to invite you to be their accountant; you can issue the invitation.

You can invite any QuickBooks user to your practice except a Simple Start user. Simple Start users must create their own companies and then invite you, the accountant, to their QuickBooks company, as described in "When a client invites you to be the accountant user" earlier in this chapter.

TIP

Your client needs to have a QuickBooks Online account before you send the invitation. If your client hasn't yet created an account, you can create it for them by using an email address that the client supplies. A QuickBooks Online company created by an accountant doesn't get a 30-day trial period, but the ProAdvisor discounts I mention in Chapter 12 can be applied to companies created through a trial-period offer.

To invite a client to your practice, follow these steps:

1. **Open QB Accountant.**

2. **Click Clients on the navigation bar.**

3. **Click the Add Client button in the top right-hand corner.**

   The Client Contact Information page appears (see Figure 13-6).

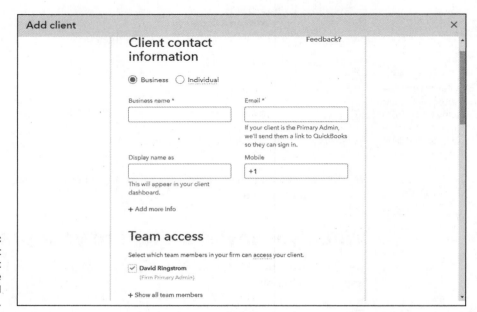

FIGURE 13-6:
The Client
Contact
Information page
of the Add
Client Wizard.

4. **Select Business or Individual, depending on whether you're adding a business or a self-employed individual.**

5. **Provide a name and an email address for the company.**

   If you provide a name and an email address for which no QuickBooks company exists, a new company will be created. Otherwise, QB Accountant adds any existing company that uses the name and email address you provide to your account.

6. **(Optional) Click Add More Info to provide billing and shipping addresses, as well as the company phone number and website address.**

7. **Identify firm team members who should have access to the QuickBooks company.**

You can change access privileges later.

8. **In the Products section, choose whether the client is billed directly or whether you want to add the client to your ProAdvisor Preferred Billing subscription.**

9. **Select a QuickBooks subscription level (Advanced, Plus, Essentials, or Self-Employed) or Payroll Standalone Subscription (Payroll Elite, Payroll Premium, or Payroll Core).**

REMEMBER

Your clients will receive your discount on payroll stand-alone subscriptions but will be billed directly by Intuit. Only QuickBooks Online subscriptions offer a choice between direct or wholesale billing.

10. **Specify whether you should become the client company's primary admin.**

If the client is the primary admin, they receive a link to QuickBooks so that they can sign in. Only your client can be the primary admin of a QuickBooks Self-Employed company. You can decide to be the primary admin of companies at any other subscription level.

11. **Click Save.**

The company is created and appears in the list of companies on the Clients page. If the new company doesn't appear, refresh your browser page or log out of QB Accountant and then log back in again.

Transferring primary rights to your client

As described in the preceding section, when you add a client company to your QB Accountant account, you have the option to assign yourself as the primary admin; in this case, you're also assigned as the accountant user for the company. But you can transfer the primary admin role to your client without affecting your status as the accountant user.

To transfer the role of primary admin to your client, you follow a two-part process:

>> You add the client to the company as a user and, in the process, invite the client to become a company admin.

>> After the client accepts the invitation to become an admin user, you transfer the primary admin role to the client — again, using an invitation process.

Inviting the client to become the primary admin

You can transfer the primary admin status to your client. Follow these steps:

1. **Click the Go To QuickBooks button at the top of the QB Accountant screen and then choose your client's company.**

2. **Click Settings, and choose Manage Users in the Your Company column.**

   The Manage Users page appears, initially showing only the accountant user who created the company.

3. **Click Add User.**

   The Add a New User Wizard starts.

4. **On the Select User Type page, shown in Figure 13-7, select Company Admin, and click Next.**

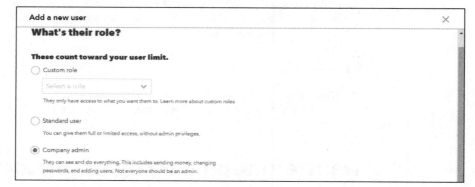

FIGURE 13-7: Select Company Admin.

5. **On the Enter User's Email Address page, provide the client's email address (and, optionally, name), and click Save.**

   The user is added to the Manage Users page, and a message appears, explaining that an email invitation will invite the user to sign in to the company. The email explains that the user must create a QuickBooks user ID unless one already exists. In most cases, if you set up a company for a client, the client doesn't yet have a QuickBooks Online login.

6. **Click Save.**

   The new user appears on the Manage Users page with Invited status.

When the client receives the email invitation to become the company administrator, the invitation contains a Let's Go! link. When the client clicks the link, a QuickBooks login screen appears, with the user's email address already filled in and a prompt for them to enter a password. Typically, the client doesn't have a QuickBooks login yet and needs to go through the process of creating a new one; when they finish filling in the password, they click Accept Invitation to be logged in. They receive a message indicating that they have successfully accepted the invitation and can access the QuickBooks company.

Transferring the primary admin role to the client

When the client has accepted the invitation to become an admin user, you're ready to transfer primary admin rights to the client. Open the client's QuickBooks company in QB Accountant and display the Manage Users page by choosing Settings ➪ Manage Users. You appear as the primary admin, and the client user's status is Active and has a User Type of Admin (see Figure 13-8). To transfer the role of primary admin to the client, click the arrow next to Edit in the Action column, and choose Make Primary Admin from the drop-down list.

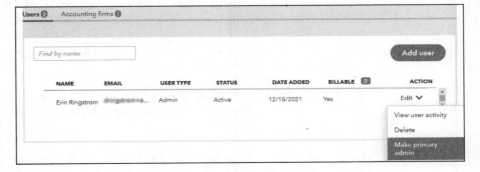

FIGURE 13-8: Assigning the role of primary admin to the client.

REMEMBER

Click the arrow next to Edit if you want to make your client the primary admin. If you click the Edit link, you'll be able to choose between Standard User and Admin. A distinction between admin and primary admin is that the primary admin is a superuser with rights that can't be changed by other admins. The primary admin can relinquish their role, but primary admin rights can't be changed or altered by other users.

QB Accountant displays a message explaining that only one user can serve as primary admin and that when you transfer that role to your client, your access changes to admin; you'll no longer be the primary admin.

An automatic email invites your client to become the primary admin; the client can accept or decline the invitation. Assuming that the client accepts, they're prompted to log in to QuickBooks, where they see a message explaining that the primary admin role has been transferred successfully and that the former primary admin — you — has been notified.

The next time you log in to the client's QuickBooks company, you'll no longer appear in the Manage Users section of the Manage Users page. Your client is the primary admin for the company, and you become an admin user.

Removing a client from your accountant-billed subscriptions

If you participate in the ProAdvisor Preferred Pricing Program (formerly known as Wholesale Pricing and Wholesale Billing), billing responsibility becomes a matter of choice:

» You can pay for the client's subscription and then bill the client for the cost of the subscription.

» You can assign billing responsibility to the client.

Further, whether the client is part of your accountant-billed subscription or the client is assuming billing responsibility, you can opt to be the primary admin or to assign that role to the client. For clients who want to be part of your accountant-billed subscription and assume the role of primary admin, you must be an invited accountant in the client's company.

If you retain the primary admin role, you can transfer primary admin privileges to the client later. See "Transferring the primary admin role to the client" earlier in this chapter.

At this writing, if a QuickBooks client that isn't already a primary admin wants to remove an accountant, the firm managing the client's QuickBooks subscription must first remove the client from their accountant-billed subscription list, even if the accountant the QuickBooks client wants to remove isn't affiliated with the firm managing the client's QuickBooks subscription.

To remove a client from your accountant-billed subscriptions, follow these steps:

1. **In QB Accountant, choose Settings ⇨ Subscriptions and Billing.**

    The Subscriptions and Billing page appears.

2. **On the Accountant-billed Subscriptions tab, scroll down to the select the company you want to remove.**

3. **From the drop-down menu in the Actions column, choose Remove from Billing.**

Your client will now be responsible for their own billing and will move to the Client-billed Subscriptions tab.

Importing QuickBooks Desktop Data into QuickBooks Online

You can import your desktop company's information into a QuickBooks Online company if both these conditions apply to your situation:

» You've been using QuickBooks for Mac 2013 and later or QuickBooks Desktop for Windows Pro or Premier 2008 or later in the United States or Canada.

» Your QuickBooks Online subscription is less than 60 days old.

Accountants can help clients import a QuickBooks Desktop company into a Quick-Books Online company. During the conversion process, QuickBooks Online makes a copy of your QuickBooks Desktop company file that it can import into an online company. Your QuickBooks Desktop data remains available for you to reference as needed.

TIP

Users in countries other than the United States, Canada, and the United Kingdom might be able to import QuickBooks Desktop information into QuickBooks Online with the help of an outside service; contact Intuit for more information. Users of QuickBooks Desktop for Windows 2007 and earlier, QuickBooks for the Mac, and QuickBooks Enterprise should contact Intuit for details on importing their data into QuickBooks Online. Accountants who import their own data into the free QB Accountant company have considerably more time to import: up to 1,060 days (almost 3 years) after creating the QB Accountant account.

Assuming that you meet the criteria outlined previously, here are the five steps of the conversion process:

1. Review general conversion considerations.

2. Examine what won't convert.

3. Update your QuickBooks Desktop software.

4. Perform the steps to export a copy of your QuickBooks Desktop data that QuickBooks Online uses for importing.

5. Review the tasks you need to complete after converting.

Preparing for conversion

Before you get started, it's important to understand several facts about converting QuickBooks Desktop data for use in QuickBooks Online:

>> You can import QuickBooks Desktop data only in the first 60 days of using QuickBooks Online. Be aware that converting QuickBooks Desktop data doesn't affect the data in the QuickBooks Desktop product; you can continue to use QuickBooks Desktop. (You definitely should consider doing this, at least long enough to confirm that QuickBooks Online will work for you.)

>> Be aware that the process of importing QuickBooks Desktop data into an existing QuickBooks Online company overwrites any list and transaction data already stored in that company.

>> Some information may not be imported when you move your file. See the next section, "Understanding what won't import," for general information and Appendix A for detailed information. Take the time to familiarize yourself with these import limitations and with the differences between QuickBooks Desktop and QuickBooks Online.

>> QuickBooks Online supports Intuit Online Payroll and QuickBooks Online Payroll to manage payroll. In some cases, your QuickBooks Desktop payroll data will update your year-to-date totals automatically. But if that data doesn't migrate, and you intend to use QuickBooks Online Payroll, you need to enter payroll totals as described in Chapter 9. Don't turn on or set up QuickBooks Online Payroll until you convert your desktop data. If you've already turned on payroll in your QuickBooks Online company, see the nearby sidebar "Payroll and Desktop data conversion."

>> Make sure that all your sales tax filings are current before you export your QuickBooks Desktop data. You may need to make adjustment entries to sales tax filings in QuickBooks Online after you import the information.

>> Make sure that you're using QuickBooks Desktop 2016 or later. For more information, see the sidebar "Using a QuickBooks Desktop trial for conversion" later in this chapter.

Before you dive into converting your data, stack the odds for success in your favor by doing some homework. First, examine your QuickBooks Desktop data file to make sure that it will convert. In your QuickBooks Desktop product, open your company and press F2 to display the Product Information dialog box, shown in Figure 13-9. In particular, take note of the Total Targets figure in the File Information section. If your data file's number of targets falls below 350,000, you can proceed.

PAYROLL AND DESKTOP DATA CONVERSION

If you've already turned on payroll in your QuickBooks Online company, don't attempt to import your QuickBooks Desktop file into that QuickBooks Online company. Instead, set up a new, empty QuickBooks Online company file, and cancel the subscription for the company in which you turned on payroll. If the company in which you've been working is a trial, you can let the trial run out instead of canceling. The theory is that you set up the original QuickBooks Online company with Payroll to see how things work, and you'll be fine if you start over and import your QuickBooks Desktop data. If you need to cancel a subscription, do so from the Billing and Subscription tab of the Account and Settings dialog box (choose Settings ➪ Account and Settings ➪ Billing & Subscription).

FIGURE 13-9:
Check the number of targets in your QuickBooks Desktop company.

Total targets

		Versions Used on File	Last accessed	08/23/2007 14:08:12
File Size	47180 K	V28.0D R1 08/08/2017		
Page Size	4096	RB 15-12-2021	**CONDENSE INFORMATION**	
Total Transactions	1219		Last run	None
Total Targets	5937	RB 15-12-2022	Last as of date	None
Total Links	2504	V28.0D R3 09/03/2017	Last payroll deleted	None
Dictionary Entries	196	V32.0D R1 08/30/2021	Last inventory deleted	None
DB File Fragments	56	RB 12/15/2022	List Information	

REMEMBER

If your data file's number of targets exceeds 350,000, condense your data. (Condensing reduces the size of your data file and removes inactive list entries, and smaller data files tend to convert better. To do so, choose File ➪ Utilities ➪ Condense Data.) If your company's targets still exceed 350,000, consider importing only lists, as described in Chapter 4.

Next, using the version of the QuickBooks Desktop product for your country (United States, Canada, or United Kingdom), verify your data file and then condense it so that it includes approximately one year's worth of data.

WARNING

Before you condense your data, make sure that you back up your data, and put the backup in a safe place. That way, you're covered in case something strange happens, which isn't likely, but it's always better to be safe than sorry. Also, create an additional backup before you export your data to QuickBooks Online.

If you suspect that the QuickBooks Desktop company data isn't in good shape — if you get errors while verifying or condensing, for example — you can try using the File ➪ Utilities ➪ Rebuild command and then rerunning the File ➪ Utilities ➪ Condense Data function. If you still get errors, consider importing lists only as described in Chapter 4.

REMEMBER

You should plan to keep your QuickBooks Desktop data file around, if for no other reason than to refer to it for historical data as needed. Many people opt to run QuickBooks Desktop and QuickBooks Online simultaneously for a month or two to make sure that QuickBooks Online is performing as they expect. This process is referred to as running the accounting systems in parallel.

Understanding what won't import

When you convert a QuickBooks Desktop company to QuickBooks Online, some data fully converts, some partially converts, and some doesn't convert at all. In addition, QuickBooks Online contains comparable alternatives for some QuickBooks Desktop features and doesn't contain alternatives for others. See Appendix A for details on data conversion.

You can import any QuickBooks Desktop for Windows company or any QuickBooks for Mac company by using a U.S. version of QuickBooks, including companies with the Multicurrency feature turned on, as long as the company falls within the limitation of 350,000 targets. You also can import QuickBooks Desktop companies by using UK and Canadian versions, again including companies that have Multicurrency turned on.

In general, the following types of files won't convert and therefore can't be imported:

REMEMBER

>> You can't import QuickBooks Desktop data into any QuickBooks Online company that was created more than 60 days earlier except for accountant company files. (You can import QuickBooks Desktop accountant company files into a QB Accountant company within 1,060 days of creating the QB Accountant account.)

When I say, "accountant company files," I'm talking about importing a QuickBooks Desktop company file into the Your Books company available in QB Accountant.

>> You can't import a QuickBooks Desktop company into international QuickBooks Online subscriptions other than UK and Canadian editions.

>> You can't import non-Intuit accounting software company files. If you need to import company data from a non-Intuit product, you'll need to work with Intuit's customer service team.

>> You can't directly import accounting data stored in spreadsheet files. But you can import this data via a third-party app called Transaction Pro, available at http://appcenter.intuit.com/transactionproimporter.

Appendix A describes the limitations you'll encounter if you import a QuickBooks Desktop company, so I suggest that you review it carefully so that you'll know what to expect.

After you review the general considerations in the preceding section and the limitations for importing in Appendix A, you're ready to import your QuickBooks Desktop company into QuickBooks Online.

It's important to understand that even if your company data meets the preceding criteria, some data still won't convert when you import; the following list identifies some of the more visible things that don't convert. For details, see Appendix A:

>> **Reconciliation reports:** Save your Reconciliation reports in QuickBooks Desktop or as PDF files in case you need to access them later. In QuickBooks Online, continue reconciling where you left off. See Chapter 8 for details on reconciling accounts.

>> **Recurring credit card charges:** In Merchant Center, cancel each existing automatic credit card recurring charge and re-create it in QuickBooks Online as a recurring sales receipt. All other recurring transactions convert and import.

TIP

On the good-news side, QuickBooks Online imports subaccounts it finds in your QuickBooks Desktop chart of accounts. Previous versions didn't support this capability.

>> **Reports:** Find a similar report in QuickBooks Online and customize it to your preference. See Chapter 10, and check out the QuickBooks Online App Center or the app store at https://quickbooks.intuit.com/app/apps/home for a list of reporting apps that can help your business.

>> **Audit trail:** Your desktop audit trail won't come over, but all changes going forward will be captured in the Audit Log within QuickBooks Online.

>> **Nonposting transactions or accounts:** These items won't convert except for estimates and purchase orders.

Updating your edition of QuickBooks Desktop

Intuit recommends using the 2016 version of QuickBooks Desktop or later to convert your data to QuickBooks Online. If you're using a version of QuickBooks Desktop earlier than 2016, see the nearby sidebar "Using a QuickBooks Desktop trial for conversion."

USING A QUICKBOOKS DESKTOP TRIAL FOR CONVERSION

If you're using a version of QuickBooks Desktop from 2015 or earlier, you shouldn't use your version to export your data to QuickBooks Online. But never fear; you can download a free 30-day trial version of the latest edition of QuickBooks available and use it to export your data to QuickBooks Online. Make sure that you pick the right country version of QuickBooks Desktop. If you've been using the U.S. QuickBooks Premier Desktop edition, download the trial for U.S. QuickBooks Pro Desktop; you'll be able to open your company in it for the purposes of exporting your data to QuickBooks Online.

Before you download and install a trial version, remember to open your current version of QuickBooks Desktop, back up your data, and put the backup in a safe place. Then download and install a trial version of the latest available QuickBooks Desktop.

To ensure that you retain access to your data, *do not* register or activate the trial version of QuickBooks Desktop. If you try to register or activate the trial, the validation will fail, and you'll be locked out. (I resisted the urge to type those last two sentences in ALL CAPS.)

The first step you should take in the process of importing data from a desktop QuickBooks company is back up your current data and put the backup in a safe place. Then, make sure that your edition of QuickBooks Desktop is up to date. And yes, even if you use a trial version of QuickBooks, you should make sure it's up to date. Follow these steps:

1. **Open the desktop edition of QuickBooks.**
2. **Choose Help ⇨ Update QuickBooks Desktop.**

   The Update QuickBooks window appears.
3. **Click the Update Now tab and select all updates.**
4. **Click the Get Updates button (see Figure 13-10).**

   QuickBooks downloads updates.
5. **When the updating process finishes, click Close.**
6. **Exit and restart QuickBooks.**
7. **Install any updates that are offered.**

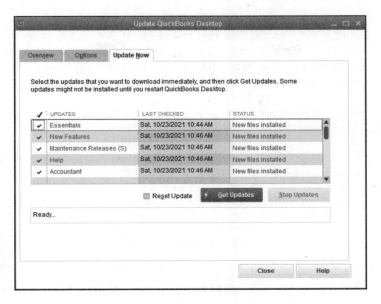

FIGURE 13-10:
Select every available update and then click Get Updates.

Next, check the following in the QuickBooks Desktop product to prevent errors during the export/import process:

» Make sure you're working in Single User mode. Open the File menu, and make sure that you see the Switch to Multi-User Mode command. Don't click it; just make sure that you see it, because its availability lets you know that you're working in Single User mode.

» Make sure that you're logged in to the QuickBooks Desktop data file as the administrator. When you log in to QuickBooks Online to import the data, you'll need to log in as a user with administrator privileges.

» To eliminate errors that might be introduced by working over a network, move the company file to your local drive.

Okay. You're ready to start the process of exporting a desktop QuickBooks company data and then importing it into a QuickBooks Online company.

Transferring data from desktop to online

You're now ready to begin the process of transferring your data. One word of warning before we continue: If you turned on payroll in your QuickBooks Online company, do *not* import into that company. See the sidebar "Payroll and Desktop data conversion" for details and suggestions.

During the transfer process, you're given the option to overwrite an existing QuickBooks Online company or create a new one. In the steps that follow, I set up an empty QuickBooks company before I started and allowed the process to overwrite it.

Follow these steps to transfer data from a QuickBooks Desktop company into a QuickBooks Online company:

1. **In QuickBooks Desktop, choose Company ⇨ Export Your Company File to QuickBooks Online.**

   QuickBooks Enterprise users should press Ctrl-1 to open the Product Information window, press Ctrl-B-Q, and then click OK to close the Product Information window. QuickBooks Pro/Premier users can also use the keyboard combination if the menu option isn't available.

   A wizard starts to walk you through the process of exporting the data.

2. **On the first page of the Export Wizard, click Get Started.**

3. **On the page that appears, sign in to your QuickBooks Online account as an administrative user.**

   If you don't have a QuickBooks Online account, you can click Create an Account and walk through the process of supplying a user ID — typically, an email address — and a password.

REMEMBER

   Because you're not signing in from your browser, you may be prompted to authenticate yourself. In this case, Intuit sends a code to your email address, and you must check your email to supply the code onscreen.

4. **On the page where QuickBooks Desktop displays the Moving-Day Checklist, click Continue.**

5. **Select the appropriate choice for turning on inventory and then click Continue.**

   If you opt to turn on inventory, select the date you want to use to calculate inventory value using the FIFO (first in, first out) method. Intuit recommends that you use the first day following your company's last tax filing period.

REMEMBER

   Only QuickBooks Plus and Advanced subscriptions support inventory. In the United States, if you opt to import inventory, your accounting method changes to FIFO, and you need to file Form 3115 with the Internal Revenue Service. If any inventory-related errors occur during the import, the process fails, and you'll receive an email with instructions on how to fix the items causing the problem. Also be aware that due to recalculations to FIFO, your Accrual Basis reports and Cash Basis reports won't match. QuickBooks flags any errors with inventory if they appear during import.

6. **Select your QuickBooks Online company (see Figure 13-11).**

I selected an existing empty company. Choosing an existing company — empty or not — makes QuickBooks Online overwrite any data that's already in that company.

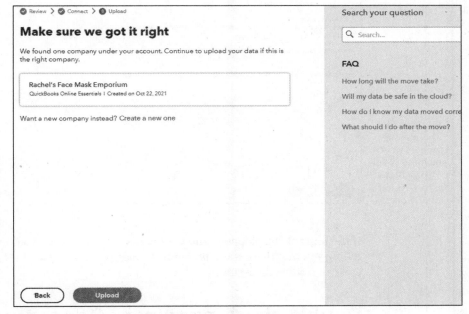

FIGURE 13-11: Select whether you want to overwrite an existing QuickBooks company or create a new one for your QuickBooks Desktop company data.

7. **Click Upload.**

8. **If prompted, type the word agree and then click Replace to confirm that you want to replace all your QuickBooks Online data for this company with data from the QuickBooks Desktop company.**

A copy of your QuickBooks Desktop company file is made. During this process, you can't use QuickBooks Desktop. Eventually, a message appears, letting you know that you'll receive an email when the process finishes.

9. **Click Got It (see Figure 13-12).**

10. **Close QuickBooks Desktop.**

You can click the Complete Your Setup button to open a new browser tab where you can log in to the QuickBooks Online company. Alternatively, you can visit https://qbo.intuit.com.

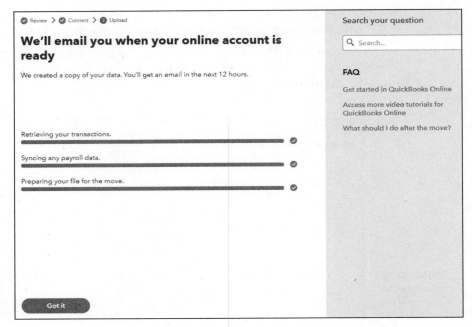

FIGURE 13-12:
This message appears when you finish your part of the export/import process.

If the unthinkable happens and your data doesn't convert, you'll receive an email telling you that there was a problem. A report will be attached for you to review so you can resolve the issues.

Double-checking things after conversion

When conversion finishes, you need to double-check the data to make sure that it looks the way you expected. At this point, I suggest that you run and compare the Profit & Loss, Balance Sheet, Accounts Receivable, Accounts Payable, sales tax liability, and (if appropriate) payroll liability reports for both the QuickBooks Desktop company and the QuickBooks Online company. Be sure that you run these reports using the Accrual basis with the dates set to All. Use the Accrual basis because reports run in both products using the Cash basis may not match.

TIP

Need a do-over? During the first 60 days of a subscription, you get a "do-over" on importing data into a QuickBooks Online company, which can be useful if things don't import as you expect. Just go through the process of importing again. This is also helpful if your attempt to run parallel didn't go as expected and you have transactions in QuickBooks Desktop that aren't in QuickBooks Online.

UNDOING AN IMPORT

Suppose that you're not happy with the results of importing and decide that you want to enter data into the QuickBooks company manually. You can purge all the data if you have an Essentials, Plus, or Advanced subscription that is 60 days old or less. Open the QuickBooks Online company and click Dashboard so that you're viewing the home page.

On the browser address bar, change the address to https://qbo.intuit.com/app/purgecompany and press Enter or refresh the page. A page appears, describing what will be deleted (everything) and how many days you have to remove the data in the company, and asks whether you're sure. Type **yes** in the bottom-right corner and click OK, and QuickBooks Online purges the data from your company. If you change your mind and don't want to purge, click Cancel in the bottom-right corner. Be aware that you can't undo a data purge; when it starts, you must wait until it finishes. Then you can start using the now-empty company.

Don't try this with the Your Books company; you'll probably cause irreparable damage. If you need to clear data from the Your Books company, contact Intuit technical support for help.

Here's a checklist of things you probably need to do to make the imported QuickBooks Online company ready for use:

>> Set up company users and sales tax items.

>> Set up payroll, either through Intuit Online Payroll or QuickBooks Online Payroll.

>> Reconcile accounts as needed.

>> Review lists and make appropriate entries inactive as necessary.

>> Set up recurring transactions to replace QuickBooks Desktop memorized transactions.

>> Re-create any necessary nonposting transactions, such as purchase orders.

>> Review inventory.

>> Customize forms and reports, and (if appropriate) memorize reports.

>> Set up a closing-date password.

See Chapter 14 for a discussion of the Client Overview in QB Accountant, which helps you identify the tasks you need to complete to bring any client's QuickBooks company up to snuff.

Switching between Client QuickBooks Companies

If you've worked through Chapters 12 and 13, you may have noticed that individual QuickBooks companies don't open in a separate tab in your browser by default. What do you do when you want to stop working in one client's books and start working in another client's books?

Well, you can click the Accountant button on the QB Accountant toolbar at any time to redisplay the QB Accountant interface and your list of clients. From there, you can click the QuickBooks logo next to any client's name to open the corresponding QuickBooks company.

But you really don't need to complete two steps to switch between QuickBooks companies. Instead, take advantage of the Go to Client's QuickBooks list on the QB Accountant toolbar.

When you're working in a QuickBooks company, the name of that company appears in the Go to Client's QuickBooks list; if you click the company name, QB Accountant displays a list of all your clients' QuickBooks companies. Just click the name of the company you want to open. You don't need to worry about saving work; QuickBooks and QB Accountant do that for you.

Chapter **14**

Exploring a Client's Company from QB Accountant

A client's QuickBooks company looks a little different in QuickBooks Online Accountant (QB Accountant) than when you view it in QuickBooks Online. This chapter explores the interface you see when you open a client company in QB Accountant. It also covers some facets of QuickBooks Online companies you may want to review for your clients to make sure that things flow smoothly.

Opening a Client's Company

You can open a client's company from the Clients page by clicking the QB logo to the left of any client's name. (See Figure 14-1.) Alternatively, you can open a client's company by using the Go to QuickBooks list on the QB Accountant toolbar to toggle from one QuickBooks Online company to another. Simply open the list and choose the name of the company you want to open.

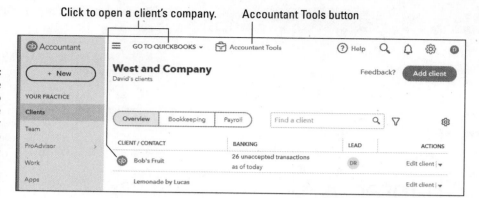

FIGURE 14-1:
Click the
QuickBooks logo
to the left of the
client's name or
the Go to
QuickBooks
drop-down menu
to open a client's
company.

TIP

If the QB logo doesn't appear next to a client's name, the client's QuickBooks subscription has expired. Click the arrow next to Edit Client in the Actions column and choose Make Inactive from the drop-down menu to remove such clients from your list. If a client becomes active again later, click Settings above the Actions column and turn Include Inactive Clients on. Then you can choose Make Active to reactivate an inactive client who restores their subscription.

When you're done working with a QuickBooks Online company in QB Accountant, you don't need to do anything special to close the company; simply open another client's company. To sign out of QB Accountant altogether, click Settings on the QB Accountant toolbar at the top of the screen.

Reviewing a Client's QuickBooks Company

You'll probably want to review the company setup information for your clients to make sure that things are set up properly. To do so, you use the Client Overview page, which provides an overview of the state of a given QuickBooks company. It's also a good idea to peruse the chart of accounts and the lists on the Client Overview page.

Taking a look at the Client Overview page

The Client Overview page can help you get a sense of where things stand in your client's QuickBooks company. To display the page, open the company by choosing it from the Go to QuickBooks drop-down menu on the QB Accountant toolbar; then, click the Overview tab on the navigation bar. At the top of the Client Overview page (see Figure 14-2), you see information about the client's subscriptions and connected apps.

WORKING IN MULTIPLE WINDOWS

You can open two or more pages at the same time within a single QuickBooks Online company. To do so, click the Accountant Tools button (refer to Figure 14-1) and then choose New Window to duplicate the page you are viewing in another browser tab. Now you can use either tab to navigate to a different page within the company.

All the major browsers let you duplicate tabs, so the New Window command is simply a convenience. In most browsers, if you right-click any tab, the shortcut menu should include a command that contains the word *Duplicate*.

Note that if you want to access two or more QuickBooks companies at the same time, you can't simply open another browser tab. Instead, you need to use separate browsers, such as Google Chrome, Mozilla Firefox, or Microsoft Edge. In Chapter 18, I show how you can use profiles in Chrome to access multiple QuickBooks companies simultaneously.

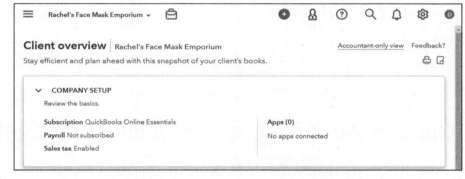

FIGURE 14-2: The top of the Client Overview page shows details on a company's subscriptions and connected apps.

In the second section of the Client Overview page, shown in Figure 14-3, you see information on the client's banking activity; the accounts in the list are set up as either bank accounts or credit card accounts.

The third section of the Client Overview page, shown in Figure 14-4, shows common issues that can arise in a QuickBooks company. This helpful information gives you a heads-up so that you can serve your clients more effectively.

The final section of the Client Overview page shows the transaction volume for a given date range. As you can see in Figure 14-5, it's designed to help you determine how much time you'll need to spend on a given client's books.

FIGURE 14-3:
The Banking
Activity section of
the Client
Overview page.

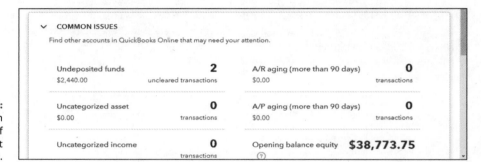

FIGURE 14-4:
The Common
Issues section of
the Client
Overview page.

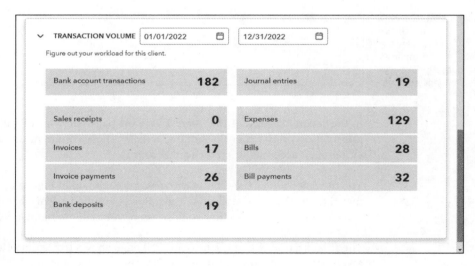

FIGURE 14-5:
The Transaction
section of
the Client
Overview page.

Be aware that the Client Overview page is purely informational. The page has no links except at the bottom of the Common Issues section, where you can click the View Chart of Accounts link (not shown in Figure 14-4).

Examining company setup information

You review company setup information to make sure that the client's company uses the correct accounting method, employer identification number (EIN), and legal business organization. You also can turn on the option to use account numbers in the chart of accounts. (You can also turn this feature off, but I've never met an accountant who didn't want to be able to see the account numbers.)

To review company settings, follow these steps:

1. **Open the QuickBooks company you want to review.**

    You can click the QuickBooks logo to the left of the client's name on the Clients page, or you can choose the client from the Go to QuickBooks drop-down menu on the QB Accountant toolbar.

2. **Choose Settings ⇨ Account and Settings, as shown in Figure 14-6.**

    The Account and Settings dialog box appears, with the Company tab selected (see Figure 14-7).

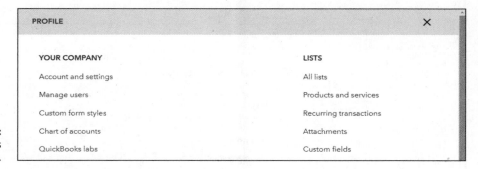

FIGURE 14-6: The Settings menu.

PROFILE	✕
YOUR COMPANY	**LISTS**
Account and settings	All lists
Manage users	Products and services
Custom form styles	Recurring transactions
Chart of accounts	Attachments
QuickBooks labs	Custom fields

3. **Review the settings.**

    In particular, set or correct Company Name, Legal Name, and EIN.

    To make changes, click any setting or click the pencil that appears in the upper-right corner of the section of settings. Make your changes and click Save.

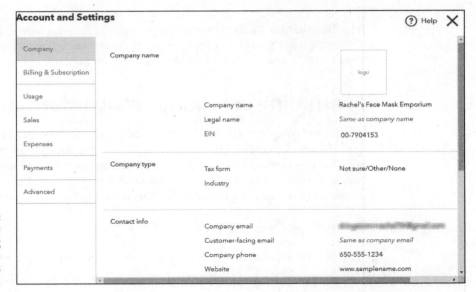

FIGURE 14-7:
The Account and
Settings dialog
box for a
QuickBooks
company.

4. **Click the Usage tab on the left side of the Account and Settings dialog box.**

The Usage Limits tab appears (see Figure 14-8), where you can review how the client subscription fits within the use limits for a given subscription. I discuss these limits in Chapter 2.

FIGURE 14-8:
Usage limits.

5. **Click the Advanced tab on the left side of the Account and Settings dialog box.**

The settings on the Advanced page of the Account and Settings dialog box appear, as shown in Figure 14-9.

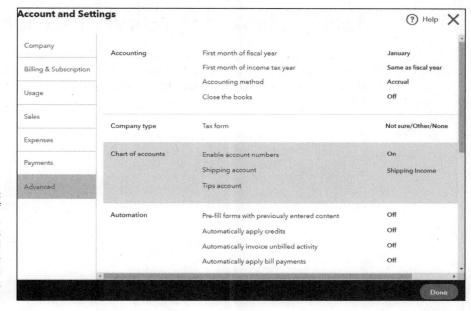

FIGURE 14-9:
Review and, if necessary, change settings on the Advanced tab of the Account and Settings dialog box.

6. **Review the settings.**

In particular, set or correct the following settings:

- *Accounting:* Fiscal and tax year information as well as the accounting method.

- *Company Type:* The tax form setting.

- *Chart of Accounts:* Whether to use numbers in the chart of accounts.

- *Automation:* Whether QuickBooks should prefill forms, automatically apply credits, invoice unbilled activity, and apply bill payments.

- *Other Preferences:* Information such as warnings when duplicate check numbers and bill numbers are used. (This section isn't shown in Figure 14-9.)

7. **Review the settings on any other pages of the Account and Settings dialog box that you feel might need your attention.**

8. **Click Done in the bottom-right corner to save your changes.**

   A message confirms that your changes were saved.

Taking a look at the chart of accounts

In addition to checking company settings, you'll probably want to review your client's chart of accounts to make sure that it looks the way you want. You can choose Accounting⇨Chart of Accounts to display your client's chart of accounts (see Figure 14-10).

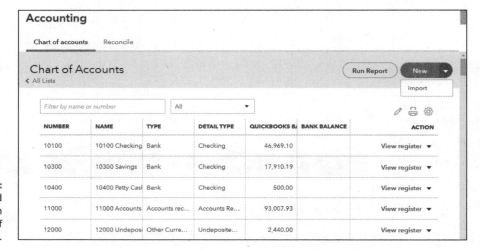

FIGURE 14-10: You can add and edit accounts on the chart of accounts page.

TIP

You also can open the chart of accounts page by clicking the Accountant Tools button on the QB Accountant toolbar. All roads lead to Rome.

If you chose to enable the option to use account numbers while you were reviewing company settings (refer to Figure 14-9), the chart of accounts page displays a column for account numbers on the left edge and a Batch Edit button in the top-right corner. You can use the Batch Edit button to add account numbers, as described in "Adding account numbers" later in this chapter.

Importing a chart of accounts

When you create a new company, QuickBooks automatically sets up the chart of accounts it thinks you'll need, but you can replace it by importing one that you've set up in Microsoft Excel, as a CSV file, or as a Google Sheet spreadsheet. If your client's company needs subaccounts, the import file can include subaccounts along with their parent accounts.

REMEMBER

To import subaccounts, use the convention *Account: Subaccount* — that is, list the parent account first, followed by a colon and then the subaccount. The file you import needs to follow a particular format, and you can download a sample file to get the hang of the layout before you set up your file. On the chart of accounts page, click the arrow next to the New button (refer to Figure 14-10) and then choose Import from the drop-down menu. The Import Accounts page appears, as shown in Figure 14-11. Click the Download a Sample File link, and open the file in Excel to see the format your file should follow.

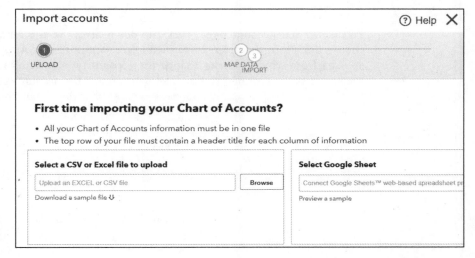

FIGURE 14-11:
The Import
Accounts page.

After you set up your chart of accounts file, you return to the Import Accounts page. Click the Browse button (refer to Figure 14-11) to select your file, and click the Next button in the bottom-right corner. On the page that appears, shown in Figure 14-12, map the headings in your file to the fields in QuickBooks by choosing your field names from the drop-down lists in the Your Field column. Then click Next.

A preview of the accounts to be imported appears. If all looks well, click Import.

Editing or adding accounts

You may need to edit an account to change an account's category type or name, and you use the Account page to make the change.

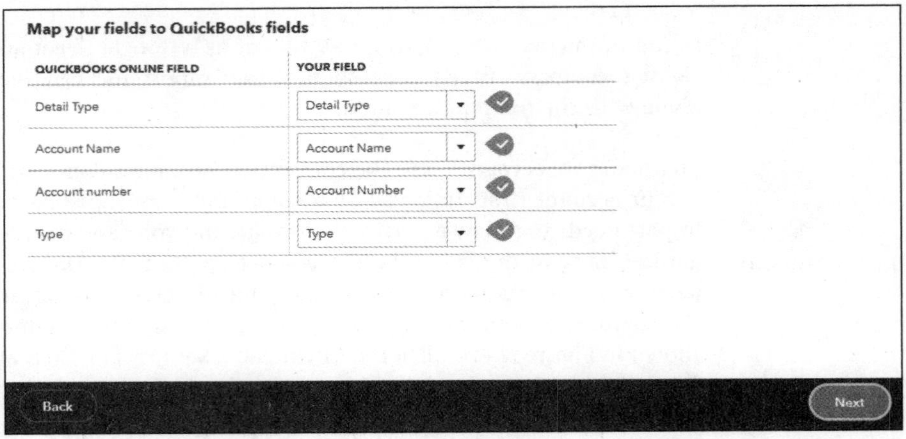

Map your fields to QuickBooks fields

QUICKBOOKS ONLINE FIELD	YOUR FIELD	
Detail Type	Detail Type ▾	✓
Account Name	Account Name ▾	✓
Account number	Account Number ▾	✓
Type	Type ▾	✓

Back   Next

FIGURE 14-12:
Map the fields in
your file to the
fields in
QuickBooks.

To display the Account page, click the down arrow in the Action column and choose Edit from the drop-down menu (see Figure 14-13). An Account window appears from which you can change the account type or detail type, amend the account name and/or description, and determine if the account is a subaccount of another account. You cannot change the currency or the account balance from this window.

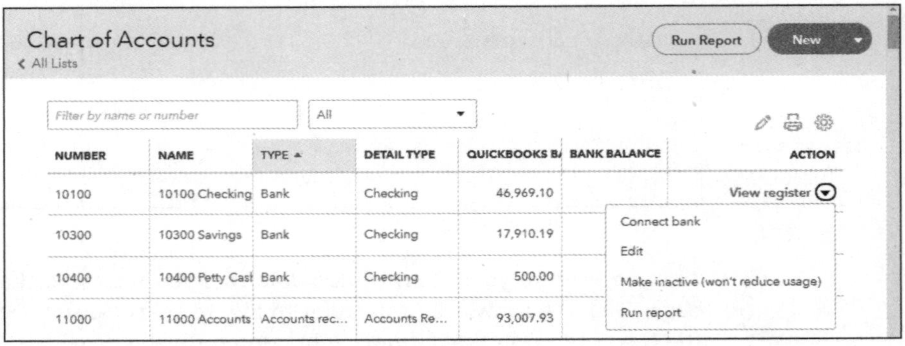

Chart of Accounts
‹ All Lists

Run Report   New ▾

Filter by name or number   All ▾   ✎ 🖨 ⚙

NUMBER	NAME	TYPE ▲	DETAIL TYPE	QUICKBOOKS B/	BANK BALANCE	ACTION
10100	10100 Checking	Bank	Checking	46,969.10		View register ⊙
10300	10300 Savings	Bank	Checking	17,910.19		Connect bank
10400	10400 Petty Cash	Bank	Checking	500.00		Edit
11000	11000 Accounts	Accounts rec...	Accounts Re...	93,007.93		Make inactive (won't reduce usage)
						Run report

FIGURE 14-13:
To edit an
account, make a
choice from an
Action drop-down
menu.

If you need to create a new account, click the New button above the list. The page you see when you create a new account looks just like the one you see when you edit an existing account.

TIP

You can choose View Register from the drop-down menu in the Action column for any Asset, Liability, or Equity account to display the account's register. Retained Earnings is the exception; it functions like Income and Expense accounts. You can click Run Report to the right of Income or Expense account to display a QuickReport for the account.

TIP

If you decide to add account numbers to the chart of accounts, you can add an account number in the Account page, but there's a much easier way, which I show you in "Adding account numbers" later in this chapter.

Adding account numbers

Here's an easy way to add account numbers to a chart of accounts. First, make sure that you enable the setting on the Advanced tab of the chart of accounts section of the Account and Settings dialog box (refer to Figure 14-9).

Then, on the Chart of Accounts page, click the Batch Edit button to display the page shown in Figure 14-14.

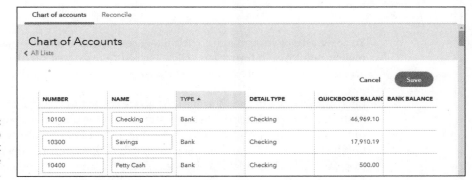

FIGURE 14-14:
Use this page to set up account numbers for the chart of accounts.

NUMBER	NAME	TYPE ▲	DETAIL TYPE	QUICKBOOKS BALANC	BANK BALANCE
10100	Checking	Bank	Checking	46,969.10	
10300	Savings	Bank	Checking	17,910.19	
10400	Petty Cash	Bank	Checking	500.00	

Type account numbers in the Number column. Save buttons appear in the top- and bottom-right corners of the page (you can't see the bottom of the page in Figure 14-14); click either button when you finish entering the account numbers.

REMEMBER

QB Accountant sessions time out after 60 minutes of inactivity, so save periodically as you enter account numbers. After you add account numbers, you can sort the chart of accounts in account-number order by clicking the Number heading of the Chart of Accounts page.

Reviewing list information

You can review list information for your clients' companies. Using the links on the navigation bar, you can view overview information about customers, vendors, and employees. To view customers, choose Sales ⇨ Customers on the navigation bar (the link might read Invoicing, depending on the choices you made when you created the company). The Customers page appears (see Figure 14-15).

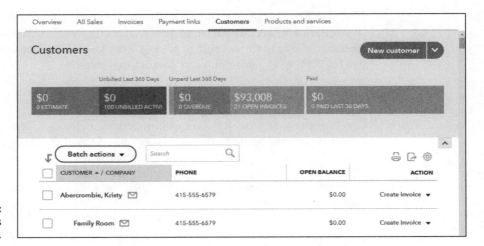

FIGURE 14-15:
The Customers
page.

To view vendor information, click Expenses⇨Vendors on the navigation bar. To review employee information, click Payroll⇨Employees on the navigation bar. When you choose Payroll⇨Contractors, the 1099 vendors set up by the client appear.

Click one or more of the filter buttons above the list to view that particular subset of the list. You can filter the list of customers on the Customers page, for example, to view only those customers with overdue invoices or only those customers with unbilled activity. And you can click the Batch Actions button (just above the table) to perform batch actions, such as emailing a group of customers. If your list is long, use the Search box to find a particular list entry. You can also sort the list by name or by open balance by clicking the appropriate heading below the Batch Actions button. Note that you can import names into a people list; for more information, see Chapter 4.

To review other lists, click Settings on the QB Accountant toolbar. In the Lists section of the resulting page, you can opt to view any of three common lists: Products and Services, Recurring Transactions, or Attachments. Or you can click All Lists at the top of the Lists section to display the Lists page (see Figure 14-16), which you can use to navigate to any list other than a people-oriented list.

For more extensive details on working with lists, see Chapter 4.

Exporting and importing bank feed rules

When your client takes advantage of bank feeds and downloads transactions from the bank to their QuickBooks company, you can help ensure that the transactions post properly. In many cases, the rules used by one client can apply to another, so rather than re-create rules, export them from one client's company and import them into another client's company.

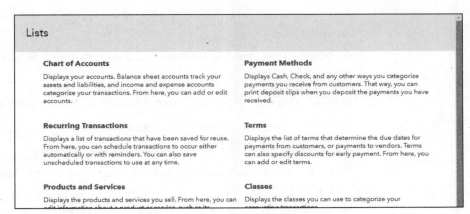

Exporting includes all the rules in a given QuickBooks company. Later, you can import rules into a different company by using the Import Rules Wizard.

To export rules from a client company, open that company and then follow these steps:

1. **Choose Banking ⇨ Rules (Transactions ⇨ Rules).**

The Rules page appears (see Figure 14-17).

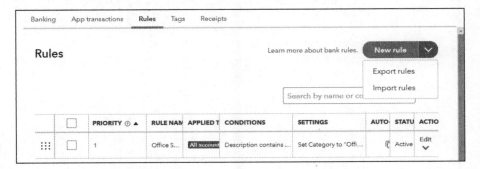

2. **Click the down arrow next to the New Rule button and choose Export Rules from the drop-down menu.**

QuickBooks creates an Excel file containing the rules and stores it in your Downloads folder. The name of the file includes the name of the client whose rules you exported and the words Bank_Feed_Rules.

The Export Rules command is disabled if a given company doesn't have any rules established.

REMEMBER

3. **Click Close.**

4. **Switch to the company into which you want to import these rules.**

5. **Repeat Step 1.**

6. **Repeat Step 2, but choose Import Rules from the drop-down menu.**

   The first screen of the Import Rules Wizard appears.

7. **Select the file you created in Step 2 and then click Next.**

8. **On the second wizard screen, select the rules you want to import and then click Next.**

9. **(Optional) On the third wizard screen, select categories for the rules that match the chart of accounts of the client to which you are importing the rules, and make any changes.**

10. **Click Import.**

    A message tells you how many rules imported successfully.

11. **Click Finish.**

    The Rules page for the client you opened in Step 4 appears.

12. **Verify that the rules you wanted to import appear.**

For more details on working with rules, see Chapter 8.

Chapter **15**

Working in a Client's Company

You work in a client's QuickBooks company in much the same way that your client does; see Chapters 3 to 9 for detailed information. In this chapter, I focus on ways you can navigate easily, search for and review transactions, and communicate with clients.

Making Navigation Easy

For the most part, navigating with a mouse is obvious: a click here and a click there. But you can use a few not-so-obvious tricks to navigate easily, including some keyboard shortcuts. Some common navigation techniques are specific to Google Chrome; see Chapter 18 for more information.

Using keyboard shortcuts

Keyboard shortcuts (see Figure 15-1) can save you time in QuickBooks. You can also find a list of shortcuts in this book's Cheat Sheet, available at www.dummies.com.

Keyboard Shortcuts

To use a shortcut, press and hold **ctrl/control** and **alt/option** at the same time. Then press one of the keys below.

On main pages, like the dashboard or customers

SHORTCUT KEY	ACTION
i	Invoice
w	Check
e	Estimate
x	Expense
r	Receive payment
c	Customers
v	Vendors
a	Chart of accounts
l	Lists
h	Help
f	Global search
d	Focus the left menu
? or /	This dialog

On transactions, like an invoice or expense

SHORTCUT KEY	ACTION
x	Exit transaction view
c	Cancel out
s	Save and new
d	Save and close
m	Save and send
p	Print
? or /	This dialog

FIGURE 15-1:
Keyboard shortcuts you can use while working in QuickBooks.

Windows users should press Ctrl+Alt+/ to view these shortcuts along with the current QuickBooks company ID. Mac users should press Control+Option+/. If you carry out this action in QB Accountant instead of QuickBoooks, the company ID you see is your own.

To use any of these shortcuts in Windows, press Ctrl+Alt+*shortcut key*. On a Mac, press Control+Option+*shortcut key*. For example, pres Ctrl+Alt+I or Control+Option+I to open the the invoice window.

Opening multiple windows

If you use multiple monitors, you'll likely want to have multiple QuickBooks windows open at the same time. Within a single company, you can duplicate a browser tab by choosing New Window from the Accountant Tools drop-down menu on the QB Accountant toolbar (see Figure 15-2). You can read about the other commands on this menu in Chapter 16.

TIP

If you're using Chrome on a Windows PC, you also can duplicate a browser tab by right-clicking the tab and choosing Duplicate from the shortcut menu; or, if you're a keyboard person, press Alt+D followed by Alt+Enter. In Chrome on a Mac, choose Tab ⇨ Duplicate Tab. In Mozilla Firefox, you can duplicate a browser tab by clicking the address bar and pressing Alt+Enter in Windows or Command+Enter on the Mac.

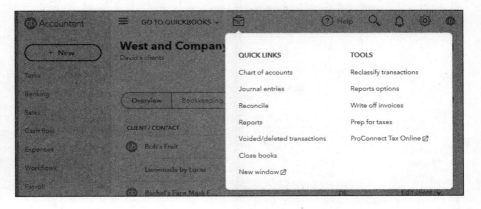

FIGURE 15-2:
Use the New
Window
command while
working in a
QuickBooks
company to
duplicate the
window you're
viewing.

When you choose the New Window command, a new browser tab displays the same information that appears on the original browser tab. From there, you can navigate to any other page within that QuickBooks company. If you have multiple monitors, you can drag any tab to another monitor.

You can also drag any tab downward to create a new window that you can toggle by pressing Alt+Tab on a Windows PC or ⌘-Tab on a Mac.

If you're a fan of split-screen displays, you can use a Windows shortcut to display two tabs side by side. Follow these steps:

1. **Duplicate a browser tab.**

2. **Drag the current tab down.**

   The browser displays the tab you dragged in its own browser window.

3. **Press and hold the Windows key (the one that appears between the left Ctrl and the left Alt keys on the keyboard) and then press an arrow key:**

   - Press the left-arrow key to pin the active window to the left side of the monitor.

   - Press the right-arrow key to pin the active window to the right side of the monitor.

4. **Click the other available window to make it the active window.**

5. **Repeat Step 3.**

There's no short, easy way to display two windows vertically. You'll have to resize manually the windows and place them where you want them.

In Figure 15-3, I displayed the Balance Sheet (on the left), created a second browser window, and drilled down in the second window to display the transactions in the checking account. Then I pinned the two windows side by side onscreen.

FIGURE 15-3:
Two windows
pinned side
by side.

You can click the collapse/expand button in either or both windows to hide the navigation bar, giving more screen real estate to the data, as I did in Figure 15-3.

When you finish working in two windows, close one and maximize the other.

Working in two companies simultaneously

Suppose that you're done working with one client and want to open a different client. As described in Chapter 13, you can click the Go to QuickBooks button on the QB Accountant toolbar and choose a new client from the drop-down menu. Or you can click the QB Accountant button to display the Clients page and then click the QB icon to the left of the company name. Either way, QB Accountant displays the information for the selected client.

That brings up the question "How do I work in two different companies simultaneously?" If you're working in Chrome, use a second profile to establish a separate browsing session. You'd effectively have two instances of Chrome running simultaneously. I discuss Chrome profiles in more detail in Chapter 18.

Alternatively, you could work with two browsers — say, Chrome and Windows Edge, Firefox, or Apple's Safari. As shown in Figure 15-4, then you can access two QuickBooks companies simultaneously. You're not limited to two companies; you can create more profiles and/or install additional browsers if you need to shift seamlessly among three or more companies.

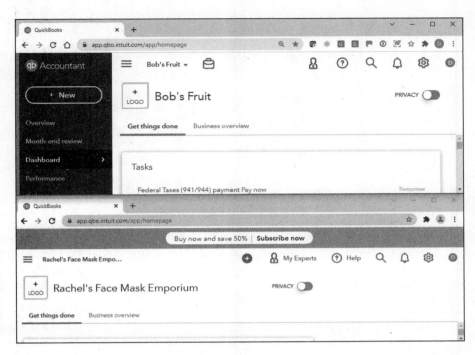

FIGURE 15-4:
To work in two companies at the same time, you can use two Chrome profiles or two browsers.

Examining Available Transaction Types

In Chapters 5 to 9, I cover transactions in a fair amount of detail, so I'm not going to repeat that information here. But you can see the available transactions by opening a QuickBooks company and then opening the New menu (see Figure 15-5).

Available transactions are organized on the menu by the type of people to which they pertain. The Other category is for transactions that don't pertain to the major categories (Customers, Vendors, and Employees), such as bank deposits.

If you want to view only a few common transactions, click the Show Less link at the bottom of the New menu. The link changes to Show More so that you can redisplay all types of transactions.

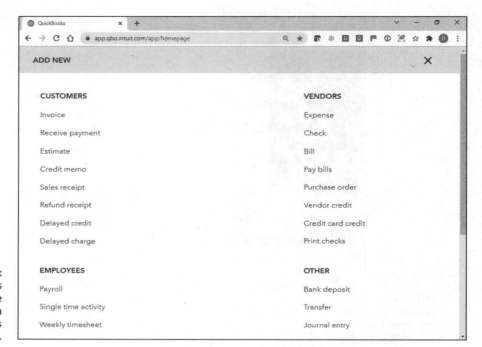

FIGURE 15-5:
The transactions
you can create
while working in a
QuickBooks
company.

Searching for Transactions

More often than not, you'll be searching for transactions in a client's QuickBooks company rather than creating them. You can search for transactions by using the Search box, shown in Figure 15-6. When you click the Search box, a list of recent transactions appears. You may also see tasks, contacts, reports, and accounts in this list.

REMEMBER

The Search box allows you to search an entire company from top to bottom, so a search term can enable to you create transactions, access contact records, view reports, and access accounts.

If you see what you want in the results list, click it to open the appropriate window. If you don't see what you want, click Advanced Search in the bottom-right corner of the menu to display the Search page, shown in Figure 15-7.

You can limit the search to a particular transaction type; search for any of several types of data; and specify whether the search should contain, not contain, be equal to, or not be equal to the search criteria.

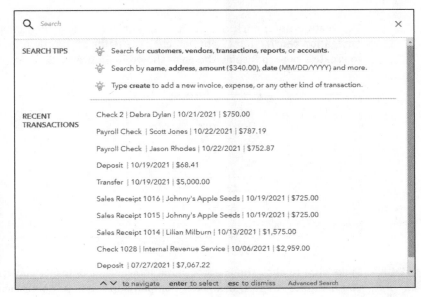

FIGURE 15-6:
Type any phrase you want to use as a search filter or click Advanced Search at the bottom of the Search list.

FIGURE 15-7:
Set criteria for a more specifically defined search.

 QuickBooks offers a transaction-specific alternative to the Search box. Let's say that you open any transaction window, such as an invoice window. Click the clock button — which appears at the top left of the screen, adjacent to the transaction type name — to display a list of recent invoices. The list that appears will always reflect the transaction window that you presently have displayed.

Making Client Notes

You and your team members can use the Notes feature in QB Accountant to document any kind of information about any of your clients. Each note automatically includes the time when the note was created and the team member who created the note. Team members who have access to the client can view and edit that client's notes. Also, you can pin notes to make them easy to find. You can think of the Notes feature as a way to create electronic sticky notes.

To create a note, click the QB Accountant button and then click Clients on the navigation bar. In your Client list, click the name of the client for which you want to create a note to display the page shown in Figure 15-8.

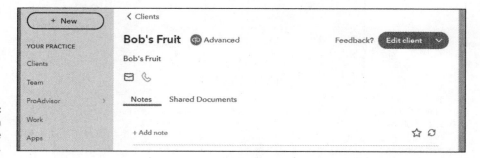

FIGURE 15-8:
The page on which you create a client note.

REMEMBER

Make sure to click the client's name to see their notes. If you click the QB icon, you'll launch their QuickBooks company instead. If no QB icon appears, the client's QuickBooks subscription has lapsed.

Type your note, and click Post. Once you've created a note you have a few options:

>> **Favorite:** Move the mouse pointer over the star icon at the top right-hand corner of the note. You can in turn filter the list of notes to see all your favorites by clicking the star icon that appears at the top-right corner of the list notes itself.

>> **Edit:** Click the three dot menu at the top right-hand corner of the note and then choose Edit. Click Save to record your changes, or Cancel if you change your mind about making any edits.

>> **Delete:** Click the three dot menu at the top right-hand corner of the note and then choose Delete. QuickBooks ask you to click Delete to confirm that you want to remove the note.

>> **Comment:** Click the word bubble icon that appears in the bottom right-hand corner of the note to add a comment. Click the Post button to save your comment. The number of comments appears adjacent to this icon, so you can tell at a glance if there's more to see. This is actually a multifunction button; clicking it not only allows you to add a comment but it also displays any existing comments.

Communicating with a Client

Communication is essential for people in all walks of life, including a client and an accountant. You can use tools in QuickBooks and QB Accountant to communicate with your clients.

TIP

You always have the option to email your clients directly, but creating requests inside QuickBooks or QB Accountant helps you centralize your client communications.

You can use Client Requests, for example, to ask your client to send you a bank statement, which then appears on the My Accountant page of your client's Quick-Books company. To do so, follow these steps:

1. **Click Work on the QB Accountant navigation bar.**

You can read more about the purpose and function of the Work page in Chapter 16.

2. **Click Create Client Request.**

The Create Client Request panel appears, as shown in Figure 15-9.

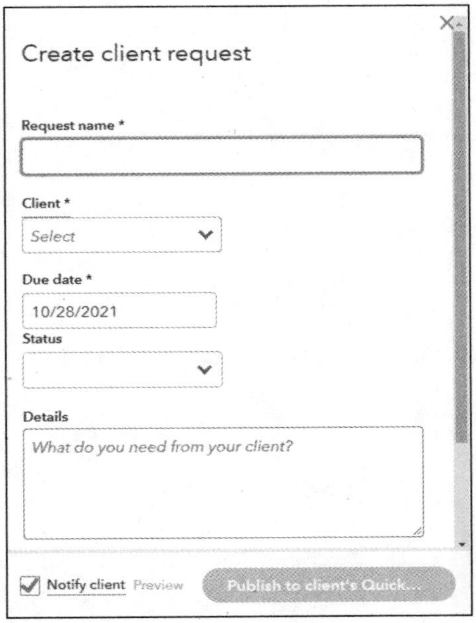

Create client request

Request name *

Client *

Select

Due date *

10/28/2021

Status

Details

What do you need from your client?

☑ Notify client   Preview   Publish to client's Quick...

FIGURE 15-9:
Client Requests gives you a centralized list of communications.

3. **Type a name for the request.**

   Think of this name as the subject line of an email message.

4. **Select a client.**

   As you might expect, you can use this method to communicate only with clients that have granted you access to their QuickBooks companies.

5. **Set a due date for the request.**

6. **Complete the remaining fields, and attach any documents you want to share.**

7. **Clear the Notify Client check box if you don't want to send an email notification to your client.**

   As shown in Figure 15-9, this check box is selected automatically.

8. **(Optional) Click the Preview link to view a preview of the email that your client will receive.**

   As shown in Figure 15-10, this generic message informs your client that they need to log into QuickBooks to see your request. Close the Preview window after you review the contents.

9. **Click the Publish to Client's QuickBooks button to close the request.**

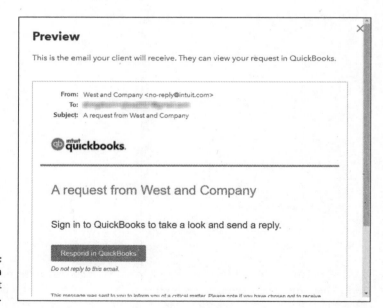

FIGURE 15-10:
A preview of a Client Request message.

As shown in Figure 15-11, your client can click My Accountant on the navigation bar to see the message. To respond, the client clicks the message on the My Accountant page to display the panel shown in Figure 15-12. On that panel, the client can write a message and attach any necessary documents.

FIGURE 15-11:
A Client Request in a QuickBooks company.

FIGURE 15-12:
The panel your client uses to respond to a Client Request.

Documents can be no larger than 20MB.

REMEMBER In turn, you can retrieve documents that your client shared with you in QB Accountant. Click Clients on the navigation bar, and in the Client list, click the name of the client. The Details page appears, open to the Shared Documents tab (see Figure 15-13). Download the document or click the link in the Request column to view or update the original request. Any changes you make appear on the Work tab.

FIGURE 15-13: The Shared Documents page allows you to access files that your client submitted.

THE MY ACCOUNTANT PAGE IN QUICKBOOKS

The My Accountant page appears within QuickBooks companies that have at least one accountant user. Accountants can't view this page in QB Accountant, however. The reasoning is that a client may have two or more accountants from different firms (perhaps one for taxes and another for bookkeeping). Each accountant can view their own requests in QB Accountant, but only the client sees the combined list of requests from the entire accounting team.

Chapter **16**

Using Accountant Tools

Accountant tools are available to QB Accountant users working in any QuickBooks Online company. You can become a user in a QuickBooks Online company in one of two ways:

» As described in Chapter 13, your client can invite you to be the accountant user on their account. Each QuickBooks company can have only two accountant users.

» As described in Chapter 12, the master administrator of the QB Accountant account can set up users. Any user established by the master administrator can log in to QB Accountant, open any QuickBooks company assigned to them, and use the tools on the Accountant Tools menu that I describe in this chapter.

In addition to describing the tools on the Accountant Tools menu, this chapter covers reporting and paying sales tax (an activity that accountants often perform for their clients, so I start with that information), as well as using QB Accountant's Work Flow feature.

Reporting and Paying Sales Taxes

You or your client can manage and pay sales tax. Open any QuickBooks company; click Taxes on the navigation bar; then click Sales Tax to display Sales Tax Center, where you'll see all sales tax returns that are due and any that are overdue. To file and pay a particular return, click the View Return button on the right side of the page next to the return you want to file. QB Accountant displays a page similar to Figure 16-1.

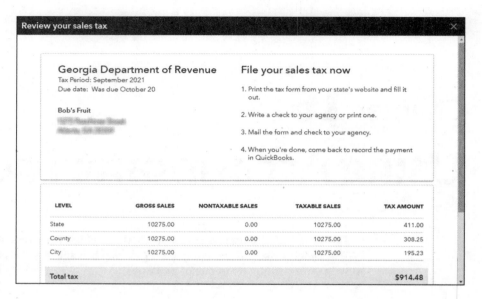

Georgia Department of Revenue
Tax Period: September 2021
Due date: Was due October 20

File your sales tax now

1. Print the tax form from your state's website and fill it out.

2. Write a check to your agency or print one.

Bob's Fruit

3. Mail the form and check to your agency.

4. When you're done, come back to record the payment in QuickBooks.

LEVEL	GROSS SALES	NONTAXABLE SALES	TAXABLE SALES	TAX AMOUNT
State	10275.00	0.00	10275.00	411.00
County	10275.00	0.00	10275.00	308.25
City	10275.00	0.00	10275.00	195.23
Total tax				$914.48

FIGURE 16-1:
Reviewing a sales tax return.

REMEMBER

You'll be prompted to use the new automated sales tax feature to set up sales taxes the first time you access the Sales Tax page. If this feature doesn't appear in your QuickBooks company yet, you'll see it in the coming months.

If you need to add a sales tax adjustment, click the Add an Adjustment link that appears below the Total Tax line. An Add an Adjustment panel appears on the right side of the screen. Provide a reason for the adjustment, adjustment date, along with an account and an amount for the adjustment. Click Add to post the adjustment or click the X at the top right-hand corner to close the adjustment dialog box.

When the Review Your Sales Taxes page appears, click the Record Payment button to display the Record Payment page. In my example, E-File wasn't available, so choosing Record Payment produced the screen shown in Figure 16-2. When E-File is available, you see the appropriate instructions and buttons onscreen.

QuickBooks calculates and displays the amount due to your sales tax agency, and you can confirm the amount or change it. Be aware that although you can change the amount due that QuickBooks supplies, if you do, you risk underpaying your sales tax liability. To see the details of the amount due on the Sales Tax Liability report, which breaks down the tax amount due, click the Report link in the first step listed on the page (Download your full report).

FIGURE 16-2:
Use this page to record a sales tax payment.

To complete the payment and sales tax filing, supply a payment date and a bank account from which to pay the liability; then click the Record Payment button, which I couldn't squeeze into Figure 16-2, but that I promise you'll see when you scroll down when you're looking at your own screen.

TIP

If you need to set up sales taxes in your client's QuickBooks company, see Chapter 4 for details on the process.

Managing Your Practice

In this section, I introduce the practice management tool known as the Work page, which you access by clicking Work on the QB Accountant navigation bar. All your team members can access this page, so it's a centralized practice management tool.

REMEMBER

Your clients can't see the Work page because it's available only in QB Accountant and only to you and your designated team members. Each team member can only see the information you grant them access to, as I discuss in the "Creating projects and tasks" section later in this chapter. See Chapter 12 if you're not sure how to add team members.

The Work page enables you to track what needs to happen for both your clients and your own firm. Although the terminology used on the Work page refers to projects, bear in mind that these projects are different from the projects that your clients can create in QuickBooks Online, which you can read about in Chapter 6.

Understanding Grid view

The default Grid view, shown in Figure 16-3, appears when you click Work on the navigation bar. You see task cards organized in date ranges: Today, This Week, Next Week, and Next 30 Days. I only had room to show the Today and This Week sections, but on your screen you'll be able to scroll down and see Next Week and Next 30 Days.

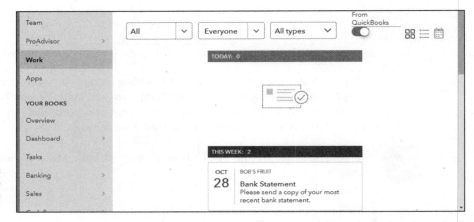

FIGURE 16-3:
Grid view of the
Work page in QB
Accountant.

Each task card of a given project identifies the client for whom the work needs to be done (or your own firm, if the project isn't for a client) as well as the project name. The task name appears on each task card as well.

You can control some of what you see on the Work page in Grid view. You can filter the page to display information for all clients, your firm, particular clients, or specific team members, for example. The Work feature also uses data in Quick-Books Online companies to display deadlines you need to meet and things you need to do, such as payroll deadlines and dates to reconcile connected banking transactions. If you don't want to see this information, you can toggle the From QuickBooks slider in the top-right corner to Off.

REMEMBER

The Work feature automatically suggests actions to take associated only with QuickBooks Online; it doesn't connect to other products, such as ProConnect Tax Online.

Because Grid view organizes tasks by due date, you won't see any type of visual connections between tasks — that is, no lines connect tasks. Grid view isn't a flow chart.

Grid view isn't the only view available on the Work page; you can read about List and Calendar views later in this chapter.

Creating projects and tasks

As described in Chapter 15, you can use the Work page to create client requests. With respect to practice management, you use the Work page to create *projects*, which represent collections of work to be completed. You break each project into *tasks*, which are subsets of the project that provide more detail about what needs to be done to complete the project. You create tasks as part of a project, but you can assign different team members to different tasks on the same project. Projects typically are general things you need to accomplish by a specified date, and tasks describe the specific things you need to do to complete the project.

As you create a project, you assign a deadline date to the project due dates to each task in the project. You identify the client with whom the project is associated and the team member who has responsibility for the project. Or you can specify that the project is internal, affecting your firm but not any of your clients.

TIP

QB Accountant contains project templates that help you quickly create common projects such as Monthly Bookkeeping and Client Onboarding. When you use one of these templates, you create not only the project, but also the associated tasks. Then you can edit the project as needed.

Creating a project

To keep this information as easy to follow as possible, I'm going to cover creating projects separately from creating tasks — even though you can, and probably will, create tasks when you create projects.

To create a project, follow these steps:

1. **Click Work on the navigation bar.**

The Work page for your firm appears.

2. **Click the Create Project button (refer to Figure 16-3).**

The panel shown in Figure 16-4 appears.

FIGURE 16-4:
Creating a project
with a template.

3. **(Optional) Choose a template from the Project Template drop-down list.**

   The template categories include Bi-weekly Payroll, Client Onboarding, Monthly Bookkeeping, or Yearly taxes. Using a template adds the tasks associated with the project along with default due dates. You can edit and reorganize the tasks; see "Working with tasks" later in this chapter.

4. **Enter a name for the project.**

5. **Choose My Firm or a client name from the Firm or Client drop-down list.**

   If the project applies only to your firm and not a client, select My Firm. You can also create a new client from this list.

6. **Set a project due date.**

   The due date you set for the project is a constraint; if you add tasks to the project, you won't be able to set due dates for the tasks that occur after the end of the project.

7. **Using the Assigned To list box, assign the project to one of your team members.**

   You can also add details for the project. Keep in mind that tasks can be assigned to only one team member.

TIP

   Click the Repeat slider to set up the time frame to use for recurring projects, such as monthly bank statement reconciliation or quarterly payroll tax filings.

Working with tasks

Now that you've created a project, you can work with the project's tasks. You can do all the following things:

>> Add and delete tasks.

>> Change the due dates assigned to tasks.

>> Reorganize the order of tasks in a project.

Follow these steps to add a task to a project:

1. **Choose Projects from the All Types drop-down list on the Work page.**

2. **Click the name of a project to display the Edit Project page.**

3. **Scroll to the bottom of the Edit Project page, and click Add a Task.**

   The task information page appears, as shown in Figure 16-5.

4. **Supply a task name, due date, and the team member to whom you want to assign the task.**

5. **Click Add Details if you want to add a note about the task.**

   The Details box shown in Figure 16-5 opens, enabling you to add notes.

TIP

   Click the Calendar button in the Due Date field to see permissible dates on which that the task can be due.

   There's no limit to the number of tasks you can create.

6. **To work with a different task, collapse the one you're currently working on by clicking Collapse in the bottom-right corner of the task card (refer to Figure 16-5), or click Add Task to add another task.**

   You don't save individual tasks; instead, you save the project, which saves the task information.

FIGURE 16-5:
Enter a task name
and due date,
and assign it to a
team member of
the firm.

7. **To delete a task or change its information, click the task.**

   As shown in Figure 16-6, the corresponding project is opened, and then the details of the task are displayed.

   - To change the task, supply the new information.

   - To delete the task, click the Remove link.

8. **To change the position of a task in the project, collapse it and then drag the square symbol at the right edge of a task up or down.**

   You can see the symbol you drag to reorder a task in Figure 16-6.

9. **Click Save to save the project and its tasks.**

   The Work page reappears, displaying your new project and any tasks.

Updating task status

As you make progress on a task, you can update its status directly from Grid view on the Work page. Click the arrow on a task card to change its status (see Figure 16-7).

Click and drag to reorder a task.

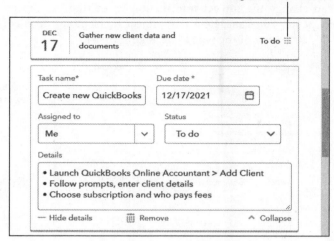

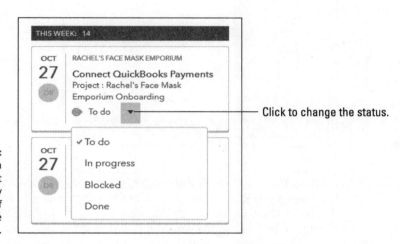

Click to change the status.

Tasks can have a status of To Do, In Progress, Blocked, or Done. You use Blocked status when something is stopping you from completing a task.

Projects can have a status of To Do, In Progress, Blocked or Done, or Canceled.

Editing and deleting project information

You can edit any project or task except those created automatically from a Quick-Books company. Regardless of the view in which you're displaying the Work page, to edit any project or task you created, click any task in the project. The Edit Project panel displays the information of the task you clicked.

You can change the project information by editing the top portion of the Edit Project panel. You can delete any project by clicking the trash-can icon in the bottom-left corner of the panel (see Figure 16-8).

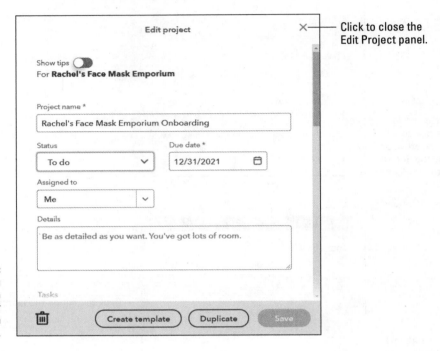

Click to close the Edit Project panel.

FIGURE 16-8:
Buttons allow you to delete, create a template, or duplicate a project.

Many of the projects you create are similar, so save yourself some work and duplicate an existing project. You also can use an existing project to create a template for subsequent similar projects. To duplicate a project, click the Duplicate button on the Edit Project panel. To create a template from the project, click Create Template. Although you can edit project and task information, you can't change a project into a task or a task into a project.

To close the Edit Project panel, click the X in the top-right corner.

Working in List view

Grid view (shown in figures 16-3 and 16-7) is limited in what it can display because the cards take up quite a bit of screen real estate. You can view your projects and tasks in List view, as shown in Figure 16-9, by clicking the List View button in the top-right corner of the Work page (below the Create Project button).

FIGURE 16-9:
The Work page
in List view.

In this view, additional filters are available. In addition to filtering for a client, a team member, and a type of work (project, task, or client request), you can filter by status and set a date range of interest. You can still edit any project or task; simply click anywhere on the project's or task's line to display the Edit Project panel (refer to Figure 16-8).

Working in Calendar view

Calendar view, shown in Figure 16-10, displays the tasks due for any selected date. On the calendar, you'll see the number of tasks due on each date. When you click a date, a panel shows the tasks due on that date.

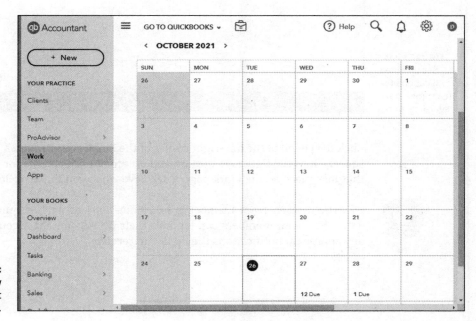

FIGURE 16-10:
Calendar view
presents project
tasks by due date.

Communicating with team members about work

At the risk of stating the obvious, communication is paramount when you're working in a team environment. You can provide notifications by email for a variety of actions associated with the projects and tasks that appear on the Work page. To specify the notifications you want to send to your team, click the Notifications link at the top of Work page (refer to Figure 16-9) to display the Notifications tab of the Company Settings dialog box (see Figure 16-11).

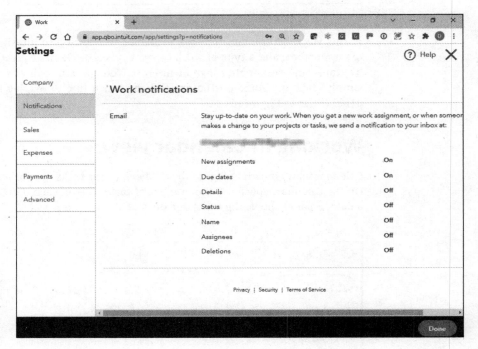

FIGURE 16-11:
Set up email notifications for team members regarding work.

 Click the pencil in the top-right corner of the Email section, which I couldn't quite squeeze into the figure, to turn on and off email notifications for various actions that take place on the Work page. Click Save when you finish, followed by Done.

 By default, each team member gets notifications of new assignments and due dates, but team members can log into their QB Accountant accounts and enable any additional notifications they'd like to receive.

TIP

Facilitating Accountant Activities

Accountants often need to reclassify transactions, examine voided and deleted transactions, write off invoices, and perform other activities. QB Accountant contains tools that make performing these activities easy.

TECHNICAL STUFF

The term *write off* is a phrasal verb representing an action, whereas the term *write-off* is a noun representing the result of said action. (In some quarters, the term *writeoff* is vying for attention, but for now, *write-off* remains the commonly accepted term.)

To view and use the accountant tools, open any QuickBooks company and then click the Accountant Tools button, which looks like a suitcase. The Accountant Tools menu appears (see Figure 16-12).

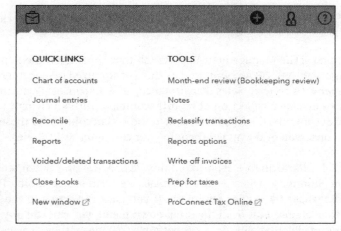

QUICK LINKS

Chart of accounts
Journal entries
Reconcile
Reports
Voided/deleted transactions
Close books
New window

TOOLS

Month-end review (Bookkeeping review)
Notes
Reclassify transactions
Reports options
Write off invoices
Prep for taxes
ProConnect Tax Online

FIGURE 16-12:
The Accountant Tools menu contains commands specifically designed to aid the accountant.

Reviewing reports

Reports in QB Accountant work the same way as reports in QuickBooks; see Chapter 10 for details.

QB Accountant contains some reports that are of particular interest to accountants. From within a QuickBooks company, click Accountant Reports on the Accountant Tools menu to display the Reports page. Reports marked as favorites appear first, and if you scroll down, you'll find all the reports organized in various groups. The Reports in the For My Accountant group (most of which appear in

Figure 16-13) may be of particular interest to you because they contains reports such as Adjusted Trial Balance and Adjusting Journal Entries. To make any of these reports appear at the top of the Reports page (so that you don't need to scroll down), click the star next to the report to mark it as a favorite.

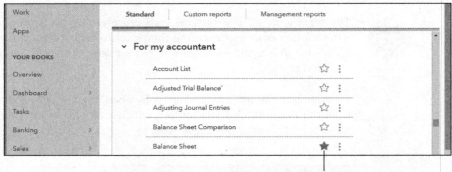

Click a star to mark a report as a favorite.

If you click the Management Reports tab that appears on the Reports page (refer to Figure 16-13), QB Accountant lists three customized management-style reports: Company Overview, Sales Performance, and Expenses Performance. All three choices display a collection of reports, complete with an elegant cover page and a table of contents. Click the View link in the Action column for these reports to view them onscreen or download them to your computer as PDF files.

The Sales Performance report contains P&L, A/R Aging Detail, and Sales by Customer Summary, whereas the Expenses Performance contains P&L, A/P Detail, and Expenses by Vendor Summary. If you click the arrow in the Actions column and then choose Edit from the drop-down menu, you can edit any report package, adding or deleting reports, or modifying the appearance of pages in the report, including determining whether pages such as the table of contents appear in the report. Using the same drop-down menu in the Actions column, you can send these reports via email, export the information to PDF or .docx files (compatible with Microsoft Word or Google Docs), or make copies so that you can make your own set of management reports.

TIP

Copying one of these reports before you change it is a rare chance to have your cake and eat it too: You keep the original report intact and create your own version of it as well.

Click the Custom Reports tab on the Reports page to view reports you've customized and saved. Click Reports Options on the Accountant Tools menu (refer to Figure 16-12) to set default report dates and the accounting basis. You also can see account reconciliation status for cash and credit card accounts, and view and set company closing date information.

WARNING

Be aware that any changes you make on the Report Tools page reset all default report dates and the accounting basis, even if you run the report from the Reports screen. So if your report comes up with an unexpected set of dates or accounting basis, check the values you set with the Report Options command. These default dates don't apply to payroll reports, because Payroll is a separate product. Neither do these dates apply to QuickReports, which you run from the Chart of Accounts page; the QuickReports period defaults to Since 90 Days Ago.

TIP

The Report Tools page shows whether the books are closed and provides a button to close the books, and the page shows you the reconciliation status of bank and credit card accounts.

Examining voided and deleted transactions

You can click Voided/Deleted Transactions on the Accountant Tools menu (see Figure 16-12) to display the Audit Log page. The default view of the page (see Figure 16-14) shows information about those transactions that have been voided or deleted. But you can use the Events list to view other types of transactions and events.

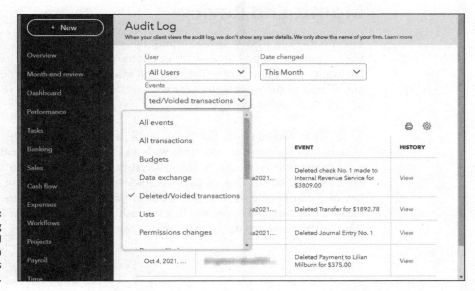

FIGURE 16-14: Use the Audit Log page to view all kinds of activity in the QuickBooks company.

Closing the books

Click Close Books on the Accountant Tools menu (refer to Figure 16-12) to display the Advanced page of the QuickBooks company's Account and Settings dialog box, shown in Figure 16-15. You can click anywhere in the Accounting section to edit the fields in that section, including the closing date for the books.

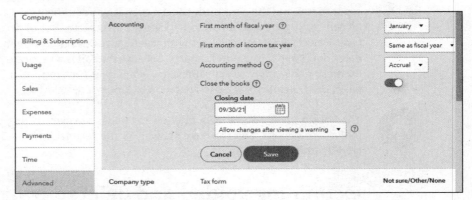

FIGURE 16-15: Setting a closing date.

You can set a closing date and then allow changes before the closing date after QuickBooks issues a warning, or you can require a password to enter changes before the closing date. Click Save to save your changes. Before you close the books, however, you'll likely want to perform a month-end review.

Month-End Review

The Month-End Review (Bookkeeping Review) command gives you a bird's-eye view of potentially problematic transactions in QuickBooks, allows you to monitor the status of account reconciliations, and offers a final review checklist. Click the pencil next to the month and year shown at top- eft in Figure 16-16 to view the Month-End Review for a period.

As shown in Figure 16-16, the Transaction Review tab displays lists of any uncategorized transactions, transactions without payees, and additional items you may want to monitor each month. If you scroll further down on your screen, you also see a To Do Checklist that includes reminders to Check for Personal Transactions, Review Loan Payments, and Record Cash Transactions. Click the Add button to create a new task and optionally link the task to a specific page in QuickBooks. You can change the status of To Do Checklist items to To Do, Waiting, and Done.

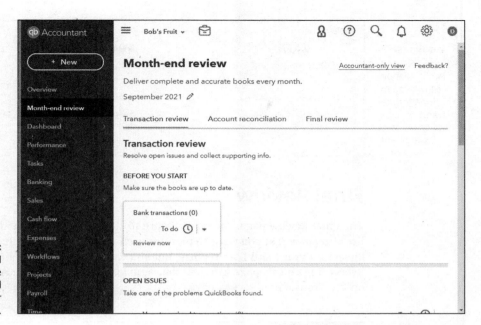

FIGURE 16-16:
The Month-End
Review page
brings potential
issues to your
attention.

TIP

Although not shown in Figure 16-16, you can click the arrow to the left of an Additional Item name, such as Check for Personal Transactions, to reveal buttons that allow you to edit or delete the item.

I couldn't squeeze this into Figure 16-16 either, but when you click Edit on a To Do List item, you can change the name and/or link name of the item; add details; and, in the QuickBooks Page Link field, provide the URL of a given page. You can copy the URL from the address bar of your browser. This task is easiest to accomplish when you click the New Window command on the Accountant Tools menu to open an additional browser window within the same QuickBooks company.

Account Reconciliation

Click the Account Reconciliation tab to monitor the status of account reconciliations. Like Transaction Review, if you scroll down this tab offers an Additional Item section that includes suggestions to Reconcile Loan Accounts and Review Reconciliation Report, as shown in Figure 16-17. You can alter these To Do Checklist items in the same fashion that you do for Transaction Review.

FIGURE 16-17:
Account
Reconciliation
allows you to
monitor the
status of bank
and credit card
statement
reconciliations.

ADDITIONAL ITEMS

Keep track of the other tasks you want to complete every month.

⌄ To Do Checklist

ITEM	LINK	STATUS
⟩ **Reconcile loan accounts**	Reconcile	To do 🕐 ⌄
⟩ **Review reconciliation report**	Review	To do 🕐 ⌄

(+ Add)

Final Review

The Final Review page, shown in Figure 16-18, allows you to maintain a running list of reports that you want to monitor each month. The list includes the Balance Sheet and Profit and Loss reports, but you can add as many reports as you want. Everything on this page works in the same fashion I describe for Additional Items on the Transaction Review page.

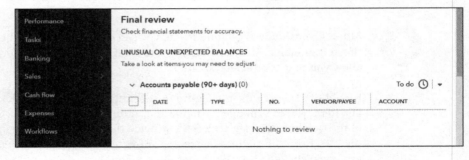

FIGURE 16-18:
Once all issues
have been
resolved, your
Final Review list
will report
Nothing to
Review.

Reclassifying transactions

When you click Reclassify Transactions on the Accountant Tools menu (refer to Figure 16-12), the Reclassify Transactions page appears (see Figure 16-19). You can use this page to reclassify transactions without worrying about the company's closing date.

You use the information in the Account section on the left side of the page and the Transactions section on the right side of the page to filter for the date range and type of accounts (Profit and Loss or Balance Sheet) you want to consider. Select an account type on the left side of the page to display transactions that meet the criteria on the right side of the page, and then choose Accrual or Cash in the Basis section. You can apply additional filters if you want and then reclassify one or more transactions in the Reclassify section.

FIGURE 16-19:
Use this page
to reclassify
transactions.

TIP

If you've enabled classes and/or locations in your QuickBooks company, you can reclassify transactions based on account, class, or location. You can always reclassify a transaction based on account, whereas class and/or location appear if you've enabled the respective setting. To do so navigate to Settings ⇨ Account and Settings ⇨ Advanced ⇨ Categories.

Follow these steps to reclassify transactions:

1. **Set the date range you want to consider at the top of the page.**

2. **Choose Profit & Loss or Balance Sheet from the Account Types List.**

3. **Choose Accrual or Cash in the Basis section.**

4. **Click an account from the list at the left to examine that account's transactions.**

   The transactions in the account appear on the right side of the page.

5. **Above the list of transactions on the right side of the page, set filters to display the types of transactions that you might consider reclassifying.**

   You can change transactions that display green circles. You can also click a transaction to open it in its transaction window and then make changes.

6. **To change several transactions simultaneously, select them by selecting the check boxes next to them.**

7. **Below the list of transactions, select the For Select Transactions, Change check box.**

8. **From the Account To list, specify a different account.**

   If Class Tracking is turned on, you also have the option to change the assigned class.

9. **Click the Reclassify button.**

Writing off invoices

Clicking Write Off Invoices on the Accountant Tools menu displays the Write Off Invoices page, which enables you to view invoices and then write them off to an account of your choice. At the top of the page, you set filters to display the invoices you want to review. You can view invoices more than 180 days old, more than 120 days old, in the current accounting period, or in a custom date range that you set. You also can set a balance limit.

As shown in Figure 16-20, QB Accountant displays the invoice number, customer name, date, age, original invoice amount, and the amount still due on the invoice. To write off any invoices, select the check box next to them. At the bottom of the page, select the account you want to use to write off the invoices; then click the Write Off button.

FIGURE 16-20: Writing off invoices.

A confirmation dialog box opens, as shown in Figure 16-21. Select an account if needed, and then click Apply to write off the invoice(s); otherwise, click Cancel.

WARNING

The Write Off feature doesn't make adjusting entries in the current period; instead, it makes adjustments in the period in which the transaction was originally created, which can affect closed periods negatively. For details on writing off an item in a closed period, see `https://community.intuit.com/articles/` `1145951-write-off-bad-debt`.

FIGURE 16-21:
Confirm that you want to write off the selected invoices.

Understanding the Prep for Taxes page

You can use the Prep for Taxes tool to adjust and review accounts before preparing the client's taxes. To do so, click the Accountant Tools button at the top of the screen and then choose Prep for Taxes in the Tools column. A new Year-End Tasks tab, shown in Figure 16-22 with the first task expanded, provides a list of common tasks that you can edit or reorder. Click any task to delete or edit it. Also, you can add document or internet links to the task.

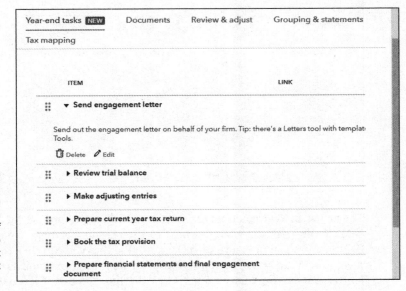

FIGURE 16-22:
The Year-End Tasks tab provides a checklist of activities to complete as part of filing the tax return.

The second tab is Documents, which you use to upload and organize supporting documents for your client's income tax return, as shown in Figure 16-23. Next, click the Review & Adjust tab to display the page shown in Figure 16-24, which allows you to compare the current tax year with the previous tax year.

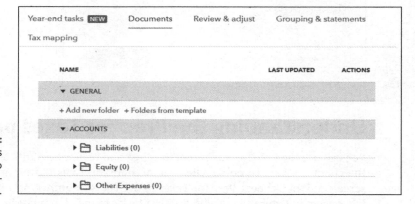

FIGURE 16-23:
The Documents tab allows you to upload support-ing materials.

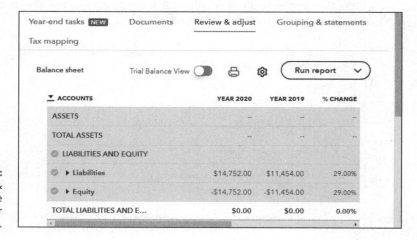

FIGURE 16-24:
The Review & Adjust tab of the Prep for Taxes page.

The values in Year columns are locked on the page to protect the integrity of the data. If you click the triangles next to the various headings (that is, Liabilities, Equity, and so on in Figure 16-24), you'll find that you can click the Make Adjust-ment link in the Actions column next to an appropriate account to create adjusting journal entries for that account. Click the link to open a journal entry window where you can record the adjusting entry. As shown in Figure 16-25, the Is Adjust-ing Journal Entry? check box is selected automatically. When you save the entry, the Prep for Taxes page indicates that you made a change. If you accept the change, the Prep for Taxes page reflects your adjustment; in addition, the balance in the Year column changes.

FIGURE 16-25:
The Journal Entry
window with the
Is Adjusting
Journal Entry?
check box clicked.

Journal Entry #2　　　　　　　　　　　　　⚙ ⑦ Help ✕

Currency

USD United States Dollar ▾

Journal date　　Journal no.　　☑ Is Adjusting Journal Entry?

12/19/2021　　2

TIP

You can delete adjusting entries after you accept them. To do so, click the amount of the adjusting entry to display a report from which you can get to the underlying journal entry. At the bottom of the page, click More; then click Delete. Confirm that you want to delete the transaction. When you return to the Prep for Taxes screen, you'll need to accept the changes that you made.

You can click any dollar value that appears as a link to view a report of all transactions that make up that balance. From the report, you can drill down to a particular transaction and, if necessary, change it. After you save the transaction and redisplay the report, you can click the Back to Prep for Taxes link at the top of the report page to redisplay the Prep for Taxes page. Once again, you're asked to accept the change, which updates the Prep for Taxes page to reflect such.

You can use the down arrow in the Actions column to add notes and attach documents to a particular line, which helps you remember why you made a particular adjustment.

You can click the check mark next to a category or account to mark it as reviewed, which lets you keep track of where you are in the review process.

The fourth tab available in Prep for Taxes is Grouping & Statements, shown in Figure 16-26. This tab allows you to group accounts in any fashion you like, which can aid the review process. You can also click Update in the Actions column to add a reference code, note, reference, and/or attachment. Click Run Report to see your regrouped report, or click the arrow next to Run Report to export the report to Excel. Use the handles represented by six dots to move accounts between groups at will. You can use Grouping & Statements with both the Balance Sheet and Profit & Loss reports.

The final tab, Tax Mapping, is for mapping your client's books to their tax return. The Prep for Taxes feature automatically maps most account balances to lines on tax forms you'll file for corporations by using IRS Form 1120 (for corporations) or 1120s, partnerships that use IRS Form 1065, not-for-profit organizations that use IRS Form 990, and sole proprietorships that use IRS Form 1040. For other business organization types, you can assign accounts to tax form lines manually. Also, you can manually assign lines on tax forms for accounts that the tool doesn't recognize, and you can change tax line assignments as needed. If you haven't set the tax form for a given company yet, the Tax Mapping page presents a Select a Tax Form to Get Started list. Once you choose a form, the Tax Mapping page updates to show you the aforementioned features.

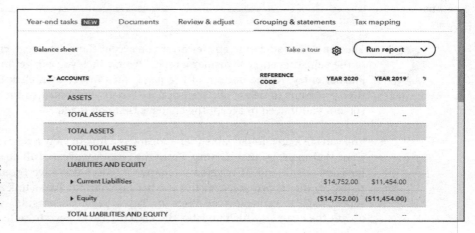

FIGURE 16-26:
The Grouping &
Statements page
of the Prep for
Taxes page.

Click the Tax Mapping tab of the Prep for Taxes page to see the page you use to map last year's QuickBooks information directly to tax forms (see Figure 16-27).

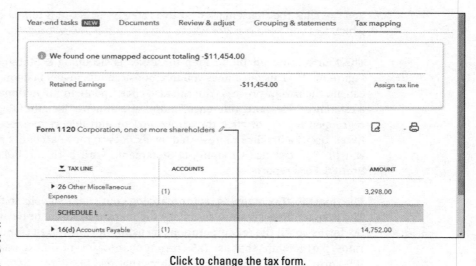

FIGURE 16-27:
The Tax Mapping
tab of the Prep
for Taxes page.

Click to change the tax form.

TIP

If you haven't yet selected a tax form for a QuickBooks company, you'll be prompted to do so when you access the Tax Mapping tab. Or you can click the Edit button (the pencil) next to the selected form at the left side of the Tax Mapping page and select a tax form; refer to Figure 16-27.

To assign an account to a tax form line or edit the line to which an account is assigned, click the Assign Tax Line link. The Assign Tax Line panel appears on the right side of the screen. Select the appropriate tax form line and then click Save.

When you finish reviewing the Prep for Taxes pages and making adjustments to entries, you can click the Tax Option button in the top-right corner of the page and then click Update Existing Return or Create New Return to transfer the information to ProConnect Tax Online and generate a tax return. You don't pay anything to use the Prep for Taxes feature; you pay only when you print or e-file a return from ProConnect Tax Online.

REMEMBER

If you don't use ProConnect Tax Online or you aren't the tax preparer, you have the option to export the adjustments to a comma-separated values (CSV) file (readable by Microsoft Excel) so that you can import them into a separate application. Choose the Export CSV File option from the drop-down menu on the Tax Options button.

Taking a brief look at other accountant tools

The Accountant Tools menu contains a few other tools that make an accountant's life easier:

>> Chart of Accounts displays the Chart of Accounts window. I describe working in this window in Chapter 14.

>> Journal Entries displays the Journal Entry window.

>> Reconcile displays the Reconcile page, where you can choose an account or review existing Reconciliation reports. For more detail on reconciling accounts, see Chapter 8.

>> New Window allows you to open a new window quickly in QB Accountant, as I discuss in Chapter 15.

>> Notes allow you to see the same notes that you can add from the Notes page that appears when you click a name on your client list.

>> ProConnect Tax Online launches a new browser window that takes you to Tax Hub in ProConnect Tax Online, another Intuit product. Tax Hub allows you to track the status of your clients' tax returns. ProConnect Tax Online connects to your QB Accountant account but is a separate product.

Chapter **17**

Automating QuickBooks Analysis with Power Query

I n Chapter 11, I explain how you can analyze QuickBooks reports in Microsoft Excel. The steps require some manual effort, which can become tedious if you need to perform them frequently or for multiple clients. In this chapter, I show you how you can automate the steps by using the Power Query feature of Excel.

First, I show how to create self-updating reports in Excel. I close the chapter with an explanation of how to unpivot data in a QuickBooks report. Unpivoting means transposing data from columns going across the worksheet into rows that travel down. You can then more easily filter the data and create pivot tables from it, as I discuss in Chapter 11.

Introducing Power Query

Power Query is an Excel feature that allows you to automate report analysis in a similar fashion to what you'd do in Excel. The difference is that Power Query keeps track of the steps that can be applied automatically to future versions of

QuickBooks reports and other data. Even better, Power Query is often referred to as a code-free solution, which means that you'll be able to automate repetitive tasks without writing any programming code.

Power Query has been around since Excel 2010 and is built into Excel 2016 and later versions. Excel 2010 or 2013 users will need to perform an online search for "Power Query download" and follow the instructions. This chapter is best suited to readers who are using Excel 2016 or later (especially as part of Microsoft 365) on a Windows computer because Power Query is not fully implemented yet in Excel for Mac.

For this chapter, I used the sample company for QuickBooks Online, which you can access at `https://qbo.intuit.com/redir/testdrive`. I chose this company so that you'll have an easy way to generate reports that have actual data in them. You also can follow along with your own data.

Connecting to QuickBooks Reports

This section explains how to automate the manual steps you may have performed in Chapter 11 when cleaning up the Transaction List by Date report. The end result is a set-and-forget approach. In other words, going forward, when you export the report from QuickBooks you'll save the new Excel workbook over the previous Excel workbook that contained the QuickBooks report. Your cleaned up data will appear in a second workbook that is linked to your report. You can choose to have the second workbook update itself automatically, or you can manually click Data ⇨ Refresh All to refresh the workbook with the latest information that you exported from QuickBooks.

Begin by exporting the Transaction List by Date report from QuickBooks. Follow these steps:

1. **Choose Reports or Business Overview ⇨ Reports.**

The Reports page appears.

2. **Start typing** Transaction List by Date **in the search field and then choose that report title in the search results.**

The search field makes it easy to locate reports without scrolling through the entire list.

3. **Select a date range, such as This Year, and then click Run Report.**

Many QuickBooks reports default to the current month, but you can designate any time period.

4. **Click the Export button and then choose Export to Excel on the resulting menu that appears.**

See Chapter 10 for more information about running reports in QuickBooks.

5. **Open and save the report in a location that you'll be able to remember.**

By default, reports that you export from QuickBooks land in your Downloads folder. In this case, you'll want a more permanent location for this report because you'll be saving over this file again in the future.

6. **Close the Excel report.**

You don't always have to close a file before you can analyze data in Excel. You can put your cursor within a list of data in a spreadsheet and then choose Data ➪ From Table/Range or Data ➪ From Sheet to load the data into the Power Query Editor. In this exercise, though, you want to access a workbook that has been closed.

7. **Press Ctrl-N or choose File ➪ New ➪ Blank Workbook in Excel to create a blank workbook.**

8. **Choose Data ➪ Get Data ➪ From File ➪ From Workbook.**

If you're using Excel 2016, choose Data ➪ New Query. If you're using Excel 2010 or 2013, a similar New Query type of command will appear on the Query menu.

9. **Browse for and select the QuickBooks report that you saved in Step 5 and then click the Import button.**

A Navigator dialog box appears.

10. **Click the worksheet that contains the data you want to access and then click Transform Data to open Power Query Editor (see Figure 17-1).**

If you were to click Load, Power Query would return the data to a new worksheet without making any modifications. If you want to automate the manual cleanup process described in Chapter 11, click Transform Data instead.

At this point, you're ready to start the cleanup process. The work that you've done so far has connected your report to Power Query and eliminated two extraneous steps that could pose issues down the line.

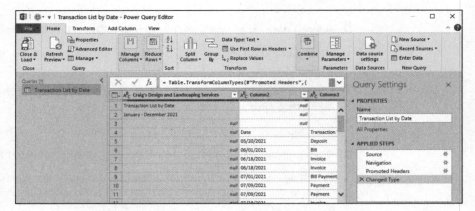

FIGURE 17-1:
The Power Query
Editor shows the
QuickBooks
report that you
just imported.

Removing header rows

As you see in Figure 17-1 earlier in this chapter, several blank rows appear at the top of the report, and the column headings appear on row 4. I show you how to remove those rows and then promote the contents of row 4 to be the true column headings. First, remove two unneeded default steps that Power Query sometimes adds by following these steps:

1. **Right-click Promoted Headers in the Applied Steps pane on the right side of the screen, and choose Delete Until End from the shortcut menu.**

The last two steps in the Applied Steps area in Figure 17-1 are extraneous. Every Power Query transformation has a Source step, and it typically has a Navigation step as well. The Navigation step allows you to see the data in the worksheet. In this case, you want to remove the Promoted Headers and Changed Type steps because they can pose conflicts down the line.

2. **When the Delete Step prompt appears, click Delete.**

You can also hover your mouse over a step in the Applied Steps pane and then click the X to the left of its name to remove it from the list.

3. **Choose Home ⇨ Remove Rows ⇨ Remove Top Rows.**

The Remove Top Rows dialog box appears (see Figure 17-2).

The Remove Rows command allows you to remove rows from the top or bottom of a report. You can also remove duplicates, alternate rows, and rows that contain errors.

4. **Enter 3 in the Number of Rows field and then click OK.**

The goal is to make the headings on row 4 move up to the first row of the listing.

Remove Top Rows

Specify how many rows to remove from the top.

Number of rows

| 3 |

[OK] [Cancel]

5. **Click the first column of the report and then press Delete on your keyboard.**

Unlike in Excel, you can remove columns in Power Query by clicking a column and pressing Delete. You can also choose Home ⇨ Remove Columns or right-click a column and choose Remove from the shortcut menu.

At this point, the report format is starting to shape up, but you can still make some additional improvements.

Promoting headers

If you scroll down on your report in its current state, you'll find that the headings in row 1 scroll off the screen. In an Excel worksheet, you can choose View ⇨ Freeze Panes to freeze one or more rows at the top of the screen. In Power Query, you can freeze only a single row at the top of the screen by choosing Home ⇨ Use First Row As Headers. This command moves the column headings from row 1 up to the frame of the Power Query grid. If you change your mind about this action, hover your mouse over Promoted Headers in the Applied Steps pane and then click the X that appears to the left of its name.

Notice that Power Query added a Changed Type step to the Applied Steps pane in Figure 17-3. Changed Type means that Power Query changed the data type for one or more columns. On this report, the dates in the first column were stored as text. I show in Chapter 11 how to use the Text to Columns feature in Excel to convert text-based dates to numeric format. Conversely, Power Query noticed the dates stored as text and converted them automatically.

TIP

Power Query isn't always this prescient when it comes to recognizing data types. You'll see an icon to the left of each column's header. Most often, you'll see ABC, which means that the column is being treated as text. If you see a column of numbers with the ABC icon, you can click the icon and choose a different format from a drop-down list, such as Decimal Number, Currency, or Whole Number.

At this point, the report is clean enough that you could send it back to Excel. First, though, I want to show you some additional actions that you can take in Power Query.

Click to format the first row as a header row.

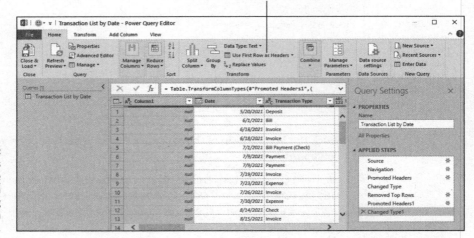

FIGURE 17-3:
The Applied Steps pane shows the transformation steps being carried out on a report.

Removing unwanted columns

In this section, I show you how to use the Choose Columns command to indicate which columns you want to keep and which you want to remove. For instance, you may not want to include the Num, Posting, and Split columns in the final data set that you're building. Follow these steps to remove any extraneous columns:

1. Chose Home ⇨ Choose Columns.

Many command buttons in Power Query are bifurcated. For instance, if you click the top half of the Choose Columns command, the Choose Columns dialog box opens (see Figure 17-4). If you click the bottom half, a menu appears from which you have to click Choose Columns a second time. On the other hand, this action also reveals the Go to Column command. The Go to Column command allows you to navigate to a specific column in your report by selecting the column name in a list.

2. Clear the Num, Posting, and Split check boxes and then click OK.

The fields in the Choose Columns dialog box are initially presented in the order in which they appear in the report. If you click the AZ button to the right of the Search Columns field, you can choose Name from the drop-down list to sort the list alphabetically, if that makes it easier for you to find the fields you want to remove.

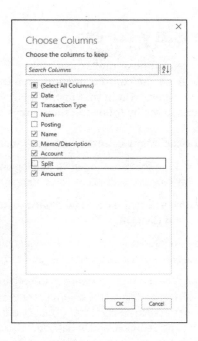

FIGURE 17-4:
The Choose Columns dialog box provides an easy way to remove unwanted columns from a report.

3. **Click Settings next to the Removed Other Columns step in the Applied Steps pane (see Figure 17-5).**

   You can revise a step that you've added to a Power Query transformation if a Settings icon appears.

4. **You can now remove any other columns you missed the first time, so you might clear the Memo/Description check box and then click OK.**

   At this point, the report should have five columns, as shown in Figure 17-5.

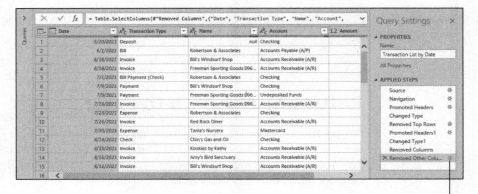

FIGURE 17-5:
The report is in a much more analysis-ready format than it was in Figure 17-3.

Click this Settings icon.

Filtering unnecessary rows

In an Excel worksheet, you can select one or more rows, right-click the worksheet frame, and then choose Delete from the shortcut menu to remove the rows. You can't remove rows from a Power Query grid in that fashion, but you can filter out transactions that you don't want to see by following these steps:

1. Click the filter arrow at the top of any column, such as Transaction Type.

In the case of the Transaction Type column, a menu containing an alphabetical listing one of each Transaction Type appears. Blank rows appear as *(null)*.

2. Clear the Select All check box, select the items you want to keep (such as Invoice and Sales Receipt), and click OK.

If you're creating a list of sales-related transactions, the Power Query grid now displays only invoice and sales receipt transactions (see Figure 17-6).

You can apply filters to as many columns as you want. Also, you're not limited to choosing options from the list. Depending on the column's contents, context-specific options on the filter menu such as Text Filters, Date Filters, or Number Filters will appear. Depending upon context, additional options such as Contains, Does Not Contain, Begins With, Greater Than, Less Than, and Between may become available as well.

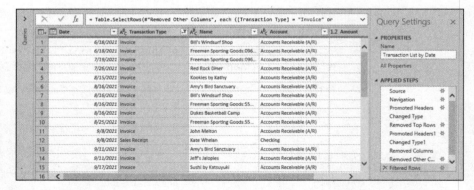

FIGURE 17-6:
You can't delete specific rows from the middle of the Power Query grid but can use filters to show specific data.

Returning the data to Excel

Choose Home ⇨ Close & Load to return the data from Power Query to Excel. Doing so closes the Power Query Editor and enables you to continue working in Excel. The data appears in a new worksheet in your workbook as a table in Excel. I discuss the table feature in Chapter 11.

Instead of returning the data to Excel as a table, you can opt to create a pivot table, pivot chart, or simply a data connection by following these steps:

1. Choose Home ⇨ Close & Load in Power Query (click the words Close & Load as opposed to the icon), and then click Close & Load To on the resulting menu.

The Import Data dialog box opens (see Figure 17-7).

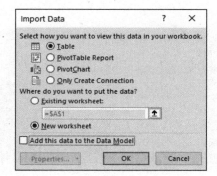

2. Choose an option in the top section of the dialog box.

The default options include

- *Table,* which creates a list of data in an Excel worksheet

- *PivotTable Report,* which creates a blank pivot table canvas in a worksheet

- *PivotChart,* which creates a blank pivot chart canvas in a worksheet

- *Only Create Connection,* which stages data in Power Query that you want to append to or merge with another data set

If you choose the Table option, your data will appear in a new Excel worksheet.

If you choose PivotTable or PivotChart, then a blank pivot table and/or pivot chart appears in your workbook. Unlike the Table option, you then won't see the underlying raw data in your Excel worksheet unless you double-click a number within the pivot table. For this reason, most users prefer to send data to Excel as a table, and then create a pivot table based on the table so that they can have the detail and a summary.

3. In the second section of the dialog box, choose an option.

You can choose Existing Worksheet and make a choice from the drop-down list to place the data in an existing worksheet instead. Keep in mind that depending on where you place the Power Query data, you could end up erasing some existing information, so it's better to accept the default of New Worksheet.

4. **Click OK.**

If you click the Cancel button instead, Power Query returns the data to your Excel workbook, and you can delete the worksheet from the workbook to remove any unwanted data.

TIP

Mission accomplished! You've successfully transformed a QuickBooks report into an analysis-ready Excel format. You can close the Queries & Connections task pane (see Figure 17-8), which appears automatically whenever you send data to Excel from Power Query.

FIGURE 17-8:
The Queries & Connections task pane appears automatically every time you import data via Power Query.

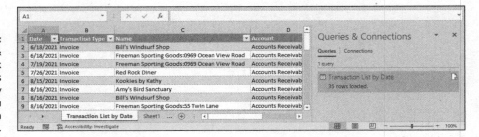

TIP

The Queries & Connections task pane allows you to monitor the data connections that you've established within a workbook. You can right-click any connection and choose commands from the shortcut menu to rename, edit, or delete the connection. Choosing Edit returns you to the Power Query Editor. Deleting the connection doesn't remove the data from the worksheet, but prevents it from being refreshed. (I discuss refreshing Power Query data later in the chapter.) If you close this task pane, choose Data ⇨ Queries & Connections to display it again.

Creating Self-Updating Reports

The gold standard for many accountants is establishing set-and-forget reports. In this case, the process is partly manual because you still have to export the Quick-Books report each time you want to update your Excel spreadsheet.

TIP

Although the topic is beyond the scope of this book, third-party ODBC drivers are available for QuickBooks Online that allow you to connect spreadsheets directly to QuickBooks, thereby eliminating the export process. After you install the ODBC driver, you can use Power Query to pull data directly into Excel. Two such drivers are available at www.cdata.com and www.qodbc.com.

Setting Power Query to refresh automatically

Although Power Query allows you to establish a connection to other workbooks and data sources, it's not a live feed to your spreadsheet. Rather, Power Query returns a snapshot of your data. If the data changes, either because you edited the data you connected to or saved a new version over a QuickBooks export, the new data won't appear in your spreadsheet until you refresh. In the "Refreshing reports" section at the end of this chapter, I discuss three ways to refresh data from Power Query, but here are the steps for the automated option:

1. **Click any cell within the list of data that Power Query returns.**

   Certain Excel features are context-sensitive, so supporting menu commands aren't available unless you click a cell containing data related to a command. For instance, you only see pivot table–related commands when you click inside a pivot table. With regard to Power Query, the Query menu only appears in the Excel Ribbon when you click any cell within data that has been brought into Excel from Power Query.

2. **Choose Query ⇨ Properties.**

   The Query Properties dialog box appears (see Figure 17-9).

   You won't see the Query menu unless you've clicked the Power Query data.

REMEMBER

An alternative way to access the Query Properties dialog box is to choose Data ⇨ Properties to open the External Data Range Properties dialog box and then click the Query Properties button to the right of the Name field.

3. Clear the Enable Background Refresh check box, select the Refresh Data When Opening the File check box, and (if available) select the Enable Fast Data Load check box.

The Enable Background Refresh option has good intentions; it's designed to enable you to keep working in your spreadsheet while data from an external source is being refreshed. In my experience, though, this option can lead to confusion because you can initiate a refresh and not be sure whether anything is happening. If you deselect this option, you won't be able to carry out any actions while the refresh occurs, but the refresh will happen much faster.

The Refresh Data When Opening the File option is where the automation happens. This option causes your spreadsheet to reach out to the external workbook automatically and grab the latest version of the data, so you see the newest information in your workbook.

Fast Data Load purportedly speeds the refresh process. I'm not convinced, but enabling it doesn't hurt.

You can change these options at any time. You might turn off Refresh Data When Opening the File if you want to archive a snapshot of a data set for a particular point in time, for example.

4. Click OK to close the Query Properties dialog box.

Query properties that you set are unique to each Power Query connection, so you need to carry out the preceding steps every time you establish a new data connection via Power Query.

Now that you've set the query properties for your Power Query connection, you need to eliminate one other speed bump to streamline the update process. Follow these steps to disable the Enable Content security prompt that otherwise appears every time you open your workbook:

1. Save and close your workbook that contains a Power Query connection.

2. Reopen your workbook.

A security prompt appears.

Don't click Enable Content in the prompt. If you do, you won't be able to prevent the prompt from appearing again. If you did click Enable Content, close your workbook, reopen it, and proceed to Step 3.

3. **Choose File ⇨ Info ⇨ Enable Content ⇨ Enable All Content to suppress the security prompt.**

As shown in Figure 17-10, the Enable All Content option makes the document a trusted document. When you mark a document as such, Excel no longer requires you to choose Enable Content before you refresh the workbook.

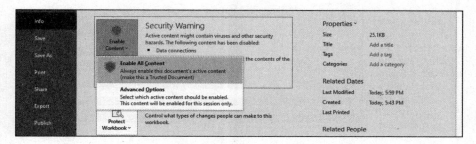

FIGURE 17-10: Setting a workbook to be a trusted document eliminates the need to click Enable Content every time you open the file.

If you're presenting the data in the form of a table, you're all set. But if you're using the pivot table feature, which I discuss in Chapter 11, you need to change one more setting to ensure that your report is completely self-updating. Follow these steps:

1. **Select any cell within a pivot table, and choose the PivotTable Analyze menu.**

The pivot table menus are context-sensitive, so the PivotTable Analyze and Design menus vanish when your cursor isn't within a pivot table.

2. **Choose PivotTable Analyze ⇨ Options.**

The PivotTable Options dialog box appears (see Figure 17-11).

3. **Click the Data tab, select the Refresh Data When Opening the File check box, and then click OK.**

This option instructs Excel to refresh your pivot table when you open the workbook.

WARNING

Make sure that you set both your Power Query connection and any pivot tables based on Power Query data to refresh automatically when you open the file; otherwise, you could find yourself reviewing stale information. Choose Data ⇨ Refresh All in Excel to be absolutely certain that everything in your workbook is updated.

FIGURE 17-11:
You must also click Refresh Data When Opening the File for a pivot table tied to Power Query to update itself automatically.

Adding a total row

Data that you return to Excel from Power Query always appears within a table. I discuss the table feature in more detail in Chapter 11. Also, you can easily add a total row to any table in Excel by following these steps:

1. **Click anywhere inside a table.**

This step displays the Table Design menu, which appears only when your cursor is inside a table.

2. **Choose Design ⇨ Total Row.**

A total row that automatically sums or counts the last column is added to your table. If the last column is comprised of numeric values, Excel sums the column. If the column is comprised of words or dates, Excel counts the number of records instead.

REMEMBER

The total row in a table tallies only the visible rows, which means that it automatically recalculates any time you filter or slice the contents of a table.

3. **(Optional) Select any cell in the total row and click the arrow to display a drop-down menu that allows you to add or remove a mathematical calculation for that column (see Figure 17-12).**

You can choose among 11 mathematical functions, but most likely, you'll opt to sum, average, or count the records.

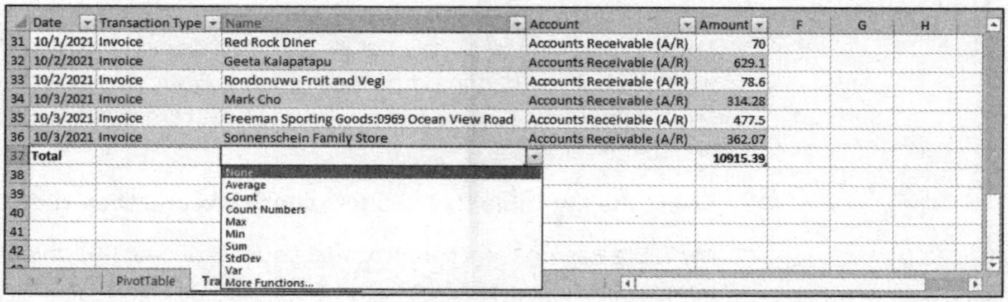

FIGURE 17-12:
You can sum,
average, count, or
perform other
mathematical
calculations in
any column of a
table's total row.

Transforming QuickBooks Data

Automating report cleanup is a huge benefit of Power Query. But Power Query can do much more. One of my favorite features is unpivoting reports.

The Transaction List by Date report makes it easy to filter because all the data appears in rows. Other reports, such as Profit and Loss by Customer, are oriented differently, with a row for each account and a column for each customer. If you want to see the total activity for a certain account for two customers at the same time, you don't have a good way to get that information quickly. Also, you can't easily create a pivot table from that type of report layout. In that case, unpivoting the data can be helpful. All the data appears in rows, and then you can filter or slice it.

Here's how to run the Profit and Loss by Customer report:

1. Choose Reports or Business Overview ⇨ Reports.

The Reports page appears.

2. Start typing Profit and Loss by Customer **in the search field and then choose the report title.**

3. Click the Export button and then choose Export to Excel from the resulting menu.

This report may be rather wide, so you may have to scroll the report to the right to access the Export button.

4. Open the report, and click the first customer name.

This positions your cursor so that Excel will recognize the list that you want to import into Power Query.

5. Choose Data ⇨ From Sheet or Data ⇨ From Table/Range.

The Create Table dialog box appears (see Figure 17-13).

Microsoft is going through what it's calling a "visual refresh" for Microsoft 365, which includes renaming certain commands. Your version of Excel may have a From Table/Range command or a From Sheet command. Both commands get you to the same place.

6. **Select the My Table Has Headers check box and then click OK.**

   My Table Has Headers confirms that your list of data has unique column headings across the first row. This report doesn't have a heading in the first column, but Excel fills in the gap with a generic heading.

FIGURE 17-13:
The My Table Has Headers setting allows you to confirm that your list has titles at the top of most or all columns.

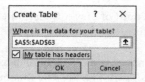

At this point, your data appears in Power Query Editor. The next step is unpivoting the columns.

Unpivoting columns

The sample report that I ran has 30 columns, which makes analysis tricky or even impossible unless you unpivot the data. The Unpivot command allows you to unpivot specific columns in a report. Unpivot Other Columns is helpful when you want to unpivot a contiguous group of columns. If unpivoting the data jumbles your data, click the X next to the Unpivoted Other Columns command in the Applied Steps pane to remove the transformation.

Follow these steps to unpivot columns:

1. **Right-click on the first column in your report, and choose Unpivot Other Columns from the shortcut menu.**

   Your report has three columns: Column1, Attribute, and Value (see Figure 17-14).

2. **Double-click the Column1 heading, replace Column1 with** Account, **and press Enter.**

   You can double-click any column heading in Power Query and type a new name.

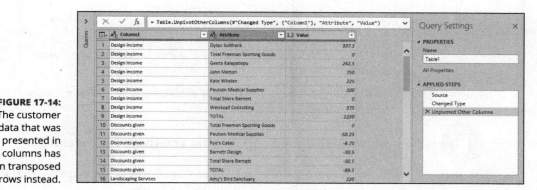

FIGURE 17-14:
The customer data that was presented in columns has been transposed into rows instead.

3. **Change the name of the Attribute and Value columns to Customer and Amount, respectively.**

   Renaming columns is a great way to prevent confusion so that no one misconstrues data in a column that has a cryptic name.

4. **Click the Filter arrow in the Amount (or Value) column, and clear the check box for 0 (zero).**

   It's doubtful that every customer will have activity in every account, so filtering out zeros eliminates noise from your report.

5. **(Optional) Click the step immediately above Unpivoted Other Columns in the Applied Steps pane, in this case Changed Type.**

   This step allows you to see what the report looked like before you unpivoted the data. Click the Unpivoted Other Column step again to see the unpivoted data. In effect, Power Query lets you walk around within the transformations so that you can see what the data looked like at various points. Click the last step in the Applied Steps pane to see the final output.

6. **Click Home ⇨ Close & Load.**

   Power Query returns the cleaned-up, unpivoted data to a new worksheet in your workbook. The original report remains in place in the form of a table.

Refreshing reports

Remember, Power Query isn't a live feed from any data source but instead returns a snapshot of your data. You can refresh Power Query data manually in five ways:

» Right-click the list, and choose Refresh from the shortcut menu.

» Click any cell in the list, and choose Table Design ⇨ Refresh in Excel.

- » Choose Data ⇨ Refresh All in Excel.

- » Right-click a connection in the Queries & Connections pane, and choose Refresh from the shortcut menu.

- » Choose Query ⇨ Refresh. This menu is available only when Power Query connects to an external data source.

REMEMBER

You need to refresh a report only when the underlying data has changed.

If you'd like to learn more about Power Query, please see *Microsoft Excel Power Pivot & Power Query For Dummies* by Michael Alexander.

5

The Part of Tens

IN THIS PART . . .

Become familiar with the Chrome browser and its features.

Learn about setting up Chrome profiles and working with Chrome windows, tabs, and bookmarks.

Examine Chrome's security and privacy.

Chapter **18**

Ten Ways to Use Chrome Effectively

This chapter introduces some browser tips and tricks that can make using Chrome easier and more effective, both in general and specifically with QuickBooks Online and QB Accountant. In particular, you see how you can use profiles in Chrome to open more than one QuickBooks Online company at a time.

Setting a Home Page

Many browsers sport a Home button that returns you to your *home page* — the page that appears when you open the browser. By default, Chrome displays a New Tab page instead of a home page, but you can display and set a home page.

Make sure that you know the web address of the page you want to set as your home page and then follow these steps:

1. **Choose Chrome ➪ Settings.**

   The Settings tab appears.

2. **Click the Home button on the toolbar.**

   This button appears between the Refresh button and the address field (see Figure 18-1). Chrome defaults to opening the New Tab page whenever you click the Home button until you tell it otherwise.

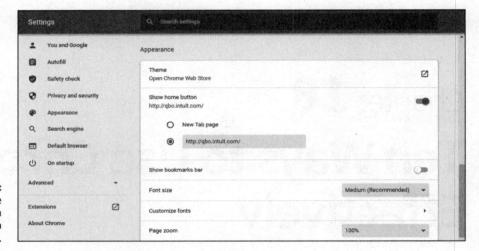

FIGURE 18-1:
Enabling the
Home button
and setting a
home page.

3. **Select Appearance on the navigation bar at left.**

4. **Click in the Custom Web Address field and type a web address, such as qbo.intuit.com if you want QuickBooks Online to launch automatically when you open Chrome.**

   The words Custom Web Address have already been replaced with qbo.intuit.com in Figure 18-1.

5. **Your changes are saved automatically, so you can close the Settings tab.**

   Now when you click the Home button Chrome displays the custom page that you set.

Duplicating and Pinning Tabs

You might find it useful to pin particular tabs so that they open automatically whenever you start Chrome. To do so, right-click the tab that you want to open automatically, and choose Pin from the shortcut menu (see Figure 18-2). An alternative to pinning tabs is creating bookmarks, which I discuss in an upcoming section of this chapter.

FIGURE 18-2: Pinning a tab in Chrome.

TIP

If you decide that you no longer want a pinned tab to appear each time you open Chrome, right-click the pinned tab, and choose Unpin Tab from the shortcut menu. As you might expect, the Unpin Tab command appears only if you previously pinned the tab.

Sometimes, you want to duplicate a tab you've already opened so that you have that tab open twice, which enables you to work in two places in your QuickBooks company at the same time. Right-click the tab, and choose Duplicate from the shortcut menu (refer to Figure 18-2). Then you can open two instances of the same page or navigate to other areas of QuickBooks Online and can return to the original tab as needed.

REMEMBER

You can access only one QuickBooks Online company at a time within a given web browser. If you need to work with two or more QuickBooks Online companies at the same time, you'll need to launch each one in a separate browser, perhaps Company A in Chrome, Company B in Mozilla Firefox, Company C in Microsoft Edge, and so on.

Using Chrome on Multiple Monitors

Here's another tab-related trick: If you have more than one monitor, you can pull one tab out of the Chrome window and drag it to your other monitor so that you can work in both QuickBooks Online and QB Accountant on multiple screens.

Again, because tabs in Chrome function independently, the work you do in each window is independent of the others.

Click and drag the tab you want to pull, and you see a preview of the new window. Release the mouse button, and the tab appears in a new window. If you didn't drag the tab to a different monitor, no problem. Just drag the new window by its title bar to your second monitor — or beyond, if you have three or more monitors.

TIP

Multiple monitors offer increased efficiency. Imagine having the Bank Reconciliation page open on one monitor and your online bank statement on the other, for example. Many accounting tasks entail transcribing information from one place, such as a bill that's been emailed to you, into QuickBooks Online. You certainly can switch among tabs and screens on a single monitor, but using multiple monitors results in an immediate productivity boost.

Zooming In and Out

At times, tired eyes need help. Fortunately, you can zoom in and out of Chrome's windows easily. Press Ctrl-+ (plus sign) one or more times to make the information in the window larger (known as *zooming in*) and Ctrl-− (minus sign) one or more times to reduce the size of the information in the window (you guessed it: *zooming out*). You can zoom into a page as much as 500 percent or zoom out to as little as 25 percent.

WARNING

Zooming is great for enlarging text, but it can also alter how web pages appear, even to the point of hiding content that would otherwise be visible. So if something seems to be missing, try resetting the zoom factor to 100 percent. To do so, open the Chrome menu and then use the − or + buttons for the Zoom command to adjust the zoom to 100 percent.

Using Bookmarks in Chrome

Bookmarks enable you to save a web address so that you can easily return to it. In this section, I show you how to

>> Create a bookmark.

>> Use a bookmark to display the associated web page.

>> Display the Bookmarks bar in Chrome to make bookmarks more accessible.

>> Organize bookmarks by renaming them, placing them in folders, changing the order in which they appear when you view them, and deleting bookmarks you no longer need.

Creating a bookmark

The dialog box shown in Figure 18-3 enables you to create a bookmark in four ways:

>> Click the Bookmark This Tab button, which looks like a star, at the right edge of the Omnibox and then choose Add Bookmark from the menu that appears.

>> Press Ctrl-D.

>> Choose Chrome ➪ Bookmarks ➪ Bookmark This Page.

>> Drag the lock icon to the left of a web address, and drop the web page's title on your Bookmarks bar.

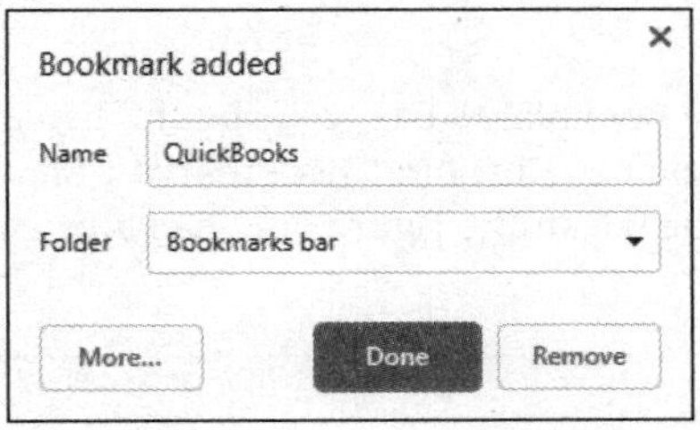

FIGURE 18-3:
This dialog box appears when you create a bookmark.

Bookmark added   ✕

Name   QuickBooks

Folder   Bookmarks bar   ▼

More...   Done   Remove

TIP

My savvy technical editor Dan pointed out that bookmarks created within Quick-Books Online are sometimes specific to a given company. If you see the word *app* in the URL, then you can create a universal bookmark that will work with any QuickBooks company. Conversely if you see *c##* where ## is a two-digit number, the page that you're presently on is specific to the QuickBooks company that you're working in.

You can change the bookmark's name and the folder in which Chrome stores it. Typically, you'll want to use the Bookmarks Bar folder, because putting book-marks in the Other Bookmarks folder can make it harder to locate your book-marks. All bookmarks you create appear at the bottom of the Bookmarks menu; choose Chrome ➪ Bookmarks to see them.

Bookmarks can display "page not found" messages (error code 404). If this happens, navigate to the page manually, and save the bookmark again, overwriting the original bookmark, or delete the bookmark if a given website or page is no longer available.

Displaying the Bookmarks bar

By default, Chrome saves your bookmarks to the Bookmarks bar, which appears below the Omnibox every time you open the New Tab page (see Figure 18-4).

Bookmarks bar

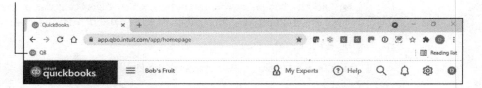

FIGURE 18-4:
Take advantage of the Bookmarks bar.

The Bookmarks bar makes using bookmarks faster and easier because bookmarks are always visible. Simply click the appropriate bookmark to display the associated web page.

To take full advantage of the Bookmarks bar, you should display it on all Chrome tabs. Press Ctrl-Shift-B or choose Chrome ⇨ Bookmarks ⇨ Show Bookmarks Bar, as shown in Figure 18-5. (The bar in the figure only has one icon.)

FIGURE 18-5:
You can display the Bookmarks bar on all tabs in Chrome.

Chrome displays as many bookmarks as possible on the Bookmarks bar, based on the names you give your bookmarks: The shorter the name, the more bookmarks Chrome can display. But you can easily get to the bookmarks you can't see by clicking the small button displaying two right arrows at the right edge of the Bookmarks bar.

Importing bookmarks

If you've been working in a different browser or on a different computer and want to copy your bookmarks, choose Chrome ⇨ Bookmarks ⇨ Import Bookmarks and Settings to display the Import Bookmarks and Settings dialog box, shown in Figure 18-6.

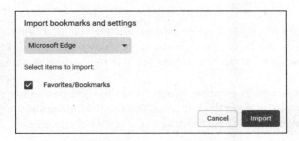

From the drop-down list, choose the browser from which you want to import bookmarks and settings. Select or clear the check boxes next to the items you want to import. (The options vary among browsers.) Then click the Import button. Chrome imports the information. The imported bookmarks appear in a folder on the Bookmarks bar, and you can use the Bookmarks tab (described in the next section, "Managing bookmarks") to reorganize these bookmarks.

Managing bookmarks

If you accumulate a lot of bookmarks, you may not be able to locate them easily when you need them. If that happens, do any of the following things:

>> Drag bookmarks into a new position on your Bookmarks bar or menu.

>> Drag bookmarks into folders on the Bookmarks bar or menu.

>> Search for a bookmark.

TIP

To create a folder, right-click an existing bookmark, choose Add Folder from the shortcut menu, assign a folder name in the resulting dialog box, and then click Save. Alternatively, display the Bookmarks Manager by choosing Chrome ⇨ Add Folder.

Choose Chrome ⇨ Bookmarks ⇨ Bookmark Manager or press Ctrl-Shift-O to display a page like the one shown in Figure 18-7. On this page, you can reorder bookmarks, create folders, delete bookmarks and folders, and rename or search for bookmarks.

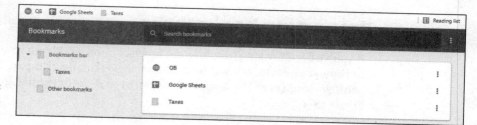

FIGURE 18-7:
The Bookmark
Manager.

TIP

The Bookmark Manager window works the same way that Windows Explorer and File Explorer work. If you're familiar with Windows Explorer or File Explorer, you already know many of the techniques you use to organize bookmarks.

The left pane displays existing folders, and the right pane shows the bookmarks in the folder you select in the left pane. You use the buttons at the right edge of the Bookmark Manager window to make organizational changes.

TIP

To remove unwanted folders or bookmarks, click a folder or bookmark and then press the Delete key on your keyboard. (*Note:* You can't delete the Bookmarks bar or Other Bookmarks folder.)

You can choose folder names when you add bookmarks, as shown in Figure 18-7. To add an existing bookmark to a folder, click the bookmark on the right side of the Bookmark Manager window and drag it to the appropriate folder on the left side of the Bookmark Manager window.

Right-click any folder or bookmark that you want to rename and then choose Edit from the shortcut menu. Type a new name in the resulting dialog box and then press Enter.

If you mislay a bookmark, type an address or search term in the Search Bookmarks field (refer to Figure 18-7), and press Enter. Chrome displays any matching bookmarks. Click the X that appears in the search field if you want to cancel the search. Simply close the Bookmark Manager tab when you're finished organizing your bookmarks; your changes are saved automatically.

Downloading Files

You can control the destination of downloads when you click the link directly, such as when you export a report to Excel from QuickBooks Online. Choose Chrome ⇨ Settings ⇨ Advanced ⇨ Downloads. In the resulting Downloads section (see Figure 18-8), click Change to set a default location other than your Downloads folder.

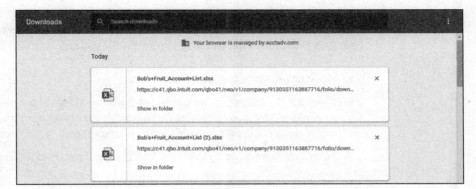

FIGURE 18-8:
Manage your
downloads in the
Downloads
section.

In addition, if you toggle on the option titled Ask Where to Save Each File Before Downloading, Chrome displays the Save As dialog box, shown in Figure 18-9, in which you can choose where to save your file. This technique is particularly useful if you don't want to dump all the QuickBooks reports that you export into your Downloads folder.

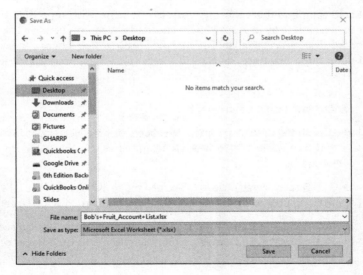

FIGURE 18-9:
You can tell
Chrome to ask
you where to
save each
download.

REMEMBER

The Save As dialog box won't appear if you set files to open automatically. You'll have to choose between having files open automatically and controlling where the files are saved if you want to save them in a folder other than Downloads.

REMEMBER

If you click a link to a file, it typically downloads automatically and possibly opens within the Chrome browser. If you want to save a file to another location, right-click the link, and choose Save As from the shortcut menu to display the Save As dialog box.

To view and open any downloaded file, choose Chrome ⇨ Downloads. On the resulting Downloads tab (refer to Figure 18-8), you can

>> Open downloaded files by clicking them.

>> Open the Downloads folder by clicking the Show in Folder link below any downloaded file or by choosing Open Downloads Folder from the menu (three dots) at the right edge of the Downloads page.

>> Search for downloads by using the Search Downloads field just below the Bookmarks bar.

>> To clear the Downloads list, open the menu (three dots) at the right edge of the Downloads title bar and choose Clear All.

Using Keyboard Shortcuts

Bookkeeping and accounting work is often rife with repetitive tasks, which you can streamline by using keyboard shortcuts. A comprehensive list of Chrome keyboard shortcuts is available at support.google.com/chrome/answer/157179, but I point out a few time-savers I like here (on a Mac, press the ⌘ key in lieu of the Ctrl key):

>> **Ctrl-W:** Close the current tab.

>> **Ctrl-Shift-T:** Use this shortcut to reopen tabs that you closed in the order in which you closed them, which is helpful when you (inevitably) close the wrong tab.

>> **F11:** Display a web page in full-screen mode, which hides the tabs, address bar, and Bookmarks bar. Press Esc at any point to close full-screen mode.

>> **Ctrl-F or F3:** Search the text of a web page, which is particularly useful when you're trying to find a piece of information within a QuickBooks report or help screen.

>> **Spacebar:** Tap the spacebar to scroll down one screen at time on a web page. Press Shift-spacebar to scroll up one screen at a time.

If you're looking for keyboard shortcuts for QuickBooks Online, visit www.dummies.com, and search for QuickBooks Online. Look for the Cheat Sheet section, where you'll find a list of keyboard shortcuts for QuickBooks Online and QB Accountant.

Working with Chrome Profiles

Multiple profiles are helpful if you're sharing a computer and each user has specific preferences with regard to the home page, bookmarks, pinned tabs, and so on.

Adding a Chrome profile

If you want to log in to two different QuickBooks Online companies from a single account, you can use different Chrome profiles. To create a profile, click the Profile button, which appears to the left of the Chrome menu and most likely shows your first initial (see Figure 18-10), and choose Add from the drop-down menu.

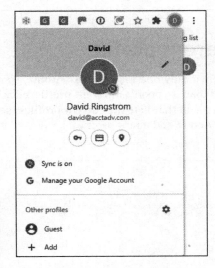

FIGURE 18-10: Use this menu to start the process of adding a profile.

On the next screen, you can sign in to a Google account if you want or select Continue Without an Account. As shown in Figure 18-11, enter a name for the profile, and optionally select a theme color. Clear the Create a Desktop Shortcut check box if you prefer not to have yet another icon on your desktop; then click Done.

TIP

Theme colors in Chrome can help you tell at a glance which profile you're in, particularly if you choose a particularly gaudy color.

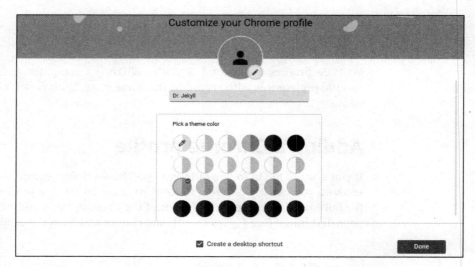

FIGURE 18-11:
Establish settings
for the new
profile.

Opening a different profile

Suppose that you have opened only one instance of Chrome, so only one button appears on the Windows taskbar. To open a different profile, click the Profile button to display a drop-down menu that lists the current profiles (see Figure 18-12). Choose a profile, or choose Add to add a new profile.

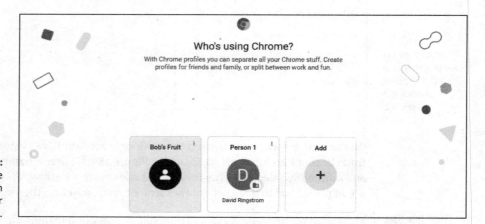

FIGURE 18-12:
Click the Profile
button to switch
to another
profile.

Assuming that you select an existing user, Chrome opens a new browser window for that user. You can toggle between these profiles by pressing Alt+Tab in Windows or Command+Tab on a Mac. You can also click the Chrome icon on your Windows task bar to toggle between open profiles.

Editing and removing profiles

Click the Settings icon next to the words Other Profiles on the Profile menu (refer to Figure 18-10) to display the Profile dialog box shown in Figure 18-12. Click a user to open a Chrome window for that user. Alternatively, click the More Actions menu represented by three dots next to the profile's icon and choose Edit from the drop-down menu to change the name or theme of the profile. Or scroll down and select an avatar. The More Actions menu also offers a Delete command that you can use to remove a profile that you no longer need. You'll be prompted to confirm that you want to delete the profile.

Managing Privacy in Chrome

Chrome enables you to control the information you share online. You can change your privacy settings, delete your browsing history, and browse in Incognito mode. To adjust privacy settings, follow these steps:

1. **Choose Chrome ⇨ Settings.**

2. **Scroll to the bottom of the Settings page, and click Advanced.**

3. **In the Privacy and Security section, click Content Settings.**

   Chrome displays a variety of changes you can make. The following sections describe the settings you may be most likely to change. If I don't cover a setting that you want to change, you can search for help on that setting at https:// support.google.com/chrome.

TIP

Use the search field at the top of the Settings screen to enter all or part of a Chrome feature that you want to configure. This approach will save you the frustration of fishing through Chrome's settings sections while muttering "I know that confounded setting is in here somewhere."

Handling cookies

You can control how Chrome handles cookies. Nope, I'm not talking chocolate chip or oatmeal raisin here — mmm, cookies — but the tiny files websites place on your computer for the purpose of recognizing your specific browser/computer combination if you return to the site. Chrome allows cookies by default because they're typically harmless, but cookies can allow sites to track your navigation during your visit to those sites. Cookies can be beneficial to you, such as by remembering your user ID for a given website or by hanging on to items you leave in a shopping cart for later. Fortunately, many websites give you the option to choose which cookies you accept, such as those that provide functionality, and to opt out of marketing or tracking cookies.

TIP

Third-party cookies are placed on your computer by one website for some other website. To increase privacy, many browsers block third-party cookies so that only the website you visit — and not any of its affiliates — knows about you and your browsing habits. Third-party cookies are typically used to mine data about you to determine which advertisements you're shown on the internet.

Enabling JavaScript

You can control whether Chrome runs JavaScript, which web developers often use to make their sites more interactive. If you disable JavaScript, you may find that some sites don't work properly.

Working in Incognito mode

If you work in Incognito mode, you can browse the web without recording a history of the sites you've visited and without storing cookies. Using Incognito mode doesn't make Chrome more secure; it simply enhances your privacy by preventing Chrome from keeping a record of the sites you visited during that particular browsing session. Even in Incognito mode, you shouldn't visit websites that you wouldn't feel safe viewing in a regular Chrome window.

To use Incognito mode, choose Chrome ⇨ New Incognito Window or press Ctrl-Shift-N. A new instance of Chrome opens. Notice that two buttons for Chrome appear on the Windows taskbar. The new Chrome instance displays an Incognito window like the one shown in Figure 18-13, and the Incognito icon appears in the top-right corner of the browser window, immediately to the left of the Chrome menu. You use an Incognito window the same way that you use the regular Chrome window.

Close the Chrome tab or tabs that are running incognito when you no longer need privacy.

Deleting browsing history

Like all browsers, Chrome typically keeps track of the websites you visit during each browsing session. One reason why browsers save your browsing history is to decrease the time you wait to see a web page that you previously visited. Also, a browser history can help you return to a website you visited previously even though you can't remember its address.

FIGURE 18-13:
An Incognito
window.

To view your browsing history, choose Chrome ⇨ History ⇨ History. A page similar to the one shown in Figure 18-14 appears. Your browsing history is organized by date and time, with the sites you visited most recently appearing first. You can click any entry to redisplay that web page.

You also can delete all or part of your browsing history, typically to maintain your privacy. To clear selected sites, click the check box next to the name of each site. A status bar appears in place of the Search box at the top of the Chrome History page and displays the number of sites you've selected. To delete the selected sites, click the Delete button that appears at the right end of the status bar. You can then confirm removal by clicking Remove in the Remove Selected Items dialog box that appears.

To clear all (or selected portions) of your browsing history, click the Clear Browsing Data link on the left side of the Chrome History page. The dialog box shown in Figure 18-15 appears. You can choose the type of data you want to delete and the time frame over which to delete that data.

History	Q Search history			
Chrome history				
Tabs from other devices	Today - Friday, September 17, 2021			
Clear browsing data ☑	☐ 6:43 PM	Bob's Fruit - QuickBooks Online	app.qbo.intuit.com	⋮
	☐ 6:43 PM	Bob's Fruit - QuickBooks Online	app.qbo.intuit.com	⋮
	☐ 6:43 PM	Expense Transactions	app.qbo.intuit.com	⋮
	☐ 6:43 PM	Expense Transactions	app.qbo.intuit.com	⋮
	☐ 6:41 PM	QuickBooks	app.qbo.intuit.com	★ ⋮

FIGURE 18-14:
Use your
browsing history
to revisit a web
page you visited
previously.

REMEMBER

If you delete all your cookies, you may need to reidentify yourself on websites where you were previously known, such as your bank's website. The process involves getting a code from the website and entering it, typically along with your password for that site, so that you can verify that you are, indeed, the user the website thinks you are.

Reviewing miscellaneous privacy settings

By default, Chrome makes certain assumptions with regard to privacy settings. I'll share these assumptions first, and then show you how you can tailor the assumptions to meet your needs.

- » Chrome asks for permission whenever a website wants to use your location information.

- » Chrome asks for permission whenever a site wants to show notifications on your computer desktop.

- » Chrome asks for permission whenever sites or apps want access to USB devices.

- » Chrome asks for permission whenever websites request access to your computer's camera and microphone.

>> Chrome asks for permission if a website wants to bypass Chrome's sandbox technology and access your computer directly.

>> Chrome blocks pop-ups from appearing and cluttering your screen.

To use Chrome (or any browser) effectively with QuickBooks Online and AB Accountant, you can't block *all* pop-ups. But you can turn on pop-ups selectively for any website. Follow these steps:

1. **Choose Chrome ⇨ Settings.**

2. **Click the Site Settings button in the Privacy and Security section.**

   The Site Settings page appears.

3. **Scroll down, and click Pop-Ups and Redirects.**

   The page where you manage pop-up exceptions appears (see Figure 18-16).

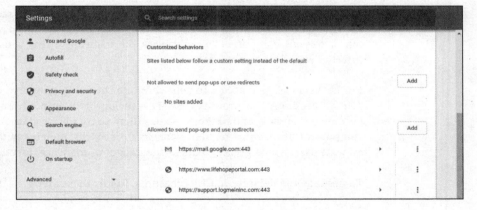

FIGURE 18-16:
Use this page to identify websites whose pop-ups you want to allow or deny.

4. **Click Add to display the Add a Site dialog box.**

5. **Type the address of the site you want to add.**

6. **Click Add.**

7. **Repeat Steps 4–6 for each website on which you want to permit pop-ups.**

Using Google tools to manage privacy

Although Google can collect a lot of information about you, you can use its privacy-management tools to control how much information it collects. Sign in to your account at account.google.com. On the resulting web page, you can adjust the ads that Chrome shows you, for example.

Managing Security in Chrome

Chrome includes several tools that help keep you safe online from bad things that can happen as you browse the internet. You might encounter phishing schemes, in which someone tries to trick you into sharing personal or sensitive information, usually through a fake website that looks genuine. You may run across websites that contain malware, which tries to install itself on your computer without your knowledge. Malware typically tries to harm you and/or your computer in some way, from simply messing up your computer's behavior to trying to steal information. Chrome includes technology that helps protect you from phishing schemes and malware, displaying a warning whenever you visit a potentially dangerous page.

Chrome also uses a technique called *sandboxing* to open websites. Sandboxing isolates computer processes from anything else that's happening on the machine. If a sandboxed process crashes or becomes infected with malware, the rest of your computer remains unaffected. Each tab in Chrome opens as a separate process, independent of other tabs. If a website contains malware, the sandboxing technique isolates the malware to that browser tab; it can't jump to another Chrome tab or to your computer. You eliminate the malware threat when you close the infected website's browser tab.

But hackers can gain access to your computer by using plug-ins, which are small add-on programs for browsers. Because they're add-on programs, plug-ins can become out of date, and hackers can use them to try to introduce malware on your computer. Chrome also regularly checks for security updates without any action on your part, which greatly reduces the danger of malware infection.

To upgrade the default security measures, follow these steps:

1. **Choose Chrome ⇨ Settings.**

2. **Click Privacy and Security.**

3. **Click Security.**

4. **Choose Enhanced Protection in the Safe Browsing section.**

   This feature warns you if Chrome detects possible malware on the site you're trying to visit, but does require that your browsing data be shared with Google.

WARNING

Don't change security settings unless you really know what you're doing.

Appendix A

QuickBooks Online, QuickBooks Desktop, and Data Conversion

You can import almost all data in a QuickBooks Desktop company into QuickBooks Online. There is mostly a one-to-one relationship between Desktop and Online, but there are features in both Desktop and Online that don't exist in the other platform. This appendix gives you a sense of what to expect if you migrate a QuickBooks Desktop company to QuickBooks Online.

REMEMBER

For best results, you should be using QuickBooks Desktop 2016 or later. If your version of QuickBooks Desktop is older, download a free 30-day trial version of the latest edition here: `https://community.intuit.com/articles/1207255-quickbooks-desktop-trial-links`. Install the trial version alongside your existing version of QuickBooks Desktop. *Don't let QuickBooks overwrite your existing installation.* Further, don't register or activate the free trial, because doing so could lock you out of your QuickBooks Desktop company. Use the trial version to convert your company data before you attempt to import it into QuickBooks Online, as shown in Chapter 14. Following these steps will allow you refer to your data if necessary. The QuickBooks Pro trial also works for QuickBooks Premier Desktop companies.

What Doesn't Import

Most of your information from QuickBooks Desktop will migrate into QuickBooks Online. Table A-1 lists what *won't* import.

TABLE A-1   ## QuickBooks Desktop Data That Won't Import

What Doesn't Import	Recommendation
QuickBooks Desktop usernames and passwords	You need to invite every QuickBooks Desktop user individually to use the QuickBooks Online company. You can limit access to certain areas of QuickBooks Online, but you won't have the transaction-level control you have in QuickBooks Desktop. If you have an Advanced subscription, QuickBooks will migrate the users rights as closely as possible; otherwise you'll need to establish the users rights manually.
Price levels	QuickBooks Online doesn't offer price levels, but in Chapter 4, I discuss a beta feature known as pricing rules that you can enable.
Reminders	QuickBooks Online doesn't offer a tickler feature, but in Chapter 16, I discuss how QB Accountant allows you to create reminders by establishing projects and tasks. You can also create tasks if you have an Advanced subscription.
Vehicle list	You can add vehicles manually to the fixed assets in QuickBooks Online.
Reconciliation reports	All reconciled items will transfer to QuickBooks Online, but you have to go back to QuickBooks Desktop if you want to review any old reconciliation reports.
Subtotal items	I describe how you can add subtotals to future transaction documents in Chapter 6.
Recurring credit card charges	You must first cancel any Automatic Credit Card recurring charges from your Merchant Center and then re-create them as recurring sales receipts. All other recurring transactions will import.
Memorized reports	Memorized reports in QuickBooks Desktop are referred to as Customized Reports in QuickBooks Online. You need to re-create all your QuickBooks Desktop reports manually. Note that QuickBooks Advanced offers a custom report writer that isn't offered in the lower versions of QuickBooks.
Audit trail	You need to refer to QuickBooks Desktop for your previous audit trail, but a new audit trail will be logged in QuickBooks Online.
Inventory from QuickBooks for Mac	You can't export inventory directly from QuickBooks for Mac to QuickBooks Online. Download the aforementioned free trial of QuickBooks Desktop for Windows, open your Mac company in that version, and then migrate your data.

TIP

Accounting software conversions always entail some amount of manual effort. There's also a learning curve during which you acclimate to the new software. Plan to give yourself three months for things to smooth out.

Features Not Fully Available in QuickBooks Online

QuickBooks Desktop users who need the following features should think twice before moving to QuickBooks Online:

» To Do notes

» Complete Job Costing

» Sales Orders

» Fixed Asset Tracking

» Estimate to Actual Reporting

None of these features is directly supported in QuickBooks Online. The fixed asset list I mention earlier is simply a list; it doesn't allow any other fixed asset tracking. But you may be able to locate add-ons to QuickBooks Online that provide the functionality you need at https://apps.intuit.com.

REMEMBER

Mileage tracking is offered only in QuickBooks Online Self-Employed. For all other versions, check https://quickbooks.intuit.com/app/apps/home for available add-ins.

Looking at List Limitations

Most, but not all, of your list information will transfer from QuickBooks Desktop to QuickBooks Online. In this section, I show you what will and won't make the transition to the cloud for your chart of accounts, customers/jobs, vendors, and various supporting lists. I talk about the items list later in "Examining Inventory and the Items List" later in this appendix. Spoiler alert: You can convert your inventory, but you might run into some trouble.

Chart of accounts

The QuickBooks Online chart of accounts uses detail types that you won't find in QuickBooks Desktop. You could consider a detail type to be a subtype of the major account categories. Expense accounts, for example, can be assigned detail types such as Auto, Equipment Rental, and Legal & Professional Fees. QuickBooks Online can guess the detail type sometimes, such as for the Undeposited Funds account;

otherwise, it assigns a generic detail type such as Other Miscellaneous Expense, which you can change. To do so, choose Reports ⇨ All Reports ⇨ Accountant Reports ⇨ Account List to review the current detail. Click any line to display the Edit Account window, where you can update the detail type. While you're here, you can add back bank account numbers and notes as well. See Chapter 3 for more information about maintaining your chart of accounts.

TIP

Many transaction windows in QuickBooks Online refer to accounts in your chart of accounts as categories. Historically, on financial statements, sections such as Revenue or Expenses were considered to be categories, whereas accounts could be line items like Miscellaneous Income or Payroll Expense. QuickBooks Online blurs theses distinctions by instead considering line items such as Miscellaneous Income or Payroll Expense to be categories instead.

Customers and jobs

Good news! The conversion process imports all your customers into QuickBooks Online. Any jobs in QuickBooks Desktop become subcustomers. Now, the bad news. The import process converts only the following customer and job information:

Customer	Phone
Company Name	Email
Mr./Ms./?	Terms
First Name	Bill to Address (except Note)
M.I.	Ship to Address (except Note)
Last Name	Tax code/item
Phone	Preferred Payment Method
Fax	Note (up to 4,000 characters)

REMEMBER

The Ship to Address converts, but not perfectly. The import process places the entire address in the main address field, leaving City, State, Zip Code, and Country blank.

Further, the following customer and job information doesn't convert:

Inactive status	Custom Fields
Customer Type	Account
Rep	Credit Limit
Price Level	Job Status

Start Date	Job Description
Projected End	Job Type
End Date	Credit Card Information

Note that Inactive status remains as long as no unbilled charges are imported.

Group items

Group items convert to bundles in QuickBooks Online for use in sales-related transactions. Any group items that appear in purchase transactions in QuickBooks Desktop become unbundled in QuickBooks Online, so you see the individual components of the group as line items in your transactions rather than see the group item itself.

Inactive list elements

You can mark customers and vendors as Inactive in QuickBooks Desktop and Online, but inactive status changes during the conversion to active for any customers or vendors who have open balances. You may want to purge inactive items in QuickBooks Desktop before running the conversion, because you can't remove inactive items from QuickBooks Online.

TIP

You can't delete list items from QuickBooks Online. If QuickBooks allows you to choose Delete, in reality, you're marking the record as inactive. You can control which lists display inactive items by clicking the Settings button above the Actions column of a list.

Users are often frustrated that items can't be deleted. What if you just want to delete an item and set it back up again? The best course of action is to rename the inactive item. (I often add a *z* in front of the item name so that the inactive items fall at the bottom of the corresponding list.) Then you can set up the item again, using the original item identifier.

Other names

Any items that appear in the Other Names list in QuickBooks Desktop will be established as vendors in QuickBooks Online.

Recurring transactions

Your memorized transactions will become recurring transactions in QuickBooks Online, but there's a catch: You must have a Plus or Advanced subscription to access them. In Essentials, your recurring transactions will be placed in cold storage, ready for use if you upgrade to QuickBooks Plus or Advanced down the line. Conversely, Simple Start users should delete all recurring transactions and templates from QuickBooks Desktop before converting to head off a passel of problems at the pass.

WARNING

You must set the schedule for each of your recurring transactions. The transaction detail will appear in QuickBooks Online, but the schedule will not. This means your recurring transactions won't post to your books until you enable them to do so by scheduling when they should recur.

Sales tax items

QuickBooks Online automatically establishes a new Sales Tax Agency Payable account for each sales tax jurisdiction. Thus, after you convert you'll have those new accounts along with any existing Sales Tax Payable accounts. Thereafter, QuickBooks Online uses only the new Sales Tax Agency Payable accounts. Use Sales Tax Center to manage your settings.

Any sales tax group items from QuickBooks Desktop will become unbundled within your transactions, but you can set up combined sales tax items in Sales Tax Center. Any three-character tax codes associated with sales tax items in QuickBooks Desktop are discarded.

TIP

Sales tax payments post as regular checks, and sales tax adjustments post as journal entries.

Ship Via list

There's no equivalent to the Ship Via in QuickBooks Online. Your Ship Via choices will be preserved within your transactions, and going forward, you'll type the information in a text field rather than choose it from a list.

Subtotals

Subtotal items in QuickBooks Desktop perform calculations, but in QuickBooks Online, they simply appear as memo entries in the description field.

Types for customers, jobs, and vendors

Any types that you've assigned to customers, vendors, and jobs will be discarded. Unfortunately, QuickBooks Online simply doesn't allow you to group list items in this fashion.

Vendors

Although you probably have some vendors you'd rather not pay again, rest assured that QuickBooks Online imports all this information:

Vendor	Email
Company Name	Terms
Mr./Ms.	Print on Check As
First Name	Address
M.I.	Account
Last Name	Vendor Tax ID
Phone	Vendor Eligible for 1099 (United States only)
Fax	

Aren't "good news, bad news" scenarios the worst? Maybe I should have led with what vanishes into thin air during the conversion process:

Contact	Credit Limit
Contact	Custom Fields
Note	Contact
Inactive	Alt Ph.
Vendor Type	

Exploring Payroll Conversion

Most QuickBooks Desktop payroll information converts to QuickBooks Online Payroll (QB Payroll) with (you guessed it) some exceptions:

» Pay types that QB Payroll doesn't support

» Invalid Social Security numbers and employer identification numbers

» Addresses in territories other than those that Intuit supports, such American Samoa and the U.S. Virgin Islands

REMEMBER

Paychecks and liability payments convert as regular checks rather than as payroll transactions in QB Payroll. QuickBooks will attempt to carry over your year-to-date amounts but check the numbers closely for payroll items that don't convert cleanly. If needed you can enter year-to-date amounts to reflect paychecks and liability payments made before conversion. Liability refunds, adjustment transactions, and opening balance transactions that affect accounts convert to journal entries.

Employee pay schedules and payroll items convert, but plan on reviewing the mappings so that paychecks get processed properly. A Complete Payroll Setup button appears the first time you display the Employees page, which prompts you to map any unmatched payroll elements from the QuickBooks Desktop import process. Search the internet for "What to do after converting from QuickBooks Desktop for Windows or Mac to QuickBooks Online." On that page, see the "Map Your Custom Pay Types" section, or visit https://intuit.me/3pZG8iz for more information.

REMEMBER

The import process doesn't convert pay types that QB Payroll doesn't support. If you don't see any choices to map a pay type, you can click the deceptively named Skip for Now option, but you can't return to the mapping screen. Instead, you need to create pay types for your employees manually to complete payroll setup.

After importing payroll information, you need to fill out an interview to complete payroll setup, establishing information such as company contributions, before you create paychecks. You might also need to enter year-to-date payroll information for each employee. Typically, you need only verify the totals, but if necessary, the interview guides you through entering these year-to-date totals to get going again.

Payroll setup

To complete your payroll setup, follow these steps:

1. **Select Workers in the left menu and then click Employees.**

2. **Click the Get Started button.**

3. **On the My Payroll screen that appears, in the Paid in [Year] column, ensure that sure each employee who received a paycheck this year is listed as Yes.**

   Employees who haven't been paid in the current year are automatically listed as No.

   The Paid in [Year] column appears only before you complete payroll setup.

4. **Click Complete Payroll Setup to enter and/or verify your year-to-date payroll totals and employee information.**

Use the Payroll Summary report in QuickBooks Desktop to enter the year-to-date numbers in QuickBooks Online as positive numbers, even though they appear as negative in the report.

You don't have to complete payroll setup in a single sitting; you can come back later, and the Payroll Setup Wizard picks up where you left off. You *do* need to complete payroll setup before you pay employees.

REMEMBER

If you reported Group Term Life Insurance or S-Corp Owners Health Insurance, the import process recalculates net pay by using QB Payroll calculations. Be sure to keep this fact in mind when comparing your QuickBooks Online Payroll Summary reports with your QuickBooks Desktop Summary reports.

Special payroll notes

Here are a few final notes about importing payroll data:

>> If you were paying or filing your taxes electronically, you need to re-enroll for this service in QuickBooks Online. Log in and follow the steps on the Payroll Preferences page (choose Settings ➪ Payroll Settings) to enroll for electronic services.

>> If you were using or want to use direct deposit for your employees, you need to add your employer information and each employee's bank account information. You can do so on the Payroll Preferences page (choose Settings ➪ Payroll Settings) or on the Employee setup page (click Employees on the navigation bar and then edit the appropriate employee's pay details on the Employee Details page).

Examining Inventory and the Items List

The Plus and Advanced subscriptions track inventory by using the first in, first-out (FIFO) method on the accrual basis. Yep, this is like the Model T; you could buy it in any color you wanted as long as it was black. You'll choose a date during the import process to be used in recalculating your inventory based on the FIFO method. You'll see your item quantities, item accounts, and details, except for unit of measure; QuickBooks Online has no provision for that.

If your inventory hasn't appeared in QuickBooks Online within 24 hours, check for an email with this subject line: "There was a problem copying your company file to QuickBooks Online." Your next step is reviewing the Inventory section of the "What data doesn't convert from QuickBooks Desktop to QuickBooks Online?" article at https://intuit.me/3dUroMi.

Examining Other Special Cases

The rest of this appendix presents notes on the way the import process treats most common areas of QuickBooks Desktop.

Bills

The import process converts item receipts to bills and discards any Bill Received status.

Bill payments

Discounts applied to bills in QuickBooks Desktop become Vendor Credits in QuickBooks Online. The address on each bill payment check is overwritten with the Vendor address in the Vendor list.

Budgets

QuickBooks Online offers only a Profit & Loss budget. That type of budget is imported; any other budget types are discarded.

Closing date

Your closing-date preference migrates to QuickBooks Online, but the Closing Date password is discarded. As with the audit log, the Exceptions to Closing Date report tracks only new exceptions that occur in QuickBooks Online as of the conversion date you choose. You can still refer to earlier exception reports in QuickBooks Desktop if you keep the software installed.

Credit card charges

Credit card charges in QuickBooks Desktop become expense transactions in Quick-Books Online. Any pending credit card credits become QuickBooks Online Credit Card Credit transactions. This is going to sound redundant, but bill payments made by credit card become bill payment transactions.

Custom fields

Oof, I hate to be the bearer of this news: You must have an Advanced subscription if you want to have custom fields for customers, vendors, employees, or items. Otherwise, anything that happened in a custom field in QuickBooks Desktop is going to remain in that custom field in QuickBooks Desktop. With that said, all subscription levels to allow you to add up to three custom fields in transactions. Also, the Sales Rep field in QuickBooks Desktop does convert to a customer field on sales forms.

Discounts

Who doesn't like a discount? I have unfortunate news if you give and/or receive discounts on customer and vendor payments: QuickBooks Online will store your terms, but it doesn't calculate the discount on any transactions you enter. You have to do make that calculation by hand. That said, any discounts applied to your QuickBooks Desktop transactions will be converted to customer and vendor cred-its, respectively.

Documents

Any documents or attachments that you're storing in QuickBooks Desktop remain there. QuickBooks Online does allow attachments of up to 20MB, but the conver-sion process doesn't migrate any previous attachments. See Chapter 4 for a list of all attachments stored in QuickBooks Online.

Finance charges

Woot! The import process converts existing finance charge invoices in QuickBooks Desktop to invoices in QuickBooks Online with no data loss.

REMEMBER

You saw that I gave you some good news in that previous paragraph? Welp, here's the bad news: QuickBooks Online can't assess finance charges. You can establish a Finance Charge element in your Products and Services List and create finance charge transactions manually. If you have an Advanced subscription, you can import transactions, so you could do the math in a spreadsheet.

Invoices

The following types of data undergo changes during the import process:

- » PO No. translates to Custom Field 1.

- » Sales Rep initials translate to Custom Field.

- » Subtotals appear in the Description field for that line in the QuickBooks Online invoice, but they don't calculate. See Chapter 6 to learn how to customize QuickBooks Online forms to include subtotals.

REMEMBER

Progress invoices — invoices based on estimates — aren't converted. When you set them up manually, you won't find any of these fields:

Estimated Quantity	Prior Average Rate
Estimated Rate	Prior Amount
Estimated Amount	Prior Percentage
Prior Quantity	Current Percentage
Prior Average Quantity	Total Percentage

But wait — there's more! These invoice elements get discarded as well:

- » The Other field and any custom fields in the Customer section

- » The Other field and any custom fields in the Item Detail section

- » Sales form templates, logos, long text disclaimers, and tax names in the Options and Others section

TIP

Chapter 3 shows you how to add your logo to sales forms.

Journal entries

QuickBooks Desktop allows you to toggle the billable status of a journal entry. All your journal entries import without issue, but the billable status is discarded.

In QuickBooks Online, you can't write a check on an income account, for example; you have to use a bank account. Thus, if the conversion tool encounters a transaction that doesn't compute, it creates a journal entry instead.

Customized sales form templates

Here I go again. You know those lovely sales forms that you so meticulously crafted in QuickBooks Desktop? You'll have to create them all over again. Chapter 3 shows you how.

QuickBooks Payments service

You need to unlink QuickBooks Payments Service account from QuickBooks Desktop and relink it to QuickBooks Online, as shown in the "Connect your QuickBooks Payments account to QuickBooks Online" article https://intuit.me/3J1Rj2Y.

Multicurrency

You can convert multicurrency transactions from QuickBooks Desktop, but there are some serious caveats. QuickBooks Desktop allows you to create transactions with up to three currency types, but QuickBooks Online allows only two, so certain types of transactions won't get imported. You may also see penny rounding differences in multicurrency transactions.

WARNING

Check the list of currencies that QuickBooks Online supports at https://intuit. me/3mgr4Mz before you convert to avoid import issues.

Online bill payment

Checks that you haven't transmitted yet keep their "to be sent" status; otherwise, the online payment status doesn't transfer into QuickBooks Online. I discuss online bill payments in detail in Chapter 5.

Pending sales

QuickBooks Online doesn't allow you to mark a sale as pending and will ignore any pending transactions from QuickBooks Desktop. Going forward, you can use the Delayed Charge form in Essentials, Plus, and Advanced.

Print mailing labels

You can't print mailing labels in QuickBooks Online. But, in Chapter 10 I do show you how you can export reports to Excel, such as a customer or vendor list. You can use that as the basis for performing a mail merge in Microsoft Word. Check out *Word 2021 For Dummies* by Dan Gookin if you need help.

Purchase orders

QuickBooks Online won't link closed purchase orders from QuickBooks Desktop to the corresponding bills.

Receive items

All three ways you can receive items in QuickBooks Desktop are converted to bills in QuickBooks Online:

>> Receive Item & Enter Bill

>> Receive Item

>> Enter Bill for Received Items

Reimbursable expenses

Reimbursable Expenses in QuickBooks Desktop are known as Billable Expenses in QuickBooks Online. Going forward, you'll specify the markup percentage when you create the purchase rather than when you create an invoice. Any reimbursable expenses and unbilled time in QuickBooks Desktop become Billable Expenses in QuickBooks Online.

Reports

Essentials and Plus subscriptions have reports that are customizable but may not always mirror reports you've used in QuickBooks Desktop. The Advanced option has a free subscription to the Fathom reporting app, as well as a custom report writer.

Accrual-basis reports that you run in QuickBooks Desktop should match Quick-Books Online, barring any transactions that the conversion tool can't handle. Cash-basis reports will likely vary, however, due to two different sets of rules in the products.

Suppose that you have a service income line of $1,000, a discount of $100, and no payments:

>> A cash-basis P&L in QuickBooks Desktop won't reflect unpaid invoices.

>> A cash-basis P&L in QuickBooks Online will show $100 of income and –100 of discount.

As partial payments are received for this invoice,

>> QuickBooks Desktop prorates the amount of the discount that appears.

>> QuickBooks Online continues to show the entire amount.

Report customization

Although your version of QuickBooks Online may not have all the report customization options that QuickBooks Desktop has, you can filter reports extensively, as well as export reports to Microsoft Excel and Google Sheets. See Chapter 10 for the lowdown on QuickBooks Online reporting, and see Chapters 11 and 16 for insights into spreadsheet analysis.

Sales rep

The conversion process will store the sales reps assigned to your existing transactions in a custom field. Then you'll have to fill in the sales rep time and again on all future transactions. You can filter reports based on sales rep.

Income tax support

QuickBooks Online users can't export information directly to tax preparation platforms such as TurboTax. Just to rub salt in the wound, that tax line mapping you set up in QuickBooks Desktop won't transfer over either. But you can approximate tax mapping by establishing detail types in your chart of accounts, as I discuss earlier in this appendix. Conversely, QB Accountant users can use its Tax Mapping feature to integrate with Intuit Pro Connect and other tax preparation software.

Terms

Your terms will import with two exceptions:

>> Jobs in QuickBooks Desktop inherit their terms from the parent customer.

>> Subcustomers in QuickBooks Online are the equivalents of jobs and can have terms that differ from those of the parent customer.

Write letters

As of this writing, QuickBooks doesn't allow you to generate customized letters. Intuit is purchasing the email marketing platform Mailchimp, so an integration is forthcoming. See the earlier Mailing Labels section for a recommended approach and resource.

Index

Q

About the Author

David Ringstrom, CPA, is president of Accounting Advisors, Inc., an Atlanta-based spreadsheet and database consulting firm. David's consulting work focuses on streamlining repetitive accounting tasks. He helps clients use software such as QuickBooks more effectively and creates automated tools in Microsoft Excel.

David spends much of his time teaching webinars on Microsoft Excel and occasionally QuickBooks. David also owns StudentsExcel, an online service that helps accounting professors teach Excel more effectively to their students. David has written freelance articles about spreadsheets and accounting software since 1995, some of which have been published internationally. David has served as the technical editor for more than three dozen books, including *QuickBooks For Dummies*, *Quicken For Dummies*, and *Peachtree For Dummies*. David is now the author or co-author of three books.

He resides in a historic neighborhood in Atlanta, Georgia, with his wife, Erin; his children, Rachel and Lucas; dogs, Ginger and Eddie; and cats, Ringo and Arlene Frances (Francie).

Author's Acknowledgments

Thank you to Elaine Marmel for handing *QuickBooks Online For Dummies* over to me. Dan DeLong is a technical editor extraordinaire whose suggestions always make my books better. I appreciate how my editors Charlotte Kughen and Keir Simpson greatly improved the readability of this book. I also tip my hat to the rest of the Wiley team who helped bring this book to fruition. I always need to thank my wife, Erin, and my children, Rachel and Lucas, for bearing with me during the writing process yet again.

Working on a book is no small undertaking, but it is always rewarding. Each time I write a book, I like to look back and thank someone who has particularly helped my career along. This time my eternal gratitude to goes to Stephanie Miller for encouraging me to create Microsoft Excel training materials for college students. I also appreciate the cautionary online banking tale that Stephanie contributed to this edition. Of course, I can't thank Stephanie without also thanking Dr. Stacy Campbell for entrusting me with imparting Excel knowledge to honors college students at Kennesaw State University. It's always a pleasure to work with you both.

Publisher's Acknowledgments

Acquisitions Editor: Kelsey Baird
Project Editor: Charlotte Kughen
Copy Editor: Keir Simpson
Technical Editor: Dan DeLong
Proofreader: Debbye Butler

Production Editor: Mohammed Zafar Ali
Cover Image: © Jovanmandic/Getty Images

Take dummies with you everywhere you go!

Whether you are excited about e-books, want more from the web, must have your mobile apps, or are swept up in social media, dummies makes everything easier.

Find us online!

Leverage the power

Dummies is the global leader in the reference category and one of the most trusted and highly regarded brands in the world. No longer just focused on books, customers now have access to the dummies content they need in the format they want. Together we'll craft a solution that engages your customers, stands out from the competition, and helps you meet your goals.

Advertising & Sponsorships

Connect with an engaged audience on a powerful multimedia site, and position your message alongside expert how-to content. Dummies.com is a one-stop shop for free, online information and know-how curated by a team of experts.

- Targeted ads
- Video
- Email Marketing

- Microsites
- Sweepstakes sponsorship

20 MILLION PAGE VIEWS
EVERY SINGLE MONTH

15 MILLION UNIQUE
VISITORS PER MONTH

43% OF ALL VISITORS ACCESS THE SITE
VIA THEIR MOBILE DEVICES

700,000 NEWSLETTER SUBSCRIPTIONS
TO THE INBOXES OF

300,000 UNIQUE INDIVIDUALS EVERY WEEK

# of dummies

Custom Publishing

Reach a global audience in any language by creating a solution that will differentiate you from competitors, amplify your message, and encourage customers to make a buying decision.

- Apps
- Books
- eBooks
- Video
- Audio
- Webinars

Brand Licensing & Content

Leverage the strength of the world's most popular reference brand to reach new audiences and channels of distribution.

For more information, visit dummies.com/biz

PERSONAL ENRICHMENT

Staying Sharp
9781119187790
USA $26.00
CAN $31.99
UK £19.99

Facebook
9781119179030
USA $21.99
CAN $25.99
UK £16.99

Guitar
9781119293354
USA $24.99
CAN $29.99
UK £17.99

Investing
9781119293347
USA $22.99
CAN $27.99
UK £16.99

Beekeeping
9781119310068
USA $22.99
CAN $27.99
UK £16.99

Digital Photography
9781119235606
USA $24.99
CAN $29.99
UK £17.99

Meditation
9781119251163
USA $24.99
CAN $29.99
UK £17.99

Pregnancy
9781119235491
USA $26.99
CAN $31.99
UK £19.99

Samsung Galaxy S7
9781119279952
USA $24.99
CAN $29.99
UK £17.99

iPhone
9781119283133
USA $24.99
CAN $29.99
UK £17.99

Crocheting
9781119287117
USA $24.99
CAN $29.99
UK £16.99

Nutrition
9781119130246
USA $22.99
CAN $27.99
UK £16.99

PROFESSIONAL DEVELOPMENT

Windows 10
9781119311041
USA $24.99
CAN $29.99
UK £17.99

AutoCAD
9781119255796
USA $39.99
CAN $47.99
UK £27.99

Excel 2016
9781119293439
USA $26.99
CAN $31.99
UK £19.99

QuickBooks 2017
9781119281467
USA $26.99
CAN $31.99
UK £19.99

macOS Sierra
9781119280651
USA $29.99
CAN $35.99
UK £21.99

LinkedIn
9781119251132
USA $24.99
CAN $29.99
UK £17.99

Windows 10
9781119310563
USA $34.00
CAN $41.99
UK £24.99

SharePoint 2016
9781119181705
USA $29.99
CAN $35.99
UK £21.99

Fundamental Analysis
9781119263593
USA $26.99
CAN $31.99
UK £19.99

Networking
9781119257769
USA $29.99
CAN $35.99
UK £21.99

Office 2016
9781119293477
USA $26.99
CAN $31.99
UK £19.99

Office 365
9781119265313
USA $24.99
CAN $29.99
UK £17.99

Salesforce.com
9781119239314
USA $29.99
CAN $35.99
UK £21.99

Coding
9781119293323
USA $29.99
CAN $35.99
UK £21.99

dummies.com

dummies
A Wiley Brand